ENGLISH RECUSANT LITERATURE
1558–1640

Selected and Edited by
D. M. ROGERS

Volume 317

JOHN COLLETON
A Just Defence of the Slandered Priestes
1602

JOHN SWEET
A Defence of the Appendix
1624

JOHN COLLETON

A Just Defence of the Slandered Priestes

1602

The Scolar Press
1976

ISBN 0 85967 331 6

Published and printed in Great Britain by
The Scolar Press Limited, 59-61 East Parade,
Ilkley, Yorkshire and
39 Great Russell Street,
London WC1

NOTE

The following works are reproduced (original size) with permission:

1) John Colleton, *A iust defence of the slandered priestes*, 1602, from a copy in the library of Emmanuel College, Cambridge, by permission of the Master and Fellows.

References: Allison and Rogers 246; STC 5557.

2) John Sweet, *A defence of the Appendix*, 1624, from a copy in the library of St. Mary's Seminary, Oscott, by permission of the President.

References: Allison and Rogers 802; STC 23528.

A IVST DEFENCE OF THE SLANDERED PRIESTES:

VVherein the reasons of their bearing off to receiue *Maister Blackwell* to their Superiour before the *arriuall of his Holines Breue, are layed downe, and the imputa-* tion of disobedience, ambition, contention, scandall, &c. *is by able arguments and authorities remoued, the ob-* iection of the aduerse part sufficiently an- swered, and the Popes sentence in the controuersie truly related.

By *Iohn Colleton.*

Curam habe de bono nomine, hoc enim maius permanebit tibi quam mille thesauri pretiosi & magni.

Ecclesiastici Ca.41. vers.15.

Haue care of thy good name, for this will remayne longer vnto thee then a thousand treasures precious and great.

Newly imprinted. 1602.

THe author of the Apollogy alledgeth the place following to shew the difference betweene his Libell and the bookes he impugneth. And we of purpose make choyse of the same, leauing the reader to iudge whether he, or we, more directly and in better temper insist in the state of the controuersie, and answere the obiections.

SApitisne inter verum falsumue discernere? inter inflatum & solidum? inter turbidum & tranquillum? inter tumidum & sanum? inter probationes & criminationes? inter documenta & figmenta? inter causæ actionem, & causæ auersionem? Si sapitis, benè & rectè; si autem non sapitis, nos vestri curam gessisse non pœnitebit, quia etsi cor vestrum ad pacem non conuertitur, pax nostra tamen ad nos reuertitur.

Augustinus contra Petil. cap. 79.

DO you know to distinguish betweene true and false? betweene solide and puffed vp? betweene turbulent, and quiet? betweene swelling and sound? betweene probations and criminations? betweene instructions, and fictions? betweene handling the cause, and running from the cause? If you know this, well and good; if you know it not, we are not sorie, that we haue had this care to instruct you, for albeit your heart be not turned to peace, yet our peace returneth to vs.

To the Reuerend Priests, and Catholicke Layty of our Country.

MAny can witnes (deerely beloued in our Sauiour) how willing I was to surcease, and did in deede breake off, when I had composed the one halfe of the treatise ensuing, holding then, the proceeding therein a labour and charge needlesse, because foure of our brethren were going to *Rome* for his Holines decision, and end in the controuersie. But in this suspence of minde, and intermission of the worke, our Arch-priest on the 26. of Ianuary last, promulgated the Popes Breue of the 17. of August next before, after he had kept the same three months or longer in his hands, as it is sayd. In which Breue, both we were demaunded *what cause we had, why we did not obey the Cardinall Protectors letters erecting the subordination,* & iudgement therein giuen: *That doubtlesse, we ought to haue obeyed, and admitted the authoritye.* Which *demaund and iudgement*, beside many other places in the Breue, were euident arguments vnto vs, that the same was graunted vpon wrong information, and *(a)* consequently of no sufficient force to bind. For had his Holines or the Cardinall Præfect of the Breues, bin truly informed of the case, neither his Holines, nor the Cardinall would without peraduenture euer haue made such a demaund, or giuen like sentence against vs. And as litle would either of their sacred persons, haue omitted to comprehend the Iesuites vnder the censure of the Breue,

(a) *Ca. si 15. de fil. præsb. li. 6. & ca. si motu proprio de præbend. li. 6.*

or letted to reproue their fault, had they knowne that the Iesuites were the prime authors, the only stiffe maintainers, and reuiuers of the crime against vs. Moreouer, at the very time of the promulgation of the Breue, there came forth first the Apollogie and then the Appendixe *with licence of our Archpriest, as written by the vnited Priestes in due subordination vnto him*: books that most sharply inueigh against vs, for not receiuing the authoritie at first, vpon sight of the Constitutiue letter. For which causes, and for that sundrie persons of good place, haue of late affirmed, that Fa. *Lister* could and would defend his position of our schisme against any scholler in the world, and also because certaine fauorites of the Iesuites hold opinion, that the Breue doth not cleere vs from schisme, but leaueth it doubtfull and vndecided; and finally, for that some of their most deuoted, are so ful spirited, as they sticke not to report, that the cause why the Pope declared in the maner he hath done for vs, was not for that our cause was iust, but vpon a prudent consideration of not giuing discontentment to the king of Fraunce and our State: I say for these causes and some other like, & to giue satisfaction to all parts, who vpon anie of the former grounds or colours haue conceiued amisse of it, I thought it my bounden dutie (especially my brethren most earnestly importuning me) to resume and finish the poore labours which I had begun and layd aside.

When the Cardinal Protectors letters were shewed vnto vs for institution of the authoritie, we tooke our selues vnbound, before God and man, to subiect our selues thereunto, his Grace not sending with the Letter Constitutiue any rescript of his Holinesse, or other Canonicall testimonie for proofe of such his iurisdiction in our countrey: and we rested the more confident, and secure in this opinion, both in respect it appeared most manifest vnto vs, that the authoritie was procured by false suggestion, and by a man much disliked

of

of our Prince and ſtate, and who ſought to rule & command our Clergie: and alſo for that it was propounded vnto vs by M. *Blackwell* with apparant falſities, and with orders directly tending to tyrannie, namely *that we ſhould not diſcuſſe the Protectors authoritie, nor the inſtitution of our Superiours, nor make any ſecret meetings for aduiſing one the other*, when as the condition of our ſtate embarreth vs to meete publikely, *nor write letters to any beyond the ſeas, without his priuitie.* For theſe reaſons, and for that the authoritie it ſelfe was moſt ſtrange, neuer heard of in the Chriſtian world, meerely penall, without mixture of any benefite to our ſelues, Church or countrey, of moſt abſolute ſoueraigntie, without tye in the proceedings to any forme of law, other then the arbitrarie pleaſure of the Archprieſt: and the receiuing of the ſayd authoritie, (the ſame being a ſuperiour prelature) expreſly, and vnder heauie penalties forbidden *(b)* by the conſtitutions of holie Church, except the partie preferred thereunto, do ſhew the Letters of the Sea Apoſtolicke (ſuch as the Cardinals were not) for proofe of his promotion.

(b) *Extrau. Iniunctæ. Bulla* 2. *Iuly* 2. *& Iuly* 3. *conſtit.* 34.

Notwithſtanding all theſe exceptions and iuſtifications of our bearing off to admit the ſubordination: we neuertheleſſe offered to obey Maiſter *Blackwell* in the meane, though not to receiue him to our Superiour, till ſuch time as the Pope ſhould make forth his Breue, or otherwiſe confirme him in his place, and likewiſe proteſted vnder our hands, that no ſooner ſhould any ſuch Breue or confirmation appeare, but that it ſhould find vs readie moſt abſolutely to receiue the authoritie. But this was not deemed ſufficient, nor ought could ſatisfie, but our preſent ſubmiſſion. Which becauſe we deferred to make, and did not yeeld to acknowledge him for our Superiour vpon teſtimonie of the Cardinals letter, father *Liſter* diuulged his condemned Treatiſe againſt vs; his Superiour father *Garnet*, and M. *Blackwel* approued the ſame. They

In Fa. Listers treatise, and in Fa. Garnets letter of the 7. of March.

taught, *that our company was to be ſhunned: that our faculties were loſt: that our ſelues were excommunicated: that none vnder mortall ſinne could inuite vs to ſay Maſſe: and thoſe that did participate with vs in Sacraments, made themſelues alſo partakers of our wickedneſſe.* Which inflaming matter of diſſention, and vntollerable reuiling againſt vs, laſted ſome moneths: and when at laſt the Popes Breue arriued, we were content notwithſtanding the ſharpneſſe of the premiſſes, to forgiue all for peace ſake, and receiued the Subordination in as large maner as it was propoſed.

Preſently vpon this atonement and remiſſion of the former defamations, Father *Iones* raiſed another paradox, farre more ſtrange and abſurd then that of Father *Liſters*, and our Archprieſt ſoothed it to be true, vidz. that whoſoeuer did ſtiffely maintaine, that we had not incurred the crime of ſchiſme by the prorogation of our refuſall to receiue M. *Blackwell* for our lawfull Superiour, he himſelfe *ipſo facto* for ſuch his maintenance incurred the cenſures of holy Church. At this time alſo M *Blackwell* publiſhed a reſolution, which (he ſaid) *he receiued from our mother citie, declaring the refuſers of the appointed authoritie were ſchiſmatikes, and commaunded that none ſhould abſolue vs in confeſſion, vnleſſe we did firſt acknowledge ſo much, and likewiſe menaced, that if we did perſeuere in the contrary opinion, he would deale with vs as a Prelate for appeaſing the ſame.*

In his Letter to Maſter Clearke.

Vpon which order, and threate of our Archprieſt, and as well for ſatisfaction of our ghoſtly children, as to make a finall end of the controuerſie, we offered to diſpute the queſtion with the Ieſuites, the authors of the Calumniation: but being denyed this iuſt requeſt by our Archprieſt, we ſent (compelled thereunto) to the Vniuerſitie of Paris, with humble petition to that venerable companie of the Sorbons, that they would vouchſafe to deliuer their opiniõ & cenſure in the caſe. Who freeing vs from ſchiſme and all ſinne in the nature of the act,

our

our Archpriest made foorth estsoones a d ecree, *prohibiting under grieuous penalties either directly or indirectly, the said censure of the famous Vniuersitie.* And within short time after, his Reuerence published another decree, *wherein he by vertue of his authoritie iudicially declared vs to haue bene truly disobedient to the Sea Apostolike, and rebellious against his office, for not admitting the subordination at first, and forbad vs vnder present losse of all our faculties, and of being ipso facto suspended and interdicted, neither to presume our selues, nor any other for vs, to defend our former disobedience any maner of way by word or writing.* Yea his Reuerence enacted further in the same decree, *that we* (as if we had bin boyes in some Colledges vnder the Iesuits, and that it behoueth also, that some iealousie were cast abrode of our demeanure) *should not haue any secret meetings, or communication together, saue such only as tended to the increase of pietie and hospitalitie, or of humanitie and peace.* A law of that qualitie, notwithstanding the smooth pretext, as the christian world neuer heard the like to be made for Priests and Pastors, sent by the sea Apostolicke for reducing others to the Catholicke faith. By which, and some other of our Archpriest his decrees following in the discourse, the reader may iudge, both what an vnworthy and seruile bondage he and the Iesuites, (whose counsell, or direction) he exactly followeth in all things) haue, and would more, of all likelyhood haue brought vpon vs ere this day, if we had not appealed and wrote to his Holines, and also whether there remayned any other refuge vnto vs then to appeale and try the accusations before that Tribunall, vnto whose iudgement both they and we must stand.

29. of May 1600.

18. of Octo-ber. 1600.

§. 5.

Further, we haue seuerall times sued for peace at the hands of our aduersaries, euen vpon vneuen conditions: namely, before the first Breue, before and after our appellation, and before our brethrens preparation to *Rome*: but they

of the other ſide euermore reiected all our offers, nor would accept of any conditions, wherein our vtter diſcredit, and their victory (though in vnrights) ſhould not appeare to the world. The holy Ghoſt writeth, and the words are true as well
Eccle.41. touching the ſpirituall as carnall parent: *the children complaine of their wicked father, becauſe they liue in reproch for him.*
(c) 22.*q*.73. *art* 4.*ad*.1. *& quodl*.10. *q* 6.*art* 13. And *S. Thomas* (*c*) with all other ſchoole Diuines teacheth, that a man is bound to defend his good name, when the wrongfull deprauing thereof turneth others to detriment.
(d) 22.*q*.72. *art*.3.*c*. Likewiſe the ſame Doctor (*d*) writeth, that one may be bound to purge his good name, euen in reſpect of doing good thereby to the defamer, *viz.* when through the checking and repreſſing of his boldnes, the party is learned to be more wary and temperate. Which is alſo the commaund of holy writ,
Proverb.26. *anſwere a foole according to his fooliſhnes, leaſt he ſeeme wiſe to himſelfe.*

We truſt by the litle which is ſaid, that both the neceſſitie, and iuſtneſſe of our defence appeareth: & ſo much the more, by how much the wrong teſtimonie which our Archprieſt lately gaue on the ninth of May 1602. concerning the Popes declaration in the matter of our imputatiue ſchiſme, rebellion, and diſobedience, was iniurious vnto vs, in that his Holineſſe cleering vs of the three foreſaid crimes, M. *Blackwell* in a publike Letter vnder his hand and name, denieth the ſame, and maketh his Holineſſe and the two Cardinals, *Burgeſio* and *Arragone* to ſpeake much otherwiſe: yea his Reuerence in an other Letter bearing the ſame date, & addreſſed to the Prieſts of our countrey, reneweth all his former decrees and prohibitions, continuing the cenſures & penalties before annexed vnto them. Whereby, if the like oppreſſions, exceeding the boundes of his iuriſdiction, and contrary to the law of God, nature, and man, (as is proued in the Diſcourſe) did or could bind, alas what infinite turmoile and harrowing of conſcien-

ces

ces do follow, when ſo many Prieſts of the Realme were ſuſpended, and depriued of their faculties, from the firſt time, that they either *diuulged any booke ſet out ſince the yeare of our Lord 1597, by which the fame of any clergie Catholike perſon of our nation may be hurt by name*; (of which quality the Treatiſe againſt the factious, the Apollogie, the Appendix with ſome other, muſt needes be accompted by the ſelfe Letter and tenor of Decree) *or directly or indirectly maintained in word or writing, the cenſure of the Vniuerſity of Paris: or preſumed in like maner to defend their diſobedience to the Sea Apoſtolike, and rebellion againſt the office of the Archprieſt, who did not at firſt ſubiect themſelues to the Subordination, vpon the arriuall of the Cardinall protectors Letter Conſtitutiue.* Which ſeuerall Decrees, each of them bereauing the offender *ipſo facto* from all his faculties, haue (if they be of force, as our Archprieſt now againe the *9*. of May affirmeth they are) ſo intangled the Prieſts, as of likelihood few, or not many, retaine their faculties, and conſequently, their penitents bound (ô the perplexitie and horror) to iterate their confeſſions made ſince that time vnto them.

In his decree of the 17. of Ianuar. 1599.

In his decree of the 29. of May. 1600.

In his decree of the 18. of October. 1600.

Father *Parſons* ſhewed his nature, when plotting the authoritie, he made the taking away of faculties the branch of the Archprieſts iuriſdiction, and our Archprieſt in my opinion, could not deuiſe a more pregnant meane, howe to diſquiet the ſpirituall repoſe of thouſands (a thing which Prelates ſhould moſt of all ſhunne, as being moſt oppoſitely contrary to the end of all Eccleſiaſtical lawes) then to annexe the loſſe of faculties to his Decrees in the maner he hath. Nor can I conceiue the reaſon why his Reuerence at this time reualidateth and inforceth the penalties of his Decrees, ſith he hath often annexed vnto them the cenſure of Interdict, a power which is not expreſſed in his authoritie, and which if he do take, as he ſaith he doth, *à iure communi*, in that he is conſtituted Archprieſt, then were the ſixe Aſſiſtants very vnaduised, and whosoeuer gaue allowance thereunto, in writing to his Holinesse Nuncio in Flaunders, for his Grace to be a meane to Cardinall *Fernesio* our Protector *that the Archpriest might haue authoritie from the Pope to excommunicate some foure or sixe of the maister ringleaders of the faction.* Because if he haue authoritie *à iure communi* by vertue of his (*e*) office, to suspend or interdict, he hath also authoritie to excommunicate. But these points are treated in the Discourse at large, where I hope the Reader shall fiud enough to acquiet all scruples, that may this way arise. For taking leaue, we heartily request the Reader, and our fellow brethren chiefly, to peruse our Reasons and proofes with indifferencie, and as their vnderstanding shall then direct, so to speake for vs in places where they heare truth and our actions expugned.

In their Letter of the 2. of May 1601. A charity well-sorting with their most sclaunderous information.

(e) *Nauar in ma. ca.27. nu.159. & 168.*

A Table of the principall points contayned in this treatise.

The fourth Reason.

lawes

The Constitutiue Letter.

Henricus Tituli Stæ Potentianæ Cardlis Caietanus, S.R.E. Camerarius, Anglicanæ nationis *Protector, Georgio Blackwello Sacerdoti Anglo,* S. Theologiæ baccalaureo formato, in vinea Anglicana *laboranti salutem.*

S*Citum est, atquè vsu fere quotidiano compertum, diuina prouidentia ad bonorum examẽ, atquè exercitationem sic disponente, vbi maiora eduntur ad Dei gloriam opera, ibi acriores etiam existere ad hæc ipsa impugnanda, vel retardanda satanæ, atq; communis hostis conatus. Neque vllum sane vidimus his annis illustrius, quam in causa Anglicana exemplum, quæ, vt insignem accepit à Domino, pietatis, fortitudinis, patientiæ, atq; constantiæ gratiam, clarissimamq; tùm confessorum, tùm etiam martyrum gloriam: sic acerrimã quoque ab hæreticis impugnationem passa esse noscitur, ita vt locum in ea habeat illud, quod de anima electa Spiritus sanctus pronunciat,* Certamen fortè dedit ei Deus, vt vinceret. *Et de vase electionis Christus Dominus.* Ostendam illi quantum oporteat eum pati pro nomine meo. *Imo Catholicos ipsos ac Sacerdotes nonnullos Seminariorum, qui cæterorum duces, atquè antesignani ad omnem excelsæ virtutis laudem hactenus extiterunt, aggredi sathanas non dubitauit, vt inter se collideret, & vnionis murum, quo omnis nititur Christianæ pietatis spes, dissiparet. Cui hostis conatui Romæ quoquè nuper emergenti, cum Smi D.N. summa prudentia, ac paternus amor remedium salutare per Dei gratiam diebus præteritis adhibuerit, cupiatq; ad huius Collegij Romani exemplum, quod summa pace, ac tranquillitate fruitur, reliquis quoque in partibus eandem curari, & conseruari animorum concordiam, sine qua nihil boni exitus sperari potest, speciali mandato nobis iniunxit, vt huic rei procurandæ omni nos qua possumus vigilantia impendamus, quod perlibenter quidem facimus, eo quod hoc cardine potissimum totius causæ momen-*

tum versari non ignoremus.

Cum igitur non parum interesse ad hoc ipsum nonnulli censeant, si subordinatio aliqua inter Sacerdotes Anglicanos constituatur, & rationes ab ipsis Sacerdotibus pro ea re redditæ à Smo D. N. probatè fuerint, nos Stis suæ pijssimam prouidentissimamque voluntatem sequentes, hoc ipsum statuere decreuimus. Atque pro ijs quidem Sacerdotibus Anglicanæ nationis dirigendis ac gubernandis, qui in Angliæ, Scotiæve regnis in præsentia versantur, vel in posterum, eo venturi sunt, dum hæc nostra ordinatio durauerit, te deligimus, cui vices nostras pro tempore delegemus, inducti relatione, ac fama publica virtutis, eruditionis, prudentiæ, ac laborum tuorum in ista vinea Anglicana per multos annos excolenda. Facultates autem, quas ad hoc ipsum tibi concedimus, hæ sunt: Primum vt cæteris omnibus Seminariorum Sacerdotibus sæcularibus (vt iam dictum est) authoritate Archipresbyteri præsis, quoad Smus, aut nos eius mandato aliud statuerimus. Deinde vt eosdem Sacerdotes dirigere, admonere, reprehendere, vel etiam castigare possis, cum erit opus, hocque vel facultatum sibi à quocunque, seu quandocunque concessarum restrictione, aut etiam reuocatione, si id necessitas postulauerit. De ijsdem præterea Sacerdotibus disponere, & de vna residentia in aliam (cum maior Dei gloria animarumque lucrum illud exigat) mouere, ac commutare: dubia quoque & controuersias exorientes audire, & pro rerum æquitate ex æquo bonóque determinare: schismata, diuisiones, ac contentiones amouere, vel etiam compescere: earumque rerum causa quemcumque Sacerdotem ad te vocare, ac conuenire: plures etiam vnum in locum conuocare, cum necesse fuerit, & cum sine probabili periculo fieri posse in Domino videbitur: congregatis vero praeesse, eisque proponere, vel quæ istis obseruatu necessaria iudicaueris, auditis assistentibus, de quibus mox dicemus, vel quæ huc, aut ad Doctorē Barrettum Collegij Duaceni præsidem (cui his etiam in rebus specialis à nobis Smi iussu tributa est potestas vt vobis assistat) scribenda duxeris. Quod si quis his in rebus (quod futurum sane de virtute omnium confisi non timemus) inobedientem se, aut inquietum, aut contumacem) ostenderit, hunc, post debitas admonitiones ac reprehensiones fraterna charitate præmissas, liceat etiam pœnis coërcere Ecclesiasticis, ablatione nimirum facultatum, vel suspensione, quoad se emendauerit: vel si hinc etiam emendatio non sequatur, tunc vel ad D. Barrettum vel ad nos scribatur, vt vel inde euocetur, qui eiusmodi est, vel grauioribus etiam censuris istic humilietur. Vt vero facilius, suauiusq; hanc sollicitudinis partem tibi commendatam exequi possis, sex quoq; consultores, seu coadiutores assignamus, qui oneris participatione nonnihil te labore leuaré possint. Ioannem nimirum Bauandum, & Henricum

Henshaum

Henſhaum Theologiæ Doctores, Nicholaum Tiruettum, Henricum Shanum, Georgium Birkettum & Iacobum Standiſium qui nuper apud nos Romæ fuit. quos ex antiquioribus eſſe optimeq; meritis multorum relatione accepimus. Tibi vero facimus poteſtatem, alios quoq; ſex præter hos iſtic eligendi, iiſdem habitis antiquitatis, grauitatis ac laborum rationibus, præcipuè tamen prudentiæ, moderationis, atque ſtudij vnionis, atque concordiæ, non parum etiam authoritatis atque exiſtimationis, quam in prouincijs habent, in quibus vices tuas noſtraſque gerunt. Omnes vero 12. *tam à te quã à nobis nominatos tibi ſubordinatos eſſe oportebit, vt melius conſeruetur vnionis ratio, ad quam omnia diriguntur tuendam. Cum vero eos delegeris ad hoc munus quos maxime idoneos in Domino iudicaueris, admonendos nos curabis de eorum nominibus, ac qualitatibus. Ipſi etiam quoad fieri ſine periculo poſſit, ſuis literis ſaltem hoc initio ſignificent, quo animo ſint ad hoc præſtandum, quod ab ijs pro conſeruanda vnione poſtulatur. Deinceps vero tum ijs, tum tibi iniungimus, vt ſexto quoquo menſe ſi fieri poſſit communibus vel priuatis literis ad nos datis de ſtatu rerum apud vos ſcribatis, vt ex ijs S^mo D. N. referamus quæ ſcitu erunt digna, vel quæ cauſæ veſtræ intereſſe iudicabuntur, vt à ſua S^te cognoſcantur. Si quis vero ex his duodecim, quos tibi in conſilium rei melius paragendæ aſſignauimus abſens fuerit, aut captus, carcereq; detentus, aut extra Angliam egreſſus, aut infirmitate, morbo, aliove iuſto impedimento retardatus, quo minus officium ſuum implere poſſit, aut rectè in eo non ſe geſſerit, facultatem tibi facimus, alium eius loco ſubſtituendi, ita vt nos deinde ea de re literis tuis admoneas. Si vero Archipreſbyter ipſe moriatur, vel ex Anglia egrediatur, vel in hoſtium manus incidat, ſic vt officio ſuo commodè fungi nequeat, tum antiquiſſimus ex conſultoribus qui Londini per id tempus, vel proximo Londino reſederit, vices Archipreſbyteri ſuſtineat quoad nos admoniti alium aſſignemus.*

Illud denique vel imprimis ſcire debetis, quod iam ſupra attigimus, præcipuam S^mo D. N. meamque his in rebus intentionem eò ferri, vt diſciplina Eccleſiaſtica quantum per temporum, hominumq; rationes iſtic fieri poſſit, conſeruetur: & præ cæteris pax vnioque animorum atque concordia inter fratres, ac Sacerdotes, nominatim etiam cum patribus ſocietatis Ieſu, qui vna nobiſcum laborarunt in eadem vinea, quod ſua S^te dignata eſt quibuſdam Sacerdotibus hinc in Angliam diſcedentibus, nuper ore proprio me præſente ſeriò, ac inſtanter præcipere, neque hoc ſinè iuſtiſſima cauſa. Nam patres illi non ſolum hic, atque alibi ſtrenuè impigreq; laborant pro cauſa Anglicana ſuſtinenda, fundandis Seminarijs, iuuentute inſtruenda, egenis fouendis, aliiſque medijs plurimis, verum etiam in Anglia quoque eadem charitatis opera proſequuntur, hocq; vſque ad ſanguinis pro-

fusionem, vt euentis, factisque demonstratum est. Cumque nullam ipsi habeant nec habere pretendant in Sacerdotes sæculares iurisdictionis, aut potestatis partem, neque vllam illis molestiam exhibere, manifesta sanè hostis astutia, ac diaboli fraus censenda videtur, ad vniuersum opus Anglicanum euertendum comparata, vt quisquam Catholicus æmulationem in eos exerceat, vel excitet, cum contra potius omni amore, ac reuerentia prosequendi sunt, quo ipsi maiore alacritate Sacerdotes, ac reliquos (vt hactenus) officijs, beneficijs, ac paterna plane charitate complectantur, & sic coniunctis animis operisque, opus hoc sanctissimum promoueatur. Vnde si quis fuerit, qui hanc concordiam labefactare studeat, eum iuxta Apostoli præceptum, & Apostolicæ sedis intentionem notare debebitis, vt vel admonitione corrigatur, vel pæna coërceatur. Reliqua si qua erunt ea vel in instructiones his annexas conijcientur, vel postea perscribentur, cum ex literis vestris intellexerimus quibus amplius rebus istic indigeatis.

Vt finem igitur imponam nescio quibus vos alloquar potius verbis quam illis, quibus toties Apostolus suos alloquebatur simili in causa, & non dissimili fortasse occasione, neque tempore. Idem sapite, pacem habetote. *Et adhuc longè instantius.* Si qua consolatio in Christo, si quod solatium charitatis, si qua societas spiritus, si qua viscera miserationis, implete gaudium meum, idem sapiatis, eandem charitatem habentes, vnanimes, idipsum sapientes, nihil per contentionem, nec per inanem gloriam, sed in humilitate superiores sibi inuicem arbitrantes, vt non quæ sua sunt singuli considerantes, sed ea quæ aliorum. *Hanc Apostoli regulam, atque exhortationem si sequamini, omnia vobis tuta erunt, atque gloriosa sicut hactenus. Si ab hac vnionis constantia vos deijci hostis insidijs patiamini, magnos scopulos incursura est causa vestra, patriæque vestræ, quod Deus auertat, vosque semper tueatur, vestrisque orationibus me ex animo commendo patris fratresque amantissimi ac R^mi^ Christi confessores. Romæ.*

R.æ V.æ

Vti Amantissimus frater Henricus
Card^lis^ Caietanus Protector.

THE

The English.

Henry of the title of S. Potentiana Cardinall Caietane, Chamberlaine of the holy Romane *Church, Protector of the English Nation: to George Blackwell* English Priest, formall Batchelour of Diuinity, *labouring in the English vineyard, wisheth health.*

T is knowne, and almost by daily experience found true, the diuine prouidence so ordaining for the triall and exercise of the good, that where greater exploits are done to the glory of God, there also are the more vehement attempts of Sathan and the common enemy, to withstand or hinder the same. Neither certes for these latter years space, haue we seene a more famous example, then in the English cause, which as it hath receiued of our Lord very singular grace of piety, fortitude, patience and constancy, and most renowmed glory both of Confessours and of Martyrs also: so in like maner is it knowne to haue endured most sharpe assaults from heretickes, in such sort, as that hath place in it, which the holy Ghost vttered of the elected soule, *God hath giuen her a strong conflict that she might ouercome*. And Christ our Lord of the vessell of election, *I will shew him how much he must suffer for my name*. Yea Sathan hath not feared to assaile Catholickes themselues, and some Seminary Priests, who hitherto haue shewed themselues leaders, and chieftaines of the rest, to all praise of noble vertue, that he might make them to bicker one with another, and breake downe the wall of vnion, whereon all the hope of Christian piety resteth. Against which attempt of the enemy beginning also of late to manifest it selfe at *Rome*, whereas the high wisedome and fatherly loue of his Holinesse, hath through the grace of God applied these dayes past wholesome remedy, and desireth that after the example of this Romane Colledge (which enioyeth great peace and quietnesse) the same concord of minds, without which nothing of good successe can be expected, should be sought for and conserued in other parts also, hath by speciall commaundement giuen charge vnto vs, that we should employ our selues for the procuring of this thing with all the diligence we can, which very willing-

God pardon the informer.

Great peace when two cannot speake together without a third, nor the students of one chamber recreate with their fellowes of another chamber.

ly we take vpon vs to do, because we are not ignorant that hereupon the moment of the whole cause dependeth.

VVe know not to this day who vvere these Priests, or what were the reasōs they yeelded.

Forasmuch therefore as some men thinke it would not a little auaile to this very thing, if a subordination were constituted among the English Priests, and the reasons yeelded by the Priests themselues for the same matter were approued by our holy Father: we following the most godly and most prudent will of his Holinesse, haue decreed to ordaine the same, and for directing and gouerning these Priestes of the English Nation that now conuerse in the kingdomes of *England* or *Scotland*, or shall hereafter reside there, while this our ordination shall continue, we chuse you, to whom for the time we commit our steed and office, induced vpon relation and the publike fame of your vertue, learning, wisedome, and labours taken for many yeares in the trimming of this vineyard. And the faculties which to this purpose we grant vnto you, are these.

First that you haue the title and authoritie of an Arch-priest ouer all the seminarie secular Priestes as is now said, vntill his Holinesse or we by is commaundement, shall institute another kind of gouernement: then, that you may direct, admonish, reprehend or also chastise those Priestes when neede shall require: and this either by restraining of faculties graunted vnto them, by whom, or whensoeuer; or by reuoking their faculties if necessitie shall constraine it. Besides, to dispose of the same Priestes, and to remoue and change them from one residence to another, when Gods greater glorie and gaine of soules doth require the same. Also to heare their doubts and controuersies arising, and for the right of things to determine them according to reason and equitie. Likewise to remoue or represse schismes, diuisions, and contentions: and for these causes to call and conuent any Priest before you, yea to summon many to repaire together in one place, when it shall be necessarie, and shall seeme in our Lord that it may be done without probable daunger, and to be chiefe ouer the assembled, and to propose vnto them either the things you shall iudge necessarie to be obserued by them, the assistants being heard, of which we wil speak anon, or the things you shall think needfull to be written hither, or to doctor *Barret* President of the Colledge of *Doway*, to whom by commandement of his Holines, we haue giuen speciall authoritie to assist you. And if any one in these matters shall shew himselfe (which truly putting trust in the vertue of all, we do not feare that it will fall out) disobedient, vnquiet, or stubborn, it is lawful,

after

after due admonitions & reprehensions first vsed in brotherly charity, to correct this party by Ecclesiastical penalties: that is to say, either by taking away of faculties, or suspension, vntill he shall amend himselfe; or if by this meane amendment follow not, then let notice be sent either to Doctor *Barret* or to vs, that he who is of such obstinacie either be called from thence, or there humbled with more grieuous censures.

And to the end you may the easier and with the more contentation execute this charge of care commended vnto you, we assigne likewise six consultors or coadiutors, who by participation of the burthen, may somewhat lessen your labour, namely *Iohn Bauen* and *Henry Henshaw*, Doctors of Diuinitie, *Nicholas Tirwit*, *Henry Shaw*, *George Birket*, and *Iames Standish*, who was lately with vs in *Rome*, which by the relation of many we vnderstand to be of the more auncient and best deserts. We also giue you authoritie to choose sixe other beside these, the same respects being had of auncientnesse, grauitie, and their trauailes, but chiefly of their prudence, moderation, and their loue of vnion and concord, not a little also of their authoritie and estimation, which they haue in the prouinces where they supply your steede and ours. All which twelue nominated as well by you as by vs, shall be subordinate vnto you, that the meanes of vnion may the better be conserued, to the maintenance and preseruation whereof all things are directed. And when you haue chosen those, whom you shall deeme in our Lord to be most fit for the office, you shall aduertise vs of their names and qualities, and let themselues also so farre as it may be done without daunger, signifie by their letters how they stand affected to performe this which for the conseruation of vnity is earnestly desired of them. Afterward we enioyne both them and you, to write euery sixth moneth if it may be, common or priuate letters vnto vs, of the state of matters with you, that of these we may relate to his Holinesse such as are meete to be knowne, or the things that shall be deemed profitable to your cause, to the end they may be knowne to his Holinesse.

A good direction, howsoeuer followed.

And if any of these twelue which we haue appointed to giue counsell vnto you, for better managing of the affaire, shall be absent, or dead, or taken, or imprisoned, or departed out of England, or letted by infirmity, sicknesse, or any other iust impediment, whereby he cannot fulfill his office, or shall not well demaine himselfe therein: we giue you power to substitute another in his place, so that afterward you aduertise vs thereof by your Letters. But if the Archpriest himselfe dye, or leaue England, or shall fall into the hands of his enemies, so that he cannot conueniently exercise his function: then let the auncientest of the consultors who at that time shall reside in London or nearest to London, execute the office of the Archpriest, vntill we vnderstanding thereof, assigne another.

Finally, you ought chiefly to know that which before we haue touched; his Holinesse principall intention and mine in these affaires to tend to this end, that Ecclesiasticall discipline so much as due consideration of times and persons will there suffer be maintained, and aboue the rest peace and vnion of minds and concord betweene brethren and Priests, particularly also with the Fathers of the society of Iesus, that haue laboured together with you in one vineyard.

The which thing his Holinesse vouchsafed of late with his owne mouth in my presence earnestly and instantly to giue in commaundement to certaine Priests departing from hence into England, neither without iust cause. For these Fathers not onely here and otherwhere, do with courage and diligently trauell for supporting the English cause, by erecting Seminaries, by instructing youth, by cherishing the needy, and by very many other meanes, but also in England too, they prosecute the same deeds of charity, and this euen to the sheding of bloud, as the euent and deeds haue demonstrated. And whereas they haue no kind of iurisdiction or authority, nor pretend to haue, ouer the secular Priests, neither any way to disquiet them; certes it seemeth to be a manifest subtilty of the enemy and deceipt of the diuell, complotted for the ouerthrow of the whole English cause, that any Catholike should practise or stirre vp emulation against them, when contrariwise all affection and reuerence is rather to be shewed towards them, whereby they may with the greater alacritie embrace the residue of the Priests (as hitherto) with good offices, benefits, and altogether with fatherly charity, and so with vnited minds and labours, this most holy worke be set forward.

VVould this were true.

Wherefore if there shall be any who goeth about to weaken this concord, your duty shall be to note him according to the precept of the Apostle and intention of the Sea Apostolicke, that either he may be reformed by admonition, or by discipline corrected. The residue if there shall be any remaining, shall either be specified in the instructions adioyning to these, or written hereafter when we shall vnderstand by your letters what further things you there want.

Where-

Wherefore to conclude, I do not know with what words better to speake vnto you, then with those which the Apostle so often vsed to his in the like cause, and perchance not in vnlike occasion nor time. *Be of one mind, haue peace.* And yet more instantly. *If there be any consolation in Christ, if any solace of charity, if any society of spirite, if any bowels of commiseration fulfill my ioy, that you be of one meaning, hauing the same charity, of one mind, agreeing in one; nothing by contention, neither by vaine-glory, but in humility, each counting other better then themselues. That euery one not considering the things that are their owne, but those that be other mens.*

If you follow this rule and exhortation of the Apostle, all things shall be safe vnto you, and glorious as hitherto. If ye suffer your selues to be throwne downe by the wiles of the enemy from this stability of concord; yours and your owne countries cause will dash vpon great rockes, which God auert, and euermore defend you: and I very hartily commend me to your prayers most louing fathers and brethren, and Christ his most reuerend Confessors. Rome.

Your Reuerences,

As a most louing brother, Henry Cardinall Caietane Protector.

The Cardinals second Letter.

Henricus Cardinalis Caietanus Stæ Rom. Ecclesiæ Camerarius, Angliæ Protector, &c. admodum *Rdo ac dilecto in Christo Georgio Blackwello Angliæ* Archipresbytero salutem in autore salutis.

ADmodum Rde ac in Christo dilecte vti frater. Vehementêr sane delectati sumus ijs literis, quas satis frequentes ad me his diebus tum charitas tua, tum consultores etiam tui Presbyteri assistentes, alijque viri graues non pauci dederunt de iusta lætitia, communiq́; approbatione subordinationis illius quam Smus Dominus iustissimis, pijssimisque de causis per nos in Clero isto Anglicano instituendam curauit; hoc enim & à virtutis vestræ singulari opinione, & vitæ quoq; professione excellentis expectandum omnino erat, vt qui ad restituendam Christi Vicario, sedique Apostolicæ obedientiam debitam tot pericula, ac labores obitis, ipsi obedire eiusdem S^tæ sedis ordinationibus non recusetis, sed alacri potius animo (quod fecistis) summi pastoris vestri statuta ad vtilitatē, pacem, & corroborationem vestram edita, obuijs (vt aiunt) vlnis amplecteremini. Itaque ex hac vestra, bonorumque omnium presbyterorum adeo prompta hilarique obedientia quam literis contestati sunt, cum S^mus Dominus, tum ipse etiam pro officij mei ratione, ac eo præterea quem in vos sentio singularem amorem, gaudium profecto atque ædificationem non mediocrem accepimus, quam optassem quidem perpetuam, vel certè diuturnam. Sed posterioribus quidem nuncijs turbari aliquantulum cepit, cum esset perlatum quosdam (vti fieri solet) refragari cepisse ac contentiones ciere, conuenticula quoque agitare, vt superiorum mandata in questionem vocentur. Tandem deniq; ad S^tem suam per ministros in partibus borealibus (vti videtur) existentes significatum est duos ex Anglia presbyteros à tumultuantibus his emissos iam esse qui huic subordinationi Ecclesiæ Anglicanæ S^tis suæ iussu institutæ contradicant. De qua re factus certior S^mus permolesto animo (prout æquum est) accepit, voluitque plenius de perturbatoribus informari. Cumque charitas tua nihil adhuc certi hac de re, neque de hominum istorum moribus vel actionibus ad nos scripserit (quod tuæ sanè modestiæ ac pietati tribuitur ne facilè ad fratrum descendas accusationem) nunc tamen S^mo id postulante, vt informatio debita de omnibus habeatur, faciendūm tibi erit omnino, vt rerum veritas per te patefiat acceptis & ad nos transmissis (quoad commodè ac sine periculo fieri poterit) bonorum tecum conspirantium sententijs, ac reluctantium etiam separatim, notatis nominibus, caussisq; percensitis quas reluctationi suæ prætendunt. Quod vt facilius citiusque ex nostræ ordinationis authoritate perficias, hoc tibi cæterisque presbyteris iniungimus, vt statim ac diligentèr fiat. Variaque harum literarum authographa ad te mittenda iussimus, quo facilius multis ad rei peragendæ breuitatem ostendi possint, Dominum præcantes vt magna bonorum suorum abundantia vos compleat, & pace veraque charitate, quæ perfectionis omnis vinculum est, dignos efficiat. Neque defatigemini animis, vt Apostolus hortatur, si difficultates ac contradictiones nonnullas in hoc vestro regimine experiamini, id enim vel optimis semper Ecclesiarum rectoribus ab initio contigit, & idem Apostolus ipsius Christi Domini exemplum vobis proponit, Qui talem *(inquit)* sustinuit à peccatoribus aduersum semetipsum contradictionem. *Sed omnia tandem ipse Dominus pacabit, fluctusque, exurgentes compescet, vosque de laboribus vestris ac patientiæ*

cumulatè

cumulatè remunerabitur. Ipse vos custodiat semper. Romæ die decimo Nouembris. Anno 1598.

Vti frater Henricus Cardinalis
Caietanus Protector.

The English.

Henry Cardinall Caietane Chamberlaine of the Church of Rome, Protector of England, &c. to *the very reuerend and beloued in Christ, George Blackwell* Archpriest of England, greeting in the *author of health.*

Erie reuerend and beloued in Christ as our brother: vndoubtedly we tooke singular great contentment in the frequent letters, which both your charity, your consultors the assisting Priests, and many other graue men sent vnto me of late, concerning the iust gladnesse and common approbation of the subordination which his Holinesse vpon iust and godly causes appointed to be instituted by vs in this English Cleargy. This truly was alwayes to be expected, as well from the singular opinion of your vertue, as also from the profession of your excellent life; that ye, who vnder-go so much danger, and take so great paines in againe-restoring due obedience to the Vicar of Christ and Sea Apostolike, your selues refuse not to obey the ordinances of the same holy Sea; but rather with chearfull mind (as you haue done) you would imbrace with open armes (as the Prouerbe is) the appointments of your highest Pastor, decreed for your profit, peace, and to make you strong. And so vpon this yours and all good Priests, their alike ready and ioyfull obedience, and which they testified by letters; both his Holinesse and my selfe, as the duty of my office required, and for the loue beside which I feele to be singular towards you, tooke certes no meane ioy and edification, which I could haue wished to haue bene perpetuall or of long continuance. But vpon later intelligence it began to be somwhat disturbed, when newes came that some (as it is wont to happen) enterprised to repugne and to raise vp contentions, also to make conuenticles to the end to call the commandements of superiours into question. Finally in processe it was signified to his Holinesse by Ministers abiding as it seemeth in the North parts, that two Priests were sent out of England by the tumultuous, which contradict this subordination of the Church of England instituted by commaundement of his Holinesse. Of which thing his Holinesse being aduertised, he tooke it (as it was meete) very grieuously, and would be more fully informed of the perturbers. And sith your charity hath not as yet written any certaintie vnto vs of this matter, nor of the manners & actions of those men (which doubtlesse is attributed to your modesty and pietie, as one who is not easily moued to accuse his brethren) yet now his Holinesse commanding the same, that due information be giuen of all, you must needs labour that the truth of things be layd open by you in taking and trasporting vnto vs (so farre forth as conueniently and without daunger it may be done) the iudgement of those good men that accord with you, and in noting the names of the contenders apart, and in signifying the causes which they pretend of their reluctation. The which thing that you may by the authority of our ordination performe with the more ease and speed, this we enioyne you and the rest of the Priestes, that it be forthwith and diligently accomplished. And we haue commaunded that many copies of these letters be sent vnto you, to the end they may be shewed to many for quicker dispatch of the affaire; beseeching our Lord to fill you with the great abundance of his blessings, and make you worthy of peace and true charity, which is the bond of all perfection. Neither be you wearie, fainting in your mind, as the Apostle exhorteth, if you meete with some difficulties and contradictions in this your Regiment, for that hath alwayes chanced euen from the beginning to the best gouernours of the Church: and the same Apostle proposeth vnto you the example of Christ himselfe our Lord, *Which* (saith he) *sustained of sinners such contradiction against himselfe.* But our Lord will appease all things at last, and allay the swelling sourges, and reward you abundantly for your trauels and patience, who alwayes keepe you. Rome 10. of Nouember, 1598.

God grant it.

As your brother Henry Cardinall
Caietane Protector.

THE

The Reasons whereupon we delayed to admit the Archpriestes authoritie, vntill *the arriuall of his Holinesse Breue.*

The first Reason.

Irst it appeared manifest vnto vs, euen by the very expresse words of the Cardinals Letter, by which his Grace instituted the subordinatiõ, that the same was procured by wrong information, and consequently voide, and of no force to bind vs to the acceptance thereof. We say voide and of no force, because seuerall Canons do so forcibly vndo & annullate whatsoeuer is procured by wrong information as they make surreption, (that is, as are the wordes of the law) [a] when a truth is suppressed, or a falshood suggested. So cleere and infallible a cause of frustrating all graunts as this manner of speech is often vsed in them: [b] *Nullius penitus esse momenti veluti per surreptionem obtentum*, & [c] *veluti surreptitium nolumus vires obtinere*, to be vtterly of no moment as obtained by surreption; and like as matter surreptious or gotten by wrong information, we will not that it should retaine any force. As though the supreme Pastours would haue said wrong information is of that certaine vndoing and destroying qualititie, as in obtaining of what grace soeuer it be found to haue place, it presently marreth and maketh the graunt of no effect. And that this is so indeed, and no wresting of the words of the law, let the best Cõmentors beare witnes for vs. The Glosse, which next after the text of the law, is of greatest authoritie, hath these words: [d] *Literæ gratiæ vitiantur, & sunt ipso iure nullæ si fuerint obtentæ per surreptionem:* Letters of grace (of which kind must needes be his Holinesse graunt for the subordination) are voide and of no force by the law it selfe, if they be odtained by surreption. To which *Panormitane* the Prince of the Canonists assenteth: [e] *Surreptio in literis gratiosis vitiat gratiam ipso facto, & quicquid vigore talium literarum secutum est:* Surreption annulleth *ipso facto*, the letters of grace, and whatsoeuer folowed by force

(a) *Ca. super literis de rescrip.*
(b) *Ca. si is de filys presb. lib. 6.*
(c) *Ca. si motu proprio de præbend. lib. 6.*
(d) *Clemen. de præbend. Ca. 1.*
(e) *Part. 2. consil. consil. 38. nu. 1.*

(f) In Ca. postremo de Appel. nu. 39.

of such letters. And *Decius* with infinite other writeth the like: [f] *Impetratio surreptitia non tenet, licet esset sanctus illequi impetrauit.* A petition obtained (of the Sea Apostolike or other prelate) by surreption is of no force, albeit he were a Saint that obtained the graunt.

(g) Sa. verb. grc.

(h) Rebuff. in praxi tit. quæ opponi possunt contra Bullam.

Neither are the aforesaid Canons antequated but still in force, that in what graunt or letters of grace soeuer the realnesse of surreption is found, the same looseth his validitie as *Sa* a diuine, and *Rebuffus* a Canonist (both writers of this age) do testifie, [g] *Gratiam Papæ surreptio facit nullam:* Surreption maketh the grace which the Pope giueth of no force, [h] *Surreptio & obreptio possunt opponi contra Bullam, & si oppositio ista vera sit, non potest euitari.* Surreption and obreption may be opposed against the Popes Bull: and if this opposition be true, there is no shift at all nor meanes of auoiding, but the Bull of necessitie looseth his force. And if surreption and obreption may be excepted against the Popes Bull, and do vitiate the same: no doubt they worke the like effect, and may be excepted against a verball graunt of his Holines, or a Cardinall Protectors Letter. It hath bene shewed before that surreption is, when a troth is concealed, or an vntruth suggested: and obreption, as [i] Pope *Innocentius* defineth is, *quando per alicuius operam factum est quod impetratæ literæ effugiunt plenam intelligentiam Papæ vel alterius qui necessitate iuris vocandus est:* when by any ones labour (that is by cunning & craftie circumuention as [k] *Panormitane* interpreteth the word) it is compassed that the letters obtained passed not with the Popes full knowledge, or with like priuitie of another, who was by order of law to be made acquainted therewith.

(i) In Ca. cũ dilecta de rescrip. nu. 5.

(k) In Ca. cum dilecta de rescript. nu 7.

(l) Ca. super literis & Ca. cõstitutus & Ca. ad audientiam. 2. de rescript. & Ca. dudum. 2. de electione & Ca. 1. & 2. de fil. presb. lib. 6. & Clemea. Ca. 1. de pres.

(m) In lib. 1. ff. de natu. rest. & in lib. præscriptione, & l. si leg. C. si contra ius, vel vti pub.

n In Ca sua nobis de offi. vicar.

Or let the case be, that there were no direct authoritie to be brought for the proofe of this assertion, as the choise is manifold euen out of the text of the law [l] Canon, and [m] Ciuill: yet it seemeth that the veritie therof might not amisse be proued in this sort. Graunts extend not their force beyond the intention and meaning of the graunter, his intention and meaning being the selfe forme, and the onely true rule and limites of what he graunteth. If therefore his Holinesse had no further intention to graunt or commaund the institution of the new authoritie, but as the information was true (as of likelihood he had not) and if not, then it followeth the causes and information being vntrue, that the graunt was of no effect in regard it had not his Holines intention, will, or meaning, to giue it life, vigour or validitie. And this we take to be one of the principall grounds, why the receiued Glosse vseth these words: [n] *Literæ per surreptionem obtentæ non conferunt iurisdictionem*

dictionem. As if one should say, what is obtained by meanes of wrong information, lacketh the Popes consent, because he graunteth it not, but vpon credence that the information was true, which being not true, he had no intention to grant it: and hauing no intention to grant it, it followeth that no iurisdiction was conferred, because the axiome hath [o] *Actus agentium non operantur vltra intentionem & mentem eorum*: Actes do not worke beyond the intention and meaning of the agents.

(o) *Ca. fin. de prebend.*

And if our aduersaries will needes here contend, that the Popes Graunt, and the Cardinals Letter for the new subordination was matter of iustice, and not of grace and fauour onely, (as how they can say it, we do not know) and therefore the authorities afore going make nothing for vs, or against them. We answer, that admit the subordination be matter of meere iustice, neuerthelesse the reason immediatly precedent doth hold, and the stronger: because in rescripts and grants of iustice, this condition *Si praeces veritate nitantur* If the causes alleaged in the petition be true, is alwayes to be vnderstood, euen by the expresse direction and commaund of the [p] law it selfe. And we adde further, that the subordination being procured by surreption, our bearing off to admit the same, could neither be vnlawfull, or iustly offensiue to any one. For although letters or graunts of iustice, are not void *ipso facto* in that they were procured by surreption, yet may the parties preiudiced by the graunt, most lawfully forbeare to obey the tenor, alleaging and prouing the surreption as the words of the glosse do most manifestly imply. [q] *Literæ iustitiæ obtentæ per surreptionem non sunt ipso iure nullæ, vt literæ gratiæ sed veniunt annullandæ per exceptionem*: Letters of iustice gotten by surreption, are not voide *ipso facto*, as are letters of grace, but they are to be annullated by excepting against the surreption. Which difference all the [r] Canonists put between letters of grace & iustice. So that we excepting against the surreption, as we did at the first shewing of the Cardinals Protectors Letter, alleaging that the meanes were not true, by which Fa. *Parsons* had procured so fruitlesse and strange subordination, what fault possibly could be in vs, doing no more or otherwise herein, then what all lawes and practise thorough out the Christian world, do licence, allow and approue.

(p) *Ca. ex parte 1. de rescript.*

(q) *In Clem. de præbend. ca. 1.*

(r) *Rebuff. in prax. tit. differentiæ inter rescripta gratiæ & iustitiæ.*

Master Blackwell himself is witnes hereof, who took exceptiõ against the exception.

Now the reasons why we did fully perswade our selues, that the causes alleaged and set downe in the Constitutiue Letter were not true: and consequently that the authoritie did not bind vs, as obtained by vntrue suggestion, were aswell seuerall truths concealed, as falsities related,and to name ſome of either ſort.

One of the truths concealed, was our deſigne at that time and readieſt purpoſe to make ſute by Supplication to his Holineſſe for creating of Biſhoppes in our Church. To which we were not onely caried by a longing deſire we had to reduce (as much as in vs lay)the broken ſtate of our Church to an vniformitie of Eccleſiaſticall Hierachie,and cuſtomarie regiment with all Chriſtendome, but alſo by a moſt ſenſible feeling of thoſe manifeſt damages we dayly ſuſtaine, and which day by day more increaſe vpon vs, for lacke of ſuch ſprituall comforts as accompanie that diuine and ſacred kind of gouernment: to wit,the miniſtring of the Sacrament of Confirmatiō,the conſecrating of holy Oyles,with many moe. The firſt whereof a comfort ſo many waies neceſſary for increaſe of ſtrength and true courage in theſe our no weak combats,as not any thing(the infinite number of our lay Catholickes conſidered, who neuer receiued the benefite of this Sacrament) can lightly appeare to be of greater or equall neceſſitie.

It is now more then 40. yeares paſt ſince we had a Catholike Biſhop at libertie in place to exerciſe his function:and for theſe latter twenty yeares and ſomewhat more,our Countrey hath not had a Catholicke Engliſh Biſhop either in priſon or out of priſon: albeit, *Ireland* an Iland ſubiect to her Maieſtie, and trauelling in like diuerſitie of Religions as England doth,was neuer in all this while deſtitute of one,two, or more, made ſucceſſiuely by the fauour and appointment of the ſea Apoſtolicke. § Vndoubtedly if our brethren and the Catholikes of our Realme, would ſeriouſly ponder on the ſeuerall graces, which iſſue from this Sacrament as from their natiue fountaine, and of other no common benefites which attend vpon that forme of gouernement,as the ſhadow doth vpon the bodie:they would not only with one conſent ſubſcribe to this our aforeſaid intended ſute, but would alſo moſt willingly ioyne in one ſupplication with vs to his Holines,that it would pleaſe him either to appoint Suffragans,or giue Epiſcopall authoritie to ſome ſuch as ſhould liue & conuerſe among vs. For to what other thing can we more impute the grieuous defectiō and fall of ſo many from the Church in the time of their triall, then to the want of the Sacrament of Confirmation, in which, the fulneſſe, ſtrength, and ſpeciall protection of the holy Ghoſt, both firmely to beleeue, and conſtantly to profeſſe our faith, are giuen in ſuch meaſure,as the grace of Baptiſme, according to the doctrine of Diuines, is thereby perfected: and the like difference wrought in the ſoule of the

Dioniſyus Eccl. Hierarchia. Ca. 2. par. 3. ad fin. Ambro. 3. ſacr. Ca. 2. & de iis qui myſt. imit. ca. 7. Aug. tract. 18. in Ioan. D. Thom. 3. par. q. 72. art. 7. Suarez ibidem, ſect 2. Bellarm. de ſacra. cōfir. ca. 11.

the receiuer, as is betwixt the state and strength of a man and a child? For as we do not receiue so great strength and quantitie of bodie in our birth, as we do after by the benefite of food and sustenance: so (the Sacrament of Baptisme & Sacrament of Confirmation working alike in spirituall matters, as do our birth and nourishment in naturall) the grace and spirituall fortitude we receiue in Baptisme, registring vs in the family of Christ, is not of that degree, actiuitie, and operation, as is the grace which giuen vs in the Sacrament of Confirmation, enrolling vs the professed souldiours of our heauenly Captaine Christ Iesus.

Certes how meanely soeuer the grace of this Sacrament is now thirsted after, or the vse thereof sued for: yet no lesse renowmed a Saint and Clarke in Gods Church then Pope *Clement* writeth, that *Omnibus festinandum est sine mora renasci Deo, & demùm ab Episcopo consignari, id est septiformem gratiam Spiritus sancti percipere, nam alioqui perfectus Christianus nequaquàm esse possit is, qui iniuria & voluntate, non autem necessitate compulsus, hoc Sacramentum praetermiserit, ut à B. Petro accepimus, & caeteri Apostoli praecipiente Domino docuerunt.* It behoueth all men without delay, to make haste to be borne anew to God, and after to be consigned of the Bishop, that is, to receiue the seuenfold grace of the holy Ghost: sith otherwise he cannot be a perfect Christian, who through iniurie to himselfe and default of his owne will, and not compelled by necessitie, omitteth to receiue this Sacrament, as we haue receiued of S. *Peter*, and the other Apostles, haue taught by our Lords commaundement. Memorable also is that saying of [s] Pope *Vrbanus: Omnes fideles per manus impositionem Episcorum Spiritum sanctum post Baptismum accipere debent, vt plenè Christiani inueniantur:* All faithful people ought after Baptisme to receiue the holy Ghost by imposition of the Bishops hands, that (in the day of resurrection) they may be found fully Christians, (beautified with the ensigne or character of the Sacrament of Confirmation.) And memorable also is that saying of [t] Pope *Melchiades: In Baptismo regeneramur and vitam, post Baptismum confirmamur ad pugnam: in Baptismo abluimur, post Baptismum roboramur: & quamuis continuò transituris sufficient regenerationis beneficia, victuris tamen necessaria sunt confirmationis auxilia. Regeneratio per se saluat mox in pace beati saeculi recipiendos: confirmatio autem armat & instruit ad agones mundi huius & praelia reseruandos.* In Baptisme we are regenerated to life, after Baptisme we are confirmed to fight: in Baptisme we are washed: after Baptisme we are strengthened. And albeit the benefites of Baptisme be sufficient to those that depart out of the

Epist. 4. ad Iuliū & Iulianū.

(s) *Epist. 1. ca. 7*

(t) *In Epist. ad Episco. Hispan.* cited de consec. distin. 5. ca. 2.

world immediatly, yet to ſuch as liue longer the helpes of Confirmation are neceſſary. Regeneration of it ſelf ſaueth thoſe that incontinent are to be receiued to the peace of the happy world: but Confirmation armeth, furniſheth, and inſtructeth thoſe that by longer life are reſerued to the conflict & warfare of this world. § By the doctrine of which three Popes and great Clarkes, it appeareth that the Sacrament of Confirmation is the complement and perfection of Baptiſme, [v] inſtituted by our Sauiour [x] to conferre the fulneſſe of the holy Ghoſt, to attaine a ſpeciall perfection, and deriue the more abundant helpes vnto vs, of confeſſing our faith when his honour and the edification of our neigbours requireth: and by it alſo to receiue a diſtinct and indelible character or badge of being aſſigned the publicke ſouldiours of Christ in the nobleſt cauſe (his faith) vpon earth.

(v) *Concil. Trid. Seſſ. 7. Ca. 1. Cō. Mogūt. Ca. 17. & Cōcil. Senonenſe in decretis morū. ca. 38.*
(x) *S. Cypria. in ſerm de vnctione Chriſ. D. Tho. 3. p. q. 72. art. 7. 8. 11. Scotus in 4 diſt. 6. q. 10. § ſed repetam Sotus in 4. diſt. 7. q vnica art. 7. Henriquez de Confirma. Ca. 4. § 1. Suarez t. 3. q. 63. art. 4. diſp. 11. ſect. 1. & q. 72. art. 7. ſect 2.*

Right excellent alſo to this purpoſe are the wordes of [y] *Damianus*: *Decretales paginæ & ſanctorum patrum inſtituta decernunt, non eſſe differendam poſt Baptiſmum ſacramenti huius virtutem, ne nos inermes inueniat fraudulentus ille contortor, à quo nemo vnquàm nocendi inducias extorſit. Delibuti igitur vtriuſquè roris vnguento, illo ſanati, confortati eſto, ſecuriùs deſcendamus ad ſingulare certamen.* The decretall pages & the inſtitutes of holy fathers haue decreed that after Baptiſme the vertue of this Sacrament is not to be deferred leaſt that guilefull racker of our ſoules (Sathan) find vs vnarmed, from whom no man euer hath wreſted the league of truce that he ſhould not hurt him. Being therefore annointed with the ſweet oyle of both deawes (Baptiſme and Confirmation) in that healed, in this ſtrengthned, we may the more ſecurely cope or deſcend to handy gripes with our ghoſtly enemie.

(y) *Serm. 1. de dedicat. Eccle.*

To conclude, [z] *Euſebius* attributeth ſuch exceeding force and working efficacie to this Sacrament, as he doubted not to ſay, that *Nouatus*, who after became an Ach-heretike, could not merit the grace and aſſiſtance of the holy Ghoſt, in reaſon of his wretchleſneſſe and lacke of deuotion, in that being baptized in a daungerous fit of ſickeneſſe, he was not likewiſe at that time ſigned and fortified with the ſacrament of confirmation. § And thus much of the importance of our intentiō & firſt truth, which as we verily thought was kept ſecret from the vnderſtanding of his Holineſſe: wiſhing euery one maturely to conſider of that litle which is ſaid, and what Diuines do further adde in this point, for exciting all Chriſtians, not onely moſt heartily to affect, but moſt ſtudiouſly alſo to get timely miniſtred to themſelues.

(z) *Hiſt. Eccle. lib. 6. ca. 35. ex Epi. Cornelij Pont. ad Fabiū.*

The second truth secreted.

Another truth secreted, was the great contention and scandalous debate raigning betweene the Iesuits and some of the secular Priests, by reason of an affected superioritie, which the Iesuits after the decease of good Cardinall *Allen*, laboured to place in father *Weston* ouer his fellow prisoners in *Wisbish*, by much his elders, as in yeares, so in sufferance also for the Catholicke cause. And it was not thought that this maner of seeking to beare rule, would take vp so or confine it self in that castle. The humour was deemed to be more actiue, and that it would soone enlarge in selfe to the Priests abroad. Neither was this opinion conceiued without cause, in respect of the question that master *Warpoole* now a knowne Iesuit and Father Minister at *Valodelide*, proposed to a student in *Rome*, demaunding of him what he would say, when no Priest should find harbour or welcome any where in England, vnlesse he came recommended by some of the Iesuits. And after the secret Iesuit (for so he was at the time when he vsed these speeches) had continued a long discourse, in shewing the ample and manifold conueniences that would ensue vpō so good an order, he would needs without deniall haue the student at the end of his tale, to declare also his conceit in the matter: and when by earnest importunitie he had wonne him therunto, and the student had shewed plainly his auersion from liking any such practise or soueraigntie ouer the Priestes, the Iesuit incontinent bewraied no litle discontentment. Againe, that which yet brought more euidence to the matter, was a Treatise which a speciall fauourite of the Iesuites compyled, and which was giuen abroade to others to reade, wherein it was discoursed, that none were fit to haue the guiding of soules: nay, speciall heede to be taken that none such be chosen to be guides, who were not addicted to Religion, or had not that way relation or dependance. Which iniurious and disgracefull assertion, being excepted against by one or moe of the auncientest Priests in our Realme, was notwithstanding so little reuersed or disliked, as more stiffely then before maintained, both by the Author of the Treatise, and by the chiefe of the society, with some other of the same company.

Now then, these and moe like particulars, which if neede require will be easily produced, yeelding sufficient coniecture, if not remonstrance, of the heartie desire the Iesuits had, to haue the secular Priests vnder their direction: we thought meete, the sooner also for auoiding the bad and ignominious reports, which were spread abroade euery where of vs for not stouping to the foresaid subiection: as that we were forsooth men, who would not liue vnder discipline, or could away with obedience, being, as it were, giuen ouer to follow the sway of our owne fancies, and vnwilling to haue either other rule, or Superior to direct vs, then our owne wil, or what the loue of liberty should prescribe: we say, to auoide this fowlest obloquy, and to the end the occasion of variance betweene them and vs, might be taken away in the roote, we desired the ordinarie gouernement by Bishops.

Which intention and petition of ours, if it had bene made knowne to his Holines, together with the ground mouing vs therunto, and the causes of the dissention (as they were not hid from the procurers of the authority) we most certainly assured our selues, that either his Holines would not haue appointed this kind of gouernment, (to which the Iesuits are no way subordinate) or not haue placed it in such a like fauourite of theirs, as themselues only had purposely culled out to serue their turns. § Or could we win our thoughts, that his Holines knowing how all things stood with vs, would neuerthelesse haue erected this kind of superiority, and haue appointed Master *Blackwell* for the Superior: yet the whole world cannot make vs to beleeue, or once to doubt that his Holines pious & prudēt disposition, his high commended vigilancie, & zeale of iustice, would if his blessed Fatherhood had bene truly and fully informed of our case, haue euer annexed such a tie and instruction to the authoritie, as that our Arch-priest should consult and take aduice in all matters of moment with the Prouinciall of the Iesuites: whereas father *Garnet*, who then had, and now hath the roome, was the chiefe of the one side in the difference: so that herby, he is become both partie and counsellour: plaintiffe and iudge: assistant, defendant, and in Commission for arbitrating his owne case, and the causes of his fellow brethren of the same societie vnder his guiding. An exorbitant most contrarie to the lawes of all Nations, and opposite to the nature of iustice, euen by the light of nature.

And let our aduersaries answer this.

The first falsitie expressed.

But to leaue to stay longer about the truths which we tooke to be concealed, as a matter wherein ignorance or forgetfulnesse may plead the informers excuse, and to come to the falsities, wherein not ignorance or forgetfulnesse can haue place, as in the former, but mis-affection or fraud, or a worse godfather must name the child. § The sole cause alledged in the Cardinals letter, and which (as there appeareth) was made the principall motiue and ground of the new institution, was, a debate or variance fained to be betweene the Seminary Priests and the Catholicke laytie of our nation. A fiction no lesse slanderous, defaming

defaming both cleargie and temporalty, then the same is open to euery mans checke. For what Priest or lay Catholike in England can warrant and verifie the assertion with any one instance, or being acquainted with what hath passed in this kind, cannot, if he hath will, witnesse the contrary? Neither is there need we should produce more or clearer euidence, for disproofe of the slander, then Maister *Blackwels* owne letter which he wrote to Cardinall *Caietane* immediatly before the institution of the authority: and which for the sundry praises it gaue to the societies high labours, and charities here, is registred in our English Colledge at Rome, as a perpetuall memory to all posterity. For the writing whereof, together with a Sermon he made in setting forth their merites, he was in many mens opinion, chosen to the office he possesseth In this letter he confidently affirmeth, that for this latter twenty yeares space and more, he neuer heard of any dissention, *Cuius afflatus paulo molestius aliquando commouit:* which was not blowne ouer without the least troubles. Which testimony of Maister *Blakwels* to the Cardinall, cannot in his owne cõscience be vnderstood of the Iesuits and Seminary Priests, but only of the good agreement betweene the secular Priests & the laity. This we say, because for the space of the latter two yeares immediatly before he wrote the said letter, not only the whole realme was grieuously scandalized, but the Pulpets rung also euery where with the great contentions, which were betweene the Iesuits and the Priests at *Wisbic.h* And these scandalous stirres were so little vnknowne to Maister *Blakwell*, as himselfe indited a generall letter vnto them, perswading to mutuall peace and concord. Yea further at the very same time when he addressed his letter to the Cardinall, he could not be but weeting to the reuiuall of the old, and increase of the new dissentions at the same place, and among the sayd persons, and which also were of no small moment, and of much disedification. By all which it is most euident, that if Maister *Blackwels* words were true, auowing that there was no dissention in our countrey, *Cuius afflatus paulò molestius aliquando commouit:* they were onely true in the secular Priestes and the laytie, and not betweene the Iesuits and the Priestes; and consequently the dissention which was suggested to be betweene the Seminary Priestes and the laytie, and for appeasing whereof the new authority was ordained, was a meere deuice and an apparant falsitie, the dissention being wholly (which was concealed from his Holinesse) betwixt the Iesuits and the Seminary Priests. And to the redresse whereof, this authority

By likelihood no holy haters of their owne praises.

The selfe words of the Letter.

no whit auailed, the Iesuits who were the brewers and principall cause of all the broyles) being altogether out of the compasse of the Archpriests authority & iurisdiction, vnlesse it be to direct him in the execution of the same.

The second falsitie expressed.

The second falshood vttered, was, that Maister *Standish* (whom the Iesuits imployed in negociating this businesse with his Holinesse, as is confessed in the Apologie, and who had at that time giuen his name to be one of their order) told his Holinesse(but by what kind of equiuocation or strange subintellection we know not)that he had the consents of the Priests in England,and came in their names to intreate the appointing of a superiour : whereas in truth he neuer acquainted the body of our Cleargy with his going, and lesse with the businesse he went about. Nay he was so cunning in cloaking his intention, that euen to those Priestes (who were not also aboue two or three) from whom he could not conceale his iourney, he pretended the cause of his voyage, to be a long desire he had to visite the holy places, and perhaps to enter into religion,forgetting therein the aduice of S. *Paul*,
2.*Cor*.4. *Non ambulantes in astutia*, not walking in craftinesse, intending one thing, and making semblance of another.

To conclude our first reason, the information being faulty, as well for truths concealed,as for vntruths deliuered,yea the very groundsell of the authority(we meane the chiefe & maine reason,& which is preferred to the first place in the *Constitutiue Letter*, & giuen as the sole & principall cause of instituting the subordinatiõ)being not only vntrue, but cõtaining beside a very grieuous touch both to the secular cleargy, & confessant Catholiks of our countrey,as that the diuel had made an assault to set vs together in tumults, when not the least breach or variance was knowne,or euer extant betweene vs : we assured our selues, the case thus standing, that we might most lawfully, and in wisedome deferre our obedience to the new authority, till we had disclosed the drift to his Holinesse, layd open the fraudulent and bad dealing, practised by the complottors and procurers of the subordination,and the likelihood of the broiles to ensue betweene the Iesuits & the Priests, whilest the Iesuites hauing thus cunningly gotten the chusing of both our Archpriest and Assistants, and consequently deriued power to themselues, to make and multiplie what ordinances they pleased in our Church,for curbing and afflicting any one that should withstand. *Res ipsa loquitur*. No moe words neede, the effects themselues do witnesse.

The

The second Reason.

THE second reason of our bearing off was, for that admitting the information to be true, which the procurers of the authority gaue vp to his Holinesse (as how little sincere it was the reason precedent sufficiently sheweth) we stood neuerthelesse morally assured that our delay could not be offensiue, being intended for no longer while, then till sending to his Holinesse (which was done with greatest speed) and vnfolding to him the true state of all matters, we might receiue direct knowledge what was done. namely whether the subordination was proposed only and vpon our liking, to be confirmed (which appeared most probable) or whether it was so peremptorily decreed (which we could not beleeue) as whatsoeuer our exceptions might be against it, it must notwithstanding be in force and continuance. And here, to make our discourse the more perspicuous, and to lay certaine grounds for supporting the same, we put downe the propositions following.

The first proposition.

NO delegatine authority, by whom, or of what matter soeuer can any way be rightfully extended beyond the limites of the cōmission and case expressed. The proues. [a] *Delegata potestas est stricti iuris, & id solum potest quod ei specialiter est commissum, & sine quo causa expediri non potest.* Delegatine authority (as writeth the Glosse) appertaineth to a strict law, and can onely be extended to that which is expresly committed, and without which, the cause cannot be effected: or not commodiously effected as ([b]) *Aretinus*, ([c]) *Decius* and ([d]) *Nauarre* do enlarge the Glosse. Againe *potestas delegata non est extendenda ad causam non expressum*. Delegatine power (as writeth ([e]) *Panormataine*) is not to be stretched to a case not expressed in the commission. Againe, ([f]) *Siue vni, siue pluribus, siue à principe, siue ab alio mandata fuerit iurisdictio, mandati forma diligenter custodienda erit, nec*

(a) *In ca. Solet de sent. excommu. verb. per superiorē lib. 6.*
(b) *In ca. De testibus Col. 3. de test.*
(c) *In ca. vt debitus honor de appella nu. 73.*
(d) *Consil. li. 1. tit. 31. de offi. Iudi. ord. nu. 4.*
(e) *In ca fin. de ver. sig. nu. 5.*
(f) *Lib. 3. tit. 1. § sed fine.*

aliquid contra quam sibi mandatum fuerit, delegatus sibi tentare audebit. The words of *Lancelot* whether iurisdiction shall be giuen to one or to many, by a Prince or by an inferiour, the forme of the Mandate must be diligently obserued, neither shall the delegate aduenture to attempt any thing beside that which shall be giuen him in cōmission. To this purpose likewise writeth (g) *Innocentius*, & (h) *Speculum* & others. And the places in the law, on which they ground their sayings, are: *in ca. Prudentiam, in ca. cum olim 2. in ca. venerabili de offic. de leg. in ca. cum dilecta de rescriptis & alijs.*

(g) *In ca. eam te de rescript. nu.6.*
(h) *Lib. 1 de iudi. de leg. § 8. nu. 10.*

The second Proposition.

WHen a cause or matter is delegated, it followeth not that all things thereupon which may any way auaile or bring furtherance to the businesse, are delegated by vertue of the same commission, but such accessories only as without which the businesse cannot be well and commodiously effected. A verity partly taken out of the text of the law, (a) *Sicut iurisdictio, sic & cætera sine quibus explicari causa non potest intelliguntur esse commissa.* As the Iurisdiction, so other things also without which the cause cannot be dispatched, are vnderstood to be committed: and partly out of (b) *Silvester Gemianus & Veru*: whom there he citeth. *Id propter quod facilius causa expediri posset, non venit nisi expresse committatur, & quamuis causa delegata intelligantur omnia commissa, sine quibus causa expediri non potest, non tamen omnia concessa sunt, quæ possunt valere ad causam expediendam.* That through the which the cause may more easily be effected, doth not fall vnder the delegation, except it be expressedly contained in the commission: and although the cause being delegated, all things are vnderstood to be committed, without which the cause cannot be effected, neuerthelesse all things are not graunted which may auaile to the effecting of the cause.

(a) *Ca. Suspitionis de offi. iud del.*
(b) *Verb. delegatus, nu. 6.*

The third Proposition.

WHen the commission runneth in generall termes without any expresse forme or limitation, the party delegate may vse his discretion, and do any thing that so serueth to the accomplishment of the affaire committed, as without it the same cannot be well

or

or commodiously effected: but if there be a certaine forme prescribed (as there is in the Cardinals letter) that forme is strictly to be obserued, and in no substantiall iot to be gone from. The first part is proued in the Chapters: *Præterea* and *prudentiam de officio & potestate Iudicis delegati*: and the latter, in the Chapter *Cum dilecta de rescriptis*. And both the one and the other are ioyntly affirmed in the Glosse (a) *Cum simpliciter mandatur sine aliqua forma expressa, delegatus omnia potest sine quibus causa expediri non potest, sed si certa forma esset data, illa seruanda est*. When the commission is in generall termes without any expresse forme, the delegate or partie commaunded, may assay and execute all things, without which the cause cannot be effected: but if there be a certaine forme set downe, that is to be kept. And how strictly it is specified in another place, where this direction is giuen. (b) *Forma mandati diligentissimè seruanda est*. The forme of the mandate is most diligently to be obserued.

(a) *In ca. præterea de offic. iud deleg verb. simpliciter.*

(b) *Gloss. in ca. cum delecta de rescriptis.*

The fourth Proposition.

WHen the forme of the commission is broken, the limites of the Mandate are transgressed. The proofe (a) *Mandati siquidem excedere fines probaretur, si quis citra formam rescripti accepti præsumeret iudicare*. He certes is proued to exceede the bounds of the Mandate, who presumeth to proceed beyond the forme of his commission.

(a) *c. prudentiam de offi. iud. del.*

The fift Proposition.

WHosoeuer goeth beyond the limites of his commission, beeing the bounds of his authoritie, (a) offendeth, but worketh nothing. Offendeth, because he vsurpeth authoritie, vsing that he hath not, and worketh nothing, because (b) *Processus delegati excedentis fines suæ potestatis non valet*. The processe of a delegate exceeding the limites of his commission is of no force. And (c) *vbi datur certa forma procedendi, processus corruit non solum si aliquid attentatur directè contra formam sed etiam citra vel præter formam*, where there is a certaine forme giuen of proceeding, the processe falleth, and is of no effect, not onely if an attentiue be made directly contrarie to the forme, but also if any thing be enterprised beside or out of compasse of the forme. Neither do any Canonists make question, but that the

(a) *Ca. venerabili de offi. del.*

(b) *Glossa in ca. hac constitutione de offic. iud. deleg. li 6.*

(c) *Panormitã in ca. prudentiam de offi. iud. deleg. nu. 5.*

forme of the Mandate or rescript is most precisely and exactly to be obserued, being as it were the needle and matter of that consequence, as if it be broken or swarued from in any one point, the whole action ensuing is ([d]) of no worth nor validitie. And which also is true by the testimonie of both ([e]) lawes, whether the particulars of the forme prescribed be pretermitted or exceeded.

(d) *Panormitã in ca publicato [illegible] & ca. cũ post.nu. 1. de elect. Ant. Fran. ibidem in ver. ipso iure. Host de offi. iud. deleg. nu 8.*

(e) *Ca. venerabili. de offi. iud. deleg. l. cum hi. § prætor ff. de transacti & in ca. fi. de restitutio. spoliat. & in l. diligenter. ff. mandati.*

The sixt Proposition.

THe formall and proper obiect of disobedience, that is the thing without which there cannot be properly disobedience, is the superiours precept. ([a]) *Tacitum vel expressum*, either tacitiue or explicitiue. Tacitiue, when the imperatiue or commanding will of the superiour becommeth kowne to the subiect after any signified manner soeuer. Explicitiue, when the precept is giuen in more expresse and plaine termes. Whence it followeth, that no one is bound vnder sinne of disobedience to obey the will of a superiour of what degree soeuer, vnlesse he signifie the same his will to be a commaundement. A proposition which ([b]) S. *Tho.* (whom both ([c]) *Siluester* and ([d]) Cardinall *Tolet* cite to this end) affirmeth in these wordes: *Licet sciam voluntatem prælati nisi tamen expressé præcipiat, non teneor.* Although I know the will of my Prelate, I am not bound to accomplish the same, vnlesse he expresly commaund me. The like also hath ([e]) *Nauar*, where he declareth when and how the sinne of disobedience is committed: *Peccat* (saith he) *qui deliberatè omittit facere quod iubetur satis apertè à superiore.* He sinneth who deliberatly omitteth to do what is plainely enough commanded by the superior: *ergo* what is not commanded, or not so plainly commanded, as it may be vnderstood to be a command, the fulfilling therof, ne is, nor can be properly an act of disobedience in the subiect: disobedience alwaies presupposing a knowne command of the superiour.

(a) *D. Tho. 22. q. 104. art. 2. Co. & in res. ad 2.*

(b) *De veritate q. 23. art. vlt.*

(c) *Verb. præceptum nu. 2.*

(d) *De sept. pec. mort. ca. 15. vers sept. est.*

(e) *In Man. ca. 23. nu. 36.*

The seuenth Proposition.

THe accomplishment of any superiours precept, may be prolonged or omitted without sinne, fault, or breach of obedience, if a reasonable, iust and lawfull cause occurre, and no peril of scandall probably appeare euident. For if the cause be iust and lawfull, the act proceeding

ceeding from the same not tainted by any ill circumstance, must needs be of like qualitie. Yea a further truth, the cause that *bona fide*[a] and to the doers vnderstanding seemed iust, though in truth and in it selfe it were not iust, excuseth the omission from mortall sinne.

(a) *D.Th.22.q.147.art.3.& Caiet.ibi.Pal. in 4.dist.15.q.4. Sil.ver.ieiunium.nu.21 & Caiet.in Sum. ver.præceptum*

The eighth Proposition.

THe subiect probably thinking that his superiour commanded the thing he did, by reason of wrong information, and that he would not haue commaunded it, had he kowne the truth, and for that cause deferring to execute the commaundement, and aduertising his superiour with speed of the truth, and reason that moued him to deferre, with expresse submission also to do as he should after direct, neither committeth the sinne of disobedience, nor violateth any other morall vertue, as it appeareth plaine not only by reason, but also by the authoritie of the[a] Canon law and the doctrine of[b] *Nauar.*

(a) *Ca.Si.quando, & ca. pastoralis de rescrip.*
(b) *In Man.ca.23.nu.38.*

The ninth Proposition.

NOne are bound to obey the commaundement of their superiour wherein he exceedeth the limites of the authoritie he holdeth ouer them, in respect the inferiour is only bound to obey his superiour in the thing in which he is his inferiour and subiect, and in no other.[a] *Non tenetur* (saith S. *Tho.*) *inferior suo superiori obedire si ei aliquid præcipiat in quo ei non subditur.* The inferiour is not bound to obey his superiour, if he commaund him any thing in which he is not his subiect, or in subordination vnto him. A doctrine so generally true, that if the Pope himselfe should commaund beyond the bounds of his iurisdiction, none are bound to obey, as writeth[b] Pope *Innocentius*,[c] Cardinall *Tolet*, and others.

(a) 2.2.q.104. art.5.
(b) *In ca.inquisitioni de sent. excom.nu.4.*
(c) *De pecca. morta.ca.15. vers.sextũ est.*

The tenth Proposition.

NO subiect is bound to obey and execute the commandement of his superiour, when in[a] reason and wisedome he cannot (as hauing cleare euidence to the contrarie) acquiet and conforme his vnderstanding to the iudgement of his superiour, or thinke the comman-

(a) *Gre.de.Val. To.3. disp.5.q.14 punct.4.& disp.7.q.3. punct.2.& To.4.disp.7.q.17. punct.2.*

dement to be right or iust,or binding,or vnder his authority. An assertion so certainly true, as to doubt thereof, were to call into question whether man should be gouerned like a beast, or that he could surprise and dispose his vnderstanding, how, and as he listed, in matters wherein he hath a demonstratiue, or euident certitude in iudgement.

The eleuenth Proposition.

ALthough in doubtfull matters that bring no detriment with them to the subiect, the subiect is bound to obey his superiour, because the superiour is in the possession of his authoritie, and consequently his title and interest the greater and abler: neuerthelesse in such doubts as on which[a] great preiudice attendeth the execution of the superiours commaundement, the subiect is not bound to obey, so long as he is prudently doubtfull whether he be bound or no. Which position is true, and holdeth if the preiudice redoundeth but to a third person, and more if to himselfe, and most of all, if to a community or multitude. The reason: because the subiect is likewise here in possession of the peculiar, be it his honour, fame, goods, liberty, life, or the like, in which his obedience would turne him to detriment. And no one is bound to surrender and depriue himselfe to his owne preiudice of that he hath in possession, vnlesse the right and interest of the claimer be very certain and manifest, which cannot be as long as the subiect prudently doubteth of the superiours authoritie in the particular commaunded.

(a) *Adrianus Quodlibet.2. Sotus de ratio. tegendi, & deteg. secre mẽb. 3.q.2. Concl.2. & 3. Salon. To. 2. disp. de tributis & vectiga. art.3. controuer.8. vers. ad intelligendũ*

The twelfth Proposition.

THe subiect may without mortall sinne disobey his Ecclesiasticall superiour annexing no censure to his commaund, so that he were not caried by contempt to the neglecting of the command. A conclusion of[a] *Angles* a famous writer of this age, and whiles he liued a publike reader of Diuinity: who for ground of the doctrine, himself being a religious man, alleadgeth common custome (the best interpreter of lawes) so to excuse and mitigate euen among the religious, the bond and law of obedience. And no lesse may be gathered out of[b] *Caietane* in his Summe, and out of[c] *Gregorius de Valentia*, where he defineth contumacie

(a) *P.2. in.4.q. de voto difficu. 16. cõcl.1. & 3.*
(b) *Verb. peccata clericorum.*
(c) *To.4. disp 7. q.17. puncto.5.*

contumacie that maketh a mortall ſinne to be diſobedience againſt a Superiour commanding vnder the threat of excommunication, this, or that, to be done or not done. Which kind of commination, or any other, the Cardinall Protector, neither did in his owne perſon, nor in the perſon of his Holineſſe ſo much as in the leaſt maner once inſinuate in any part of his Graces *Letter Conſtitutiue.*

The thirteenth and laſt Propoſition.

A Superior proceeding vniuſtly (as he doth when he commandeth more then the place and authoritie he holdeth giueth him leaue) may without all imputation of blame (the peril of ſcandall euer excepted) be as lawfully reſiſted as an [a] aduerſarie, as a [b] theefe, as a [c] wolfe, as a [d] tyrant or forraine enemie. So that to diſobey a Superior, enlarging his precepts beyond the vtmoſt bounds of his authoritie, is ſo farre from the nature of criminall diſobedience, as it cannot be ſaid to be the leaſt ſinne: yea the caſe may be ſuch, as it were ſinne and perhaps great ſinne to obey. For none will deny, but that there is [e] a kind of obedience which is indiſcreet or vnlawfull, agreeable to that Canon of holy Church collected out of S. *Gregorie*, *Admonendi ſunt ſubditi ne plus quam expedit ſint ſubiecti, ne cum ſtudent plus quam neceſſe eſt hominibus ſubijci, compellantur vitia eorum venerari.* Thoſe that liue vnder ſubiection are to be admoniſhed that they be no more ſubiect then is meet, leſt whiles they endeuour to ſhew more ſubiection to men then is neceſſary, they be compelled to worſhip their vices.

(a) *Nauar in ca contingat cauſa 5. nullitatis n 8*
(b) *D. Tho. 22. q. 69. art. 4. c.*
(c) *Ezech. ca. 22*
(d) *Molina Tõ. 1. de iuſtitia & iure tract. 2. diſp. 23. verſ. conceſſa.*
(e) *D. Tho. 22. q. 104. art 5. ad 3. & D. Bernard. Epiſt. 7.*
(f) *3. p. paſtoralis cura. 2. q. 7. ca. admonendi.*

THeſe grounds being laid, we proceed and affirme that the Cardinals Letter, as it is plaine to the Reader, maketh no mention at al of any Mandate or Commiſſion which his Holines ſhould giue, other then that he ſhould imploy his indeuour to make peace in our Countrey, to the example of the peace and quietnes eſtabliſhed in the Engliſh Colledge at Rome. And how this commaundement did communicate authoritie to the Cardinall to inſtitute an Archprieſt ouer vs, with like iuriſdiction and ſoueraigntie as is expreſſed in the *Letter Conſtitutiue*, appeared a more ſtrange point vnto vs, then we could vnderſtand, or find out any ground, or ſhew of reaſon, how the ſaid commaundement of his Holineſſe could any way be in ſuch ſort poſſibly extended, and retaine force to bind. For what neceſſary connexion is there betweene making of peace in our Country, and inſtituting of an Archpriest ouer one part of those that were at variance, with iurisdiction to spoile them of their faculties, to remoue them from their places of residence, to depriue them of the vse of their Priestly functions, and to afflict and vnable them to do good in our Church, and in no degree to subordinate the other more principall part of the contenders to the least iot of the same iurisdiction? We say, what necessary and straight coniunction is there between the two precedents, that Commission being graunted to labour and effectuate the one, viz. peace in our Countrey, authoritie must thereby be thought to be graunted to erect and appoint the other, viz. an Archprist? Must the assigning of an Archpriest with such iurisdicti on be holden alike intrinsicall or dependant an accessorie to the taking vp of dissention, and of making peace, as not ordaining the one, the other could not be effected? None will say it that shall compare them together, and none can say it, that haue wel looked vpō the sequell: contētiō, strife, debate, variance, broiles, scandall, parts-taking, enmitie, slaunders, calumniations, wrongs, iniuries, being now most rife in our Church, and neuer heard of before. Neither any maruell at all, whiles one who was vnknowne vnto vs to haue any such authoritie, nor many yeares euer holden but for our backe friend, would institute in our Church a new forme of gouernement, the like neuer heard of in the world, meerely penall, wholly consisting in punishing, and in punishing contrarie to the forme of law, that is, without citing, without triall, without proofe of the accusation. And to bring this intollerable burden vpon vs, without making so much as any one of our bodie priuie thereunto, and also to giue vs none other satisfaction of this his Graces straunge proceeding in our Church, but onely the warrant of his owne Letter, and the same not addressed to vs neither, but to the superiour onely, whom himselfe without all our consents or weeting preferred to the office, by the sole information of him, whose busie head and actions haue bene the cause and increase of much trouble and persecution in our Church and Realme. And who being a member of another bodie: and professing also a mortified state, and to haue relinquished the world, seeketh neuerthelesse to be our great maister, and to rule all: and would to God but to rule, and not to domineere or tyrannize rather.

Let any practised Gouernour Ecclesiasticall or temporall, or any one of common vnderstanding in the world, tell vs whether this platforme, this new and strange kind of gouernement, and as straunge a manner maner of proceeding in it, were a meane to make peace, or not rather the high way to breake peace, to kindle debates, to multiply dissention: and as it were to strike vp an alarum of troubles in our poore afflicted Church, too manifoldly (if it pleased God to the contrarie) alreadie tossed?

The new authoritie therefore being in it selfe no greater a helpe to the setting forward of peace, and in the sequell so preiudicious; the first, second, third, and fifth Propositions, shew that his Holinesse commaunding the Cardinall to bestow his paines for the establishing of peace and concord, to the patterne of the peace wrought in the English Colledge at Rome, did not therin for ought appeareth, or may be gathered out of the Constitutiue Letter, giue commission to his Grace to enact the foresaid iurisdiction.

Againe, the second, third, and fifth Propositions declare, that the enacting of the like authoritie, not being so nigh linked and vnited an accessorie to the principal in charge, as the one might not be wel effected without the institution of the other, declare we say, that we were not bound by any law of holy Church or duty of obedience, to subiect our selues to such his Graces ordinance: because his Grace seemed eue͂ by the tenour of the selfe Constitutiue Letter, to haue exceeded the limits of his Holinesse Commission vnto him, in that receiuing but a commaundement to make peace, he made an Archpriest, and indued him with largest punishing iurisdiction and soueraigntie ouer vs. Neither of which were behooueable, or not so behooueable to the making of peace, as that peace could not be made without these, as is already shewed. And therefore his Graces decree, touching the subordination could not, at least in the iudgement of our owne thoughts bind vs, the same appearing vnto vs to be an excesse or too great an enlargement of the delegation committed. Plaine by the authorities and proues laid downe in the said Propositions.

But if our aduersaries shall here say, that the Constitutiue Letter maketh mention how his Grace in ordaining the new authoritie, followed therein the will of his Holinesse: we may answere, that imagining as we did, and vpon most pregnant grounds, that father *Parsons* was the inditer of the letter, we had little reason knowing him as we do, to credit euery word therin, especially the matter being so greatly preiudiciall to our selues, Church, and Realme, and so fit a rise or step besides, to his further designes.

Another reason also, and which more induced vs not to beleeue euery word in the Cardinals Letter, was the report it made of the fatherly charitie which the Iesuits exhibited towards all Priestes in our countrey, and that they molested no one. An affirmance so farre from truth, as to doubt whether it be true or no, were to doubt whether yce be cold or fire hote, or whether there be a Sunne in the element. For who can deny, vnlesse he be resolued to deny any thing, how apparant or demonstrable soeuer, but that all the Cleargy and sociall dissention in our Realme proceeded from some of the fathers of the Society? The dissention at *Wisbich* from fa. *Weston* assuming superioritie, the dissention now on foot, from fa. *Lister* the author, from fa. *Garnet* the approuer: from fa. *Iones* the increaser, from fa. *Holtby* the maintainer, and from some other of the Society, the abettours of our most grieuous wrongs and infamie.

Thus no doubt we might answer, and neither idlely nor vntruly, yet we will not thus answer, but referre our selues to the sixth Proposition, which yeeldeth another kind of reioynder, and bringeth more light and helpe to our cause and innocencie.

For the said Proposition teacheth, that the formall obiect of obedience is the knowne precept of a Superiour, not the sole will, vnlesse it be an imperatiue or commanding will, and so notified as the subiect vnderstand it to be a commaund.

So that admitting we had bene bound to beleeue euery word in the Cardinals Letter, as how little we were bound it will appeare anon, and more in the next reason: yet the Cardinall vsing but these words (*Nos S^tis^ suæ pijssimam prouidentissimamq́, voluntatem sequentes, hoc ipsum statuere decreuimus*. We following the most godly and the most prouident will of his Holines, haue decreed to appoint a subordination among the English secular Priests) we could not see how this related will of his Holines did put on the nature of a precept, especially after so expresse and certain a maner, as that we were bound (all causes how iust soeuer set aside) to obey forthwith the new authoritie, & not respite our absolute submission therunto, no not so long as til we could sēd to his Holines for more direct & assured knowledge in the matter.

Beside, the reasons were neither few nor vulgar, but many and very materiall, which droue vs to thinke, that if his Holinesse had possessed such a determination, as at vnawares without any one of our assents or priuitie, to appoint vs a superiour, and with so large soueraigntie ouer vs, yet that he would neuer haue vsed so little fauour towards vs, who liue in the midst of so many miseries, and dayly spend our liues for the

truth

truth and primacie of that Chaire, as to enact the authoritie in so powerable a manner, that euen at the first appearing thereof, and by the bare Letter of one Cardinall only, it should be the crime either of notorious disobedience or schisme (an impossibilitie) euen not to prostrate our selues, and surrender our full and absolute obedience thereunto, without either making question how it came, or so much as to send to his Holinesse for vnderstanding whether it was his ordinance or no.

First the milde and sweete disposition of his Holinesse nature forbad vs so to thinke: then the quality of our pressures: the ancient Canons of the holy Church allowing Priests the election of their Archpriest: the deserts of our poore estate, seruing God in the degree of Priesthood without either enioying or expectance of Church liuing; yea and which did most of all deforce vs from entertaining so hard a thought of his Holinesse loue and pastorall regard towards vs his afflictiue labourers, was the most respectiue and honourable speeches, which himselfe vsed to some of our brethren: namely that he would not appoint any order of gouernemēt in our country, before the good Priests in England (so gracious were his Holinesse words) should aduertise him, what kind of gouernement were fittest & best sorted with the miseries of our Church.

Distinct. 63. Ca. Si in plebibus.

A ground of surreption.

That his Holinesse vsed these speeches, there be two Priests or moe in England that will depose it: and father *Parsons* himselfe hauing more then once reported so much, cannot without doing wrong to his religious profession, denie or vnsay the same. So that the question rested, whether of these two we should sooner and were more bound to beleeue, the Popes owne word or the Cardinals Letter. Either the Popes word related vnto vs by seuerall of our brethren of good report, and the immediate hearers thereof, or the Cardinals Letter penned as we no whit doubted, by our boldest aduersarie containing apparant vntruthes, as before is shewed, and will hereafter more appeare.

And now, the matter of our choise to whom we should giue more credite, being of this quality: whether sooner to beleeue the Popes owne word, or the Cardinals Letter, was it possible that father *Lister* or any other of lesse holy profession and of meaner parts, could embolden their pens and tongues to by-name vs so prodigally as he and some of his complicers haue done? Or could it be thought credible, that our superiour, who by his place and order of charity, is the more inuited to loue vs, and bound by iustice wherein he may to defend vs, would intreate his children (our trespasse no greater) in so vnkind and hard a manner as he hath done and continueth ? Let others, who can, aunswere. We will returne and proceede in our proues.

Senior *Acrisio* one of the Popes Fiscals, and who had commission to examine maister *Bishop* and maister *Charnocke* in their imprisonment at Rome, hath giuen very good testimony, & with like circumstances as not lightly any euidence may deserue more beliefe. For this officer hauing by himselfe and father *Parsons* taken the examination of the two prisoners, and demanded of like as many questions of them, as were thought necessary, he told them that now he was to make relation of all things to his Holinesse, and therefore counselled them to commend the cause to God by prayer, adding that it were not amisse also, if they would enioyne to themselues three dayes fast that weeke, for better prospering of the affaire. A spirituall taske which the prisoners gladly vndertooke, and performed in the time prescribed.

The next weeke Senior *Acrisio* came to the prisoners, and among other matters very confidently affirmed to them both apart, that the new superiority was not instituted by his Holinesse command, as his Holinesse himselfe (with whom the day before he had conference about the same point) told him, and yeelded for reason, that he durst not enact a forme of gouernement in our countrey (ô the strange information that was giuen against vs) for that he would not aduenture to haue his authority contemned of the Priests in England.

What better proofe (if Senior *Acrisio* Priest and his Holinesse Fiscall, be an honest man in his words) can be demanded then this, for iustifying the delay we made in subiecting our selues to the Archpriests authority ? What argument taken from th e euent of the matter, can be of more force to shew, that we had reason to suspēd our beliefe in many particulars of the *Constitutiue Letter*: or what more pregnant coniecture can there occurre (the Fiscals words being true) then that Fa. *Parsons* of likelihood hath told many a good tale to his Holinesse for inducing him to conceiue alike hardly of out whole secular Cleargy, as scarcely harder could be conceiued, had we bin the lozels of the world, and not our loyaltie, obedience, respect, loue, dutifulnes, and sufferance for the eminency of that Sea, equall with the merites of any Cleargy in the world ?

The

The same officer also, or another of greater calling, which is more likely, told maister *Bishop*, as himselfe witnesseth in his letter to Fa. *Parsons*, that his Holinesse had at the most, no other purpose touching the bond and imposition of the authority, then that it should be proposed to the Priests in England, for triall whether they thought that kind of gouernement fit & sorting with the state of their countrey, & then as they should make knowne their opinions therein, his Holinesse intended to establish or change it.

This letter is in the English booke.

And beside the report of the Fiscall herein, strengthned by so solemne and particular circumstances, the busie, busie endeuours of the society to get Priests to set to their names to a letter beginning with *Olim dicebamur*, in testimony of their applause and thanksgiuing to his Holinesse, for appointing the authoritie, and his Holinesse long delay (a full twelue moneth or thereabout) to cõfirme the same, is argument euident inough (if no inuincible proofe) that the truth and processe of matters, were no other then is sayd.

Or if in so probable a truth, there need moe coniectures, the hardnesse of our two brethren their intreaty by Fa. *Parsons*, the like, as neuer had a president in that place, doth not a litle confirme that all was not sound and iustifiable. For vndoubtedly if there had not layd a pad in the straw, or some secret hid in the decke of the stratageme, which Fa. *Parsons* would not haue his Holinesse and others to see: what need was there for him to procure (doubtlesse by no charitable or true information) the imprisoning of his countrey-men, of Priests, of labourers in Gods vineyard, of those who for zeale of religion, had made themselues incapable of fauour in their owne countrey, and one of them relinquished a rich inheritance; to procure the imprisoning of those who for many yeares space, had continually ventured their liues, and with good profit, for reducing of soules to the obedience of the Sea Apostolike: to procure the imprisoning of those, who with all submissiuenesse of duty came a long and a chargeable iourney to his Holinesse foote, out of loue and conscience to vnfold all things to his wisedome, and for truer vnderstanding of his Holinesse pleasure? What neede was there not onely to imprison them before they were heard, or could come to the presence of his Holinesse, but to apprehend them with Isberze by night, with torches most infamously, and himself (a religious mã) to be the leader & chieftaine? What need was there to imprison them apart, to rifle them of all the instructions, letters, and notes they brought, to keepe them close without licence so so much as to heare Masse, euen vpon some of the chiefest feasts in Gods Church? What need was there for himselfe to be their Iailour, and keeper of the keyes of both their chambers? What need was there to deny them to haue their learned counsel or Aduocates which they seuerally and earnestly requested, and which seemed so iust a petition as father *Holby* in his discourse of the last of Iune 1601. auoweth vnder serious protestation, that they had it graunted vnto them, and bringeth it in, to imply their greater guiltinesse, for that hauing their learned counsell and pleaders allowed, were neuerthelesse condemned and found worthy of the punishment layd vpon them, which was to be banished, and confined in the banishment, without any contribution or reliefe at all towards their maintenance? What neede was there, their arrest and imprisonment being so publickly knowne as it was, and the whole course and manner thereof being so straunge, as it could not but giue token to euery one of some notable and hainous crime in them, to try them after in secret in the Colledge, and to suffer neither scholler of the house, nor externe, nor any at all, to be present at their triall, beside the two Cardinals their Iudges, Senior *Acrisio* the Fiscall, father *Tichborne* the Notary, Doctor *Haddocke*, & master *Martin Array* aduocates for the Archpriest, himselfe, and the two prisoners, to the ende no doubt, that none might witnesse, lament, and admire, for what sinfull trespasse (so to call their Christian intents) they were so long and so straightly imprisoned, and condemned to the sufferance of so greatly infamous and extreame punishment? What neede was there neuer to release them of their durance, no not after their triall before the two Cardinals, vntil such time as his Holinesse had cõfirmed the authority by his Breue? What need was there that in the verie graunt of the prisoners liberty, they must be enioyned vnder heauiest penalties to depart the city within twelue dayes, and that the dayes of the one must be expired too, ere the other might be enlarged, or set foote out of the Colledge? What need was there that the prisoners being to be exiled and confined, might not yet (as they instantly desired) be confined together in one place or prouince? In fine, what need was there that our two brethren might not at least going both one way for many hundreth of miles to the places assigned of their confinement, could neuerthelesse vpon their instant desire be suffered to take comfort one of the others company, being both Priests, in so wearisome, dangerous, and desolate a iourney?

New yeares day and Twelfe day.

Vndoubtedly these & other like vsages insinuated something: they had

had their meaning: fa. *Parsons* is wise, and therfore how little soeuer his complexion inclineth him to pittie, yet he would not shew the like extremities for manifesting his inclination and potencie onely. He deuised the platforme of the gouernement: our brethren disliked it. Enough: Or if we should adde more, what must we say? The authoritie being a bird of fath. *Garnet* and father *Parsons* own hatching, and the man whom they promoted thereunto of their owne chusing: also the forme of the subordination creating themselues in truth and vnderhand, the appointers of the Archpriest, the designers of the Assistants, the makers of our lawes, the dispensers, the disposers, the directors, the commaunders, and our great masters in all things. Their stomackes were too great not to haue the subordination to go forward, howsoeuer father *Parsons* his soule lay at pawne in the *Interim*, as wel for his vsage towards our two brethren, as also for abusing therein of the Sea Apostolicke.

Neither among so many strange wonders, could we maruell at any thing more, then what the cause or drift might be, why father *Parsons* comming on a time from his Holinesse, told one of the prisoners M. Charuock that he had neuer so much ado, as to perswade his Holines, that he and his fellow Agent were Catholicke Priestes and not heretickes; a thing as father *Parsons* auowed, which his Holinesse would not beleeue of a long while. O good God, to what times are we reserued to liue in, either for that so vniust an information should be giuen to the highest Pastour against vertuous Priests, or that an auncient religious man, should in such sort glose and counterfeit? For it cannot be possible, if his Holinesse stood so conceited, but that very impious vntruths and with greatest colour of truth were inculcated to his Holinesse, ere his practised and aged iudgement could entertaine and ground so bad an opinion of English Priestes, as they comming so farre off vnto him, should be of any other religion then Catholicke.

Two Priests to come out of England to Rome, and purposely to his Holinesse Chaire, and in a message and supplication from Priestes: whereof a good many were then, are now, and had bene a long while in durance for the Catholicke cause, and in an affaire meerely belonging to the Romane Religion, with a prest readines also to follow and obey his Holinesse order in the same, as vnder their booke-othes they assured, are (we trow) no tokens of heresie, but ablest demonstration of conuincing the contrarie.

What should then be the cause that his Holines was possessed with so hard an opinion against them, and consequently against vs all, from whom, and in whose names they came? Was it the matter they came about? Impossible, if right information had bene giuen: because they came only to vnderstand the truth cōcerning the institutiō of the new authoritie, and to open to his Holinesse wisedom, our difficulties about the same: and to acquaint him with the spiritual wants of our country, with humblest petition for supply. Cardinall *Caietane* (who had most cause to stretch the action to the hardest sense against vs, in that it might beare some semblāce of an opposition against his ordinance) & Cardinall *Burghesio* openly acknowledged at the time when our two brethren appeared before them, sitting in iudgement vpon their cause, that they could not find fault with the intention and matter they came for. And if the intention & matter were lawfull or not iustly to be blamed, as both their Graces affirmed, let our aduersaries tell what might the trespasse be, why his Holinesse mind was so greatly auerted, or rather his holy zeale incensed?

The messengers were reported, the one to be a Maultster and a Horse-courser, the other for an incontinent person. O tongue libertie whither runnest thou? O father *Parsons* how credulous are you in bad matters? Let but this latter be proued, notwithstāding you said (who perchance counteth such a saying no bad pollicie) that a Priest sware it, and two other Priestes tooke their othes that they heard him sweare it, and we do all here yeeld our selues without further conuiction to be traytours to God and his Church, and craue the fagot.

There was a night-cappe with a border of blacke silke two fingers deepe, a dozen of silke points, fine sockes, a sword, and a dagger found in their chambers, and matter of much good sport made therat: father *Parsons* the chiefest doer, hauing now forgotten how himselfe went attired when he liued in England, and how some of his brethren here now go more costly then any Priest.

The messengers were accused, that they came to *Rome* to renue the stirs in the Colledge. The apprehension of M. *Dudley*, M. *Barrowes*, M. *Rowse*, and M. *Watson*: the remoue of Fa. *Weston*, M. *Archer*, M. *Southworth*, and M. *Pound*, from *Wisbich* to the Tower: the great search made by the Officers for our Archpriest, was laid to their charge, as a complot agreed on before their going, and after executed by vs here their confederates. To make the bead-rowle long inough, it was obiected that M. Doctour *Bagshaw* had a pension of fiftie pound a yeere

of

of her Maiestie: that we dealt with the Counsell and tooke direction from them. The fall of M. *Ithell*, and the Apostacie of Frier *Sacheuerill*, were laid warmely in their dish, with a long rable of surmises, what would become of some others if they hold on? Were not these fine exceptions (we appleale to the whole world) or accusations rather? Who would euer think they could haue bin spoken without a vizard, or obiected by any who before had not shaken hands with all shamefastnesse? Alas alas, whither do vnruly humours driue such, as serue them? For could there be grosser tales deuised, if one would haue fabled for the whetstone? or more infamous slaunders coined, if there had beene a dispensation graunted to forge at pleasure? That these things were laid in the dish of our two brethren, & against vs their fellows, it cannot with any truth be denied, or but with the abandoning of a great deale of modestie be stood against. For sundry Letters containing the greatest part of the premises, and which father *Parsons* had the perusing of, and was the inditor or prompter of all, or most of the contents, and which also himselfe sent open into England, to and for our Archpriest and others to reade, are yet extant, and both the priests liuing against whom the said counterfeit crimes were obiected, and who are ready to witnesse, or if need so require, to depose so much as before is rehearsed.

But what would we inferre out of all these? Verily not that father *Parsons* did accuse them and vs to his Holines in al the foresaid crimes, for then vndoubtedly his maners had bene so far discrepant from the etymologie of his religious name, as blacke is from white, or hell from heauen. Neuerthelesse we cannot but assure our selues that he or some other (and none but himselfe hath the office of informership in the English affaires) plaid a monstrous bad part in inciting his Holinesse by vntrue and vngodly suggestion to conceiue so infinite hardly of our two brethren, as not to be brought but vpon long perswasion to thinke them to be Catholicke Priests.

Now although the reasons, testimonies, and probabilities already alleaged may sufficiently declare, what grounds we had to beleeue that his Holinesse did neither commaund the institution of the new authoritie, nor was priuie to the particulars: yet because we desire to abound in the purgation of our good names (being all that we haue to leese, and *better then great riches*) we will adde a few more for fuller *Prouerb. 22.* proofe and testimonie of the issue.

It seemed then a matter most improbable vnto vs, that his Holinesse carrying a singular praise for his wisedome and clemencie in gouerning, would euer appoint so barren an authoritie in our poore distressed Church, as this appeared to be, consisting wholly in a libertie and freedome to punish without the admixture of the least comfort redounding to any thereby. Yea it appeared incredible in our vnderstanding, that his Holinesse after so many tokens of fauour and compassion towards our miseries, would ordaine the like strange and penall gouernement, and not so much as to giue vs notice thereof from himselfe by Breue or missiue letter: knowing that without such immediate notice or other Canonicall certitude, we could neither in discretion, wisedome, nor conscience, admit so meere a burthen void of all maner of commoditie in our Church.

Note the precedent.

When his Holinesse made Cardinall *Allen* of blessed memory, our Superiour, he declared it by a Breue, notwithstanding the state and rich deserts of the man, our founder in learning and common parent. Which president and foregoing example, did in a sort commaund vs to beleeue, that if the new subordination (farre more straunge and in some points more ample too, then the authoritie of the good Cardinall) had bene the binding ordinance of his Holinesse, his pastorall wisedome would in like manner haue vouchsafed (specially conferring so large iurisdiction vpon a priuate man, not in dignitie before, nor of any marke or reckening in comparison of the true vertuous, a like wise, and most learned *Allen*) to publish and attestate such his fact to our Church by a Breue or some other kind of Apostolicall writ. And we were alike thorow setled in this opinion, as we reckned the contrary a plaine derogation to his Holinesse wisedome, clemencie, iudgement and compassion.

Another probabilitie. The *Constitutiue Letter* as M. *Blackwell* read it vnto vs, directed (except our memories do much deceiue vs) that the rest of the Assistants who were left to the Arch-priest to chuse, should be selected out of the number of the auncientest Priests, that had their places of residence in or nearest about London, to the end (as the reason was adioyned) that he might vpon euery occurrance, haue some readie at hand to consult withall. The breaking of which prescript, forme and direction, did secure vs that the *Letter Constitutiue* was not the ordinance or commaundement of his Holinesse. For if it had bene either, as there wanted not reason to moue vs, so did we throughly presume, that neither M. *Blackwell* nor the Iesuits (in truth the chiefe Electors) receiuing expresse direction to chuse the rest of the assistants

among

among the elder sort of Priestes, residing in or nearest about London, would euer haue bene so venturous, as contrarie to the selfe-forme of the Commission, not only to chuse two, three, or foure of the Assistants, but the whole number of them in places furthest remote from the place assigned. And that such a direction was expressely contained in the Cardinals Letter, as it was shewed vnto vs by M. *Blackwel*, M. *Charnocke*, and my selfe (who were first of al sent for before him to acknowledge the authority) are ready to witnes, and beside the record of both our memories, the presumptions ensuing do not a little seeme to confirme the same.

Anon after that M. *Blackwel* had chosen the ful number of the Assistants, a Gentleman very inward with him in these affaires, brought their names vnto me in writing, which when I had read and saw that some of thẽ which were chosen, dwelt in the North, another in *Wales*, a nother in the West Country, and others in place farre distant, and no one in, or neare to London, the place assigned: I demaunded why M. *Blackwell* had not chosen his Assistants according to the direction of the Cardinals Letter out of the number of the auncientest Priests in and about London. The Gentleman not denying but that the Cardinals Letter so prescribed, gaue this answere: that if M. *Blackwell* had chosen the Assistants according to the direction of the Cardinals Letter in and neare about London, this inconuenience had followed, that he could not haue had, or not so conueniently by much, so ready aduertisements from those parts and quarters of the Realme, where he hath now chosen the Assistant, as by this meane (his Assistants there residing) he shall haue.

Which reason how weightie soeuer it appeare, yet because in Delegations, and no lesse in subdelegation, the [a] forme of the rescript is of the substance of the Commission, and strictly to be obserued, and not to be gone from, or what is done to the contrary to be of no force and void in law, as the third, fourth, and fifth, Propositions teach. For which respect, and also because the reason alleaged in the Cardinals Letter, for hauing the rest of the Assistants to be chosen in and neare about *London*, was expedient and very behouefull: we could not thinke that M. *Blackwell* or the Iesuits would euer (in any such ouert & actual maner at least) transgresse the direction and selfe-forme of the Commission, had he, or they taken the *Constitutiue Letter* to be the ordinance of his Holinesse, and not for the plot of father *Parsons*, receiuing reputation by bearing the Cardinals name, but the thing it selfe left

(a) *Ca. Cum dilecta. de rescriptis, & glossa ibidem. Ca. si cui de elect. li. 6. & glo. ibidem & glo. in ca. Praeterea de off. de leg. verb. simpliter. Panormitan. in ca. Cũ post, de elect. nu. 1. & Ant. Frã. eodem ca. verb. ipso iure Hostiensis de offici. iud. deleg. nu. 8. Speculum eod. tit. §. 5. n. 1. & alii.*

wholly to the others order,framing,and direction.

Another proofe or presumption , though not so forceably concluding , and which time (a good decypherer of matters) hath sithence discouered , is the appearing of a second forme of the *Constitutiue Letter* as we take it , or at leastwise of a copie of the *Constitutiue Letter*,subscribed and signed with the Cardinals hand and seale, as was the *Constitutiue Letter* it selfe. And that this is true, thus we make plaine. The *Constitutiue Letter* which M.*Blackwell* first shewed vnto vs,bore date the 7.of March, 1598. as himselfe will not deny,nor can, if he then shewed vs the true Letter, because the Popes Breue confirmeth it by that date : and about some foure moneths after the attonement made vpon the arriuall of his Holinesse Breue, my selfe intreating M. *Blackwell* for a sight of the Cardinals Letter, to the end I might once throughly see (as wisedome and conscience did require) to what I was bound : he sent me the Letter which is *verbatim* set downe in the beginning of the booke, and which was subscribed and sealed with the Cardinals name and signet : and his name so farre as we could gesse (for moe Priests saw it beside my self) was written also with his Graces owne hand. But this Letter bore no date at all,either of the day of the moneth,or yeare of our Lord,as I can wel proue (if it be denied) by sufficient witnesses.

And being in this maner infallibly sure that there were two seueral *Letters Constitutiue*,both attested with the Cardinals hand and seale, the one with date,the other without date:and therefore not to be said that the Cardinall out of his prouident wisedome, sent two Letters of one purport into England,to the end that if one miscarried,the other might come to M. *Blackwell* his hand : for that a Letter bearing no date,can carry little credence,and consequently not sufficient to work so great and effect as was intended,the erection and establishment of a subordination , both meerly penall,and without example from the beginning of the world.

Hereupon,I for my part do not see the counter-euidence, why M. *Charnocke* and my selfe should distrust, or not rather trust our memories agreeing both in one, and little doubt but the *Constitutiue Letter* which M.*Blackwel* first shewed to vs both,differed frõ the other which he sithence sent vnto me to reade. And not onely in the matter about chusing the Assistants,but in another point also more importãt:which was,that the offenders should *dicta causa*,be heard to speake & answer for themselues,before condemnation or punishment inflicted:a right

that

that nature and all lawes prescribe. I vse the Latine words (*dicta causa*) because I seeme and haue since euer seemed to remember the very words themselues, which maketh me as in this, so in the former also the lesse doubtfull by much, whether my memorie faileth me, yea or no in the said particulars.

Neither can we yeeld a reason why fa. *Parsons* or some other might not as well alter the *Constitutiue Letter* in these points, as he or some other altered the sentence of the two Cardinals, *Caietane* and *Burghese*, in the exile & confinement of our two brethren. And that their honours sentence was altered in the copy, which was sent into England by fa. *Parsons* (vnles some other besides fa. *Parsons* writeth to our Archpriest of such matters) & which M. *Blackwel* read to M. *Mush* & me, & shewed the same to others, is so apparant a truth, that M. *Blackwell* can in no sort deny it. The sentence in the originall was, that in vertue of holy obedience & vnder censure of present suspension from diuine offices, they should not (*pro tempore* for a time) presume to go into *England*, *Scotland*, or *Ireland* without the expresse leaue of his Holinesse or the Lord Cardinall Protector: but in the copie it was thus changed, that vnder the foresaid censure they should not presume to returne or go into any of the said kingdomes for the space of 3. yeares. So that the wordes (*pro tempore* for a time) in the originall signifying an indefinit space of time, were altered in the copy which was sent into *England*, went here currant & none but it, into a determined & set space of time, contrary to the wordes of the originall, and more then could be collected out of the tenor, nor the sentence euer so interpreted to our brethren on whom it passed.

Now if fa. *Parsons* dealt thus boldly in the sentence of the two Cardinals, what reason can be yeelded why we should discredit our memories standing vpon so many presumptions, rather then thinke that fa. *Parsons* would straine curtesie to change or get to be changed the *Letter Constitutiue*, a deuice and plot of his owne, and whereof he hath the whole managing.

That which we would adde further in this point, is: that his Holines confirming onely that Letter of the Cardinall which bore date the 7. of March, in which the abouenamed particulars were expressed (vnlesse as is said, our memories do wonderfully deceiue vs, whereof yet we haue no more doubt then of what we doubt least) it followeth, if so the said particulars were indeed expressed in the *Constitutiue Letter* which his Holinesse confirmed, that the election of the Assistants made by M. *Blackwell* is fruſtrate, and likewiſe all ſuch cenſures and penalties as he hath impoſed vpon vs, otherwiſe then the forme of his Commiſſion gaue him authoritie to do. And conſequently reſteth bound by the preſcript [a] rule of law and conſcience to make vs rateable ſatisfaction to the meaſure of the infamie and damages ſuſtained: great and very great both.

For proofe of the premiſes Pope *Innocentius* the third writeth, [b] *Proceſſum contra formam reſcripti attentatum, irritum decernimus & inanem.* We define that the Proceſſe be of no effect and voyd which was either begun or proceeded in, cōtrarie to the forme of the Cōmiſſion. The like to this, hath Pope *Bonifacius* the eight. [c] *Si cui eligendi poteſtas data fuit, & iuxta traditam ſibi formam non eligerit talis electio non valet nec robur obtinet firmitatis.* If power of electing be giuen to any one, and he ſhall not chooſe according to the limit or forme preſcribed, ſuch an election is voide (* *ipſo iure*) and retaineth no force.

Now, that he who receiueth Commiſſion to chuſe for ſuch a cauſe, ſuch perſons to his Aſſiſtants, as haue their reſidences at ſuch a place, breaketh the forme of his Commiſſion if he chuſe them otherwhere, there can be no queſtion made thereof, and conſequently the [d] act he doth therein is of no validitie, nor can bind any one to take them for Aſſiſtants.

(a) *Ca. fin. de iniuriis. ca. ſacro de ſent. excom. Gloſſa in ca. quoniam cōtra de probation. v'b. negligentiam. Nauar in man. ca. 25. nu. 12. Silueſt. v'b. iudex 1. nu. 17. & omnes.*
(b) *Ca. Cum dilecti, de reſcriptis.*
(c) *Ca. Si cui de elect. lib. 6.*
* *Gloſſa. Ibidē v'b. valere.*
(d) *Panormit. in ca. prudentiā de offi. iud dele. nu. 5. & Ant. Fran. in ca. cum poſt de electione.*

The third and laſt principall reaſon, why we could not thinke the new ſubordination to be the ordinance of his Holineſſe, or appointed by his commaundement, was in reſpect of the rigours it contained, a note fartheſt remoued from his Holineſſe nature, and courſe of proceeding. For inſtances.

Firſt, it appeared incredible that his Holineſſe tender compaſſion towardes the ſeuerall and heauieſt afflictions that the lawes of our Country lay vpon vs, would to the increaſe of our burthen inſtitute a meere penall iuriſdiction in our Church, carrying only power to puniſh & afflict vs more: yea, and in ſuch ſort (as we tooke the caſe) to puniſh and afflict vs, as not after any condigne ſatisfaction and worthieſt amendment, the Superiour had authoritie to reſtore the offender, to that which before he depriued him of, namely his faculties, the onely inſtrument and meane of doing good to others, and for himſelfe to liue by. For although in Cenſures of holy Church regularly he that hath authoritie to bind, hath alſo authoritie to looſe, and contrarywiſe he that hath authoritie to looſe, hath authoritie to bind: yet

24. q. 1. ca. Si Petrus. & diſt. 21. ca. inferior. & de pænit. diſt. 1. ca. verbū & Silueſter. verb. Abſolu. 1. nu. 3.

yet it followed not at least in our vnderstanding (the taking away of faculties being no censure) that because the Archpriest had authoritie giuen him to take away faculties, graunted by whom or whensoeuer, therefore he could giue or restore them againe, after he had once taken them away, in regard his authority being delegatiue and after a prescript forme it could not (at least as we thought) be extended beyond the cases expressed. And therefore no expresse signification being made of any such authority in the *Constitutiue Letter*, that he might restore againe all such faculties as he had for any cause taken away, we thought the subordination to be much more rigorous or defectiue in this point, then that it could be the ordinance or commandemement of his Holinesse.

A second instance. It appeared incredible that his Holinesse bearing so great commendation for mercifulnesse and lenitie as he doth, would neuerthelesse enact a new kind of punishment for the Priests of our countrey onely, fighting in more bloud for maintaining the soueraignty of that Chaire, then any other Cleargy at this day in the world. We presume to say a new kind of punishment for the Priests of our countrey only, because the auncient and vsuall manner of punishing Priests in other countries, that shew themselues disobedient, vnquiet, or stubborne, against their Ecclesiasticall superiours, is by imposition of censures, that is by debarring them the vse of their Priestly functions, not by taking their faculties quite from them. But in the new subordination, authoritie is giuen not onely to suspend or debarre vs from the vse of our faculties, but as if that tye and punishment were too slight, or brought not misery inough vpon vs, we must haue all our faculties taken quite and cleane from vs, giuen by whom and whensoeuer. A kind of iurisdiction seldome heard of, and neuer vsed vpō any Pastors, such as al the Priests in our country are after a sort reputed to be, & so named in the 9. Instruction. Nor was the iurisdiction euer practised in England while good Cardinal *Allen* liued, but an extremity taken vp only since Fa. *Par.* began to sit at sterne, & therby become more bold to vnmaske his violent nature. Yea as M. *Blackwell* now demeaneth the matter, and sayth he hath good warrant for it, not only al our faculties must be taken wholy away from vs vpon due conuiction of a fault, but the like prosecution must be made vpon vs without triāll, without proofe, without summons, meerely at the arbitrary disposition of himselfe, that is (as the euent hath hitherto shewed) when & so often as he shall imagine or be pleased to pretend a cause.

A third instance. We could not beleeue (the action being without an example in Gods Church) that his Holinesse determining to make a superiour ouer our whole secular Cleargy, would institute no greater a prelate thē an Archpriest to take the charge: especially if his Holinesse then meant so much, as in his later Breue is sithēce appointed, that he should also be a superiour ouer the laity, as well honorable as worshipfull. And not onely to gouerne all the secular Priests residing within the realme, but to gouerne, direct, and command vs if so we do or shall reside in the kingdome of Scotland,

A scope which conuinced our vnderstanding, that the subordination was not the appointment or decree of his Holinesse, but some fine descant or politicke deuice plotted by father *Parsons* for seruing some turne appertaining to state matters. We wish it were not so, but it is too plaine: for if consideration of matters of this quality were laid aside, what reason can be giuen that an Archpriest residing in England, should direct and gouerne his Countrey-priests in Scotland, where also no English Priests at the time of instituting the authority, or since is knowne to reside? But father *Parsons* harbouring some watchfull bugs in his brest, and forecasting matters a farre off, thought it good wisedome to preuent the contingent, which his owne feare or surmizes suggested, and to forelay what might fall in time: verifying therein the words of our Sauiour, *The children of this world, are wiser then the children of light in their generation.* (*Luke* 16.)

A fourth instance. On the one side it appeared straunge, that his Holinesse hauing set so long in the Chaire as he hath, and receiuing aduertisements of the miseries of our Church, could be so little weeting to the state of Priestes and lay Catholikes in our countrey, as to thinke Priests might be remoued from one residence to another by authority, and not great and open daunger to ensue. And on the other side, if so his Holinesse were ignorant of the lawes of our country, or did not vnderstand the miseries and dangers we liue in, what sinne could our prolonging be, of not subiecting our selues to the new authority, till we had informed his Holinesse therein, and shewed how inconuenient, nay how dangerous, or truer, how impossible it was for any such iurisdiction to be practised in our countrey, vnlesse we did wilfully lay open, not onely our selues, but our Catholike friends to the hazards of a thousand ieopardies? Let that point of the subordination, the termes of our realme, and the nature of requisite circumstances be considered together, and the demonstration is made of as much

much as is auerred.

We will here let passe in silence that one of the Assistants (the Iesuits chiefe solicitor in forwarding this new authority at Rome) was the man, who first suggested that clause of remouing Priests from their places of residence to be inserted in the iurisdiction of the Archpriest, alleadging such a cause for his good deede, as howsoeuer his discretion serued to tell it, yet our conscience, and feare of preiudice to manie, especially if the faculty should happen to be practised as hath bene already threatned, will not giue vs leaue to recite it.

Alexander the third writing to the Archbishop of *Rauenna*, and pointing out the respect and duty we should beare to the Sea Apostolike, vseth these words: *Aut mandatum nostrum adimpleas, aut quare adimplere non possis rationabilem causam prætendas.* Either regardfully fulfill our commaundement, or alleadge a reasonable cause why you cannot. As if the good Pope would haue sayd, the commandement of the Sea Apostolicke, or of any other superiour ought to be carefully executed, vnlesse there be a reasonable cause to the contrary. Neither is this a false glosse or an enlarging of the Popes words, being the same with the written Glosse: *Mandatum superioris debet adimpleri vel reddenda ratio quare non adimpletur.* The commandement of a superiour ought to be accomplished, or a reason rendered why it is not accomplished. And in another place: *Oportet mandatum Domini Papæ adimplere, nisi subsit ratio non adimplendi.* It behoueth to fulfill the commandement of the Pope, except there be a cause of not fulfilling it.

Ca. Si quando de rescript.

Glossa ibidem.

Glossa in ca. cum teneamur de præbend.

And it is likewise a receiued doctrine among all [a] diuines, that an exception of reasonable cause excuseth from sinne, and is to be admitted in all precepts soeuer in positiue lawes.

A document which our aduersaries seeme by the nature of their proceedings to be little acquainted withall, in that they did so rashly and most wrongfully condemne vs, we wote not of how many enormities, without so much as suspending their iudgements, till they had heard or enquired after our reasons, or knowne what we could say for iustifying, or excusing our bearing off, by them so peremptorily condemned.

(a) D. Tho. in sen. dist. 15. q. 3. art. 4. ad quartum quest. ad 3 Sil. verb. lex. nu 8 Graff. p. 1. Li. 2. c. 1. 36. nu. 16.

O Lord, who could thinke, the contrary being not seene and felt, that men of learning, men of religion, men that must be accounted of a passing mild spirite, would censure, adiudge and diuulge that action of ours to be so grieuous a crime as they made it, being in his nature no other, then which Popes themselues haue decreed to be lawfull, and millions of true obedient children haue without scruple committed?

To wade further, be it that we knew the Archpresbitership and the iurisdiction adioyned, to be the commaundement, or immediate act of his Holinesse, as before the arriuall of his first Breue (the whole time of our bearing off) we ne did, nor could win our thoughts to suspect any such matter: what, must it by and by put on the nature of enormious disobedience, and we wote not what else, to deferre the accomplishment of the sayd commaundement vpon manifest euidence of vntrue and most ignominious suggestion expressed in the front of the same Letter, wherein the commaundement it selfe was signified, and alledged also for the chiefe and sole cause, why the subordination was instituted? Verily if such auouance be throughly and vprightly looked into, there cannot but appeare in them matter of dishonoring the Sea Apostolicke and supreme pastours, as that hauing made forth their cõmandements, vpon information cannot, or must not, after permit that any delay be made by the subiect in executing the commandements, how wrong & detractiue soeuer they shall thinke, or know, the information to be: then which, what is farther from reason, or can deeper distaine?

But leauing to others to comment vpon the paradoxe, we desire the aduersarie that can say most in the cause, to particulate the reason, which in our duty and loue towards his Holinesse, should haue moued vs to thinke that his mild and sweet course of proceeding with all other nations, had so maruellously chaunged it selfe towards the professant Catholikes of our Realme, his oppressed children, as to graunt authority to the Archpriest to place and displace Priests in their houses, harboring them of charity, when but an inckling of receiuing any Priest into their house is matter inough to occasion trouble, and the proofe or knowledge thereof a sufficient cause vtterly to vndoe thẽ & their whole family. A iurisdiction therfore farre more inconuenient & hurtfull, then we could any way beleeue his Holinesse euer appointed: nay our vnderstanding gaue vs that we could not but with breach of bounden duty thinke that his Holinesse would euer assigne such a faculty as we for the foresayd cause and preiudice, as also for that it giueth authority to the Archpriest to dispose of the persons of secular Priests, a thing neuer heard of: yea in the consequence to dispose of our liues too, in regard that all Catholike houses, whither he may remoue vs, be not alike safe and free from danger.

What

What shall we say? We could no way imagine that this so rare & ample iurisdiction came from any other then from the heads of father *Garnet* and fathers *Parsons*, as bearing the right stampe of father *Parsons* nature, and sorting with other his forcible pollicies. For by inuesting the Archpriest (their owne at commaundement) with this soueraigne kind of iurisdiction, they knew they had a meane alwayes ready at hand, to helpe when they would, their brethren the Iesuites and other their deuoted friends to the best places in our Realme, and thereby, to draw to their party such of the laity, as they would fainest haue to comply and aduance their proceedings: First by remouing the Priest they keepe, if he be thought an impediment thereunto, and after by placing another Priest in his roome, who must prepare and win them, in the maner he shall be directed.

A fifth instance. It seemed most improbable vnto vs, that his Holinesse knowing in what deepe disgrace we liue with our Prince, and in what vtter contempt and scorne with the greater number of our Realme by infinite (and this for no cause more, if for any so much, as for honouring and maintaining the supreme dignity of that Chaire) would neuerthelesse, adde this hard fauour and increase of dishonour to our other afflictions: as that we should in no chaunge, haue the election of our superiour, but the Cardinall Protector (a straunger, and who being a chiefe patrone of our oppositors, hath shewed himselfe alwayes a backe friend to our party) should without any of our voyces, or the least aduice taken from vs, euermore of himselfe appoint our Archpriest. A greater disgust then we could perswade our selues, that his Holinesse for the compassion and respect he beareth toward our miseries, would euer shew, specially to our whole Cleargy.

And certes we could not recken this so straunge a prouiso, but for a cunning deuise of they two foresayd Iesuites, both to preuent that none might be chosen to the place, but such as themselues should well like, and haue the preferring of, and by the intersession and meane of this fauour bestowed, euermore to make themselues the proprietaries and commanders of our Archpriest, and haue him ready to execute all their designes: punish, remoue, disgrace, whom, when, and how they should appoint.

In briefe, the speeches that M. *Blackwell* himselfe vsed not long after the receit of the *Constitutiue Letter*, bred at that time an assured opinion in vs, that the authority he claimed, was not the institution of his Holinesse. The speeches were these: [That if we would accept of the ſubordination appointed, and ſhould obediently demeane our ſelues thereunto, his Holineſſe intended, after ſome triall of our cariage vnder this forme of gouernement, to make Biſhops in our Church, and to allow them as large pentions as the reuenewes of Biſhoprickes in our countrey amounted to in a Catholicke time.] Which words ſounding very vnlikely in our eares, what could we in reaſon thinke, but that, if the authority had bene the act of his Holineſſe, ſuch groſſe inducements little needed: and conſequently the vſing of them did more and more confirme vs, that the ſubordination was only a platforme of the Ieſuites, put in execution by the Cardinall without any commandement of his Holineſſe, for erecting the ſame in particular with the faculties adioyned.

And to make this of the more probability, there occurred three other ſpeciall preſumptions, the one was certaine ſpeeches, vttered by a Senior Aſſiſtant: The ſecond, the deuiſing of [*Olim dicebamur*] for gathering of names: The third, the order of ſwearing Prieſtes of the Colledges ere they ſhould haue faculties giuen them for England.

A letter of thankeſgiuing the eighth of Nouember 1599.

Touching the firſt, maiſter *Terwit* the ſecond Senior Aſſiſtant very inward with the Ieſuites in moſt of the affaires ſpake (as we were told) vpon what occaſion himſelfe better knoweth, that the new authority, meaning the ſubordination was but to continue for a yeare or two, being only procured for curbing maiſter *Muſh* and *Collington*, with a few others. Which words howſoeuer we deſerued them at his hands (as I for my part neuer ſaw the man in England but once, and then, but for a dinner while onely, when alſo there paſſed no occaſion to my knowledge, that might conceit him ſo hardly againſt me, but rather the contrary) yet they could not but giue vs cauſe to doubt, & the more we knew him to be great with Fa. *Parſons* & Fa. *Garnet* (the only archcontriuers of the ſubordination) the better ground we thought we had to beleeue the ſpeeches, and his words being true, we aſſured our ſelues that the ſubordination was not the act nor commandement of his Holineſſe: for then, it could no way probably be in their power to let it dye in the time mentioned, as it did eaſily lye in their power to let it fall at the end of that time, if the ſubordination were the meere ordinance of the Cardinall his grace, he being ſo neare alyed in affection to father *Parſons* in particular, and to the whole body of the ſociety in generall.

Touching the ſecond. The Ieſuits or our Archprieſt, either, or both aduertiſing father *Parſons* that ſome refuſed to receiue the ſubordination

tion, and excepted against the Cardinall Protector his letter, as insufficient to establish the kind of gouernement it appointed: What did father *Parsons* but presently inuented (as notice was giuē vs) this peece of finenesse, that forsooth his friends here, the Archpriest and the Iesuites, should frame a letter of thanksgiuing to his Holinesse for instituting of the new subordination in our Church, and procure the subscription of as many Priests hands thereunto as they could. Whereupon a common letter was anon penned for rendering thankes to his Holinesse, *in making vs happy and fortunate through the very great, wholsome and singular benefit which it had pleased his Pastorall care to bestow vpon vs, by commanding our most Illustrious Protector Cardinall* Caietane *to institute the forme of gouernement, now by him erected in our countrey.* The words *Olim dicebamur.*

To which letter (oflike for the better drawing on of others to follow) the Iesuites who were not within the lists of the subordination, did first of all put to their names. Neither did their charity or forwardnesse content it selfe with this, but as, if the blame should haue lighted onely on them, if any had bene slacke or neglected the homage, they and their friends spared no labour or perswasion of mouing and soliciting others to giue their names: yea the businesse was so effectually prosecuted, as some were made to beleeue it was sinne, others told to be schisme not to giue their names, and all brought to beleeue, that his Holinesse looked to receiue thankes.

Strange, that the greatest personage in the world, an old man, vertuous, holy, humble, wise, cumbred with a thousand affaires, so as he can hardly giue audience to heare matters of waight, should looke to receiue thankes, and in a letter subscribed with two or three hundreth names, and for conferring no greater a benefit then for commanding Cardinall *Caietane* to institute an Archpriest with iurisdiction only to punish (for at that time maister *Blackwell* had no other authority) such as were before ouerwhelmed in miserie, and euery houre in daunger of leesing their liues, for defending the diuine rights of his Papacy, & for maintaining Christs truth, and the nobliest cause vpon earth. And with whose names must this letter be subscribed? with a Catalogue of names of poore Priests, distressed persons, beggars, neither knowne, nor euer heard of by his Holinesse, and distant by more then a thousand miles from him.

But had his Holinesse expected or exacted thankes at the Priestes hands of our country, yet who would thinke that our Archpriest and the twelue Assistants, being our heads, and consequently the principall persons in our body, had not beene a competent and sufficient number, or at the most with sixe or ten other of the ancientest Priests, to haue ioyned in such a letter of humbling thankes to his Holinesse in their owne, and in the behalfe of the rest. Or admit it be *decorum* to subscribe such a multitude of names in a letter to his Holinesse, and in no greater affaire then to giue him thankes, yet the procuring of euery Priests name mattered little, but was rather superfluous or a vanity, the rest giuing thankes in the person of all, except his Holinesse should haue taken tale how many by name had thanked him.

We should maruell if father *Garnet* and father *Parsons* did not laugh in their sleeue, notwithstanding themselues were the plotters of the deuice, when they saw the ouersight of our brethren, and how easily most of vs were won to giue thanks for a subordination, being a staffe for themselues, their deputies, and successours, to beate vs withall at their pleasure, except we did still sing *placebo*, and bow downe our neckes to what yoake soeuer their enterprising natures thought meet to lay vpon vs.

But howsoeuer they delighted themselues with this, yet if father *Parsons* were made acquainted with all particulars, he could not but wish that maister *Blackwell* had vsed some better pretence for suspending three Priests from the vse of their faculties, then because they would not vpon his command confirme, *his authority vnder their hand writing, as a certaine witnesse of their obedience, and by putting too their names*: the Priests thẽselues knew not to what, vnlesse it were to [*olim dicebamur.*] A cause we dare say, that since the beginning of Christianity, there was neuer Priest suspẽded for the like. For the subiect to be punished because he wil not confirme the authority of his Ecclesiasticall superiour vnder his hand writing (an exaction of al incongruency, for what inferiour can confirme the authority of his superiour, that being an office of a superiour to the superiour) or put his name to a letter of thanksgiuing for a new increase of subiection, is a course so contrary to reason and iustice, and so repugnant in it selfe, as it can hardly admit any colour, cloake or euasion.

The words of our Archpriests letter of the 4. of Aprill 1599. which is set downe in the booke to the Inquisition.

Neither in truth do we thinke that the rendering of thankes to his Holinesse was the ground, and true cause indeed why so many names were gathered with like ado: but rather that the impulsiue and reall cause thereof, was, for that the Iesuits hauing deuised the authority to subordinate (as it seemeth) our whole Cleargy to themselues by

chusing

chusing and directing the Archpriest, got the Cardinall Protector to erect the same by his letter , not doubting but that by the place and power of the Cardinall, we would all swallow the hooke. But seeing themselues deceiued in the conceit, they threw about with speed how they might beare out the action, and in fine maugre the might of such as withstood them, atchieue their desire (a desire perchance neither a little nor a short while lōged after)& resolued: that a Letter of thanksgiuing should be drawne to his Holines, and as many Priests labored, as the Arihpriest, themselues, and their friends could preuaile with, to put to their names, that so hauing once gotten their names, fa. *Parsons* might after vse them to his Holinesse and the Cardinals , for a proofe and contestation of the Priestes great willingnesse and applause to the subordination , and that they all with one voice intreated the confirmation thereof: when the truth was that most of those, or rather all (a very few excepted) who gaue their names, would neuer haue done it, but vpon conceit that his Holines had already decreed the subordination, and did full heartily repent the folly when it was past , and they saw the pollicie.

Loe , the onely ground and true cause impulsiue and finall , and which deeds themselues haue sithence witnessed, of framing (*olim dicebamur*) of gracing it with the Iesuites names in the first ranke , and of procuring the subscriptions of Priests therunto, with greatest expedition, importunitie, and with all sorts of postulation. Lo also one forceable motiue , which then induced vs to thinke that the subordination was neither the commaundement, nor the ordinance of his Holinesse: for then what needed the like shifts of descant or so much cunning, or plainer, so guilefull a proiect and prosecution?

To come now to the other presumption of swearing of Priestes, or binding them by solemne promise to obey the Archpriest , ere they may haue faculties giuen them in the Colledges from whence they are sent. Which exaction or constrained oath, we tooke to be most needlesse , had the subordination bene the ordinance of his Holinesse and so knowne. For who can in reason or with good conscience doubt, whether the Priests that come into England vpon zeale with perill of life, to reduce others to the obedience of the Sea Apostolike, would in themselues as ring-leaders , first abandon the same by withdrawing their bounden obedience from any Superiour , whom they should know , or probably vnderstand to be lawfully appointed ouer them? So that the hearing of this exaction, did so little stagger and appale vs in our conceiued opinion, as it much fortified, and brought vs in a thorough beleefe, that the subordination was not the act or commaund of his Holinesse. For if it had bene, and that it could haue bene so proued, (as if it had bene either, it might most easily haue bene proued) no doubt but wisedome, loue, and charitie, in the Rectors of the Colledges would haue inuited specially father *Parsons*, both in respect he liued in Rome, when the subordination was graunted, and gouerned al or the chiefest Colledges, rather to haue giuen satisfaction and Canonicall sertitude of the subordination it selfe to the Priestes, then through default thereof to leaue them doubtfull in mind, and oblige their consciences by oath.

And when was it euer seene, that any, much lesse Priests, the franchised children in Gods house, should be compelled to sweare obedience, before they knew, or any legall or sufficient proofe made binding them to know (as neither was done) that the party to whom they should sweare obedience was their superiour?

To shut vp this our second reason, we will grant to our aduersaries, that his Holines commanded a subordination, and inioyned the Cardinall most directly to ordaine gouernement among vs, as to our vnderstanding the same did not appeare in any part of the Cardinals Letter and his Holinesse Breue was not then extant (for no sooner was it extant, but that we presently submitted our selues without the least exception or repugnancy) yet the principall marke and end of his Holinesse, being to establish peace, no doubt his bessed fatherhoods will and pleasure was, that such a subordination & forme of gouernement should be instituted, as might auaile to the making and continuance of peace. Therefore the Archpresbytership accompanied with no benefite at all, but onely with iurisdiction to afflict vs, as namely to restraine or suspend our faculties, to take them quite away, to remoue vs from our places of residence, to commaund what he listeth, and as the authoritie is now practised to suspend, from vse of al Priestly function, to interdict both Cleargie and Laitie, to multiply Decrees vpon Decrees, and in such maner and matter, as if we were no longer *the chil-*
Gal. 4. *dren of the free woman, but of the bond woman*, and our state and persons become so seruile, as there remaineth no right in vs to resist any iniurie, defamation, or oppression soeuer.

Now if this kind of subordination bringing no cōmoditie with it, but all plentie of discommodities, hurts, and annoyances, be, or could be, a meane to make peace, the motiue and end of instituting the authority, authoritie, or as much as tend that way in it selfe, or not rather yeeld occasion of hasting new quarrels, a thing quite contrarie to his Holines designe in graunting the delegation to the Cardinall:not only our wits and iudgements,but common reason also,is vtterly eclipsed in vs. For we confesse, we cannot see how by common reason, it may appeare likely to any man of iudgement,that peace would folow,or that peace could be any way effected(which the sequel hath hitherto verified)by the erecting of this subordinatiō including the seminary Priests onely,while the totall masse and life of the whole contention,was not betweene the seminarie Priests among themselues,or betweene them and the Laitie,but betwixt some of the secular Priests and the Iesuits, ouer whom the Archpriest hath so little iurisdiction, as the chiefe of the Iesuits is by a speciall prouiso added to the Cardinals Letter, ioyned after a sort in commission with the Archpriest, in that the Archpriest is directed by vertue of the said Instruction, to do nothing of waight,without the priuitie and aduice of the other.

What more plaine, then if two be at variance,the meane of according them by authoritie, ne is, nor can be, by hauing iurisdiction and command ouer one of them,and none at all ouer the other,but by carrying authoritie ouer both,as our Archpriest doth not.

Againe,what equitie or iustice, (the parent,Nurse,and preseruer of peace,) can any one in reason exspect, when he that is most engaged in the difference,and a party also,is appointed Counsellor and aduiser to the Iudge,& the Iudge prescribed to do nothing of moment without him? Too strange a forme of Iustice,as we thought,for his Holines to be the setter downe of,and so vnfit a meane to peace,as what can able and further contention most.

Touching also the composing of the dissention, pretended to be betweene the secular Priests and the lay Catholickes, this authoritie appeared in like maner very defectiue in the means of taking it away, if there had bene such a difference, in regard the Cardinals Letter giueth the Archpriest onely authoritie ouer the Seminarie Priests, and maketh not euen the least mention of any iurisdiction or power giuen him ouer the laitie,as he that peruseth the *Constitutiue Letter*(the true and sole lists of his whole authoritie) cannot but see.

Or if any will shew themselues to be of so weake iudgement, (as once a speciall Agent of our aduersaries did, vpon warrantise as he said from father *Parsons*) as to auow, that the Archpriest holding authoritie ouer the Priests, Confessours to the Laitie, he holdeth likewise authoritie ouer their ghostly children, it were vndoubtedly a strange consequence, and which bringeth a new doctrine into the world. For hereby it cannot but follow, that when a religious man (a thing most common) is Confessor to a King, or Pope; the chiefe of the house or companie whereof the religious man is a member, hauing by the rules and vow of religion iurisdiction ouer the Confessor: he hath likewise iurisdiction by this reason ouer the King, or Pope, to whom the said religious mã is ghostly father. But let the sequel be good, as in common reason it is most absurd, yet euen in this maner the authoritie is in it selfe farre short of effecting peace. For not all the Lay Catholickes, and most probably not such, between whom and the Priests the contention was, or was like to be, are vnder the charge of the Seminarie Priests, but vnder the guiding of the Iesuits, and consequently no whit at all vnder the iurisdiction of the Archpriest, if the former doctrine were currant, that he that retaineth iurisdiction ouer the Confessor, retaineth iurisdiction ouer his ghostly children.

Further, these that were in this maner vnder the direction of the seminarie Priests, were not, neither would be, nor perhaps could be so tied to continue with them, but that they would leaue them at their pleasure, and when they thought good. Nay it cannot be doubted, but they, meeting with such an occasion, would not faile to change their ghostly father, and go to confession to the Iesuits for ridding themselues from all such authoritie of the Archpriest. An inconuenience as none greater, and which by likelihood would in short while, set our whole Church on fire. Wherefore the authoritie of the Archpriest appearing vnto vs, neither auaileable to the making of peace between the secular Priests and the Catholicke laitie, if they had bene at variance, as it was suggested: neither a meane to attone the debates betweene the Iesuits and the Priests, which was concealed: and his Holinesse motiue and intent of commaunding a subordination to be instituted, being a pious and zealous desire of according all differences, and making perfect peace: it seemed cleare vnto vs, that his Holinesse neuer meant, that this kind of subordination afflicting onely, and furthering nothing els but the increase of our miseries, should be brought into our Church: but some other more profitable kind of regiment, that might encourage, strengthen, and support the naturall infirmities of man, in these troubles and hote times of Catholike triall. All which considerations and precedent profes, did more then probably assure vs, that it could hide neither offence before God or man, and lesse the

crimes

crimes obiected, to deferre our absolute submission, vntill such time as his Holinesse should make knowne his particular commaundement, or ratifie and approoue the Cardinals act after some authenticall manner.

The third Reason.

OVR third reason was, that supposing the information had bene true, and that his Holinesse had giuen also a plaine, and direct commaundement to the Cardinall to ordaine an Archpriest with like power and soueraigntie ouer vs as is challenged, and that himselfe likewise had nominated M. *Blackwel*, & appointed the Cardinall to choose him to the office, and further that all these particulars had bene cleerely and most expressely set downe in the *Constitutiue Letter*, as how little any of them were, the Letter it selfe doth best testifie, and the former reason hath sufficiently shewed: yet not knowing these things otherwise to be true, but by the sole testimonie of the Cardinals Letter, we did and do still think, that we were not bound to beleeue, in such a generall innouation and preiudice of our Church, the like vntestified, & single relation, without Canonicall certitude of such his Holinesse delegation to his Grace, or Commission by word of mouth, or other deriued authoritie, in what manner, or vnder what title soeuer.

For who can doubt, but that it is most meete and requisite, that the greater and more strange the authoritie is, which is claimed, the more Canonicall and euident ought the proofes to be, by which it is claimed. To make an Archpriest superiour ouer the Cleargie of a whole Realme, to direct, to reprehend, to chastice, and prescribe as he listeth vnto them: to remoue them also from their places of residēce, the same being in temporall mens houses, and of almes: and not onely in this nature to commaund them, while they reside in the same kingdome with him, but also to hold & exercise the same iurisdiction ouer them, if so they reside in an other kingdome, gouerned by an other Prince, and distant by many hundreth miles from the place of the others abode. These are so rare nouelties without example in holy Church, as no proues, but such as are legall, can seeme warrantable or sufficient inough in the case.

And because this very point which we are now entring into, is the hardest knot in the whole controuersie, & in which the principall issue most lieth, we thinke good for the more perspicuitie of the discourse, first to make a diuision of the meanes, by which the Cardinall might receiue authoritie from his Holinesse, to constitute such a subordination in our Church. And then, to proue that his Graces Letter (whether patent or sealed, as to my remembrance it came sealed vp according to the Romane maner with a labell) was no such proofe as could either in law or conscience bind vs to admit the subordination appointed without further specialty of such his Holines Commission vnto him, then the credence and testimonie of his Graces Letter either patent or close sealed.

Touching the first, it seemeth cleere that his Grace receiued authoritie from his Holinesse, to constitute an Archpriest ouer vs, either by way of formall delegation, or by way of Cōmission by word of mouth. This is so euident and manifest by the tenor of the Constitutiue Letter (if a commaundement to make peace, be a Commission to institute an Archpriest) that if our aduersaries shall gaine-say it, they seeme not to loue truth, but rather to affect contention.

And if his Grace receiued authoritie from his Holinesse by way of formal delegation, then his Grace not shewing vs the Popes rescript, or a contestified copy thereof for testimonie of the delegation, we were not bound by law or conscience, to admit the subordination vpon the sole credence of his Graces Letter patent or close sealed.

Pope *Innocentius* in his decision to the Bishop of *Baia* registred among the Decretals, priuiledgeth all persons not to beleeue another to be a delegate, vnlesse he first proue the Delegation: his wordes be these.[a] *Nisi de mandato sedis Apostolicæ certus extiteris, exequi non cogeris quod mandatur.* Except thou remaine certaine of the madate of the sea Apostolicke, thou art not bound to execute the thing commaunded. But what manner of surenesse or certaintie that is, here it resteth to be explaned, which is here vnderstood by the words (*nisi certus extiteris,* except thou remaine sure.) The expositors both ancient and moderne affirme, that to the making vp of this kind of surenesse, is necessarily required

(a) *Ca. Cum in iure de offi. dele.*

quired either the sight of the originall of the delegation, or at least a contestified copie thereof. [b] *Delegato non creditur dicenti se delegatum nisi id literis probet, idq; probare debet per originale, vel per exemplum ex originali solemniter sumptum.* Credence (as writeth *Zecchius*) is not to be giuen to a Delegate affirming himself a Delegate, vnlesse he proue the same by a rescript, and he ought to proue it by the originall, or by an example taken solemnely (that is, according [c] to order and forme of law) out of the originall. The very same hath *Panormitane* touching the meanes of prouing a Delegation. [d] *Mandatum delegationis primo potest probari per orginale: secundo per exemplum solemniter sumptum ex originali.* The mandate of a delegation, may first be proued by the originall: secondly by an authenticke copie of the originall. The like do the authorities also conclude that follow. *Innocentius,* [e] *Delegatus nō probat mandatum nisi literas ostendat.* The delegate doth not proue his madate except he shew the letters. *Durandus,* [f] *Delegatus nihil potest facere nisi ostendat literas suæ delegationis.* The Delegate can do nothing vnlesse he shew the letters of his delegation. *Egidius,* [g] *Delegatio Papæ non potest probari nisi per literas.* The Popes delegation cannot be proued but by Letters. *Bouerus,* [h] *Delegatio potest probari per testes postquam fuerit literatoriè semel præsentata, alias secus.* A Delegatiō may be prooued by witnesses after it hath bene once shewed by a rescript, otherwise not. *Bellemera,* [i] *Delegatus ante receptas literas suæ potestatis, non potest vti iurisdictione sibi demandata.* The Delegate cannot vse the iurisdiction committed vnto him, before he haue receiued the Letters of his authoritie. Pope *Boniface* the eight. [k] *Dicenti se delegatum sedis Apostolicæ, non creditur vel intenditur nisi de mandato Apostolico fide doceat oculata.* Credence is not to be yeelded or his words to be harkned vnto, who shall affirme himselfe a Delegate of the sea Apostolicke, vnlesse by eye-witnesse he proue the Apostolicall mandate. The Glosse, [l] *Nisi delegatus ostendat iurisdictionem suam, non est ei credendum si dicat se delegatum.* Except the Delegate doth shew the instrument that witnesseth his iurisdiction, he is not to be beleeued if he affirme himselfe a delegate. And in another place, [m] *Scriptura requiritur in Delegato Papæ.* A Letter instrument is required in the Popes delegate for proofe of the delegation.

(b) *In sua Ecclesiastica rep. de iudice delegat. nu.5.*

(c) *Ca. pen. & vlt. de fide inst. & ca. Significauit & ca. Albericus de testib.*

(d) *In ca. cum in iure de offic. del. nu.6.*

(e) *In ca. cum olim essemus de priuil & excess. priuil. nu 4.*

(f) *Li.2. de probationibus. §.3. nu.1.*

(g) *Decisione 7. de off. deleg.*

(h) *Verb. delegatio. nu.10.*

(i) *Conclu. 110. nu.15.*

(k) *In extrauagante iunctæ de elect. §. Sane.*

(l) *In ca. cum in iure, de off. dele.*

(m) *In ca. 1. de sensibus exact. li.6. § Postquam verb. in scriptis casu.25*

All which authorities, and other that might be alleaged make the case plaine, that neither credence is to be giuen to a Delegate, vnlesse he proue the delegation, nor that the delegation can be otherwise proued, but by shewing either the originall, or an authenticke copie thereof, and consequently neither being shewed vnto vs, as our aduersaries themselues will confesse, we were not bound to beleeue the delegation. And here we might end this member, saue that perchance our oppositors will reply and say, that we take our marke amisse, in regard the partie Delegate was a Cardinall, and therefore not tied to make either of the two foresaid proofes, but that his Graces owne word was of authoritie enough to bind vs obey the ordinance, without further proofe of the delegation or tenour of his Holines graunt. To which we answer.

First, that *Imola* and *Antonius de Butrio*, with sundrie others of the best writers, affirme that the aforesaid wordes of the Canon (*Nisi de mandato sedis Apostolicæ certus extiteris, exequi non cogeris quod mandatur:* Vnlesse thou be certain of the Popes mandate, thou art not bound to execute the thing commaunded) haue their full force and strength, and are to be extended to the estates and personages of Cardinals, and that they as wel as other Delegates are bound by this place of the law to proue their delegation, or no tie to ensue. Which is also the opinion of *Benedictus Vadus.*[a] *Cardinalis qui asserit se delegatum, non creditur ei nisi ostendat literas.* A Cardinal auouching himselfe a Delegate, is not to beleeued vnlesse he shew the rescript of the delegation. And it is likewise the opinion of *Conradus,*[b] *Non creditur Cardinali asserenti se esse delegatum nisi ostensis literis suæ delegationis.* Beleefe is not to be giuen to a Cardinall, affirming himselfe to be a Delegate, except he shew the letters of his delegation. Semblably to this also writeth *Felinus,*[c] *Sicut dicenti se delegatum non creditur nisi ostensis literis, ita nec Cardinalibus.* As beleefe is not to be giuen to one auowing himselfe a Delegate except he shew the Commission, so likewise neither to Cardinals.

In ca. quod super his. de fide instrumentorũ. Ca. cum in iure de offi. deleg.

(a) In repertorio verb. Cardinal.

(b) *Li.2.ca.2. de Cardinalibus §.3.nu.22.*

(c) Ca. super his de fide instru. nu.10.

Again the same author handling this question of purpose: whether a Cardinals word be sufficient to proue a delegation to himselfe, resolueth no in the Silogismes following.[d] *Credere alicui propter eius dignitatem est stare præsumptioni: sed textus in Canone dicit (nisi de mandato sedis Apostolicæ certus extiteris exequi non cogeris quod mandatur: Ergo non sufficit iuris præsumptio.* To beleeue another in regard of his dignitie, is to rely vpon a presumption: but the text of the Canon sayth (except thou remaine sure of the mandate of the sea Apostolicke thou art not bound to execute what is commaunded:) Therefore a presumption of the law doth not suffice. And in another place in words and sense almost coincident.[e] *Vbi requiritur certitudo, non sufficit probatio presumptiua,*

(d) In ca. Super his. de fide instr. nu.12.

(e) In ca. cum in iure de offi. del. nu.7.

tiua, sed credere dignitati est adhærere præsumptioni: ergo non satisfit isti textui (nisi certus extiteris de mandato sedis Apostolicæ exequi non cogeris quod mandatur.) Where a certaintie is required, a presumptiue probation is not sufficient, but to giue credite to dignitie, (*that is to a Cardinall in respect of his dignitie*) is to adhere to a presumption: therefore it doth not answere or satisfie this text of the law (except thou remaine sure of the mandate of the sea Apostolicke thou art not bound to execute what is commaunded.)

Gloss. in l. c. de fide instrum.

What plainer proues can be desired, or which can more conuince the authorities being taken out of the best writers in the argument? To descend therefore to the second member.

If the Cardinall receiued authority to institute the subordination by way of commission from the mouth of his Holinesse only, and not by way of delegation in writing: yet that we were no way bound to accept of the subordination, vpon credence of the Cardinals sole letter, without further proofe of such his Holinesse commission vnto him, we declare and make manifest by the authorities following.

Panormitane[a] *Non creditur Cardinali asserenti aliquid in præiudicium alterius, & ideo si Cardinalis dicat Papam sibi commisisse aliquid viuæ vocis oraculo, tendens in præiudicium alterius, non crederetur sibi nisi aliter probaret*. Beliefe is not to be giuen to the word of a Cardinall if he affirme any thing to the preiudice of another; and therefore if a Cardinal say that the Pope hath committed such or such a thing vnto him by word of mouth tending to the preiudice of another, he should not be beleeued, except he otherwise prooue what he affirmeth. *Filinus* [b] *Non creditur etiam Cardinali quando agitur de præiudicio tertij. Et hoc est adeo verum quod Papa non potest facere de potestate ordinaria quod credatur vni soli in præiudicium alterius.* Beliefe is not to be giuen euen to the word of a Cardinall, when a third person is to receiue damage thereby And this is so vndoubtedly true, as the Pope cannot appoint by his ordinary power, that credit should be giuen to one only in preiudice of another. *Decius*[c] *Non creditur etiam Cardinali vbi tractatur de præiudicio alterius*. One ought not to beleeue, no not a Cardinall wherein the preiudice of another is treated. The Doctors of the *Rota* [d] *Non creditur assertioni Cardinalis nisi circa iurisdictionem eius.* The assertion of a Cardinall is not to be beleeued, but in matter belonging to iurisdiction, rising out of his office and not in other. The additions vpon the chapter, *quod super de fide instrumentorum in Panormitane* [e] *dicto Cardinalis in hijs quæ concernunt alterius præiudiciū non creditur.*

(a) *In ca. sicut nobis de sententia excommu. nu. 5.*

(b) *In eodem ca.*

(c) *In ca. causam quæ de off. deleg. nu. 25.*

(d) *In decisio 33. de probationib. in anti. nu. 1.*

(e) *Sub. nu. 5. lit. e.*

Beliefe is not to be giuen to the word of a Cardinall in matters that concerne the preiudice of another. Which Position the foresayd writers proue by seuerall [f] passages of the Canon law, specially by this that followeth [g] *Canonica & Ciuilia iura sequentes districtius inhibemus ne vnius iudicis quantæcunq; fuerit authoritatis verbo credatur in causis siue super testamentis, siue quibuslibet alijs contractibus quæstio agitetur, salua in omnibus sedis Apostolicæ authoritate.* Following the Canon and Ciuill lawes we very strictly inhibite that credite be giuen to the word of one Iudge of how great authority soeuer he be in causes whether the question be made vpon testaments, or vpon other contracts whatsoeuer, the authority of the Sea Apostolike reserued in all things. Neither is this only an ordinance of the Canon law, Ciuill, and Nationall, but a Decree beside of nature her selfe in cases of moment, as witnesseth S. *Thomas* and his Expositors.

(f) *Ca. licet. 2. de testibus & 3 q. 9. ca. iudices.*
(g) *Ca. cum à nobis de testibus.*

2. 2. q. 80. art. 2.

Neuerthelesse because the Canonists write in the vtter shew diuersly in this point, some that beliefe is to be giuen to the assertion of a Cardinall: other that beliefe is not to be giuen: they, meaning in matters not preiudiciall: these in matters that bring detriment with them: and in these matters also which bring detriment with thē, some write that a Cardinall his auowance is to be beleeued, some other the contrary that it is not, the former authors vnderstanding in matters of small or indirect domage, the latter in matters of great and direct preiudice. Therfore to the end that no exceptions be taken, nor place left to counterplead, we thinke good to annexe the words of *Nauar*, who as he caried a most singular account ouer all Christendome for learning and sound iudgement in his faculty, so doth he open this difficulty and discusseth it farre more distinctly then any other, and reconcileth the authors in the differences aforesayd. His words be these.

Lib. 3. consil. de testament. cōs. 11. nu. 8. & 9.

Credendum est Cardinali etiam in preiudicium tertij tribus concurrentibus. Primum quod testetur de commissis à Papa sibi aut alijs per eum deferrendis. Secundū quod sint solita concedi. Tertium quod non vergant directè in præiudicium aliorum, sed tantum indirectè & per quandam consequentiam. A Cardinall is not to be beleeued yea to the preiudice of a third, three things cōcurring. First that the testimony he giueth be of things committed by the Pope vnto them. The second that his testimony be of such things as are vsually or wont to be granted. The third, that the things do not redound directly to the preiudice of others, but onely indirectly & by a certaine sequell or implication.

Of which three specified conditions, all and euery one of them being

ing requiſite, the firſt onely is to be found in our caſe, and neither the ſecond nor third. Not the ſecond, becauſe the ſubordination which the Cardinall by his *Letter Conſtitutiue* erected, is not a cuſtomarie kind of ſubordination, or which is vſually graunted, but rather an authority whoſe like in all circumſtances was neuer graunted, as is manifeſt by that which hath bene rehearſed in the ſecond reaſon. And the third falleth in as little with our caſe, becauſe liuing by the vſe of our faculties, it cannot be, but a very great, direct, and immediate preiudice to be depriued of them, meerely at the arbitrary pleaſure of another, without iuridicall proofe or lawfull conuiction of any condigne or proportionable demerit. Which preiudice appeareth alſo by ſo much the greater or more infinite, as the retaining and vſe of our faculties, are the ableſt, if not the ſole meanes both of gaining and releeuing ſoules, the end why we tooke Prieſthood vpon vs, a profeſſion in ſo great diſlike and perſecution with the ſtate.

Againe, what more apparant preiudice either to Prieſts or to the Catholike laity, then that authority ſhould be giuen (the ſtraight condition of the lawes of our Realme conſidered) to change and remoue Prieſts from one reſidence to another, we being indued with no Church liuing, nor the lay Catholikes bound by as much as the leaſt ſhew of charity, to maintaine any one in their houſes, but ſuch as thẽſelues ſhall chuſe or caſt affection vnto, in regard they muſt venter therein the vtter looſing of all their goods, life, ſtate, & the ouerthrow of their whole poſterity. And neither muſt they make this venter for a weeke, two, or three, but muſt ſet downe their dwelling in the hazards of the caſualty, ſo long as they entertaine the Prieſt, and euer after during their liues, and the lawes of the preſent ſtate.

Moreouer can a ſeparation be made by authority of the Poſtour from the flocke: of the Guide from the charge: of the Prieſt reſiant from his acquaintance and place of aboad, and no ſpeeches to grow and be ſpread thereof? Moſt improbable. And not much leſſe vnlikely is it, but that the walking vp and downe of ſuch ſpeeches in many mens mouthes, will quickly lay open the ſtate of ſuch Catholikes from whom they are, and to whom they ſhal be in ſuch ſort remoued, to danger, hauocke, and ruine.

Another preiudice, and which doth not ſo much directly follow vpon the ſubordination, as it is intrinſecall and incorporate thereunto, the preiudice being expreſly and by ſpeciall prouiſo enacted in the *Conſtitutiue Letter* it ſelfe; to weete, that the nomination and chuſing of the Archpriest, should not appertaine (notwithstanding the large iurisdiction and commaund he carrieth ouer all) either to the company of the twelue Assistants, or to the whole body of Priestes within our Realme, who are to obey and liue vnder his rules, but that in euery change of the Archpriest, either by death, apprehension, leauing the Realme, or other accident, the successour is to be assigned by the Cardinals Grace onely, a forrainer to our nation, aparted by many hundreth of miles from vs, a stranger to our affaires, and neither acquainted with all the sorts of our pressures, nor with their measure and qualitie. Which prouiso seemed also the more straight and preiudicial vnto vs, in respect the Cardinall Protector was like to receiue no other information, to direct his honour in the election of the next Archpriest, but that which father *Garnet* and father *Parsons* the authours of all our troubles, and the maister parties of the one side of the difference, should then againe suggest, and rule all in the second, third, and euery change, as they did in the election of M. *Blackwell*, and consequently our poore cleargie neuer lacke matter of disturbance, vnlesse we accommodate and prostrate our selues to father *Parsons* humour and the direction of the Iesuits in all things.

And here we cannot but wish to God that father *Parsons* pollicie and the seeking of himselfe, would once at length redound more then it doth, to the good of our Church and Countrey: we meane his cunning pollicie in preuenting that none of our nation come to preferment or credite in the Court of Rome, or haue meanes to enforme his Holines of the true state of matters, but that himselfe must be the sole agent and informer, or some such his creatures as shall not faile to second his driftes, and runne in one and his owne currant with him.

We hope none of iudgement, and acquainted with the ouer-ruling humour that raigneth in some persons, but will soone affirme the precedent inhibition of debarring vs the choise of our owne Superiour, being so many as we are in number, to be no little or light preiudice, specially if he maturely consider of the reasons that S. *Leo* the great, giueth in a case not vnlike to ours. *Vt nullus inuitis & non petentibus ordinetur, ne plebs inuita Episcopum non optatum aut contemnat, aut oderit, & fiat minus religiosa quam conuenit, cui non licuerit habere quem voluit.* That no one be ordained ouer others, whō to haue they are vnwilling or not desirous, lest the people so constrained either contemne or hate the Bishop whom they wished not to haue, & thereby become lesse religious thē is meet, in not being licenced to enioy whom they desired.

Neither

Neither can we name or report this barre, leſſe then a preiudice vnto vs, becauſe holy Church her ſelfe gouerned by the wiſedom of heauen, hath ordained that euery Eccleſiaſticall congregation and Colledge of Prieſts ſhould haue the chuſing of their owne Prelate: yea and that the Prelate not after this wiſe choſen, may be lawfully refuſed as one promoted contrarie to the diſcipline of Canonicall order. *Ca.1.de electione,& gloſ.ibid.* Hard, that we being ſo many in number as we are, and the whole Cleargie of a Realme, and neither liuing all vncollegially through our owne default, but by the neceſſitie of the time, ſhould thus, both firſt and laſt, and in euery chaunge, be depriued of hauing the election of our Prelate.

At the firſt, whiles we liued without a Superiour, it might perhaps ſeeme no great diſfauour to haue a Superior appointed vnto vs without our aſſent, or priuitie, or voice, or aduice in the election: but now when we appeare in a ſort collegiated, by liuing all in obedience vnder one Superior, and vnder a receiued and ſet forme of gouernement, to haue the ſame meaſure and diſfauour neuertheleſſe continued, yea to haue the continuance thereof expreſly and by particular caution enacted, it cannot but be deemed a preiudice by any vpright iudgement, and a much higher diſgrace and impeachment to our whole Church, then (as we hope) our long trauailes, the burden of our pouertie, the waight of our other preſſures, the daily venturing of our liues for the gaine of ſoules, the ſtore of bloud we haue that way yeelded, the fruite which hath come therof, and our maintaining the rights of the Romane ſea, either haue, or by Gods grace with our wittingnes euer ſhall deſerue of *Peters* Chaire, or at the hands of his Holineſſe.

Now if our aduerſaries can anſwere and ſhew wherein we are miſtaken, or how the precedent reaſons or authorities conclude not for vs, whether the Cardinall receiued his authoritie by way of formall delegation, or by way of verball commiſſion: we beſeech them of charitie to communicate their knowledge, and we promiſe them, they ſhall find vs thankfull, and moſt readie to recant our errour and aske them pardon.

And this being proued, that we were not bound by law or conſcience (for that cannot be againſt conſcience in which ſo many approued authors do agree to be lawfull) to ſubiect our ſelues to the ſubordination his Grace erected vpon the ſole credence of his Letter without further teſtimonie that his Holineſſe gaue him Commiſſion to inſtitute the ſame in *ſpecie*, with all the branches and faculties: it reſteth for cleerer remonſtrance of the truth and ſatisfaction of al doubts, that we anſwer the reaſons which our aduerſaries make for proofe that we were bound to beleeue and obey the Cardinall Protector his Letter, before the appearing of his Holineſſe Breue in Confirmation thereof.

M. Blackwell in his 12. queſtions to the Prieſts, 14. of March 1600. Fa. Holtbey in his diſcourſe the laſt of Iune 1601. and in the Apologie fol. 108.

ONe of the chiefe reaſons that our aduerſaries bring for proofe of ſuch our bounden dutie is, that his Grace was Lord Protector of our Nation, and the diſtributer of faculties to Prieſts in their miſſion from Rome for England.

De ſtatu Ill. DD. Card. nu. 9.

To which we anſwere: firſt, of the two dignities Cardinalſhip and Protectorſhip abſtracted and conſidered apart each from other, no doubt the title of Cardinalſhip is the greater, and by ſo much, that hardly there is any reſemblance to be made betweene them, as is to be ſeene by comparing the prerogatiues together, recounted and laid downe by *Zecchius* in his booke *de repub. eccleſiaſtica.* And therefore if we were not bound, (as is abundantly proued before we were not) to beleeue a Cardinals word in a matter of like preiudice, much leſſe were we then bound to giue credence to the word of a Protector in the ſame.

But be it for further proofe-ſake, and declaration of moe our aduantages, that the office of a Protector doth in right challenge more beleefe, then doth the ſtate of a Cardinall, and that the two ſoueraigne dignities and offices meeting and reſiding in one perſonage, as they did in Cardinall *Caietane*, could not but impoſe a ſtraighter bond by much vpon vs to beleeue and obey the particulars of his Graces Letter ſubſcribed and ſigned with his own hand and ſeale, then could the like Letter of any other Cardinall, who was not our Protectour, nor had the diſtribution of faculties in the miſſions.

To this we ſay, that the authoritie of our Protector thus compounded and enlarged, remaineth neuertheleſſe a definite authoritie, and falleth vnder the name of authoritie: but the text of the law aboue cited is, [a] *Quantæcunq; authoritatis, &c.* How great authoritie ſoeuer the affirmer is of, he is not in things hurtfull to another to be beleeued vpon the ſole teſtimonie of his owne word. And [b] *Panormitane* cited by [c] *Sylueſter* writeth, that *quantumcunque eſt perſona authorizabilis*, what high & ample authoritie ſoeuer the perſon beareth, he is not in *præiudicialibus* in matters of preiudice, to haue beleefe built vpon the credence

(a) *Ca. cum à nobis de teſtib.*
(b) *In ca. præterea de dilat. n. 5*
(c) *Verb. delegatus nu. 5.*

dence of his owne word onely. What need moe proues? It is very manifest by the vnanswerable authoritie of the text it selfe aboue cited, *salua in omnibus sedis Apostolicæ authoritate*, that the priuiledge of being beleeued vpon the sole warrantize of his owne word in cases of preiudice, is a respect peculiarly reserued and appropriated to the supreme dignitie of the Sea Apostolicke. *Ca. cum à nobis de testib.*

Or if on the other side, our opponēts wil, as a principal man among them did once boldly affirme, that the Cardinall did not so much institute this kind of subordination in our Church by vertue of any delegation receiued of his Holines, as he did it by vertue & office of his Proterctorship. A conceit that M. *Blackwell* himselfe in some of his Letters, which he wrote incontinent after the receit of the *Constitutiue Letter*, seemeth to beate about, if not to inferre, calling the subordination, *Statuta, constitutionem, institutionem, ordinem, prudentissimam prouisionem Ill^mi Domini Protectoris*. The statutes the constitution, the institutions, the order, the right prudent prouision of our most illustruous Protector. To my selfe the 8. of August, & to M. D. *Bishop*, and my self the 17 of Aug. 1598.

Now if our aduersaries beaten from their other holds, will retire (as some of them haue, to the succour of this poore shift) alas the fortresse they flie too is but a paper wall, a descant fit onely to deceiue the ignorant. For the office of a Protector consisting (as *Zecchius* relateth) in proposing the elections and other causes of the Prouince, or Country, whereof the partie is Protector in the sacred consistorie: and in answering the reasons, doubts, or exceptions, which the Pope, or any of the Cardinals shall there moue, touching matters by him propounded, neither did nor could impart like iurisdiction and soueraigntie to his Grace, as thereby to institute of himselfe any kind of gouernement, and much lesse so strange a kind of gouernement in our whole Church. For why, is there any kind of semblance or societie, any alliance or coniunction between authoritie to propose elections, to preferre the sutes of our Country, to yeeld satisfaction to what is obiected in that most honourable assembly of the Pope and Cardinals (the offices of a Protector) and the iurisdiction of erecting a subordination, the like wherof in all points was neuer heard of in our Church before, if euer any where else in the Church of God? The sequence is so incongruent, that none of iudgement will make it, and none but such as are wedded to their owne folly, will euer stand therein, carrying no more coherence then that chalke being white, must needes without doubt be cheese, or because the aduocate moueth and pleadeth his *De stat. Ill^orum D^orum Card^in. nu. 9.*

clients cause, therefore without question he hath authoritie to determine and giue finall sentence in the same.

Touching the other part or mēber of the reason, that we are bound to admit what Cardinall *Caietane* assigned, in respect his Grace had the distribution of faculties to our Priestes that come from thence, we thinke no answer fitter then silence, in respect it bewrayeth so great shallownesse and defect of iudgement. For if we were in this regard bound to beleeue the Cardinall on his word, because he had authoritie to delegate faculties, it followeth directly, that we are in like sort bound to beleeue the President of *Doway*, the Rectour of the Colledge at *Valedolid*, father *Parsons* and so many of the Iesuits as haue authoritie to giue faculties, vpon credence of their owne word: yea the ground and respects being one, we are likewise bound if the former reason be good, to beleeue our Archpriest and his successors, of what bad qualitie soeuer they happen to be, vpon testimonie of their owne word, because authoritie to delegate faculties, is now annexed to the office: and so any of this number may at his pleasute, by borrowing leaue of his conscience, innouate, set vp, pull downe, chop and change what he listeth in our Church, by saying onely he had a commandement from his Holinesse without shewing script or scrowle, or other assurance for proofe thereof, then his bare word, and we bound forsooth vnder crimes of greatest infamie, to admit the same and subiect our selues: thē which, what greater folly, what fouler distain to the dignitie of our Priesthood, or what in his nature or consequence layeth open a wider gap, to let in intrusion, confusion, and all vtter hauocke both of order and discipline, in the house and Sanctuarie of Almightie God, and spouse of our Sauiour?

ANother reason which our aduersaries vse for confirming their Position against vs, is the variety of the testimonies they shewed vnto vs besides the *Constitutiue Letter*, for proofe that the subordination was erected by his Holinesse priuitie and commaund: namely a second Letter of Cardinall *Caietanes*, signifying that his Lordship receiued a charge from his Holinesse to institute the subordination he did: a Letter of the Popes *Nuntio* in *Flaunders*: a Letter of Doctour *Stapletons*, an other of Doctour *Barrets*, an other of father *Bellarmines*, since Cardinall: an other of Doctour *Worthingtons*: and two other, from our two brethren which went to *Rome* in the affaire, all attesting (as our aduersaries are pleased to report) the subordination to be

the

the commaundement of his Holinesse.

A faire shew, to carrie away the vulgar and credulous, but of too light substance by much, to perswade any of iudgement, who haue but looked vpon the Canons of holy Church, were all true that is said, as when the particulars come to scanning, we trust neither all, nor the most part will so fall out.

And first it is cleere by the authoritie aboue rehearsed out of *Innocetius, Panormitane, Speculator, Felinus, Egidius, Bellemera, Bouerus, Zecchius, Conradus*, the very choise of both the ancient and moderne Canonists, that all Papall delegation especially communicating iurisdiction in penall matters, must of necessitie, ere any be bound to obey, be first proued either by shewing the rescript of the delegation, or an authenticall copie thereof. Neither can such a delegation, iustly according to the forme of the law be proued by record of witnesses, saue when as *Bouerus* noteth, the originall hath bene shewed before, as the originall of this delegation (if so the Cardinall his grace receiued authoritie from his Holinesse by way of formall delegation) was neuer, if euer extant to be shewed. Which saying also of *Bouerus* is not generally to be vnderstood in all kinds of Delegation, but in such onely, as do not deriue a pluralitie of particular iurisdictions, the contrarie whereof the new subordination doth, containing at least ten seuerall iurisdictions, and as many moe instructions. For in delegations of this sort, proofe is to be made by shewing of the original, or an authentike copie thereof, and not by the sole record of witnesses, as after the allegation of [a] *Barbatia*, the Doctors of the *Rota*, haue [b] in plaine termes decided, & who also quoteth these words of [c] *Baldus* for ampler proofe of the assertion. *Gratia Papæ facta super iurisdictione non potest probari per testes.* The grace that the Pope giueth communicating iurisdiction, cannot be proued by witnesses.

Verb. delegatio. 7. nu. 10.

(a) *In prohemio super Clement.*
(b) *Decisione quæ incipit, Quod licet Romana curia.*
(c) *In ca. 1. de allodÿs col. 3. in tit.*

And the reason is plaine and inuincible: for where many particulars are delegated, and those vndepending one of other, as in the new authoritie, there the volubilitie of humane memorie, and the strict necessity of neither adding nor detracting considered with other circumstances: namely, that wordes may often beare diuerse senses, and do take their limitation and truest exposition from that which went before or followed after in the same Commission, there we say where these thing meete, the proofe of the delegation, cannot without suspition of errour be made by report of witnesses, but ought onely to be made by shewing the originall, or a testified copie, as the authours before cited do write.

Which reason also seemeth as strongly to conclude that the faculties and iurisdiction giuen to the Archpriest, and particulariz ed partly in the Constitutiue Letter, partly in the instructions, and partly in the additions, being many in number, and distinct without dependance each of other, cannot well for the same cause and ficklenesse of memorie, be proued by witnesses, but rather require for due proofe the shewing and comparing of an authenticke note, or abstract of the things in particular, which were graunted to the Archpriest or Cardinall by his Holinesse, which hitherto we neuer saw, nor heard tell of, nor, which perhaps was euer extant, notwithstanding the iust necessitie thereof. Neuerthelesse we wil yeeld to our aduersaries, to the end to make our iustification the cleerer, and the lesse impugnable, that the like delegation or commission may be proued by witnesses, though the originall, nor anie authenticke copie were euer shewed before. Which was neuer affirmed by any writer, or euer practised (as we thinke) no not where oppression and bondage raigned most.

Yet here we trust that yeelding thus much voluntarily, our aduersaries wil not (an inch so freely and friendly being giuen them) take by and by an ell, and thinke it enough to proue the delegation or commission in generall, and not also to proue the tenour in particular. For if this large scope were once in vre and admitted, the next may be to bid all order farewell, as wherein discipline is rifled, tyrannie set free, the practise of holy Church turned vpside downe, and the arayes of all Christian peace and quietnesse vtterly broken: in regard it followeth hereby, that whosoeuer can prooue a delegation or commission, may forthwith incroch and challenge therupon to order all matters, either out or in his commission, as he listeth, without restraint, limit, checke, or gainestanding of any, as hauing by the former scope authoritie for his warrant: which is so very absurd, that he scarcely deserueth the name of a man, and lesse the praise of scholership, who shall shew himselfe so very a babe as once to affirme it.

And now here we demand, who in the rankes of the foresayd witnesses (which are yet all that our aduersaries themselues claime witnesse of) doth in his record descend to the specifying of any one particular contained in the commission? Let the testimonies be reuiewed and compared with the *Constitutiue Letter*, and we are content to make the aduersary, who is most against vs, our Iudge in the case. For to begin with the first and take them all in order: The second letter of

Cardinall

Cardinall *Caietane*, which is ſet downe *verbatim* in the beginning of the booke (were it not contrary to the naturall forme of iuſtice obſerued among all nations, be they Chriſtians, Iewes, or Pagans, for any one in the exterior Court to beare witneſſe in his owne cauſe) neither auerreth nor ſpecifieth any one particular of his Holineſſe commiſſion vnto him, other then the commiſſion it ſelfe in generall termes, as all men may be their owne informers that will reade the Letter.

Angles.p.2. in 4.q.de reſt. leg.penal. diff. 1.con.1.

Moreouer there be certaine clauſes or points interlaced in the ſayd Letter, which did ſo little inuite vs to beleeue the reſidue therein mentioned, or what his Grace had written before in the *Conſtitutiue Letter*, as they moſt mightily, more then euer before, cauſed vs to doubt of the proceſſe. For ſome part of the contents curteouſly findeth fault with maiſter *Blackwell*, for that he had not written to Rome of our manners or actions in ſo long while, and rendering his excuſe, layeth it in his modeſty and charitie, in that he would not be eaſily moued to accuſe his brethren: a property wherein one of his greateſt facilities did, and doth conſiſt, as we then knew, and haue ſithence more abundantly felt: nor can himſelfe deny this much, and father *Parſons* letter to maiſter Doctor *Biſhop* of the ninth of October 1599. and the late Apologie do verifie it apparantly.

Another peece of the letter impoſeth a commaundement or two vpon our Archprieſt, both to certifie the names, manners, and actions of the tumultuous, and the cauſes which they pretend of their reluctation, for ſo the letter termeth vs, and the iuſtifiable demaund we made for Canonicall proofe of his Holineſſe commiſſion, ere we did abſolutely engage and ſubiect our ſelues therunto. Iniunctions which certes we could not beleeue nor ſuſpect to proceed from order of his Holineſſe, notwithſtanding ſo much was expreſly ſignified in the letter. [*Nunc tamen S^mo^ id poſtulante, vt informatio debita de omnibus habeatur faciendum tibi erit omnino.* Yet now his Holineſſe commanding the ſame that due information be giuen of all, you muſt needes do it.]

The reaſons why we could not beleeue or ſuſpect thus much, were: firſt becauſe his Holineſſe was at *Ferrara* three hundreth miles, or thereabout from Rome at the time when the Cardinals letter was written: for his graces letter bore date from Rome the tenth of Nouember 1598. and his Holineſſe maried the King of *Spaine* and the Duke of *Burgundy* at *Ferrara* on the 12. of the ſame moneth, two dayes after the date. Againe, his Holineſſe for a good while before had not bene in Rome, being in his iourney towards *Ferrara*, nor was the Cardinall one of his attendants in the iourney. And to thinke that aduertisements of like quality, and small moment, as this businesse of ours was, passed this while too, and fro, betweene his Holinesse, and the Cardinall, were a very improbable conceit, considering the continuall trauell of his Holinesse, and the hourely accesse of all sorts of people vnto him, and for that his Holinesse intended ere long to returne to Rome, where the Cardinall might haue personall conference with him about the affaire, and in time conuenient inough, the matter being but onely to inquire how a few poore Priestes haue liued, and to vnderstand from their aduersaries the causes they pretend, in dislike of a gouernement already in being.

And albeit these were the respects which inclined vs to doubt whether his Holinesse enioyned any such commaundement as the letter specified, yet that which indeed farre more setled the doubt in our thoughts, was the partiality or iniustice, in that our aduersaries, and those that made a chiefe party, and were most interessed in the controuersie, should haue the certifying of what we could say either in clearing of our selues, or against them, and so haue the telling of both tales, theirs, and ours. Beside, it seemed straunge that we being defamed but of one crime (if it be a defamation and a crime to do as the lawes of holy Church licence and direct when doubt is made either of the commission, or of the specialties therein contained) we must haue our manners or actions without any specification of, or in that particular ransacked, and layd open to the world. The first kind of partialitie or iniustice not tollerated among the Heathens, and the later (if by our manners and actions the course of our life be meant, as the exception taken against the negotiators and other our brethren do verifie) as contrary as what may be most contrary to the expresse Canons of the Sea Apostolicke. *Inquisitio fieri debet solummodo super illis (criminibus) de quibus clamores aliqui præcesserunt*. Inquisition ought onely to be made concerning those crimes of which some clamorours reports haue gone before.

Ca. si quando de potest. iudicis deleg.

Ca. inquisitionis de accusat. § ad hæc & ca. qualiter el. 2, eodem.

That maister *Blackwell* was willed to make inquisition of our manners or actions by way of authority, and consequently by way of inquisition, the words of the sayd letter do attestate. For the Cardinall hauing before signified the Popes commandement to maister *Blackwell*, that he should not faile but send notice of our names, manners, or actions, his grace immediatly addeth: *Quod vt facilius citiusque ex nostra ſtræ ordinationis authoritate perficias, hoc tibi cæteriſque Preſbyteris iniungimus vt ſtatim ac diligenter fiat.* The which thing, that you may by the authority of our ordination performe with the more eaſe and ſpeede, this we enioyne you and the reſt of the Prieſtes, that it be foorthwith and diligently accompliſhed.

But the moſt we would inferre of the premiſes is, that theſe things being part of the contents of the Letter, and ſounding ſo hardly both againſt the common forme of iuſtice, & the decrees of Gods Church, we could not imagine, either the ſame to be written by any order receiued from his Holineſſe, or written at all by the Cardinall, but we tooke the letter for an extrauagant of father *Parſons*, ſubſcribed by the Cardinall without peruſing it before, only vpon confidence of father *Parſons* iudgement and ſincerity in managing the affaire he had begun. Neuertheleſſe we can but muſe, why father *Parſons* would haue other mens liues and actions informed, when if his owne life and diſpoſition were vnripped, they would perchance bring as little edification to the world, as the life and tranſgreſſions of ſome other. But the old ſaying is, *Non videmus manticæ quod in tergo eſt*, we do not ſee the part of the wallet that hangeth behind, where, father *Parſons* of likelihood (as this his forwardneſſe ſhould ſhew) hath bundled vp the frailties of his owne life, and there keepeth them without looking on them, and thereby commeth to haue leiſure and appetite to gaze vpon the life and cariages of ſome of the ſecular. But to proceed in examining the reſt of the teſtimonies.

Secondly his Holineſſe *Nuncio* in *Flaunders* in his Letter to maiſter *Blackwell*, and which our aduerſaries alleage as a teſtimony againſt vs, made no mention at all of the tenor of the commiſſion, nor of any particular that ſhould be contained therein. Our aduerſaries themſelues will not deny this, or if they do, we muſt ſay there is no truth in their words. The whole that his Lordſhips letter can be drawne to make againſt vs, or to teſtifie for them, was in that his honour writing to M. *Blackwell*, wrote vnto him by the name and title of Archprieſt: which alſo hapned (as we thinke) through this occaſion. After father *Parſons* had won the Cardinall to ſolicite and erect a ſubordination in our Church, the like as himſelfe thought fitteſt, he ſent a copie of the *Conſtitutiue Letter* to the *Nuncio* in *Flaunders*, and to others there to reade. Whereupon the *Nuncio* ſeeing maiſter *Blackwell* to be conſtituted Archprieſt by the Cardinall, gaue him alſo that title. And what is this for proofe of the commiſſion, ſpecially for proofe of the tenour, the thing which is to be witnessed,(as is declared before) or else what is witnessed to be little worth?

Thirdly touching the testimony of D. *Stapleton*, the most and all that he wrote to the *Nuncio* concerning the authority of maister *Blackwell*, and which our aduersaries lay hold on for reckord against vs, was, that his Holinesse had made him Archpriest. Which thing also he did neither write by way of affirmance, or to testifie so much, but onely accidentally by occasion of another matter, to weete, what he thought fittest to be done about maister *Tempest*. For at that time the *Nuncio* had sent M. *Tempest* vnto him with his accusers to be examined in the points, for which the Cardinall Protector had taken away his faculties, while he was in the way downwards from Rome, and giuen likewise order to the *Nuncio*, that he should be stayed in the Low-countries, and not suffered to go into England.

Now when Doctor *Worthington* and maister *Cæsar Clement* his accusers, had charged him before Doctor *Stapletō* with as many things, as they thought good, or as their instructions from father *Parsons* directed, and he had made his answer and purgation thereunto: Doctor *Stapleton* aduertising the *Nuncio* by letter, how the matter passed before him, & withall giuing his honor to vnderstand, what he thought meetest to be done in the cause, wrote: that maister *Tempest* might wel be dismissed and suffered to depart into England, and as he should there demeane himselfe, so to receiue againe his faculties of the Archpriest, whom his Holinesse had constituted superiour in England. By all which, being the whole summe of that Doctor *Sapleton* wrote to the *Nuncio*, what more may be gathered, then that Doctor *Worthington* and maister *Cæsar Clement*, relating the contents of the *Constitutiue Letter*, or shewing a copie thereof vnto him, which at that very season was newly come to *Bruxels*, and made common to many, the other incidently thereupon inserted in his foresayd Letter to the *Nuncio* the words aboue mentioned. Which in no sence can iustly be reckened a testimony, the writer by euidence of all circumstances thinking nothing lesse in vsing the words, then as a witnesse to testifie the commission, or that the subordination was the ordinance of his Holinesse by what he did say.

But whatsoeuer Doctour *Stapletons* intention was therein, either to witnesse or not to witnesse the subordination, as it could not be to witnesse it, vnderstanding the same but by report: yet our aduersaries themselues wil not say, that the good man did parti-

cularize

cularize or testifie the tenour of the commission, or any one iurisdiction contained therein. Or had he rehearsed in his letter some moe or few particulars of the commission, as he did not, yet we desire to know, what reason or satisfaction can be yeelded, why he might not as well haue erred in relating the tenour (and consequently neither bond, nor wisedome in vs to beleeue his words) as he did in saying that M. *Tempest* vpon desert of his good cariage in England, might haue his faculties restored vnto him by the Archpriest, whẽ M. *Blackwell* at that time had no authority at all (as himselfe both confessed & practised) either to restore him, or giue faculties vnto any other vpon what necessity soeuer.

We will not stay here to aske the cause, why D. *Stapletons* letter addressed to the *Nuncio* vpon the aforesayd businesse, was brought ouer with other like into England, and here shewed for testimonies. But although we will not stand to demand the reason hereof, yet we cannot but giue all men to know that our suspition, doubts, and mistrust of the validity of the new authority, were no whit lesned thereby, but very much increased, seeing what meane proues were mustered, and as it were marshalled in the forefront of the army of prooues against vs.

Fourthly, concerning the testimony of M. D. *Barret*, there was yet much lesse cause why he should be brought for witnesse, vnlesse the necessity be such, that any thing must serue that can make the least shew of sounding against vs, we neuer saw or heard but of two letters that he should write, the one to the Popes *Nuncio* in *Flaunders* concerning matters belonging to Maister *Tempest*, the other to maister *Blackwell* himselfe. In either of which, no other testimony was giuen, then that he named maister *Blackwell* Archpriest, and wished that those effects might follow vppon the authority, which the author in the institution of the authority intẽded, without naming who he was. And what we pray could this possibly make to the proofe of that which was then in question, and which we stood vppon to know after an assured and requisite manner, viz. whether the Cardinall receiued a commaundement from his Holinesse to erect such a subordination with like iurisdiction in all points ouer vs. Well, it must needes argue a rich wardrope, and good proues no doubt to lye in store, where such poore stuffe is brought forth for shew.

Fiftly, touching the testimony of father *Bellarmine*, (of whose letter our impugners seeme not to make the least account) first we ſay that to this day there be very few of our company who euer ſaw the letter: and for certaine, neither of theſe two, whom Maiſter *Blackwell* calleth the Princes in the action (and hath foreſt puniſhed for defending their owne and their brethrens good names againſt the ſlaunders impoſed) euer caſt eye thereon, or the ſame euer ſent by any or offered vnto them to reade, till after the arriuall of his Holineſſe Breue, and our abſolute admittance of the authority. And therefore whatſoeuer teſtimony it caried, it could little condemne or blame thoſe, that knew no more thereof. But what might the contents be of the letter, or to whom was the ſame written, and to what purpoſe?

The letter was written to father *Parſons*, in aunſwere of a letter of his, & to do him to vnderſtand, that the two English Prieſts, of whom he wrote vnto him, were not as then come to *Ferrara*, and that his Holineſſe was much incenſed vpon newes of their intention of comming, and determined to impriſon them. Againe, that father *Parſons* needed not to come to *Ferrara* about that buſineſſe, in reſpect his Holineſſe intended to make no long ſtay there, & that if in the meane, the two Prieſts hapned to come, he aſſured that their audience ſhould be put off, till his Holineſſe came to Rome.

This for ſo much as our memory ſerueth, was the contents of the letter. And now what proofe of the tenour or any particular of the commiſſion is there named in all this, no word, or ſillable ſo much as pointing thereunto? Neuertheleſſe we will not gainſay if father *Bellarmine* wrote ſuch a letter, but that the diſpleaſure which his Holineſſe is ſayd to take for their comming (if ſo the cauſe of his diſpleaſure was their comming and not rather wrong and ſiniſter information) may in ſome ſort not amiſſe argue that his Holineſſe was priuie to the erecting of the ſubordination, but it can no way argue that this or this was the tenour of the commiſſion, or theſe the particulars of the iuriſdiction giuen. A point much more important to be teſtified, then the commiſſion in generall, ere any be bound to render their particular obedience. For being in poſſeſſion of our particular freedomes, no reaſon to render them vp by conſtraint (as euery bond bringeth a conſtraint) into the hands of another, before he hath ſufficiently and according to law in that matter proued his right thereunto, as was ſhewed at large in the eleuenth Propoſition. And the ſame appeareth alſo plaine by this place in the Decretals: *Antequam exprimantur res,*

delegatus

delegatus nequit iurisdictionem exercere. Before the things be expressed (*wherein the Delegate hath authoritie*) the Delegate cannot exercise iurisdiction: and consequently none bound to obey in the same. And what in this respect is true in Delegations, holdeth also in commissions by word of mouth. *Ca. Pastoralis de rescript. in fine.*

We omit to lay downe the reasons we had of not giuing ouer light credit to what was auerred in the Letter, if so it had bene shewed vnto vs before the comming ouer of his Holinesse Breue, and our acceptance of the authoritie. The stile sauoured little or nothing at all of the temper and mildnesse wherewith the good religious father was knowne to abound: Then the Letter was taken not to be of his hand writing: and sithence it hath bene acknowledged that it was but a copie, and not the originall it selfe. Againe the contents greatly derogated from the natiue and sweete disposition of his Holinesse, as in like measure and without knowing the cause, to be offended with any, for repairing vnto him, and much lesse with Priestes comming from a Realme so farre off, and so well deseruing of holy Church, and in the generall cause of many. Lastly the Letter passed through the hands of father *Parsons*, and some other vnto vs, whom we accounted of no such integritie, but that circumstances considered, we might in wisedome mistrust least something therein might be added or altered, for making the famous Clarke to speake harder against vs.

Fiftly touching the testimonie of Doctour *Worthington*: none of vs know, or were euer told to this day, what he either said or wrote in witnesse of the authoritie or tenour thereof, or in commendation of our delay. Neuerthelesse let his record be what it can be, we hope by Gods grace (when one opponents or himselfe shall acquaint vs therewith) to be able so to answere it, as that it shall neither conuict vs of the crimes obiected, nor of any other faultie transgression.

Lastly concerning the testmonie of our two brethren the negociators of the affaire: we maruel why either * our Archpriest in his twelue proposed questions, or * father *Holtby* in his discourse, should so earnestly obiect their ioynt testimonie against vs, when the first Letter of all that we receiued from M. *Charnocke*, came to our hands together with the Breue, at which time we presently yeelded our obedience. * The 14. of March, 1600. *The last of Iune 1601.

We do not deny but that M. *Bishop* in his Letter of the 22. of February 1599. according to the Romane account, which was deliuered vnto vs some seuenteene or eighteene dayes before the receit of the

Breue, made mention that M. *Charnocke* had written vnto vs at the same time, but we did not receiue his Letter, before the comming of the Breue, as our Archpriest, father *Garnet* and some other can witnes, if they please to remember themselues. So that what testimonie soeuer M. *Charnock* gaue in the said Letter, it maketh little against vs, because we absolutely admitted the subordination, and subiected our selues so soone as euer we saw his Holines Breue, before the reading of M. *Charnockes* Letter, as the Gentleman can testifie who first brought vs the copie of the Breue testified with the hands of our two brethren in *Rome*, M. *Bishop* and M. *Charnoke* to be a true copie, wherby it vnquestionably followeth, that the breach of promise wherewith father *Holtby* chargeth vs for not submitting our selues vpon certificate receiued from our two brethren, is an vntruth, as there be many moe in that Letter-treatise.

These notwithstanding, let vs heare what were the letters and acknowledgements of our 2. brethrē, by mean wherof they are brought for witnesses, or as a confirmation of blame against vs. They both wrote that they heard Cardinall *Caietane* affirme, that what was done touching the Archpriest, was done by order from his Holines: & that they heard so much also by others, not expressing the parties names of whom they did heare it. Againe that they repented themselues of taking the iourney, chiefly of the inconsideration they committed therein, and that they requested their humble commendation and dutie might be done vnto our and their Superiour the Archpriest.

Loe the auowances and writings of them both, and which M. *Bishop* signified in a Postscript onely, vpon occasion by like, that father *Parsons* reading his Letter (as he did, and prescribed or approued the points to be treated of, in all the letters that either of them wrote vnto vs, during the whole time of their imprisonment, which was full foure moneths) and finding that principall Verbe (the former signification) missing, he would not, but needes haue the said complements added in a poscript.

Certes that they repented themselues of taking the iourney, being kept before the writing of the Letters eight weekes (from the 29. of of December till the 22. of February, in close and straight durance, vnder the iaylourship of father *Parsons* their chiefe aduersarie and examiner, was no strange newes, and lesse strange that they sorrowed the inconsideration they commited, which as themselues haue sithence expounded, they principally meant in not taking the names of moe

Priests

Priests with them, or in a better forme then they did, and specially because they omitted the procuring of the King of *France* his Letter in their behalfe to his Ambassadour in *Rome*, which was promised, and another to his Holinesse himselfe for request of fauourable audience in their sute: matter of iust sorrow, they smarting after the rate they did for omitting of the helpes, vpon confidence only of the most behoueable and reasonable petitions they were to propose.

But of what persons, beside the Cardinall his Grace did our two brethren remaining close prisoners, heare that the Archpresbytership, and the faculties adioyned, was the order of his Holinesse? Had any of those accesse vnto the prisoners, which liued neare about his Holinesse, or were often in his presence, and so by likelihood might heare when the commission was giuen, or after talked of? Were other straungers or their countrey-men in the city allowed to come vnto them? Were the students of the Colledge licensed at that time to visite the prisoners, and haue communication with them?

No, no, they were alike straightly kept, as they were not suffered to consult or speake with any, nor the one of them with the other. What then? did his Holinesse Fiscall (who was appointed to examine the prisoners, but not long after surrendred the office to father *Parsons*) report so much vnto them? It cannot be sayd, because the same man at the end of all their examinatiõs & resiftings, told the prisoners (as they both witnesse) that the subordination was not the ordinance of his Holinesse. Of whom then had the prisoners that intelligence? vndoubtedly either from father *Parsons* or father *Owen*, who onely had recourse vnto them: relators that must needes haue beliefe giuen to their words, because the one was a chiefe deuiser of the authority, and his reputation lay in gage to haue it go forward: the other, a profiting scholler in father *Porsons* studies, and his right hand in this busisinesse, as the seruice following declareth.

When maister *Charnocke* wrote his letter vnto vs, by the appointment of the Cardinals for a finall end of their durance, as father *Owen* reported, and father *Parsons* had the perusing thereof a night and a day, it was brought againe vnto him by father *Owen*, with order from father *Parsons* to adde that the subordination erected was the order of his Holinesse, who answering he could not write so, because he knew it not, the other replied, that the Cardinall protector sayd it when he sate in iudgement in the cause, and that father *Parsons* affirmed the same, and therefore he might well and truly write, that to his knowledge the Archpresbitership was the appointmẽt of his Holinesse. Whereupon the prisoner being willing to giue the fathers the most contentment he could, for his speedier riddance out of prison, promised him to write in so large a maner in that point as possibly he could with any truth, and accordingly signified in his Letter, yet not that he knew the subordination to be the order of his Holinesse, but that he heard the Cardinal to affirme it, and also vnderstood it by credible relation of others. The like wrote M. *Bishop*, and not vnlike vpon the same perswasion.

But neither the one nor the other of our brethrẽ, nor the Cardinall Protector in the *Constitutiue Letter*, nor any other, of whom witnesse is claimed, did euer in the least word affirme that the faculties and iurisdiction annexed to the Archpresbitership, (the onely point which was most needfull of all other to be descended vnto, being the most materiall, and which alone for the amplenesse, rigour, & vnusualnesse thereof, caused our delay) were the ordinance or commandement of his Holines. A thing worthiest of special note, as that most manifesteth the headie violence of our aduersaries, and how beyond all colour of reason, they haue proceeded in their accusations and outcries against vs.

Now touching the commendation and dutie our two brethren sent to be done, to our and their superiour the Archpriest: who could thinke, reading the passage, but that somwhat lay hid, & was insinuated by the words, that they being prisoners in Rome, should as it were, hunt after so impertinent an occasion of calling M. *Blackwell* their Superiour, and direct commendations vnto him by that title, when as we were right sure, they both well knew that the Cardinals Letter made him but Superiour ouer the Priestes residing in *England* and *Scotland* only, and not ouer any, whiles they liued any other where. And one of them being sithence asked the meaning of the said words, aunswered, that the authoritie of the Archpriest, not stretching to any out of *England*, this clause [*so farre as I can, so farre distant*] vsed in the same sentence where he rendred his dutie, did shew that he wrote it onely to make faire weather with father *Parsons*, and the sooner to get himselfe released of the imprisonment he indured.

But would our aduersaries indeed vnderstand the truth, how much or wherein our two brethren do either beare witnesse against vs, or condemne our standing off, to yeeld our obedience vntill the comming of his Holinesse Breue? Let them reade M. *Bishop* his answere to father

father *Parsons* Letter, and the censure vpon the same, both printed in the English booke, and written when they were not in hold, and then tell vs the particularities wherein they giue testimonie against vs, or find fault with our delay. In the meane, there are none but must see that all the testimonies which are brought against vs, proceeded from one head, & take their whole force from the Cardinals word, and not from his Graces word as auowing the particular faculties & iurisdiction annexed to the Archpresbytership to be the command or appointment of his Holinesse, but from his Graces word onely that he receiued a Commission to make peace in our Country, and that following the will of his Holinesse he decreed a subordination. We therfore being not bound to beleeue (specially to obey, as hath bene sufficiently proued before) the Cardinals word, himselfe writing and affirming it, we were lesse bound by al consequence to beleeue and obey the same related or witnessed vnto vs by others.

And here I thinke good to aduertise, touching the report I haue made of all the precedent testimonies, that I do not so auow it, as that I engage my word, the report to be in euery iot one with the Letters themselues: for this were (the imperfection of mans memorie considered) to ground certaintie vpon vncertaintie, especially the time being long since I read most of the Letters, and neuer read them but once, nor could be admitted to copie them forth: whē also I feared no accident lesse, then that matters would fal out as now they do: or that we should euer haue had occasion to proue our selues no disobedient run-agates from the Church of Rome, or from the supreme Pastour thereof, who with semblable perill of life, and renunciation of worldly preferment, haue for many yeeres laboured to reduce other to the sheepfold, and due obedience of the same Church, and highest *Pontifex*.

That which I haue said is the whole truth of my owne thoughts, and as much, and not otherwise then my memorie vpon best recalling of matter could suggest. If our aduersaries will haue the foresaid persons to speake more for them, or in another tune against vs: let them produce their Letters, and out of them all, inforce the most they can against vs. The qualitie and maner of their dealing with vs hitherto doth not put vs in hope, they will much spare vs: and we on the other side, haue as little feare (truth and sinceritie encouraging) but that we shall be wel able to free our selues of as much, as all corners being sought, can be obiected in our rebuke. And certes the force of the foresaid testimonies (if such farre off speeches from the point, vnintended and accidentall, may be called testimonies which Pope *Calixtus* denieth) will appeare very weake, and be most easily auoided, if the ground they stand vpon be aduisedly pondered. For if any of all the parties, of whom our aduersaries claime testimonie should be demaunded (Cardinal *Caietane* excepted, who neither might fitly beare euidence in his owne cause) the reason why they so wrote, or what knowledge or certaintie they had of the thing they affirmed: would they, or could they truly, yeeld another reason for such their affirmāce, thē that they heard it to be so by report, or that they had read the *Letter Cōstitutiue?* We beleeue verily no, & how cā we beleeue otherwise, one liuing at the time of the grant of the Commissiō in *Louaine*, others in *Bruxels*, an other in *Doway*, an other we wote not where, all distant a thousand miles from *Rome* where the authority was granted, saue onely Cardinall *Caietane* and father *Bellarmine*, since made Cardinall.

3.q.9.testet.§ si debitum.

4 q.2.& 3.si testes §. nullas idoneus.

Siluest. verb. testis nu.2.

And first, to heare a thing by report, is no good ground or sufficient warrantise, for any one thereupon to witnesse the same to be true. For the Ecclesiastical Canon hath *Testes nō de alijs causis, vel negotijs dicant testimonium, nisi de his quæ sub præsentia eorum acta esse noscuntur.* Let not witnesses giue testimonie of other causes or matters, but of those which are knowne to be done in their presence. And *Innocentius* affirmeth, that if one bearing witnesse of a thing, and being asked how he knew it to be so, as he witnesseth it to be: his testimonie is nothing worth, if the can render no surer cause of his testimonie, then that he heard it by report. *Si dicit, ego scio quia sic omnes dicunt, non valet eius testimonium, quia malam & insufficientem causam reddit sui testimonij.* If the Testis say, I know it, because all men do so report, his testimonie is not good, because he assignes too weake or insufficient a cause or ground of the testimonie he beareth. And the same holy Father and Pope reputed the glorie of the Canonists, hath these wordes in the same place: *Officium testis est propriè dicere veritatem de ijs quæ percipit quinque sensibus corporis.* It is properly the office of a witnesse, to tel the truth of those things, which he knoweth by one of the fiue senses of the bodie. Consonant to this is that also which *Siluester* writeth: *Requiritur quod testis testificetur de auditu proprio, scilicet quantum ad sonos, vel devisu quantum ad visibilia, & idem de alijs sensibus, non de alieno: *quia non est propriè testimonium.* It is required that a testis should beare witnesse of the things himselfe heard or saw, and so the same of other senses,

3.q.9.testes.

In ca.cum causam de testi. & attest.nu.3.

Nu.2.

Verb. testis nu.6.

* Glos. in l. in sum. ff. de aqua pluuia, arcen.

ſenſes,and not of things he taketh by report, becauſe this kind of euidẽce is not properly a teſtimony.Neither do other authors new or old diſagree in this poſition.*Benintendus*[a] *Teſtis de auditu non ſolum non plenè probat,ſed etiam non facit præſumptionem ſufficientem ad transferendum onus probandi in contrariũ:* A witnes ſpeaking by hearesay doth not only not fully proue,but faileth to make ſo much as a ſufficient preſumption of inforcing the aduerſarie to proue the contrarie.Again,& which cōmeth a little nearer and more diſtinctly to our caſe , the ſame authour hath theſe words almoſt immediatly enſuing the other: [b] *Teſtimonium de auditu & relatione alterius nullam facit probationem in negotio de recenti geſto.* Teſtimonie giuen by heare-ſay and vpon report,maketh no preſumption in a matter newly done.*Speculum* [c] *Teſtimonium de auditu alieno,ſcz. quod audiui dicit non valet* . A witnes vpon hearesay is little worth.*Panormitane* [d] *Teſtis interrogatus quo modo ſcit,debet dicere, quia vidi & audiui* . A witneſſe being asked how he knew the thing he teſtifieth,ought to be able to anſwer,becauſe I ſaw it and heard it.For that as *Barbatia* recordeth[e] *In vſu & auditu,fundatur teſtimonium.* Teſtimony touching mattet of fact,is founded vpon aſſurance of the eye and eare. The author compriſing the verdict of the other three ſenſes, vnder the nobleneſſe and generalitie of the eye and eare.

(a)*Conclu.67.nu.*10.

(b)*Ibid.nu.*11.

(c) *Li.*1*.de teſt.* § 1*.nu.*53.

(d)*In ca. ex literis de conſuetu.nu* 4.

(e)*Super Clem. in rubrica de elect fo.97.col.*4

On the other ſide,if our aduerſaries ſhall ſay,that the aboue named witneſſes or any of them did reade the *Conſtitutiue Letter* , and therefore wrote as they did : we aske them what maner of ground this is,& wherein it differeth from the kind of teſtimonie that followeth? *Iohn* imagineth that *Peter* gaue him a boxe on the eare,and thereupon frameth a bill of cōplaint againſt *Peter* : and when he had framed it, ſheweth the ſame to ſundry of his friends.After,the matter is brought to triall: *Peter* denieth the giuing of the blow,*Iohn* auerres it:the fact reſteth to be proued by witneſſes. *Iohn* in this meane while vnderſtandeth,that thoſe his friends to whom he ſhewed the bill, haue ſithence addreſſed ſome Letters to certaine of their friends, and vttered ſome words concerning the contents and drift of the bill, and thereupon calleth them to witneſſe , and bringeth their ſaid Letters into the Court : and they comming to giue euidence, the Iudge asketh whether they were preſent, and did ſee when *Peter* gaue *Iohn* this blow, and they anſwer no . The Iudge demaundeth further, what then is it which they can ſay for teſtimonie of the fact . Marie quoth they, we did reade his bill of complaint before the ſute was commenced , and thereupon wrote the Letters we did , thinking that *Peter* had giuen

Iohn the blow. Surely if ſuch a peece of euidence and claime of teſtimony, being one with that which is brought againſt vs, ſhould come before the Iudges of the Kings Bench, or Iuſtices of Oyer and determiner, they might perhaps ſport themſelues not à little at the folly. But the leaſt cards muſt be all coat-cardeś againſt vs.

For concluſion of our anſwer to this ſecond obiection, and for a briefe recitall of that hath bene ſaid before in this third reaſon, we beſeech our impugners to conſider vnprightly and ſeriouſly, as before God in the court of their owne vnderſtanding: firſt, whether truth, reaſon, demonſtratiue practiſe, and the voice of all lawes ſpeake not more for vs then for them: nay whether they all do not combine and pleade wholly for vs, and altogether againſt them: namely that euery delegation muſt be proued by ſhewing of the Commiſſion or autheticke copie thereof, and not by witneſſes, eſpecially if the delegation or verball commiſſion ſhall impart a many of particular iuriſdictions, as this of his Holineſſe did to the Cardinall with like number of faculties. Then whether teſtimonies not founded vpon euidence of the eye or eare, but grounded onely vpon report or hearesay, are of any force, or make a preſumption in law, in a matter lately done.

Thirdly, whether it be enough in law or conſcience, when a delegation or verbal commiſſion is granted to one, deriuing many diſtinct and ſeuerall iuriſdictions, each bringing their porper and increaſing preiudice to others, whether it be enough we ſay to teſtifie the commiſſion in generall, and not for the witneſſes to deſcend to the teſtifying of the particular tenour of the commiſſion. And if in all theſe three vnderſtanding be conuinced by the euidence and proues aforegoing, then we inſtantly pray them for the loue of their owne ſoules, not to be aſhamed to confeſſe the truth, and ſurceaſſe further contention, remembring what the holy Ghoſt writeth: *Eſt confuſio adducens peccatum, & eſt confuſio adducens gratiam & gloriam*: there is a confuſion that bringeth ſin, and there is a confuſion that bringeth grace and glorie.

A Third reaſon that our impugners make againſt vs, and ſeeme in the force thereof to take no ſmall contentment, is, that at our firſt comming ouer, we were, and are ſtill beleeued to be Prieſts vppon our word, without ſhewing our letters of orders, and that folke come to vs, without making queſtion either of our Prieſthood, or of our iuriſdiction to heare confeſſions: and how then? our ſelues being in this ſort beleeued vpon credit of our owne word, could we refuſe

to

to beleeue our Cardinall Protector, vpon euidence of his Graces letter, hand, and seale? Do we looke that others euen in that tribunall of loosing from sinne, should rely vpon, and trust our bare word, and vse vs without scruple in the court of their soule, and we in the sensible feeling and continuance of this supreme credence and fauour, so to forget our selues and our duty, as not to giue beleefe to the word of a Cardinall, of our Protector, of his Holinesse Counsellor in all matters incident to the gouernement of the Vniuersall Church? A fault that can no way be excused, and which cannot but condemne vs with as many as are wise. Well: let vs notwithstanding the peremptorinesse of the accusation, haue leaue to aunswere and cleare our selues as we can.

First we desire to know of what kind of fault did this our reproued demeanor condemne vs? Not of the crime which was first obiected. For to refuse to obey a Cardinall Protector his letter in matter of like preiudice, and in authority deriued by commission from his Holinesse without further proofe, then his Lordships owne letter for testimony thereof, hath no more affinitie with that crime, then white hath with blacke, or things that are lawfull with things vnlawfull. Of what other offence then, did our foresayd demeanor condemne vs? Forsooth of enormious disobedience. What, is the matter so certaine? Yea. Then against whom immediatly did we commit this enormious disobedience, against his Holinesse, the Cardinall, or maister *Blackwell*? Not immediatly certes against his Holinesse, because there is no disobedience, and much lesse that, which can be called enormious, (a) but consisteth in the breaking of a knowne precept: and we neither vnderstood at that time, nor did know before we read it in his Holinesse Breue, when we presently yeelded our obedience, that his Holinesse had giuen commaundement for such a subordination to be directed with like iurisdiction as is set downe in the *Constitutiue Letter*, ne did the Cardinall any where specifie or relate so much. So that we hauing no vnderstanding of such his Holinesse commandement, before the comming ouer of the Breue, and then submitting our obedience thereunto without any delay, how could our demeanor be immediate and enormious disobedience against his Holinesse?

(a) *D.Tho.2.2. q.105.art.1. cor.Greg.de Vale.ibidem punct 3. Siluester verb inobedientia & omnes.*

If our aduersaries will gainsay any of the premises, as we hope the euidence of the truth, nor their owne consciences will giue them leaue, it resteth (and it is our request vnto them) that they would tell vs, when, to whom, and in what forme his Holinesse gaue such a commaundement,and that we had also vnderstanding thereof,whiles we detracted to obey the subordination. An issue, which we are sure all the world, nor the Angels of heauen can make true against vs, and which not verified, it remaineth vnpossible to proue that we were in the action of our bearing off, enormiously and immediatly disobedient against his Holinesse.

Not against the Cardinall as our Protectour, because we neither knew nor heard that his Lordship was by prerogatiue of authority, any otherwise a superiour to the Priestes in England, then as other Cardinall Protectors are ouer the Cleargy of the countries or Prouinces whereof they are chosen Protectors. Who neither practise nor claime,as all Christendom is witnes,any such iurisdiction ouer the Priests, as either to ordaine new superiorities amongst thẽ, or to haue the chusing of their prelate, or to increase the rules of their subiectiõ, or any otherwise to alter the forme of their vsuall gouernement.

Not against the Cardinall as Delegate or Commissioner, because we were not bound either to beleeue or obey him in that place, before his Grace had shewed vs the rescript of the delegatiõ,or otherwise authentically proued his Holinesse commission vnto him, as hath bene abundantly declared before.

Not against the Cardinall as the distributer of faculties to Priestes in their commission for England, because the authority to institute an Archpriest with like iurisdiction as is specified in the *Constitutiue Letter*, was not delegated in that commission, nor euer so claimed, nor yet to this day so interpreted.

Not against maister *Blackwell* and the twelue Assistants, because we being not obliged(as is said)to obey the Cardinal in regard of the none-proofe of the delegation or commission by word of mouth: we could not be bound to obey master *Blackwell* or the twelue Assistants, taking their whole authority from the Cardinall. *Nemo in alium potest plus iuris transferre quàm ipse habet.* No man can transferre more right to another then himselfe posseseth. And therefore being not bound as is proued before to obey the Cardinall in constituting the subordination,by reason his Grace had not first shewed or proued his commission,we rested lesse bound to obey maister *Blackwell* & the twelue Assistants, because what was defectiue in his Grace the principall, or of no sufficient power to bind,must needes by all necessary sequell,be as much if not more defectiue, and of lesse force to bind in the secondaries, or his Graces subdelegates.

Gloss. in c. Si cui de elect. li. 6

Or

Or if now our reprouers ſhall ſay that although our detracting to ſubiect our ſelues to the Cardinals order, were neither the crime they firſt tooke it to be, nor enormious diſobedience, yet the ſame could not but make vs guilty of ſome other great offence. Of what by name? Surely, of the like offence by coherence (the argument being brought *à ſimili*, of likeneſſe betweene matters) as thoſe ſhould commit, who ſhould refuſe to beleeue vs to be Prieſts vpon our word, and would not but vpon ſurer proofe, vſe vs in that function.

Now then what kind of offence might this be? To heare Maſſe, is by the ſtraight condition of our lawes, the forfeiture of an hundreth markes: to helpe a Prieſt at Maſſe, or to be confeſſed of him, is made an act of felony: to relieue, abet, harbour, or maintaine him, no leſſe. What fault then not to beleeue ſuch or ſuch an one to be a Prieſt, or not to partake with him in Prieſtly functions, except he know him to be a Prieſt by other prooues, then vpon the bare reckord of his owne word? Verily the faulte is ſo little, as none of iudgement will take it, but for an act of prudence: and the contrary, for a faile of due conſideration, if not for a fact of too much aduenturouſneſſe or temeritie.

And our cōſcience here prompteth that our fault-finders, as full of exceptions as they are againſt vs, ne haue, ne will, entertaine any one as Prieſt, and leſſe ſubiect themſelues in confeſſion vnto him, of whom they ſhall haue no further ſurety what he is, a ſpie, or an honeſt man, then the parties bare affirmation of himſelfe.

But we wot how our contradictors wil reply at laſt, when all other pretences be taken from them, to weete, that our diſtruſt and prolonging to obey the Cardinals order, was an iniurie to his Grace, and could not but derogate from the honour of his high eſtate. This is the moſt that we thinke can be obiected, and to this we anſwer. Firſt, that it is a receiued propoſition in the ciuill and common law, and reaſon conuinceth, that *Non facit alicui iniuriam qui vtitur iure ſuo.* He doth iniurie to no one, that vſeth his owne right. We therefore vſing no more then our owne right in the aboue mentioned delay (and that kind of right too, which the Canons of holy Church, the vniforme conſent of all writers, and the generall practiſe ouer all Chriſtendome, doth abſolutely affoord and aſſure vnto vs) can neuer acknowledge, that our precedent demeanour, was, or could be poſſibly, any iniurie to his grace. For can contraries be both true, or one and the ſelfe action, be iuſt and vniuſt, right to one, and iniurious to ano-

Ca. cum eccleſia de electione & l. iniuriarū § 1. ff. de iniurijs.

ther? *Silueſter* declaring the Etymologie, or interpretation of the word [*Iniuria*] writeth: *Iniuria, eſt quaſi non iure.* Iniurie, taketh her name of a defect of right. And the Philoſopher oppoſeth iniurie, as a contrary to law or right. So that what is done lawfully, or by good right according to law, cannot without the abuſe of the terme, be counted an iniurie.

Verb. iniuria ante. §. Ariſtoteles. 5. Ethn. ca. 1.

Againe, the not yeelding of that to any man of what high degree ſoeuer, which the law of holy Church doth prohibite, or not graunt it ſhould be yeelded vnto him, is neither iniurie nor the diminiſhing of reputation. And that our demurre to admit the new authority was of this quality, it is plaine by the authorities that haue bene alleaged, and will yet appeare more euident hereafter.

Lib. 19. contra Fauſtum ca. 25. 14. q. 1. quod debetur.

Saint *Auguſtine* writeth, and his words be regiſtred in the Decrees, *Peccat qui exigit vltra debitum.* He ſinneth who exacteth beyond his due. Which without peraduenture holdeth as well in points of ſoueraignty and command, as in matters of worldly ſubſtance, if not more, in reſpect that the abridgemēt of freedome is more irkſome to man, then any meane loſſe of the goods he enioyeth. And therefore whatſoeuer our hard-friends be pleaſed to deliuer abroad of his Graces intention, yet we cannot thinke that he intended to exact that beliefe in vs, and obedience to the contents of his *Letter Conſtitutiue*, as vppon the ſole view thereof (his honours iuriſdiction being a delegatiue power) we ſhould incontinent captiuate our vnderſtanding and bowe downe our neckes to the yoake, without asking for other proofe of the delegation and the tenour thereof, then the credence of his owne word alone.

Or if his Lordſhip had this meaning, as we ſhall not beleeue he had, to exact ſo vndue a tribute at our hands, yet that being more then our debt, and repugnant to the order in Gods Church, how could our prolonging or not taking his Graces word for full and ſufficient warrantiſe of what he ſayd, be either ſinne in vs, or an iniurie to his honour, when the learned writ and the doctrine is receiued of all men.

Gloſſ. in inſtitut. Lancelot. li. 1. de confirmatione electionis tit. 9. §. patet, vreb. literas.

Quamuis aliàs iniuria fiat ei cuius dicto credi deberet, ſi ab eo exigeretur ſcriptura: ſecus tamen eſſet in caſibus requirentibus à iure ſcripturam. Although it ſhould be otherwiſe an iniurie to exact of him the ſight of his commiſſion, whom it is meete to beleeue vpon his word: neuertheleſſe it is not ſo in theſe caſes, in which by the aſſignement of the law a letter or written teſtimony is required. And that the law not onely licenſeth, but appointeth the proofe of a delegation to be made

by

by ſhewing the Delegators letters, the authorities before quoted do verie amply demonſtrate, as alſo that commiſſion giuen by word of mouth in matter of preiudice, ought and muſt be atteſtated otherwiſe then by the ſelfe and ſole auowance of the commiſſioner, and likewiſe that beliefe in caſes of * great preiudice is not to be giuen to the word of a Cardinall.

Bart. in l. palatinos cod. de collation. fiſc. l. 10. Iaſon. conſil. 72. nu. 3. & cõſil. 104. Alciet. in ca. cum contingat nu. 35. de iureiur. Cõradus li. 2. ca. 2. de Cardinalibus. §. 3 nu 22.

But now let vs conſider of the arguments, that our opponents make againſt vs. The Catholike laity of the Realme (ſay they) beleeue vs to be Prieſts vppon credite of our owne word, without ſhewing them our letters of orders: *Ergo* we were bound to beleeue our Cardinall Protector, affirming that he receiued a commaundement from his Holineſſe, to erect a ſubordination. Againe, the layty beleeuing vs to be Prieſts vpon our word, reſort in confeſſion vnto vs without mouing queſtion of our authority: *Ergo* we ought to haue ſubiected our obedience to his Graces order, & ſubordination appointed without making ſtay, or demaund for any further proofe or confirmation thereof.

Good conſequences: whether the antecedẽts be true or no. What, muſt the fauour we receiue of the laity in not examining whether we be Prieſts or haue faculties or no, bring an obligation vpon vs to obey our Cardinall Protectour vpon teſtimony of his owne word alone, and not onely in things of direct and greateſt preiudice, but euen in things wherein the lawes of holy Church giue vs leaue not to obey? Straunge, that the voluntarie fauour of the laity, and in a caſe too, wherein themſelues receiue commodity, as they do by partaking with vs in the exerciſe of our Prieſtly functiõs, muſt be of conſequence to bind vs to accept of, and endure the foreſayd detriments. Surely ſuch fauours are leſſe worth then thankes, and ſuch ſolide arguments or fond deductions, fitter to be vſed in a matter of ſport, then for condemnation of Catholike Prieſts.

To beleeue one to be a Prieſt vppon the affirmance of his owne word, or becauſe he ſaith ſo, is no matter of preiudice to the beleeuer, or to any third perſon: for neither is the beleeuer or any other brought thereby within compaſſe of an enforced ſuperioritie, or of hauing their former liberty abridged, and penalties impoſed at the arbitrarie diſpoſition of their hard friends: but in our caſe, and ſuppoſed obligation, it fareth much otherwiſe, becauſe the preiudices that attend the *Conſtitutiue Letter*, are many, and of mightieſt preiudice, as hath bene declared in the beginning of this reaſon. And therefore by the rule of common wisedome, stronger and more assured proofe was both to be made and expected, for beleeuing the authority and all the particulars thereof, commaunding a present subiection, then for beleeuing *Iohn Astile* to be a Priest, so long as none are bound, but all left wholy to their owne choise, either to heare his Masse, or receiue Sacraments, or enter acquaintance with him.

Moreouer the law of humane curtesie inuiteth to beleeue the word of another in auowances of no preiudice, the like as this is: to beleeue *Iohn Astile* to be a Priest so long as there is no band to partake with him in any spirituall or indomageable action; but neither mans law, or Gods law, celestiall or worldly wisedome, doth prescribe that we should beleeue another vpon warrantise of his only word in matters, that after, will we nill we, bring with them store of preiudice, and a constrained bond of obedience, which euermore and with all persons, is reckned for most irksome. But on the other side, it cannot be shewed any where certaine, neither is there any such custome in the Church of God, as that the laity are left free at their owne choise, whether to beleeue or not to beleeue a Priest to be Priest, vnlesse he first shew them his letters of orders, this being an [a] exaction which only belongeth to Bishops and such Curates to make, as shall admit vnknowne Priests to say Masse or minister Sacraments in their Dioces or iurisdiction.

Or let vs graunt to our aduersaries, that the lay Catholikes of our Realme haue Pastorall or Episcopall authority to call vs to proue our ordination. What may they do? No more certes by the Canons of holy Church, then to examine and call such to this reckning as are [b] *Vagi & ignoti* [c] *de quorum ordinatione non constat*, wandering and vnknowne Priests of whose ordination there is no certainty. *Lyndwood* commenting vpon our countrey constitutions, hath these words: [d] *vir bene notus & bonæ famæ, qui vbi conuersatus est, longo tempore habitus est pro ordinato, non cogitur nec per literas nec per testes probare ordinationem suam*. A man well knowne and of good fame, who in the place where he liued was a long time counted a Priest, is not to be constrained to proue his ordination either by letters or witnesses. And Pope *Innocentius* the third, resoluing the doubts which the Patriarch of Ierusalem moued vnto him touching such as came into his Dioces without their Dimissories or testimoniall letters, writeth: [e] *Nisi legitimè tibi constiterit siue per literas, siue per testes* ([f] *siue per idonea argumenta*) *de illorum ordinatione canonica, qui penitus sunt ignoti, non debes ipsos permittere*

(a) *Tit. de Clericis pereg. per totum. dist. 71. & 52. per totum. Lindvvod, const. lib. 1 ca. cum quanta de Cler. pereg. Concil. Tredent. sess. 22. Decret. de obseruandis & vitandis in celebratione Missæ.*
(b) *Concil. Trid vbi supra*
(c) *Lyndvvood vbi supra.*
(d) *Lyndvvood lib. 1. in ca. cū quanta de cler. pereg. verb. constiterit.*
(e) *Ca. tuæ fraternitatis de Cler. pereg.*
(f) *Inter eodem tit.*

tere in tuis plebibus celebrare. Vnlesse thou dost assuredly vnderstand either by letters or witnesses, or by sufficient arguments their Canonicall ordination who are vtterly vnknowne, thou oughtest not to permit them to celebrate before thy Diocesians.

Now how can it be conceiued, that we are wandering persons vtterly vnknowne, or that our initiation or receiuing of Priesthood appeared neither by letters, witnesses, or other able arguments, being trained vp as we were in a knowne Seminarie, and taking holy orders by the appointment of the superiour, the whole house likewise witnesses thereof, and many of our fellowes here in England ready from the eye to attestate the same, the frequent correspondence also betweene the chiefe of the Seminaries and others in our countrey, and almost a weekely entercourse of persons too and fro, with many other pregnant and most forcible presumptions: we aske how it can be conceiued, notwithstanding the counterpleading of all these contrarie apparances, that we be persons vtterly vnknowne, and by sequell such as may be suspected whether we be true Priests, or but disguisers and miscreants? If our iudgement shall be taken in our owne case, we thinke there is little reason for any man to call our Priesthoods in doubt, were our owne words of no credit, and consequently the auauncing of the fauour we receiue in being beleeued to be Priests vpon our owne relation without sight of our letters of orders, to be but an idle florish, and as weake an argument, as what is weakest to proue that we were bound to obey what our Cardinall Protector ordeined, without making question of his Graces authority, or looking for further proofe then the testimony of his owne word for warrantise therof; but such truthes must haue like proues.

To end all in few words, we aske our aduersaries what is our dutie to do if the laity shall refuse to beleeue one, two, or moe of vs to be Priestes, and will not haue communion in diuine Seruice and Sacraments with vs as with Priestes, vntill we shew them our Letters of orders, or shall otherwise according to law proue our selues to be men of that calling? Will they out of their wisedome, and charitie giue vs other counsell, then to haue patience in the *interim*, and to procure with most conuenient speede satisfaction and legall testimony to their doubts and exceptions? No truly: well, then we not holding our selues bound to admit the subordination vpon credence of the Cardinals word, vntill such time as his Grace had either shewed the rescript of the delegation, or proued his verball commission, or obtained from his Holinesse a confirmation of the authoritie erected,what was the part of our Archpriest,the societie,& their adherents to do in this point?not as ours was in the former,to patient our bearing off,and procure so soone as they could one of the foresaid proues for our due satisfaction,either a sight of the Commission it selfe,or an authentical proofe thereof, or else some Papall instrument for testimonie of that which his Grace had brought into our Church and imposed vpon vs. It cannot be denied the cases being alike, or rather our case infinitely more demaunding that right of iustice.

And if this had bene their dutie,as the lots changed,it would soone haue bene proclaimed, then what thankes did we deserue in sauing them that labour and charges,and vndertaking to our great cost, the discharge of that businesse for them?We desire not to be our owne iudges,neuerthelesse can we thinke but that our paines therein craued a gentler recompence at their hands,then to imprison those that were sent about the businesse,and not only to imprison them (a thing neuer heard of as we thinke since S. *Peter* sate first in the Chaire,the nature of the affaire considered) but to raise most fabulous and sinfull reports of them,and dub both them,& vs,with the surnames of all impietie, as of faction,emulation,ambition,scandall,rebellion, highest sacriledge, disallegiance to the Sea Apostolicke, renegacie from the spouse of Christ,and of what not,implying turpitude in this kind? A strange requitall,and so strange,as inhumanitie it selfe could hardly deale lesse charitably, or more vnconscionably with vs, had we bene Iewes or Turkes,and the onely drosse of either nation: but our Lord Iesus giue vs euer his grace to possesse our soules in patience, and incline our disturbers to reuerse at length their most vncharitable slanders,the cause and continuing occasion of all the scandalous broile among vs, past, present,and to come.

We haue bene the longer in refuting this weake and vngrounded reason,because not onely the vulgar,but father *Holtby* in his discourse of the 30. of Iune, 1601. and diuerse other both of the Laitie and Cleargie, Secular and Religious, haue it most frequently in their mouths, and enforce the obiection as a most mightie and choking argument to conuince what they most ignominiously burden vs withal.

(a) In his said discourse the 30. of Iune.

A Fourth reason that our oppositours bring for proofe and maintenance of the crimes they impute vnto vs,is,the fewnesse of our number, being as father [a] *Holtby* writeth, but twelue or thirteene in all:

all, or as[b] other make the account but ten: and[c] after father *Parsons* manner of numbring vs, much fewer then ten.

First let vs admit that these men write a truth, as how farre their wordes swarue from all truth, it commeth after to be examined, yet we are to demaund of them and the rest of our impugners (who think the fewnes of our number, matter & euidence cleere enough to condemne vs by) whether the cause we stand in be naught in that we are but fiue, ten, or twelue which defend it. If they say yea, as they must, or else bewray their own reason: then must it follow by force of the same reason, that the cause of S. *Thomas* of Canterbury in defence whereof [d] no one Bishop adhered vnto him in the whole Realme, nay, all subscribed to the Articles he stood against, was treasonable, rebellious, or vnlawfull: then the cause that Bishop *Fisher* died for, and the causes that infinite other of great Holinesse maintained, hauing fewer and incomparably fewer of the cleargie vnited to them in open defence of the same, then are now, or were at first of our companie, were likewise either treasonable, or rebellious, or vnlawfull: which we are sure our aduersaries will not say, and yet they cannot but say it, if they stand to the triall of the reason they make against it, or shall not acknowledge the vnsoundnesse or inualiditie thereof.

(b) Doctour Haddock and M Array in the libel dated the 10. of Ianuary 1599. & giuen vp to the two Cardinals Protector and vice-protector against M. Bishop and M. Charnocke.
(c) In his letter to M. Bishop the 9. of Octo ber 1599. and in the Apologie.
(d) *Gulielm. Neubrigensis lib.2.ca.16.*

For further satifaction in this point, we refer our aduersaries to the dayly iudgement, which experience maketh the surest confutation of all other; whether the small number of open defendants (especially when the sword of authoritie is drawne against the matter or action defended, as it is in our case) be a sufficient warrantie in conscience, for any one of vnderstanding to infer that the cause they stand in, is wicked or vngodly, or not meete for men of quiet natures, or Priests to be seen in. Verily the question is so cleare and demonstrated by dayly experience, as he that should make doubt hereof, might not amisse seem to haue liued out of the world, nothing being more frequent in the world, then for truth to find fewest defenders, when authoritie, humane fauour, and temporall gaine be her impugners.

But to vnderprop this weake reason, founded vpon our small number, father *Holtby* fortifieth and gildeth the matter in this wise. *It is well inough knowne* (saith he) *that those who receiued the authoritie, farre exceeded the other, who deferred their obedience, not onely in number, being twentie for one, but in all things else, setting their presumptuous minds and busie heads aside.* And, *it is too too cleare, that the refusall came not either of ignorance or infirmitie, but of plaine malice, of an obstinate will not to obey,* *Pag.2.& 5.*

and from a proud presumptuous mind and seditious spirite. Also, *it is manifest that some of the best among them, were euer noted for busie and seditious spirites, yea no one of their chiefest almost, but he was noted with some particular fault or exception: but among their brethren* (who embraced their authoritie) *there were many which liued without touch of discredite, and euery way better qualified then any of them.* Thus much father *Holtby*. And father *Parsons* in the Apologie striketh this key oft, as the musicke perhaps that best contenteth his eare: yet because the vntruthes in that booke be innumerable, and because another intendeth to display them in part, we meane not here to insert any of his course reports, but will returne to father *Holtby*, and demaund of him the reason, why, if the ill habites and sinnes he vpbraideth vs with be notorious, he did not name the persons he meant, but vseth the deprauing wordes in such generall manner, as the Reader is left (a condemned [e] kind of detraction) to apply them to whom, and to so manie as he listeth of our companie. Or if the wicked qualities and enormities he obiecteth, be not commonly knowne to raigne in vs, why did the religious father (he and his complices being the [f] assailers, and we the partie assailed, a materiall difference and which putteth great oddes in the case touching the lawfulnesse or vnlawfulnesse of reuealing secret sinnes) thus inordinately publish and blaze our dishonours to the world, in addressing the discourse to one, but communicating the same to many ere it came to that one bodies view.

(e) *Nauar. in Man. ca.* 18. *nu.* 18.

(f) *Sotus de inst. li.* 5. *q.* 7. *art.* 3. *Valenti Tom.* 3 *disp.* 5. *q.* 14. *punct.* 3.

We expect his answere, and how he will cleare himselfe of both, either being a foule transgression: and in the meane do hold this position, that truth out of what mouth soeuer it commeth, ought to be [g] preferred and not impugned. A lesson of Christian doctrine and which our Sauiour in his owne fact did not let to manifest in commending the censure of [h] the Pharisie with a *recte iudicasti*, thou hast iudged aright, albeit he perfectly knew him to be most enuious and arrogant. So that how exorbitant soeuer our naturall inclination and qualities be, and with what particular faultes or exceptions neuer so greatly distaining, the chiefest of our company go marked, yet if we maintaine a truth, the maintenance is not to be calumniated, either in that we are but few, or because we are (admitting the relgious mans slaunders) *busie headed, proud, and presumptuously minded, seditiously spirited, and wel knowne to be euer noted with particular faultes or exceptions.* In which treatise also, the same discrupulous father forbeareth not to condemne

(g) *Gloss. in ca. quæritur* 2. *q.* 7. *verb. præponimus.*

(h) *Luke* 7.

vs,

vs, for not yeelding our obedience at first before notice of his Holinesse Breue, *of* (to vse is owne words) *a most grieuous and damnable, most enormious, notorious, publike and hainous sinne, breeding open scandall, and making vs infamous for rebellion comming from plaine malice, and conuincing vs to haue a seditious and most presumptuous spirite, &c.*

Touching the lesser faultes or ill properties imputed, we answere no more, but that we know now *who can first throw the stone at vs*: for it were indecent, or a point of hypocrisie, to twite other with particular faults, except he himself were free. And concerning the criminous, we are to put him and his Superiour in mind, that there is [i] satisfaction due vnto vs, and we demaund it, vnlesse he shall proue (to which we challenge him) both that we were culpable in the manner he specifieth, and that the offences were notoriously knowne.

Ioh.8.

(i) D.Tho. 22.q. 62.art.2.ad 2m Caietanus ibid. Sotus de iustitia lib.4.q.6. art.3.ad 4 arg. Nauar.in Man. ca.18.nu.45. Valent.To.3. disp.5.q.6.punc. 5 assert.1.& 2. Bannes de iure & iust.q.62. art.2. dubit.8. Petrus à Nauar. lib.3.ca.4.nu. 375.& sequent. Salon.Tom.1.q 62.art.2.controu.20.

Now for the comparison, we are very sure that not all nor the most part in our Realme, do thinke that M. Doctor *Bagshaw*, M. Doctor *Bishop*, M. *Bluet*, M. *Mush*, M. *Taylor*, so much inferiour as father *Holtby* maketh them to any of the elder Priests that are of the contrarie side: nor yet M. Doctour *Norres*, M *Champney*, M. *Bennet*, M. *Drurie*, second by so great oddes to any of the yonger sort in any one quality or talent soeuer: nay rather if the matter were to passe by verdite of most voices, it is certaine that father *Holtby* would be found partiall, if not detractious in the comparison.

And concerning the report that he and others make, and seeme to glory much therein, that we were but ten or 12, at most, who stood off, to admit the authoritie, we say no more but that fath. *Parsons* (through whose irreligious dealing our two brethren were spoiled of their notes and schedules they carried, and which he sent afterwards into England or the most part of them) can witnesse that there were thrice ten within one who gaue their names: whereof some also wrote that there were many moe of their brethren, which disliked the forme of the gouernement appointed, or rather that they were but few, which were willing to receiue it, if they might any way chuse. And indeede what one commoditie spirituall or temporall, either to Priest or lay person did the authority bring with it, to inuite any one of iudgement to like thereof: vnlesse apparant preiudices, slaunder, that the secular Priests and Laitie were at great variance, and the mightie increase of our miseries or new seruitudes must be counted commodities?

Aggredi Sathanas non dubitauit, vt inter se collideret.

But howsoeuer our aduersaries do please themselues in our small number, yet there are few in our Realme of any acquaintance with

Priests,but know there be mo then ten inwardly for vs,for one against vs. We wish from our hearts that euery Priest would shew himselfe outwardly, as he is affected in his thoughts, and then we should little doubt but that our small number (so great a beame of the eye of our cause)would quickly waxe the greater part,and the reckning that our aduersaries make of twentie for one, to be on their side against vs, would farre fall out to be truer in the count for vs.

A Fifth obiection which our oppositours make against vs, is the grieuous condemnation that publickely passed vppon vs at *Rome*,by sentence of the two Cardinals, *Caietane* and *Burghesio*, and by the contents of the Breue and his Holinesse iudgement. The auowances of our Archpriest in his decrees of the 29. of May, 1600. & of the 18. of October following, and in his Dimissories to me,and refutories to all the other Appellants of the 20. of December.

His wordes in the former decree are these. *Whereas after the condemnation at Rome of the two Embassadours* (he meaneth Maister Doctour *Bishop* and Maister *Charnoke*) *together with all their complices here,and also the Popes Breue confirming the Cardinals Letters,as,Validas ab initio*, (that is of force from the beginning) *and vtterly condemning and inualiditing all things done to the contrarie.*

His wordes in the latter decree, these: *Vt omnes occasio in posterum tollatur,vel minimæ litis de hac præterita controuersia commouendæ: quoniam ex literis nostræ institutionis datis Romæ die 7. Martij 1598. potestas nobis concessa est, de dubijs ac controuersis inter nos exorientibus determinandi, eaq; literæ à S^mo D. N. die 6. Aprilis 1599. confirmatæ sunt; omniaq; & singula illis literis contenta de expresso mandato & ordine, & cum participatione & certa scientia sua facta & ordinata fuisse declarante,adeo vt suum plenarium effectum sortiri & plenissimam roboris firmitatem obtinere debeant:atque irritum & mane sit quicquid secus per quoscunq; commissarios aut iudices attentari scienter,vel ignoranter contigerit:propterea nos ex authoritrte hac nobis à S^mo D.N.commissa pronuntiamus & declaramus primas illas literas institutionis nostræ omnes Catholicos in Anglia verè obligasse : eosq; qui nostræ authoritati scienter quouis modo repugnarunt, verè inobedientes fuisse sedi Apostolicæ, & in nostrum officium per eandem sedem institutum rebelles.*

The English.

That al occasiō hereafter may be takē away euē of mouing the least strife of this controuersie past,because by the Letters of our institution giuen

giuen at Rome the 7. of March 1498. authority is graunted vnto vs to determine the doubts and controuersies that rise betweene vs: and these letters were confirmed by his Holinesse the sixth of Aprill 1599. and declaring all and singular the things contained in these letters to haue bene done and ordained, by his expresse commaundement and order, and with his participation and certaine knowledge in so much as they ought to haue their fullest effect, and obtaine greatest firmenesse: and that it be voide and of no validity whatsoeuer shall happen otherwise to be assaied wittingly or ignorantly by what Commissioners or Iudges soeuer. Therefore we by this authority committed vnto vs by his Holinesse, do pronounce and declare these first letters of our institution really to haue bound all the Catholikes in England, and those who wittingly any maner of way impugned our authoritie, to haue bene truly disobedient to the Sea Apostolicke, and rebellious against our office instituted by the same Sea.

The words he vseth in the dimissorie and refutory letters, are these: *Manifestum est quod ipsorum progressus etiam ante Breue Apostolicum in grauem condemnationem Romæ duorum Illmorum Cardinalium, & etiam suæ Stis iudicio prolapsi fuerint.* It is manifest that their proceeding, (he meaneth our delay and sending to Rome) euen before the comming of the Apostolicall Breue were sharply condemned at Rome by the sentence of two most illustrious Cardinals, and also by the iudgement of his Holinesse.

Were not our deseruings very ill if these things be true? Or being vntrue, was not our superiour forgetfull in reporting after this maner, that is: vntruly of the Cardinals, vniustly of his Holinesse, and most wrongfully against vs his subiects and brethren? None can deny it. Let vs then examine the matter, and see whether the reports be true or no. And here first we protest that we cannot coniecture the reason why his Reuerence calleth maister Doctor *Bishop*, and maister *Charnocke*, two Embassadours (by which name they are also stiled in the Appendix) considering they were imprisoned before they were *Fol.22.* heard, and after exiled a part and confined in their exile, a kind of intreaty which was neuer vsed by that Sea towards any Embassadours if towards any other person. To thinke our Superiour vsed the word as a mocke, placing it as he did in a publike Decree, seemeth so much or infinitely to derogate from the grauity requisite, as we cannot well admit the thought, albeit we know not what other meaning he could haue.

But to let this paſſe and come to what is more materiall.

After the condẽnation at Rome of the two Embaſſadors together with all their complices here] we are verie ſure that our greateſt aduerſaries themſelues will not ſay that there paſſed any other condemnation vpon our two brethren at Rome or elſewhere, ſaue that ſentence only which the two Cardinals *Caietane* and *Burgheſio* gaue in writing vnder their names, and in this there is no mentiõn made of their complices, nor any word in the whole ſentence that can in the leaſt maner ſound that way. And to the end we be not our owne iudges, but that other may ſee the truth as well as our ſelues, the ſentence is verbatim ſet downe, and after tranſlated into Engliſh.

R^do^ in Chriſto P. Rectori vel Vicerectori *Collegij Anglorum de vrbe. Decretum* Ill^orum^ Cardinalium Caietani & Burgheſij de *cauſa Gul. Biſhopi, & Rob. Charnochi.*

Reuerende in Chriſto pater vti frater. Cum audita his diebus atque examinata duorum ſacerdotum Anglorum cauſa nobis à S^mo^ commiſſa Guli.mmirum Biſhopi & Rob. Charnochi, qui ſanctitatis ſuæ iuſſu per menſes aliquot in iſto Collegio detenti fuerunt, viſum nobis fuiſſet nullo modo cauſæ Anglicanæ expedire, vt dicti preſbyteri ſtatim ad eas partes reuertantur, vbi controuerſias cum alijs ſui ordinis hominibus exercuerunt, idipſum modo, re cum S^mo^ collata, eiuſq; deſuper voluntate iterum explorata, decernendum atque ſtatuendum duximus. Quapropter præfatis Guli. & Rober. ſacerdotibus S^tis^ ſuæ noſtróque nomine ordinamus, ac in virtute ſanctæ obedientiæ ſub pæna ſuſpenſionis à diuinis ipſo facto incurrendæ, alijſq; cenſuris pænisq; S^mi^ D.N. iudicio infligendis ſtrictè præcipimus, vt niſi de expreſſa S^tis^ ſuæ aut Ill^mi^ Cardinalis Protectoris licentia, Angliæ, Scotiæ, vel Hiberniæ regna pro tempore adire non preſumant, ſed apud alias Regiones Catholicas quibus à nobis præſcriptum eis fuit, quietè, pacificè, ac religioſè viuent, curentq; tam literis, quam nuncijs, alijſq; modis omnibus quibus poſſunt, pax vnioq; inter Catholicos

Anglicanos

Anglicanos tam domi quam foris conseruetur. Quæ si ipsi verè ac rebus ipsis præstiterint, citius deinde licentia reuertendi restitui eis poterit. Hæc vero interim legitimè ab eis obseruari fideliterq́, executioni mandari præcipimus, hocq́, nostro nomine R[tia] V[a] eis significet. Datum Romæ ex ædibus nostris die 21. Aprilis 1597.

R[a] V[a] Vti frater *H.* C[lis] *Caietanus* Protector.

Vti frater *C.* Car[lis] *Burghesius.*

The English.

To the reuerend in Christ, Father Rector or Vicerector of the Colledge of the English in the *Citie. The Decree or definitiue sentence of the most Illustrious* Cardinals Caietaine and Burghesio in the cause of *William Bishop and Robert Charnocke.*

Reuerend father in Christ as our brother. Whereas of late by commission from his Holinesse we haue heard and examined the cause of two English Priests, to wit *William Bishop* and *Robert Charnocke*, which haue bene for the space of some moneths detained in this Colledge, it appeared vnto vs to be in no case expedient for the English cause, that the sayd Priests should immediatly returne to those partes, where they haue bene at variance with other men of their order; and now hauing conferred the matter with his Holinesse, and being againe certaine of his pleasure therein, we thinke meete to decree and appoint the very same. Wherefore we ordaine in his Holinesse and our owne name, and do strictly commaund the foresayd Priests *William* and *Robert* in vertue of holy obedience, and vnder paine of suspention from diuine offices, to be incurred in the fact it selfe, and vnder other censures and penalties to be inflicted at the appointment of our holy father, that without the expresse leaue of his Holinesse, or the most Illustrious Cardinall Protectour, they do not for the time presume to go to the kingdomes of

England, Scotland, or Ireland, but liue quietly, peaceably, and religiouſly in other Catholike countries, where we haue aſſigned them: and endeuour as well by letters, as by meſſengers, & by all other meanes, that peace and vnion be conſerued among the Engliſh Catholikes at home and abroad. Which things if they truly and really performe, their licence to returne may the ſooner after be graunted vnto them. But in the mean while we command theſe things to be rightfully obſerued & faithfully executed, & that your Reuerence ſignifie thus much vnto them in our name. Giuen at *Rome* from our Pallaces the 21. of Aprill 1599.

Your Reuerences
as brother, H. Cardinall Caietane Protector,
as brother C. Cardinall Burgheſio.

NOw let him whoſoeuer would ſooneſt find a hole in our coate, teach vs in what part of the ſentence we *their complices here* are mentioned, or point vs to that word in the whole Decree, which can any way iuſtly or colourably be ſtretched to ſuch a meaning or implication. And if neither of theſe can be ſhewed, as moſt ſure it is they cannot, how can we with any regard of truth, or moderation of ſpeech be ſayd to be condemned?

Againe delegatiue Iudges of what eſtate ſoeuer they be, receiuing authority by Commiſſion from their ſuperiour, to heare and determine the cauſe of ſuch and ſuch perſons by name (as did the two Cardinals from his Holineſſe, as their ſentence it ſelfe beareth witneſſe) cannot extend their cenſures & condemnation to any of the ſayd perſons complices, not expreſſed in the Cõmiſſiõ, how guilty ſoeuer they know them to be. The reaſon is, becauſe they haue no authority nor iuriſdiction ouer them, as the firſt, fourth and fifth Propoſition teach in the ſecond Reaſon, and may be further declared by this ſimilitude of the caſes. The Queenes Maieſtie giueth a Commiſſion to two of her priuie Counſellors to arraigne *Iohn Aſtile* and *Iohn Anoke* for treaſon cõmitted: Now we aske whether theſe priuie Counſellors, may by vertue of this limited and particular cõmiſſion proceed vpon and condemne ſuch cõplices of the ſaid traitors as their honors by ſifting matters may find to haue had their finger in the treaſon, without any perſonall triall or ſummõs of thẽ: for thus alſo it fared in our caſe. We aſſure our ſelues that none will ſay they can, and thoſe that are ſtudied in the lawes do knew they cannot; and that the lawes of our country

(reaſons

(reasons voice) haue prouided punishments condigne for so exorbitant a presumption.

Furthermore howsoeuer the condemnation giuen by the Cardinals vpon our two brethren, may be lengthned to reach vnto vs, yet the punishment imposed (a correlatiue in a kind to the condemnation, and which cannot but concerne all those on whom the condemnation passed) ne did nor could possibly any way agree, or so much as point to *their complices here*. For this being, that those on whom the condemnation was giuen *should not presume to go into the kingdomes of England, Scotland or Ireland without expresse leaue of his Holinesse or the Lord Protector*, it could in no congruencie in the world appertaine to vs who were in England long before, and at the same time euen to the knowledge of the Cardinals themselues, when their Graces deliuered the sentence, if both their Graces did expressely set downe such a sentence (as the speeches and cariage of Cardinall *Burghesio* to M. *Charnocke* seeme in a sort to admit a doubt, least the inditing therof were the left-hand worke of father *Parsons*, as the words [*in isto Collegio detenti* detained in this Colledge] contained in the sentence, and the sentence being dated from their Pallaces, yeeld no improbable conceit, together with other grounds touched in the censure vpon father *Parsons* letter to M. *Bishop*.

Pregnant suspition of father *Parsons* cloaked dealing.

Moreouer, if condemnation passed vpon vs at Rome, as complices of our two brethren, then doth it necessarily follow, that we were their complices in the crime they were condemned for. And what crime was that? for maintaining controuersies as the sentence expresseth, with other men of their order. Well, but what kind of controuersie did they maintaine? and with what men by name? and how came our partaking with them so notorious, as that we might rightfully be codẽned (for what was not rightfully done, can neuer be but iniuriously obiected) without summons or relation from vs, what we could say for our selues? The sentence doth neither specifie what were the controuersies, nor name the men, with whom they maintained them. Wherefore it were well, and but the due tribute of charitie (considering the infamie that groweth vnto vs by so publike an affirmance of our condemnation at Rome) that declaration were made both what the controuersies were in particular & the names of the persons with whom they were maintained, and also our notorious participation in the same, that so our countrey might be informed of the particular: and our selues take notice of the offence we committed, which without ſuch helpe,we cannot hitherto call to mind.

To ſay that the controuerſies, and the perſons with whom they were maintained, was the delay which our two brethren & our ſelues made in admitting the new authoritie after ſight of the Cardinal Protector his Letter: and in their going to Rome by our perſwaſion,for more certaine knowledge of the ſubordination, and how fully it was eſtabliſhed,and for informing his Holineſſe, aſwell of the inconueniences thereof,as of the needs that abound in our conntry,were,as we thinke,to charge the two Cardinals with ignorance or error,or both. For if this were the controuerſie, and the Archprieſt the partie with whom it was maintained(as if not,the whole world cãnot proue vs to be their complices in any other cõtrouerſie)then we muſt ask this queſtion:whether M. *Blackwell* was at that time, when we delayed to ſubiect our ſelues vnto him ſo authorized our Archprieſt, as we were bound vnder ſin or other bond to admit him before the comming of his Holines.Breue. If he were not,as the foregoings ſhew he was not, and the enſuings God willing ſhall proue that we could not admit him without tranſgreſſing the lawes of holy Church, thẽ the non-admittance of him was not to maintaine controuerſies,but to defend, we ſay not our freedome (though if it had bene ſo, the endeuour had beene moſt lawfull and honeſt) but to defend trueth, to ſhunne penalties, and for conſeruing order and the Hierarchie of Gods Church inuiolated. Actions which no way approach to that degree of deformitie, as to deſerue exile and alſo confinement in exile, and in Catholicke Prieſtes, that had many yeares ventered their liues in Chriſt his cauſe, and the baniſhment and confining therein to be inflicted vpon them by perſonages of Eccleſiaſticall preeminence.

If on the other ſide, M. *Blackwell* was ſo fully and abſolutely conſtituted our Archprieſt, as we could not without ſinne protract the ſubmiſſion of our obedience vnto him: then muſt we craue pardon to thinke that the two Cardinals miſtooke in their ſentence, *quid pro quo*, one kind of ſinne for another,the leſſe for the greater.For the only and ſole cauſe which their honors alleage in the ſentence of baniſhing and confining our two brethren,was for that *they had maintained controuerſies with men of their owne order.*

So that if the bearing off to receiue M. *Blackwel* in the authority he claimed, were indeed the maintaining of the cõtrouerſies which their graces meant in their ſentẽce(as needs it muſt be if M. *Blackwel* wrote

a

a truth in affirming vs to be condemned at Rome as their complices, we being at no time their complices in any other controuerſie) then as we haue ſaid, their Graces miſtooke the leſſe ſinne for the greater, controuerſie for diſobedience, or truer for rebellion: [a] rebellion being when one will not obey, or ſhall impeach the iuriſdiction of his Superiour: or for a far greater ſinne, if all be true which hath bene obiected againſt vs. Neither were their honours, as it ſeemeth, only miſtaken, or ſpoke improperly in this, but alſo in another point of like moment, viz. in that M. *Blackwell* being lawfull Superiour to our two brethren (as it is ſuppoſed) and in manie reſpects of more then Epiſcopall iuriſdiction ouer them, neuertheleſſe their Graces did not otherwiſe name or more particularly ſtile M. *Blackwell*, then by compriſing him vnder the general terme of *other mē of their own order*, for ſo runne the wordes in the ſentence, as the Reader may ſee: nor is there any other cauſe at all alleaged why they were baniſhed & confined, but for that *they had maintained controuerſies with other men of their owne order, and therefore not expedient to the Engliſh cauſe that they ſhould anon returne to thoſe parts where they had ſo demeaned themſelues.*

(a) *Panorm. in ca. ſane 2. de offic. iud. deleg. nu. 4.*

Errours of that nature, as it were hard to thinke their graces would commit, conſidering their long practiſe and place, but chiefly in reſpect of the vnuſuall and grieuous puniſhment impoſed, and for that by this generall or improper ſpeech, neither the puniſhed were let to vnderſtand the nature of their offence (a default in iuſtice) nor ſatiſfaction giuen to the world, why ſo heauy chaſtiſement was taken of Prieſts comming ſo farre off to the Sea of Rome.

Conſiderations which force vs to thinke, that their Graces meant not by the ſaid words of the decree, the controuerſie which our two brethren had with the Archprieſt, in not admitting his authoritie vpon ſight of the *Conſtitutiue Letter*, but the maintaining of ſome other controuerſie, albeit we wote not, nor can geſſe what controuerſie that ſhould be, or with whom.

Againe the wordes of the decree are *for maintaining controuerſies with other men of their owne order.* Which being ſpoken in the plurall number, and none can ſay that either of our two brethren maintained controuerſies, or had ſo much as vnfriendly ſpeech with any one Prieſt (M. *Blackwell* excepted) in reproofe or diſlike of his admitting the ſubordination Which conuinceth except the ſentence were erroniouſly giue, that their Graces could not not vnderſtand by *maintaining controuerſies with other men of their owne order*, the difference betweene the Archpriest and them concerning the receiuing or not receiuing of the Subordination.

And to shew the aduantages that commonly concurre with all truth, and do abound in this, we will grant to our aduersaries that the Cardinals vnderstood no other controuersie in their sentence, then that which our two brethren had with our Archpriest about the subordination, and wherein we were their complices, and that also the punishment inflicted, was such as it might aswell appertaine to vs as to them (as how meerely impossible it was so to do, it hath bene declared before) yet what sequence can be inferred either in equitie (which is iustice tempered with the sweetnesse of mercie, and euermore chalengeth her due place in iudgements giuen by such personages because iustice without mercie is crueltie, as S. *Chrysostome* writeth) or in rigour, extending all things to the highest seueritie that can be? Must the condemnation that passed vpon our two brethren be stretched, & needes inuolue vs their complices, neither summoned to the triall, nor named in the sentence, nor specified in his Holinesse Commission to the Cardinals, or we otherwise vnder like authoritie or iurisdiction of their graces? Certes both reason, learning common sense, and the custome of all Nations, Heathen and Christian do counterpleade: nor all ages, as we thinke, can yeeld one president from the beginning of the world to this present day, where and against whom any iuridicall condemnation (as that is maintained to be which passed against our two brethren) hath bene in like sort extended, were the persons to whom it was extended of neuer so base calling, and the fact they committed neuer so notorious and execrable. Circumstances or materiall points which greatly alter our case: for Popes, Councels generall and prouinciall, and famous Emperours haue decreed sundrie priuiledges for the more iust and respectfull proceedings against men of our function. Yea the holy Apostle for the more reuerence of Priesthood, omitted not to giue direction likewise in this affaire, and the fact also wherein our two brethren were condemned not the most hainous euen by that *species* or kind of the offence, to which the Cardinals themselues raunged, and intituled it by: viz. *the maintaining of controuersies with other men of their owne order.*

Dist.86 siquid 2.q.1.in multis capitibus & eadem q 7 ca.ipsi & ca. testes 15 q.7 per totum ca. qualiter 2. de accusationib. Concil. Trid. sess.13 de reform.ca.4. 1.Tim.5.

(a) Ca. dilecto de prebend. & dignit. & ca. cum super de sent & re iud. & eod ca. quamuis.

It is a receiued Proposition among the Canonists, and alleaged by Pope *Innocentius* the third, and Pope *Gregorie* the ninth that [a] *Regulariter alijs non nocet res inter alios iudicata.* Regularly a matter past in iudgement betweene others, hurteth none but the parties themselues

against

against whom the iudgement was giuen. Which saying howsoeuer it may be vnderstood and limited (as it beareth [b] seuerall exceptions, and hardly can our case though racked neuer so hardly, be brought vnder any of them all) yet it is most certaine that the preiudice it can bring to their complices or fellowes in the action, is but [c] a presumption, or at the worst hand, according to the opinion euen of those that are most large in the matter, but [d] a halfe proofe.

And al learning teacheth (iudgement requiring a certitude) that not [e] a presumption only or half proofe, but a ful proofe, that is an euident, cleere, & open proofe, ought to go before condemnation in matter of crime, such as the edict auoweth & diuulgeth vs to be condemned of.

Or if there were no authoritie or verdict of generall practise to proue that a iudgement passing vpon certaine persons by name, ne doth nor can extend it selfe to the inuoluing of their complices, yet the drift of common reason and the auoiding of seueral inconueniences ensuing thereupon, would conuince no lesse. For such a consequence and order of iustice, once in vre and admitted, none that had fellowes in any action (how iust and honorable soeuer the same were) could assure themselues not to be condemned therein, or not feare probably to be condemned, in regard the aduerse part might single out one or mo of the companie (to which attempt such ministring of iustice would be a good allurement) and call them to triall, who either by errour, negligence, or ill pleading, or by vnderhand packing or cousinage, might leese or betray the cause: and then the iudgement giuen vpon them, must by this new forme of iustice inuolue and condemne all the rest of the partizans or complices, neither cited to appeare, nor weeting to the trial, or yet named in the condemnation. An enlargement and subintellection which the [f] lawes of holy Church forbid, and which going once for iustice, would soone occasion a thousand trecheries, and put out of ioynt all the common weales in the world. Which we do not say to insinuate a fault in our brethren, but to shew the *non sequitur* or discoherence of the inference, that because forsooth our brethren were condemned, (vpon what vnconscionable information father *Parsons* better knowes) therefore we being their complices were also condemned, notwithstanding we were neither summoned, nor priuie to the trial, nor named at all in the sentence, nor specified in the Iudges Commission.

Panormitane the choisest expositour of the law, giueth seuerall ex-

(b) *Vide glossa verb. res inter alios, & leg. res inter C. quan. res iudic. non noc. & Bald. in margarita, ad inno. verb. sententia & Iaso. in li. 1. § huius studij ff. de iusti. & iur. & alberi. de statutis part. 3 q. 65.*

(c) *Panor. in ca. quamuis de sen. & reiud. nu. 3. & Couarunias pract. quaest. ca. 13. nu. 4.*

(d) *Bartholus in l. admonendi ff. de iureiur. Ant. de Butri & Imol. in ca. finali supra iureiur.*

(e) *Deut. 17. & 19. D. Tho. 2. 2. q 70. art. 2. Sotus lib. 5 de instit. q. 6 art. 2. Valentia Tom. 3. disp. 5. q. 13. punct. 2. Siluest. verb. probatio nu. 1.*

(f) *3. q. 9. ca. Omnia. ca. caueant. ca. absente & per totam quaestionem. ca. causam quae, de rescrip. ca. 1. & ca. susceptis de causa poss. & prop. ca. dilecto de praeb. ca. cum super & ca. quamuis de sent. & re iud. Clem de verbor. sign. ca. saepe contingit.*

amples wherein the ſentence giuen againſt one offender, doth not dilate it ſelfe and damnifie the complice or concurrent in the ſame fault, as namely [g] one being condemned for producing falſe witneſſes, it followeth not thereupon that the witneſſes were falſe. Likewiſe [h] a notarie condemned of making a falſe inſtrument, doth not inferre the condemnation of the partie through whoſe ſolicitation he did it. Againe, [i] two brothers by father and mother, marrying with two ſiſters of like ſort, within the degrees of conſanguinitie, the condemnation of the one brother, doth not extend it ſelfe to the condemnation of the other brother, nor indomageth his cauſe or plea. In briefe, the condemnation [k] of the Adulterer, implies not the condemnation of his fellow the adultereſſe, or the contrarie, but the partie not confeſſing the fault is left to his or her purgatiō. The reaſon of all which is (as hath bene ſaid before) for that conuiction might happen to paſſe vpon the ſuſpected delinquent, either by fault of not ioyning iſſue wel, or by default of vnskilfull pleading, or by corruption of iuſtice, or by teſtimonie of falſe witneſſes, or by partialitie of the Iudges, or the like. But of this enough, the aduerſaries aſſertion being alike weake, and contrarie to all forme of law.

(g) *In ca. quāuis de ſent. & re iud. nu. 25.*
(h) *Nu. 26.*
(i) *Nu. 27.*
(k) *2. q. 4. interrogatum.*

To come now to another part of our Archprieſts affirmatiō, viz. that *the Popes Breue confirmeth the Cardinals Letters, as, Validas ab initio*, hauing force from the beginning, *and vtterly condemneth and inualidateth all things done to the contrary*. Firſt, howſoeuer ſome of thoſe particulars may be deduced, as illations out of the Breue, yet it is moſt cleare, that not all, nor the moſt part of the wordes are to be found in the Breue. And to the end, that all which we are to ſay in diſproofe of theſe auowances, may the more eaſiy be vnderſtood, and that all perſons may conſider the inferences and maner of proceeding on both ſides, we thought good to annex and Engliſh his Holineſſe Breue word for word as exactly as we could.

Clemens Papa Octauus.

AD futuram rei memoriam, &c. Inter grauiſſimas noſtræ paſtoralis ſolicitudinis curas, illæ de Catholica nimirum religione conſeruanda & propaganda præcipuum locum obtinet, propterea quæcunq́ ad hunc finem mandato noſtro per S. R. F. Cardinales geſta & ordinata ſunt, vt debitum conſequantur effectum Apoſtolica licæ confirmationis robore communimus. Nuper siquidem dilectus filius noster Henricus tituli Sta Potentianæ presbiter Cardinalis Caietanus S. R. ecclesiæ Camerarius, ac nationis Anglicanæ apud nos & Apostolicam sedem Protector, pro fœlici gubernio & regimine ac mutua dilectione, pace, ac vnione Catholicorum regnorum Angliæ & Scotiæ, ac pro disciplina ecclesiastica conseruanda & augenda de mandato nostro dilectum filium Georgium Blacuuellum sacerdotem Anglum sacræ theologiæ Bacchalaureum, ob eius pietatem, doctrinam, Catholicæ religionis zelum & alias virtutes in Archipresbyterum Catholicorum Anglorum cum nonnullis facultatibus per eum & alios duodecim sacerdotes illius Assistentes respectiuè exercendis per ipsius patentes literas expeditas, quarum initium est, Scitum est atque vsu fere quotidiano compertum, &c. Finis vero, vestrisq; orationibus me ex animo commendo patres fratresq; amantissimi Christi confessores die 7. Martij, anni millesimi, quingentesimi 98. deputauit, prout in prædictis patentibus literis quarum tenorem præsentibus ac si ad verbum insererentur pro expressa habere volumus, plenius continetur. Nos autem cupientes duputationem prædictam ac omnia in præfatis literis patentibus contenta tanquam de mandato & ordine nostro & cum participatione ac plena scientia nostris facta & ordinata, plenariè executioni vt par est demandari. Et vt illa omnia pleniorem roboris firmitatem obtineant, prouidere volentes motu proprio & ex certa scientia & matura deliberatione nostra deq; Apostolicæ potestatis plenitudine deputationem supradictam ac prænarratas Henrici Cardinalis Protectoris patentes literas desuper expeditas cum omnibus & singulis in illis expressis facultatibus priuilegijs, indultis, instructionibus, declarationibus, ac alijs quibuscunque contentis, in omnibus & per omnia perinde ac si omnia hic nominatim expressa & specificata essent, authoritate Apostolica tenore præsentium confirmamus & approbamus: illisq; Apostolicæ ac inuiolabilis firmitatis robur adijcimus, & omnes ac singulos defectus si qui in eisdem interuenerint supplemus, eaq; omnia & singula de expresso mandato & ordine, & cum participatione & certa scientia nostris facta & ordinata fuisse, & esse, ac propterea valida, firma, & efficacia existere & fore, ac plenissimam roboris firmitatem obtinere, suumq; plenarium effectum sortiri & obtinere, sicq; ab omnibus censeri, & ita per quoscunque iudices ac commissarios iudicari definiri debere: ac irritum & inane quicquid secus super his à quoquam quauis authoritate scienter vel ignoranter contigerit attentari decernimus: non obstantibus constitutionibus & ordinationibus Apostolicis cæterisq; contrarijs quibuscunq;. Datum Romæ apud S. Petrum sub annulo piscatoris die 6. Aprilis, anno 1599. Pontificatus nostri anno octauo.

M. Vestrius Barbianus.

Pope Clement the eight.

FOr future memorie of the thing, &c. Among the weightiest cares of our pastorall sollicitude, that surely of conseruing and propagating the Catholike Religion possesseth the chiefest place: and therefore what things soeuer are done and ordained to this end, vpon our commaundement by the Cardinals of the holy Romane Church, we, that they may take due effect, do fortify the same with the strength of a pastoricall confirmation. For as much as of late our beloued sonne *Henry*, presbyter Cardinall of the title of S. *Potentiana*, Chamberlaine of the holy Romane Church, & Protector of the English nation with vs and the Sea Apostolike, hath by our commandement for the happy administration and gouernance, and for the mutuall loue, peace, and vnion of the Catholikes of the kingdomes of England and Ireland, and for the conseruing and augmenting of Ecclesiastical discipline deputed by his letters patents dispatched, which begin in this maner, (*It is knowne and almost by dayly experience found true,*) and end after this sort: (*And I very hartily cōmend me to your prayers most louing fathers and brethren, and Christ his most reuerend confessours, the 7. day of March* 1598. our beloued sonne *George Blackwell* English Priest, Bacheler of Diuinitie, for his pietie, literature, zeale of Catholicke Religion, and his other vertues to be Archpriest ouer the English Catholickes, with certaine faculties by him, and other twelue Priests his Assistants respectiuely to be exercised, as is more at large contained in the said Letters patents, whose tenor we will haue reckned or expressed, as if they were word by word in these presents inserted. And we desiring the foresaid deputation, and all things contained in the aboue mentioned Letters patents, as done and ordained by our commaundement and order, and with our participation and full knowledge, to be put, as meete is, in full execution. And being desirous to prouide that all these things may haue the greater firmenesse of strentgh, we of our proper motion, and certaine knowledge, and mature deliberation, and of the fulnesse of Apostolicall power, do by the tenour of these presents confirme and approue with Apostolicall authoritie the abouenamed and rehearsed Letters patents of Henry Cardinall Protector * sent from hence, with all and singular faculties, priuiledges, fauors, instructions, declaratiōs expressed in them, and

* *Desuper expeditas.*

and other things whatſoeuer contained, in and by all reſpects, as if all things here by name were expreſſed & diſtinguiſhed: and we do adde vnto them the ſtrength of Apoſtolicall and inuiolable firmeneſſe, and do ſupply all and ſingular defects if any hapned in the ſame, and all and ſingular theſe things to haue bene, and to be done and ordained by our expreſſe commandement, and order, and with our participation and certaine knowledge, and therefore to be & remaine of force, firmeneſſe, and of efficacie, and to obtaine moſt ample ſtrength, and take and hold their fulleſt effect, and ſo ought to be cenſured of all men, and to be ſentenced in like ſort, and defined by what iudges and Commiſſioners ſoeuer: and we do decree to be void and of no validitie whatſoeuer otherwiſe in theſe things ſhal fortune to be attempted by any man of what authoritie ſoeuer, wittingly or ignorantly, notwithſtanding the conſtitutions and ordinances Apoſtolicall, and whatſoeuer els to the contrary. Giuen at Rome at S. *Peters* vnder the fiſhers ring the ſixt day of Aprill, the yeare of our Lord 1599. the yeere of our Popeſhip 8.

M. Veſtrius Barbianus.

TO auoide all doubtfull vnderſtanding of words, and here firſt to agree of the iſſue, that when the point is debated, the difference be not found in the end to conſiſt only in the diuerſe taking of words, and in no diuerſitie of matter: we requeſt leaue of our Archprieſt to moue this one queſtion, whether by the foreſayd aſſeueration, viz. that the [*Popes Breue confirmed the Cardinals Letters, as validas ab initio, and vtterly condemned and inualidated all things done to the contrary*] he meant that the ſayd Breue did ſo confirme the Cardinals *Letter Conſtitutiue* as it had force from the beginning, to bind vs vnder the crime of ſchiſme or enormious diſobedience to accept preſently of the ſubordination, without delaying our ſubmiſſion in the maner we did, that was, vntill the appearing of his Holineſſe Breue; or whether his meaning by the foreſayd words were onely that the ſayd Letter had an obligatiue force from the beginning in it ſelfe, in that it was written by lawfull and ſufficient authoritie, to wit, by ſpeciall commaundement of his Holineſſe: but yet it had no force actually and forthwith to bind vs to receiue the ſubordination aſſigned, becauſe there wanted either ſome Papall inſtrument, or other, more authentike proofe, then the Cardinals owne affirmation for testimony of such his Holinesse commaundement, and graunt of the particular faculties enacted. If our Archpriest vnderstand this latter sense in his auowance (as the cause whereupon, and the ende why he vsed the words, with the circumstances of both, do all gainsay and most plainly contradict that his Reuerence had any such meaning) we assent and say the same with him, that the Popes Breue confirmes the Cardinals letter as *validas ab initio*, and vtterly condemneth and inualidateth all things that from thence should happen to be attempted to the contrarie. But on the other side, if our Archpriest meant by his words, that the Cardinals *Letter Constitutiue* was of force from the beginning, to bind vs to admit of the subordination appointed, without staying for further proofe or confirmation (as with no colour it can be denied but that his Reuerence had this meaning, for otherwise how could he possibly declare, especially in a publicke Decree, that all the Catholickes in England who any way before the comming ouer of the Breue had impugned his authority, were therein really disobedient to the Sea Apostolicke, and rebels against his office, and that the Pope in his Breue declared no lesse by condemning vtterly all things done to the contrary, vnder which no doubt our prolonging must needes be implied) then vnder his good leaue, we must say that he is much mistaken, and offereth wrong to his Holinesse, in reporting him to write, that he doth not, and perhaps that too, which in equity he could not. Or howsoeuer this be, yet his Reuerence may do well to tell vs and the world beside, being possessed with his former charge against vs, in what words of the Breue either expresly or implicitiuely is the sayd condemnation contained of all things done to the contrarie? We say done, signifying actions that passed before the promulgation of the Breue, as did our deferring, and not actions enterprised since the publishing thereof. For as we will most willingly graunt that his Holinesse annulleth all actions succeeding the date of the Breue, attempted by whom soeuer: so must we agnize that we can neither see nor cõiecture in what part of the Breue, or by what words thereof his Holinesse either condemned, or taxed the actions performed before the setting forth of the Breue.

If the Cardinals letter was of actuall force to bind from the beginning, from whence did it take vigour? It is a generall proposition among the Canonists, that *Creditur literis cuiusque de hys quæ facere potest vel debet ratione officij sui*. Beleefe is to be giuen to euery mans letters,

Speculum de probat. § 3. nu. 15.

letters, in the things he can, or belongeth to him to do by vertue of the office he beareth. But it hath bene made verie manifest before, that the Cardinall could not institute such a forme of gouernement in our countrey by vertue either of his Cardinalship, or Protectorship: and therefore the letter his Grace wrote for enacting the same, was by vertue of some extraordinarie iurisdiction, and not by any quality of his foresayd dignities, and consequently the iurisdiction being extraordinary, we were not bound to giue such infallible credite, and height of obeysance to his Honours letter, as by and by to prostrate our selues to the subordination his Grace appointed, being alike vnprofitable, imperious, and most burthensome, before his Grace had proued the commission by other meanes, then by witnesse of his owne word. A verity so clearly shewed before, and with that force of authorities, as it were superfluous to seeke to confirme it with moe.

To say the Pope hath declared that the Cardinall his letters are from hence of force, and that all things therein passed with his Holinesse full knowledge and participation, maketh no more for proofe of the crimes obiected against vs, then the promulgation of a law doth proue those to haue transgressed the law, who betweene the making of the law, and the promulgation thereof, committed such acts as the sayd law prohibited. Which is so feeble a proofe (the promulgation being of the [a] essence of the law, and without which the law not binding,) as none can be weaker.

(a) *distinct. 4. ca. in istis. D. Th. 1. 2. q. 90. art. 4. ca. de legibus l. leges & in authentica & omnes tum Canonistæ tum Theologi.*

And now to come to the last part of the foresaid auowance, where our Archpriest writeth, *that our proceedings euen before the comming ouer of the Breue were sharpely condemned by the sentence of the two Illustrious Cardinals, and also by the iudgement of his Holinesse.* It hath bene shewed that no such condemnation passed vpon vs, either by sentence of the two Cardinals, or by the iudgement of his Holinesse. And we further affirmed, that what condemnation soeuer passed vpon our two brethren, by sentence of the two Cardinals, yet that, that condemnation and sentence cannot truly and properly be called the iudgement of his Holinesse. For although the said Cardinals tooke their authoritie from his Holines of being iudges in the cause of our two brethren, neuerthelesse the sentence they gaue was their owne act and iudgement, and not the act and iudgement of his Holinesse, as is most cleare by this, that their graces were delegatiue iudge, in the cause, and his Holinesse the Delegator. For to delegate and to be delegated, being two distinct things, and not competible in one person, in one and the same respect: it followeth that the sentence of the delegatiue Iudge or Iudges, is not the sentence and iudgement of the delegator, as witnesseth Decius in these words, *Licet*[a] *delegatus habet potestatem à delegante, tamen iudicio suo iudicare dicitur, vt est textus in ca. Prudentiam de officio deleg.* Although the Iudge delegate haue his iurisdiction from the delegator, yet the iudgement which he giueth in the cause committed, is his owne iudgement, as hath the text in the Chapter *Prudentiam de offic. deleg.* Which position is also manifest, in that Appellation from the Iudge delegate to the delegator, is very frequent, and holden by[b] all writers for the most orderly Appellation. Which could not be, if the sentence of the Iudge delegate were the sentence or iudgement of the delegator: for then such Appellations were from a sentence to the giuer of the same, neither fit, nor like to releeue; nor euer vsed, but when sentence was giuen vppon wrong information, and by the supremest Iudge only.

(a) *Decius in ca. decernimus de iudicijs n. 35*

(b) *Decius in rubrica. de offic. deleg. nu. 5. Siluester verb. Appellatio. nu. 9. li. ff. si quis, & à quo l. præcipimus. c. de Appel.*

The inferēce we would make out of these is, that admitting the two Cardinals giuing sentence vpon our two brethren, had inuolued and condemned vs their complices in the same sentence; as there is no such thing nor by iustice could be, yet their Graces giuing that sentence as delegatiue Iudges, neither did, nor could but make the same sentence their own sentence, and not the sentence and iudgement of his Holinesse, and consequently we cannot but recken this auowance of our Archpriest [*that our proceedings yea before the comming of the Breue were very grieuously condemned by the iudgement of his Holinesse*] among the manie of the other wrongs that his Reuerence hath done vs, vnlesse he shall proue the defaming assertion otherwise, and more substantially then because the two Cardinals condemned our brethren to be banished and confined.

And to end our answer to this fifth obiection brought against vs, we do most certainly assure our selues, that if his Holinesse were made acquainted with the manner and nature of things as they proceeded, he would so little giue our Archpriest and father *Parsons* thankes for making him the prompter or approuer of the sayd sentence against our two brethrē, as he might peraduenture sharply rebuke their boldnesse therein. For who can thinke that his Holinesse compassionable and bounteous nature, would not onely inflict banishment and confinement in banishment for an action lawfull, yea, prescribed by the Ecclesiasticall Canons, as when[c] doubt is made (as sincerely and before God we had great doubt of the Cardinals authority to institute

(c) *Ca. Si quando de rescript.*

such

ſuch a kind of powerable ſubordination in our Church) of a delegates commiſſion, then to intreate the ſtay of execution, till the graunter of the commiſſion might be aduertiſed of the matter, and the truth vnderſtood. Offices, which we performed: for, both we requeſted maiſter *Blackwell* very earneſtly to forbeare the abſolute aſſuming of the authority, with promiſe notwithſtanding to obey him though we would not fully and perfectly admit the ſubordination, before more certaine knowledge came, that his Holineſſe ſtood priuie and conſenting to all and euery branch of the ſubordination and iuriſdiction graunted to the Archprieſt: and alſo made him acquainted with our intention of ſending to Rome about our doubts. Yea maiſter *Biſhop*, the Sonday before he & our brother began their iourny, went to him, renewed the petition, gaue him a note vnder his hand and name, of the particulars about which he meant to deale with his Holineſſe, & receiued a counterpane or another like note of maiſter *Blackwell* (which he caried to Rome with him, and which of likelihood the Fiſcall or Fa. *Parſ.* rather, tooke from him, with the other ſchedules, when at their apprehenſion he bereft them of al the writings they brought) teſtifying that ſuch and ſuch were the matters that he went to Rome for, and to propoſe to his Holines. What more plainer or honeſt dealing could be deſired on our part? Or what ſhould we further adde? Maiſter *Blackwell* himſelfe, in the ſixth of his twelue queſtions which he propoſed to vs to aunſwer vnto, dated the fourteenth of May, acknowledgeth, that, *Quòd ante ſuum diſceſſum agnoſcere ſuum Archipreſbyterum viſi ſunt, & quod illo conſcio, & non contradicente, quamuis improbante, iter arripuerint*, That both our brethren did ſeeme before their departure to acknowledge their Archprieſt, and that they tooke their iourney with his priuity, and not contradicting though not approuing.

Another materiall euidence of diſprouing that which hath bene obiected againſt vs was, that when our brethren were firſt committed priſoners, they both took a corporall oath, and one or both proteſted vnder the ſame as well for themſelues as for vs their aſſociates, that if his Holineſſe thought not meete to incline to our petition for chaunging the ſubordination into ſome more profitable kind of gouernement, but would ratifie or confirme that which was erected, yet that we were content and ready to yeeld all obedience thereunto. We aske here againe, who can thinke that his Holineſſe compaſſionable and bounteous nature, would not only enioyne baniſhment, & confine them in baniſhment, for an action of this quality, and veſted

Agnized in the Apologie fol. 130.

with no other circumstances, but would also beside the nature of the punishment, which drew infamie vpon their persons, and consequently sure to alienate mens mindes and charities from releeuing their necessities, not so much as contribute one peny of maintenance, hauing the distribution of the fragments that remaine in the twelue baskets, we meane of all the charities abounding in Gods Church, either to carie them to the places assigned being Priests, or there to liue by after their comming. We therefore as we haue said, do most confidently assure our selues, that if his Holines should once come to know (as we doubt not but God in time will worke it) the true storie of these stratagems, that his mature consideration will giue father *Parsons* and our Archpriest little thankes, in making and diuulging him to be the decreer, or director of the iudgement that passed vpon our two brethren.

Luke 9.

A Sixth reason which our aduersaries forme against vs, and seeke to vndershore it with authoritie, is an argument they draw from this place of the glosse: *Octauum priuilegium quod Cardinali asserenti se legatum creditur absq; literis. Dist.27.ca.nobilissimus.* It is the eight priuiledge of a Cardinall, that if he say he is the Popes Legate, beliefe is to be giuen to him though he shew no letters. Out of which place father *Parsons* in the Apologie inferreth, that because the superioritie and iurisdiction of a Cardinall Legate is a farre greater matter, then was the authoritie which our Cardinall Protector tooke vpon him in ordaining the new subordination, and because the assertion of a Cardinall in affirming himself the Popes Legate, is to be credited though he shew no letters for testimonie thereof in regard of the knowne priuiledge due in this case, to the highnesse of his estate, therefore our Cardinall Protectour testifying and professing to vs and the whole world in his Letters patents vnder his hand and publicke seale, that he instituted the subordination (this authoritie whereby he did it being not so great as the authoritie of a delegate *de latere*) *ex speciali mandato Smi* vpon speciall commandement of his Holinesse, was to be beleeued without shewing the Popes Letters, or making other proofe then his Graces owne affirmation for the truth or testification of the Commission.

In extrauag. excerabilis Ioã. 22. de præbend. verb. sublimitatem eorum. Ca.8 fol.108.

Vbi supra & fol.114.

This is the deduction & argument that father *Parsons* maketh, and in his owne wordes so neare as they could be vsed, the forme and strength of the argument not omitted. To which we answere, first, that the consequence is not good, then, that what is alleaged for fortifying

tifying the same is either false or of no moment. For declaration. First it commeth to be noted, that the words which immediatly follow in the place where fa. *Parsons* taketh the foresaid passage, be these, *Licet aliqui hoc reuocent in dubium*, albeit some doubt of this eight priuiledge. And certes all men do not thinke, if the Pope should send a Cardinall Legate into *France* or *Spaine*, or into any other Catholike kingdome, especially about matter disgustfull, that either of their two Maiesties most Christian or most Catholicke, would readily receiue him as such a person, and admit the execution of his office without shewing the Popes letters for testimonie of the legation. Neither in shew (be it spoken vnder leaue, & with due submission to holy Church) doth such refusall deserue any great censure, because seuerall [a] Popes beside the demonstration of dayly practise, haue testified that it is not the maner of the Apostolicke Sea to receiue an Ambassage from any person whatsoeuer without letters in the credence of the Ambassadour. And therefore that holy Sea, not accustoming to receiue or beleeue any Ambassadour without letters from the Prince or Potentate he commeth from: it seemeth to follow not amisse, this action of the highest Sea being as an exampler for other, that Kings or other temporall and supreme Magistrates are not bound to receiue, and giue credite to the word of a Cardinall Legate, vnlesse he shew the Popes letters for witnesse of his commission. But these notwithstanding we graunt as the truth is, that a Cardinall Legate ought to be beleeued vpon his word, without shewing the Popes letters for testimonie: yet we resolutely denie, that a Cardinall delegate is to haue the like credite giuen to his word in the charge or matter committed vnto him, as father *Parsons* inferreth, except he first shew the Popes letter, or otherwise proue the Commission. A veritie which hath bene sufficiently, if not more then enough confirmed before by diuerse authorities out of all the chiefest writers new and old vpon the law. Neuerthelesse to abound in our proofes of this materiall point, we will adde one authoritie more, and such an authoritie as concludeth for vs & against our aduersaries, whether the Cardinall instituted the subordinatiõ, as his Holines delegate by a rescript, or as his cõmissioner by word of mouth only. *Si de magno alicuius praeiudicio agatur non creditur Cardinali testanti sibi aliquid à Papa viuae vocis oraculo mãdatum, nec creditur ei asserenti esse delegatum nisi literis ostensis*. If the question be (saith *Zecchius*) of a matter that is very indomeageable to another, a Cardinall is not to be beleeued vpon his word, testifying that the Pope enioyned him such a commaunde-

(a) *Steph. Papa dist. 63. ca. lectis Nicholaus Papa dist. 97. ca. nobilissimus & ca. de man. prin. l. vnica.*

Pag. 58. 59. & sequentib.

De statu. Illrum Cardinalium nu. 9. vers. 6.

ment by word of mouth: neither is beleefe to be yeelded vnto him, if he affirme himselfe a delegate, vnlesse he shew the letters. And the author proues both partes of the assertion, by the testimonies of sundrie other writers which he there citeth.

Further, beside the pleading of authority, the reason is manifest why credit is giuen to the word of a Cardinall, naming himselfe a Legate, without shewing the Popes letters, and not to the word of a Cardinal affirming himself a delegate, or to haue receiued such a Cōmission by word of mouth, except he shew the Popes letter for testimonie of the delegation, or proue the verbal commission after a farre more autheticall maner then by the sole record of his owne word or missiue Letter patent or sealed.

Zecchius de statu Ill^mi Legati nu.2.

For when the Pope sendeth a Legate *de latere* to anie Prince, Country, or Prouince, he neuer sendeth him but with the aduice and consent of the residue of the Cardinals, which maketh the mission very notorious. Againe, a Cardinall legate departing vpon like occasion from the Court of Rome, taketh his dispatch and leaue of his Holinesse and the other Cardinals with great solemnitie, goeth likewise towards the person and place assigned after a most honorable maner of attendance, accompanied with others of rare parts. and when he commeth neare to the confines of the Countrey or Prouince whereof he is made Legate, he aduertiseth the nighest Bishop of his approching at hand, who presently is to commaund his Cleargie to giue their attendance and meete the Legate on his way comming, and to bring his Grace to the Cathedrall Church or any other that is nearer, with all sutable preparation and entertainement. Which kind of ceremonies with other complements, do euer make all laterall legations most aparant: but in delegations, and more in commissions by word of mouth, there is no such solemnity nor manifestation vsed: which yeeldeth a most materiall cause why credite is and ought to be giuen to the auowance of a Cardinals affirming himselfe a Legate, without shewing the Popes Letters, & why the like credite is not by any bond due to be giuen to the word of a Cardinall, if he affirme himselfe a delegate, or shall say he receiued Commission from the Pope by word of mouth to do this or that.

Idem ibidem nu.3. & speculum de Legat. § 4. superest.

**Speculum vbi supra, nu. 14. Zecchius vbi supra. nu.4. Siluest. verb. Delegatus. n.22 Cucchus lib.1. Tit.25. de off. & potest leg. Staphilus eodem tit. & alij.*

To put another difference betweene the cases, a Cardinall Legate receiueth the masse or body of his authority* *à lege communi* from the supreme dignitie and office he holdeth: but a Cardinall delegate Commissioner or executor, taketh not onely the subiect, but the limits

mits and ſpecialties of his whole iuriſdiction from the Popes reſcript or verball direction, and therefore ought to proue the particular tenour by other meanes then by the ſole credence of his owne word, eſpecially becauſe, as [a] ordinarie iuriſdiction, the [b] like as is legation, is matter fauourable: ſo all delegatiue iuriſdiction is matter diſpleaſant, or burdenous: and matter that is burdenous requireth in common reaſon a more full and ſtrict proofe then matter importing fauour. And further, that which maketh yet the caſe ſomewhat more cleare, is the receiued poſitiō among the Canoniſts, that although [c] a Cardinall is to be counted a Legate vpon his word, neuertheleſſe if he claime any iuriſdiction more then he hath from the conſtitutions of the law by office of his Legateſhip, he is not to be beleeued vpon his word, but muſt proue his claime and ſaying, either by ſhewing his commiſſion, or by teſtimonie of witneſſes, or after ſome legall maner: which maketh plaine in the conſequence, that where a Cardinall hath not the authoritie he claimeth by vertue of ordinarie iuriſdiction founded in his perſon as in an ordinarie, there he is not to be beleeued vpon credence of his ſole word, but muſt authentically proue what he affirmeth ere any be bound to obey.

(a) *Gloſſ. in ca. 1. de reſcript. verb. proceſſius.*
(b) *ca. 2 de offi. Legat. li. 6.*
(c) *Panorm. in ca. quod tranſlatione de off. leg nu. 10.*

Which precedent differences and diſparitie if father *Parſons* had conſidered, he would neuer haue made ſo ignorant inference, as he did vpon the place of the Gloſſe before cited: nor would he haue ſo weakly reaſoned if the ſubiect he wrote of had bene matter of ſtate, or belonged to the genealogie of Princes. Yet why ſay we thus, ſith euen in his booke of Titles he reaſoneth as ſhallowly or more vnaptly, making (forſooth) the ſucceſſiue raigne of two Queenes immediatly one after another, a let and cauſe why a woman ſhould not ſuccede her Maieſtie in the Crowne, for that as he writeth, our Nation will not endure a third Queene, meaning the old Counteſſe of Darby who was then aliue, and ayming perchance alſo in the ſpeeches at the Ladie *Arbella*, groſly forgetting in the meane, how the principall drift of the whole booke tended to the aduancing of anothers title, and a forrainer of the ſame ſexe. The like feeble reaſons he alſo maketh for diſcrediting the titles of other great perſonages. But to proceede to anſwer his other former auowances in our owne matter.

He affirmeth, *that to be the Popes Legate, is a farre greater caſe then this of ours is*, meaning the authoritie of Cardinall *Caietane* in inſtituting the ſubordination: and we affirme that a delegate in the cauſe committed vnto him by his Holineſſe (as the inſtituting of the ſubordination was by his owne words committed to Cardinall (*Caietane*) is of greater iurisdiction in the same cause, then is a Legate generall. And that which we say is the expresse law [d] and so interpreted by the best expositors:[e] *Is cui aliqua causa specialiter delegatur, maior est Legato generali quantum ad illam.* He to whom a certaine cause is delegated by speciall commaundement, is greater in the same then is a Legate generall. To which words of *Durandus*,[f] *Panormitane*,[g] *Iohannes Andreas*, and [h] *Felinus*, most agreeably consent.

(d) *Ca.constituisti de off legat.*
(e) *Speculum de legato, § 4. supereſt. nu. 48.*
(f) *In ca 2. de offic. leg. nu. 6.*
(g) *In ca sane 2 de offic. delegat. nu. 1.*
(h) *Ibid nu. 1.*

Yea we adde, that the iurisdiction of Cardinall *Caietane* was not onely superiour and greater in the cause committed, then the iurisdiction of a Cardinal Legate in the same, if there had bene any such resiant in our country, but that the iurisdiction & authoritie granted vnto his Grace therein was farre more ample, then custome or the constitutions of holy Church do allow to a Cardinal Legate, as is to be seen by comparing the faculties which his Grace subdelegated to Maister *Blackwell* with the iurisdiction that [i] *Durandus*, [k] *Staphilus*, [l] *Cucchus*, [m] *Zecchius*, and other that particularize these seuerall iurisdictions ordinarily belonging to a Cardinall Legate. For what Cardinall Legate can giue authority to an Archpriest, to remoue Priests frō out the houses where they are harboured of charitie, & know not how otherwhere to hide their heads? Againe, what Cardinall Legate can subdelegate authoritie to an Archpriest, to recall faculties graunted by the Pope himselfe? Iurisdictions surpassing the ordinarie authoritie of any Legate. But of these and some other like, more will be said in the next reason.

(i) *De Legato § 4. supereſt.*
(k) *Titul. de legato.*
(l) *Lib. 1. de institu. iur. can. Tit. 15.*
(m) *De statu. Illmi Leg. nu. 4.*

Fol. 108. & 114

Further, the religious man affirmeth, that *the Cardinall testified and professed to vs & the whole world in his letters patents vnder his hand and publike seal, that he instituted the subordination by special commandement of his Holinesse.* Alas, what needed this amplifying of words or vntruths rather? For first how can it well be verified that his Grace testified and professed so much to vs, and the whole world, when he neuer wrote a word of that or of any other matter vnto vs, and addressed the Constitutiue Letter by name to M. *Blackwell* onely? Againe, how can it be truly said, that he testified and professed it in his Letters patents and vnder his publicke seale, when the Constitutiue Letter came close sealed, according to the Romane fashion of sealing missiue Letters with a labell? A particular which I seeme very perfectly to remember, and the more perfectly by this token, viz. that when M. *Blackwell* shewwed the said letter vnto me to reade, he bid me beware of brusing the seale.

ſeale. Which wordes the Letter being foulded vp, and conſequently the ſeale not to be ſeene that was put too in the inſide after the ſubſcription, made me to vnderſtand them, of the ſeale which I ſaw on the backe of the letter remaining (the labell being cut and the ſeale not touched when the letter was firſt opened) faire in his full print or purtraite.

Notwithſtanding, becauſe our memories may deceiue vs, we will not ſtand vpon it, nor was it alleaged to the end to weaken thereby the validitie of the contents of the Conſtitutiue Letter, the force therof being one and of equall degree, whether the ſame came patent or cloſe ſealed. Neither was the ſaid Letter euer denied by any, to be the Cardinals Letter, though we al did moſt aſſuredly acertaine our ſelues that you father *Parſons* had the ſole penning thereof, and not of the Letter alone, but of the inſtructions and additions alſo.

Tholoſanus in Tit. de reſcript. li. 1. ca. 2. nu. 13

The only cauſe why we touch theſe, is, leaſt ſome hearing the Conſtitutiue Letter to be named Letters patents, may thereupon imagine it to be of ſuch irrefragable authoritie as the word ſignifieth in the lawes of our Realme. And perchance not to vnlike purpoſe was that added, which followeth (*vnder his hand and publicke ſeale*) to the end that others reading the wordes, might conceiue the ſeale fixed to the *Conſtitutiue Letter* to be the ſeale of ſome publike office, and therfore great rebelliõ to diſobey, or except againſt any iot of the contẽts. And as by theſe we wold not deny, but that the Canoniſts affirm the known ſeale of a Cardinal, to be an authentike ſeale, & to make the contẽts of the letter whereunto it is put, of a very reuerent and ſingular reſpect: ſo likewiſe it is certain, that the ſame Canoniſts affirm, that a letter ſigned with a Cardinal his ſeale, cõtaining matter preiudicious to another, & receiued by Commiſſion from his Holineſſe, he doth nor can claime the like ſoueraigne credite, as the parties preiudiced, remaine obliged either by law or conſcience to obey the ſame. Marie, that a Cardinall his ſeale is called a publicke ſeale, as father *Parſons* phraſeth it, is more (as we thinke) then he euer read, or Canoniſt euer wrote.

Panorm. in ca. quod ſuper de fide inſtrument. nu. 5. and the other Authors quoted fol.

But the truth of the other aſſertion, to wit [*the Cardinall teſtified and profeſſed to vs and the whole world, that he inſtituted the ſubordination by ſpeciall commaundement of his Holineſſe*] is more doubtfull by much as being vnder the checke and controlment of ſo many, as ſhall happen to reade the Conſtitutiue Letter. For in what place thereof, can ſo much or halfe ſo much be ſhewed, vnleſſe the letter muſt be read with ſpectacles, that haue vertue to make that to appeare to be writtẽ therin is not? The Cardinall onely affirmeth, that *his Holinesse enioyned him by speciall commandement to make peace in our countrie, after the example of the peace and quietnesse made in the English Colledge at Rome.* Which commission or authoritie to make peace, is (vnlesse we be infinitly deceiued) a farre different thing in nature, from the authoritie to institute an Archpriest, with like ample and exorbitant iurisdiction in our whole Church. Verily the proportion seemeth to be so little, and the dissimilitude between the meanes of making peace, and it, (the quality of the subordinatiō & the maner of bringing it into our Church considered) as there could well no hope be conceiued of peace to follow, through the institution of such a subordination, except we would make the fathers of the Society our directours, and remaine euermore their obseruant pupils.

If it be replied, that the Cardinall wrote in the Letter Constitutiue, *how in decreeing the subordination, he followed the will of his Holines:* We answere, that to follow the Popes will in doing of a thing, differeth much from receiuing of a speciall commaundement of doing the same. Neither doth it appeare in the Cardinall his Letter that his grace followed the will of his Holinesse, in erecting this subordination *in specie*, with the iurisdiction, faculties, and instructions adioyned: nay the contrary seemed plaine, in that his Holinesse willed the Cardinall by speciall commaundement (as his Grace relateth the words in the Constitutiue Letter) to labour the effecting and establishing of peace in our countrie, which standing, his Holines intention and will could not be, but that such a subordination should be ordained amōg vs, as might most auaile to the making and continuing of true peace, and in which principall qualitie, the new subordination being most defectiue (if not part of the faculties annexed of a quite contrary nature) what inference more direct, then that the Cardinall only followed the will of his Holinesse in the name of a subordiuation, (a point of lesse moment) and not in the substance, matter, specialties and forme thereof, points incomparably more important? Which, how vnperfect a manner it is of following his Holinesse will, we leaue to others to iudge.

Finally, where you father *Parsons* do say, that his Holinesse commanded the institution of the subordination in *respect of the diuision and dissention raised in England betweene Priestes and Iesuites, or Priestes and Priests,* we are glad to see you to correct the defaming errour (though the whole Realme could reprooue you if you did it not) which your selfe

ſelfe inſerted, in the Conſtitutiue Letter, making the cauſe of inſtituting the ſubordination, to be diſſention betweene the Secular Prieſts and the Lay Catholickes. And as we are glad of this, ſo may we not omit to note the pollicie, that you, labouring to erect a ſubordination, concealed that frõ his Holines which was true, & which moſt needed reformation, (to wit, great diſſention betweene Ieſuits and ſome ſecular Prieſts) and pretended other vntrue matter, viz. ſtrife among the Secular Prieſts, and debate betweene them and the lay Catholickes, a moſt iniurious calumniation. And when by this cunning fineneſſe of masking matters, you had obtained your deſire, that is, ſuch a forme of gouernement as your ſelues made choice of, neither compriſing your brethren here, as it had bene reaſon it ſhould, being the more potent part of the contenders, but in ſteeed of this iuſtice and equality, made you and them in truth the electours of our Archprieſt, and *our Archprieſt commanded in matters of waight to ſeeke your iudgement and aduiſe:* In the ninth instruction. then when matters be compaſſed, and all things that your ſelues aſſigned, moſt ſtrongly cõfirmed, to agnize or colour the former vntruth (which as it ſeemeth could not be but a ſtudied falſhood) by rehearſing many diſtinctiue cauſes, is proofe of wit, and the more, by doing it in ſuch a language, as thoſe who by authoritie ought moſt to puniſh and remedie the fault, cannot vnderſtand the abuſe.

For concluding our anſwere to this ſixth obiection, we ſay no more but wiſh the Composer to arme himſelfe with patience, by conſidering theſe words of holy Scripture, *qui inconſideratus eſt ad loquendum* Prouerb.13. *ſentiet mala:* He that is inconſiderate in his ſpeeches againſt another, muſt not thinke but to feele the rebukes due vnto his folly.

A Seuenth obiection which our aduerſaries alleadge againſt vs, is, that we being the perſons, who [a] *went about to erect ſodalities, to* (a) In the Apologie. fol. 101. [b] *ordaine new aſſociations, to* [c] *make a certaine gouernment among our ſelues* (b) *Ibidem fol.* 105. *without conſent, counſell, or notice of any Superiors, and this to the preiudice* *of others (the moſt part of our brethren reclaiming and miſliking the ſame.)* (c) *Ibid. fol.* 90. And *were* [d] *ſo feruent in this point to haue a ſubordination and gouernment* (d) *Ibid. fol.* 100 *among our ſelues, as without all ſuperiours authoritie we would haue ſet vp* (e) *Ibid fol.* 104 *our aſſociation:* Did neuertheleſſe [e] *when the inſtitution of the Archprieſt came into England, and was promulgated by the prudent and godly letters of the Protectour, and ordained for conſeruation of peace by the higheſt authoritie that is vpon earth, begin (hauing reſolued to be vnquiet) firſt to ſtagger and doubt, and then to diſcuſſe our ſuperiours commandement, and*

(f) In the letter of the six Assistants to the *Nuncio* in Flāders, 2. of May 1601. §. 7.

lastly to contemne it. Which sinne of ours[f] *can no where else be placed, but in the highest greece of disobedience, seeing it was cōmitted against the supreme Pontifex himselfe, and against the dignitie of the whole Romane Court.* The obiection is laid downe in their owne wordes, as it is to be seene in the places quoted, neither haue we wittingly omitted ought, that themselues adde of waight to this purpose. And now to answere directly hereunto.

First we acknowledge, that some of our companie went about (though after, and not with like feruour, as M. *Standish* now an Assistant did, being the first motioner of the matter and chiefe prosecutor) to erect a sodalitie of such as would giue willingly their word and names to obserue certaine rules that should be agreed vpon and deemed fit for the good of themselues, and manie other, during the present state of things. The cause of this proiect, were certaine hard speeches which some indiscreete persons (either the too zealous followers of the societie, or some of the fathers themselues, or both) gaue forth, against the secular Priests in generall, that they liked not to liue vnder obedience, or to haue other Superiours then the direction of their owne wils. Which report (put away the working of diseased humours) grew chiefly and outwardly of this cause, for that many of our brethren in *Wisbich* refused to accept father *Weston* to their Superior, and to accept such orders as he the said father *Weston* and his partie (wherof many were secret Iesuits, and none so ancient either in yeeres or in sufferance for the cause, as were sundry of the other side, and of lesser talents also,) thought fit to appoint. To remoue this exception, and to let the authors of the report to see in our deedes, that we were no such worshippers of our owne wils, nor so auerted from the duties of obedience, but that we would in the degree that becommed secular Priests, both relinquish the one, and bind our selues to the other, and also to giue helpes and prouocation to our nature (dull by inheritance) of going the more forward in vertue, we thought good, if not necessarie, to vnite our selues and agree vpon some certaine rules, and choise of a superiour, for the better obseruing of discipline and the said rules.

The rules that were set down to be obserued by the sodality intended, were first some eighteene (as M. *Standish* can record, who taking them to translate, shewed them to fa. *Garnet*, & not vnlike, to other of the societie) containing chiefly, matter of increasing sociall and mutuall loue: and this not onely betweene Priests that should be of the sodalitie,

dalitie, but betweene them and all Priests, as the rules themselues yet extant in the first draught can witnes: namely of furnishing Priests at their first comming: of releeuing the needes of other, especially of prisoners and persons fallen into trouble, or decayed for harbouring of Priests: of preaching monethly or catechizing weekely: of aduenturing vpon any daunger for sauing or comforting a soule in extreme necessitie, being requested thereunto: of disliking no one, for not being of the sodalitie: of declining al such occasions as might breede variance with others, especially with the fathers of the societie, & if any like cause be offered by them, to acquaint the superiour of the sodalitie with it, that he might forthwith, before the matter grew to head, or be knowne to many, conferre with the Superior of the societie for redresse, and a charitable end of the difference: of spending daily some time in meditation, or in reading some spirituall booke: of conferring about difficult and intricate cases, and neuer vpon his owne iudgement to resolue such, without taking the aduice of other his brethren: of making a generall confession euery halfe yeere, for the halfe yeare past, and of other like points. And none of all the rules to bind vnder mortall sinne, saue onely, that the superior should not incorporate, or vow himselfe a member of another bodie, before such time as he had relinquished the office. If they of the North not knowing what we had done in the South, drew other rules, or moe, what skilled that, sith they stood contented to accept of those rules which most voices should approoue, and ours of the South, not theirs of the North were approoued?

And now, this being the designe intended, the cause why it was intended, and the breuiate of the rules, we aske the sixe Assistants, that sent the letter of information to his Holinesse *Nuncio* in Flaunders against vs, we aske father *Parsons* the writer of the Apologie, and (so farre as in dutie we may) we ask also their superiours, by whose allowance the said Apologie was printed, what it was, that was so greatly amisse, either in the circumstances, or nature of the designe, as might deserue the reproches, which the said letter to his Holinesse *Nuncio* layeth vpon vs, for hauing such a purpose?

When the matter was broken to father *Garnet*, for vnderstanding his liking and opinion in the same: he answered, that it *was the best thing which was taken in hand in all this Queenes time, if it could be effected.* Likewise when the affaire was communicated to father *Weston*, he seemed to like it very well. And if they haue since changed their mindes, yet we request father *Parsons* (the maker of the Apologie) and our Archpriest (the allower of the printing thereof and of the Appendix) to shew the reason why they terme the setting downe of [g] Rules in *Wisbich* by the eighteene Priests, and the electing of father *Weston* for [h] *their Iudge, Correctour, and Censurer ouer them,* [i] *a holy and quiet purpose,* and so [k] mainely depraue and condemne the sodalitie we intended, wheras the rules of that [l] Academie or congregation as they call it, are neither [m] *more easie or commodious,* nor more [n] *auance honest, and ciuill conuersation among those* that should liue vnder the orders (the qualities which the Apologie attributeth to the said rules) then were the rules of the sodalitie we went about to make, and perhaps not equall to ours in the foresaid qualities, and incomparably behind ours in other respects, more generall, and releeuing the distressed.

(g) *Fol.* 72. (h) *Fol.* 73. (i) *Ibidem.* (k) *Fol.* 90. (l) *Fol.* 66. (m) *Fol.* 65. (n) *Fol.* 72.

Or howsoeuer their rules exceeded ours in goodnes, or ours theirs in that, and in forwarding a common good, yet it cannot be denied, but that we, who laboured, or rather proposed the instituting of a solliditie, did surpasse them in this one point, viz. in desisting from prosecuting our purpose, assoone as we first vnderstood that some two or three of our brethren misliked our endeuors, holding it for more charitie to surceasse that for peace and quietnesse sake, which might occasion good to our selues and others, then by proceeding in a matter we were not bound too, to kindle the ire or emulation of a few. The like, if the greater and better part of the prisoners in *Wisbich* (for so our Archpriest and father *Parsons* styleth them) had bene pleased to haue done, as by no perswasion they could be brought vnto: O Lord, what tumults, what broiles, what scandall, what infinite detraction had there bene left vncommitted? And it is worth the labour to note, who they were that principally opposed themselues against the institution of the sodalitie, albeit none were to be of that companie, but with their owne liking and intreatie.

M. *Blackwell,* M. D. *Bauine,* and M. *Tiruit.*

Doctour *Bauen* the senior Assistant, stood so stifly opposite against the introduction of the sodalitie or association, as he letted not to affirme when his opinion was asked therein, that if the Pope should appoint a Bishop in our countrey, during the present state of matters, he would be one that should resist, and informe his Holinesse of the inconuenience and hurt, which the bringing in of such authoritie would worke in our Countrey. And M. *Blackwell* only of all the Priests in our contrey, wrote certaine reasons in dislike and condemnation of the Sodalitie: to wit, that as by the rules of Phisick and Philosophie, it was no wisedom for any, who had a long while kept their health by liuing in such an ayre, or by feeding on such meates, after to change the same ayre, or alter their customarie diet: and as it is a dangerous errour in ciuill pollicie to seeke to change the forme of gouernement, vnder which they haue enioyed lõg peace & happines: so is it folly, or great temeritie, hauing liued so many yeares in peace and quietnesse in our Countrey, as we haue, without any association, or other superior, to begin now to set vp new authorities, and bring in innouations. Yea he added further, how vnfit, how vnprofitable, and how preiudicial it was for any one person to take vpon him the Ecclesiasticall gouernement in our Countrey, and that if he liued to the change of Religion, he would deale for deuiding the Bishopricks into moe Diocesses. Which reasons concluding directly and most strongly against the new authoritie, were anon of likelihood either soon forgot, or began to appeare of no force when himselfe was chosen Archpriest.

Iu like manner, when father *Parsons* last trauelled from *Spaine* to *Rome*, he so greatly disliked the making of a superior in *Englãd* among the secular Priests, as he made it the ordinarie subiect of his talke during the whole iourney, deuising moe and new reasons dayly for remonstrance and proofe of the inconueniences. But after his arriuall in *Rome*, and conference with M. *Standish* and father *Baldwine* (whom father *Garnet* had imployed as his agents in the businesse vnto him) he soone altered his mind, vnderstanding of like, by intelligence from father *Garnet*, how probable it was, that in short time the Priests would agree vpon some forme of gouernement, and therfore it imported him with speede to preuent our intentions, least we hapned in the meane, to make choice, of a kind of gouernement and gouernor which would impeach their designes, and make way to the diminishing of the reputation they now carried in our Country, which was and is the swaying of all things as themselues think meete.

Inconstancie in the Noter of incõstancy.

Neither is it vnlike, the thing being constantly auerred by many, but that father *Garnet* sent father *Parsons* notice of the man whom he should promote, and of the authoritie and particular iurisdiction which he should procure vnto him ouer vs. Hence came that place of Scripture into father *Parsons* head, together with his analogicall exposition. *Crescente numero discipulorum, factum est murmur Græcorum aduersus Hebræos, &c. When the multitude of Priestes increased, and the former spirite in many of them decreased, there began presently murmuration and emulation against the fathers of the society.* Hence proceeded the

Act. 6.

manifold and long faction laid downe in the eight Chapter of the Apology, where father *Parsons* cunningly fashioneth a narration lasting for foure of the first leaues, but with addition of moe vntruths then he vsed full points in the tale. Hence sodainely arose an vrgent, or as it were, a fatall necessitie in fa. *Parsons* conceit, of making a Superiour in *England* ouer the secular Priests, an affaire which himself a little before in his iourney from *Spaine* to *Rome* (as hath bene said) spake so much and often against, and from prosecution whereof, himselfe aduised vs by M. *Champney* to desist, as from a matter of contention. Hence finally are the words of the Apologie, (o) *It seemed in all good mens opinion (and in the Iesuites aboue the rest) that the onely or chiefe remedie of auoiding murmuration & emulation in the secular Priests, against the fathers of the societie, would be to haue a subordination of the secular Priests among them selues, whereby the fathers of the Societie might remaine forth of all occasion of contention.* Good Lord must the taking away of emulation and heart-burnings in the secular Priests against the fathers of the Societie, be made the motiue and end why this subordination was instituted? Who can beleeue it, that shall looke into the particulars? or who will not but auow the contrary, that shall consider how and by whom the same was procured? For is it likely or possible in reason, that that kind of subordination should extinguish emulation, or make agreement, or not increase murmur and debate, which the more principall and oppressing partie in the contention should deuise, and get to be ordained without consent or notice of the other partie that suffered the oppression? And who we pray, plotted this kind of subordination but father *Garnet* and father *Parsons*? Who nominated the Archpriest but they? Who deuised the iurisdiction but they? Who framed the authoritie? who annexed the instructions? who made the additions? who chose the assistants but they? Who conferred with Cardinall *Caietane*? who informed his Holines? who procured the confirmation, but father *Parsons* onely, or such as himselfe did set on worke, and put in their mouthes what they should say? In briefe, who euer had part, voice, or consent in any point belonging to the particulars of the subordination, saue these two, and perhaps some other few of their consorts, whom they thought good to acquaint with the affaire?

Lo, the deceiuing and presuming nature of the man.

(o) *Fol.* 100.

And this which we say, is so cleere to euery one that will not blind his owne vnderstanding, as the Sunne when it shineth. Neuerthelesse if witnesses be demaunded at our hands, we will name no other but father *Garnet* and father *Parsons* themselues, hauing their own words

for

for teſtimonie. For when father *Garnet* asked M. *Iohn Bennet* for his name to *olim dicebamur*, that is, as hath bene ſignified before, to a pretenſed letter of thankſgiuing to his Holineſſe, for inſtitution of the authoritie, and ſeeing him to be vnwilling to giue his name, told him that the ſubordination was the fact and proſecution of father *Parſons* his old friend, and therefore ſtood aſſured he would not denie the graunt of putting too his name. Likewiſe father *Parſons* in his ſpeeches with M. *Charnock* at Rome among other things freely acknowledged, that hearing how we went about in England to make a ſuperiour among our ſelues, he thought it wiſedome to preuent the effecting of ſuch our endeuours, by chooſing and promoting one to the roome whom they knew to be their friend, and would comply with them. But why ſtand we about the proofe of theſe? the apparant managing of the affaire, the condition of the particulars, the manner of the proceſſe, the nature of the circumſtances, the ground, the end, the ſcope, and all other acceſſaries being more euident then boldneſſe (we will not ſay impudencie) it ſelfe can denie? Pag. 50.

Neither was this forme of gouernement, deuiſed onely by the foreſaid paire of fathers, and by their meanes brought vnweetingly vpon vs, but they keepe themſelues euermore cloſe at the ſterne directing, ruling, preſcribing, guiding, as vniuerſally and abſolutely, as if themſelues were the Archprieſt or any other higher ſuperiour ouer vs. And whether now this kind of ſubordination thus plotted, thus effected, thus executed, thus continually caried againſt vs, *be the onely or chiefe remedie* (as father *Parſons* auoweth) *of auoiding murmuration and emulation in the ſecular Prieſts againſt the fathers of the Societie, and whereby they might remaine forth of all occaſion of contention*, this we leaue to the indifferent to iudge, the contrarie appearing plainer to vs, then that any doubt can be made thereof. But to returne.

We aske of father *Parſons* and the ſixe Aſſiſtants, who ſeem to haue beaten their wits for finding matter wherin and how to condemne vs, whether by ſeeking to vnite and prouoke our ſelues to vertue through the erecting of a Sodalitie, among ſuch onely, as ſhould like and deſire to be thereof, we became thereby obliged in conſcience to accept of any ſubordination which himſelfe and his conſorts ſhould by wrong and ſiniſter ſuggeſtion, get to be propoſed or ordained againſt vs? If they ſay yea, it reſteth, that they proue the bond, a worke impoſſible: or if they ſay no, then why doth he in the Apologie, and the other in their letter to the *Nuncio* in *Flaunders* of the ſecond of May, dilate as Ca. 1. 6. & 8.

they do, and so iniuriously inferre thereof against vs? It hath bene e-uough and enough declared before, that we were not bound to admit the subordination vpon credence of the Cardinals Letter, and being not bound by any vertue of the said Letter, we trow, our trauels to make a sodalitie, did not bind vs thereunto: if so, they had not bene broken off as they were, before the institution of the subordination, and we all conioyned in the sympathie or mutuall embracing of one desire to sue to his Holinesse for obtaining of Bishops in our country. We say no more, but that if father *Parsons* or the sixe Assistants had stood so indifferently inclined to fauour our attẽpts in going about to ordaine a Sodalitie, as he sheweth himselfe prone and readie not only to excuse, but to commend and iustifie the league and orders of the Agency begun and prosecuted in the Castle of *Wisbich*, calling the same
(p)Fol.66. [p] *a congregation according to the fashion and example of those priuate congregations of our Ladie, allowed by the Sea Apostolicke in diuers Countries:* no doubt both he and they, had lessened their account in the day of their doome, when they must answere for the wrongs they do vs.

Touching the preiudice which by instituting the Sodalitie should be intended to others, we would faine know, what preiudice that could be in particular, when euery man was left free to his own choice, and no one to be misliked if he would not be a member thereof, and others tied by a new obligation to loue, reuerence, and stead him wherein they could. Neither do we take it to be true, that *the most part of our brethren did reclaime and mislike the institution of the Sodalitie*, as may be gathered by the small number of those that manifested their dislike, being as we haue said before, but very few, three onely of note, M. Doctor *Bauen*, M. *Blackwell*, and M. *Tirwit*, and by the companie of those that expressed their good liking therof, which were more thẽ 20. times so many as those that impugned the same, by the account & reckord of such as negociated the affaire, and dealt with others for vnderstanding their affection or auersion therein.

To that wherewith the obiection chargeth vs, that [*when the institution of the Archpriest came into England, and was promulgated by the prudent and godly letters of the Protectour, we (hauing resolued to be vnquiet) began first to stagger and doubt, and then to discusse our Superiours commaundement, and lastly to contemne it:*] we answer, that if the Cardinals Letter had bene the Popes Letter, or an Apostolicall Breue or Bull, as it was not, and the degrees of beleefe due to the one exceedingly surmounting the degrees due to the other, yet doubting as we did,

did, or truer, being right assured as we were in our own vnderstanding, that the said Letter was procured by surreption or obreption, or both; what fault was it in vs to *stagger and doubt, and discusse our Superiours commandement*, when no writer ancient nor moderne, but holdeth the same for most lawfull? [q] *Non negamus literas Apostolicas recognosci quidem & discuti debere, cum sint dubiæ, sint necne subreptitiæ an legitimæ.* It is not to be denied (writeth *Azore*) but that Apostolicall Letters may and ought to be considered of, & discussed, when they appeare doubtfull, whether they were procured by wrong or right information. And the same Author in another place hath these words, [r] *Fas est etiam Laico de literis pontificijs cum dubiæ sint & incertæ, bona fide probabiliter, ambigere, disputareve, sint necne Pontificiæ, sint necne subreptitiæ.* It is lawfull, euen for a lay man, hauing no corrupt intention, probably to question and dispute, whether the Popes letters appearing doubtful and vncertaine, were indeede his Leters, or gotten by surreption.

(q) *Institut. moral. p. 1. li. 5 ca. 14. quæritur. 4.*

(r) *Idem ibidem quæritur 7.*

Againe, the Canonists note many things which may be opposed against the Popes Bull, and [s] *Rebuffus* putteth downe 29. exceptions, whereof some, if they be found in the Bull, cannot be salued, but do vtterly inualidate and frustrate the same: some other that may be amended, and the Bull after to be of force. Now if it were vnlawfull (as father *Parsons* maketh it to be (though all the learned besides himselfe do with one voice witnesse the contrarie) to scanne and discusse the Popes Bull, how should the said defects or matter of exception be opposed? And if this libertie be graunted against the Popes Bull, or Apostolicall Letters, no doubt, the same freedome or much greater, is allowed against a Cardinals Letter, instituting a strange subordination afflictiue and most rigorous. But the father would haue vs (and we commend his wit therein) to practise perfect obedience, that is, as Diuines teach, [t] not only promptly and readily to do whatsoeuer we are commaunded, without considering the authoritie or end of the Commaunder, but to preuent also the commaundement of our Superiour in all things wherein we know before, his will or pleasure. And yet, if we should follow the fathers exhortation in this point, and not content our selues with performing the obedience we are bound too, and which [v] sufficeth vnder tie of sin, we do not see, how, shewing this perfect obedience, we ought to haue admitted the subordination, because the *Extrauagant Iniunctæ*, and the [x] constitutions of other Popes do forbid to receiue any such superiour Prelate to the office, and dignitie he claimeth, without sight of the Popes Letter for testimonie of

(s) *Rebuffus in praxi. Tit. Quæ apponi possunt contra Bullam.*

(t) *D. Tho. secunda secundæ q. 104. art. 5. D. Bonauẽ. q. vlt. Durandus q. 4. Cordubensis in exposit. Regulæ ca. 10. q. 2. Valẽtia To. 3 disp. 7. q. 3. punct. 2. Angles par. 2. in secundũ. lib. Sent. dist. 44 q. 2 diff. 5. & Sũmistæ verb. Religiosus.*

(v) *D. Tho. vbi supra ad tertiũ.*

(x) *Paulus 3. Const. quæ incipit, cum nobis. Iulius 2. Constitut. quæ incipit, Romani Pontificis. Iulius 3. constit. quæ incipit, Sanctissimus.*

ſuch his graunt, and the parties promotion. Neither can that in truth be called perfect obedience, but rather indiſcreet and ſinfull, which tranſgreſſeth the ordinances of holy Church, as vndoubtedly we ſhould haue done, had we receiued M. *Blackwell* to the office of the Archpresbyterſhip, before the ſhewing of the Popes Letters for his preferment thereunto.

No doubt, but the vtter face of the perſwaſion which the ſonnes of
Gen.34. *Iacob* vſed to *Sichem*, was good and holy, as being the act of Circumciſion, the chiefeſt Sacrament of the old law, yet *Sichems* obedience thereunto, was the cauſe of his death, and of the ſlaughter of many mo.
2.Reg.11. Againe, if we looke vpon the outſide of *Dauids* counſell to *Vrias*, in exhorting him to take his eaſe after his weariſome iourney, there appeareth nought but goodwill and kindneſſe, and yet *Dauid* had a ſubtile fetch therein, and more reſpected his owne good in the counſell, then he did the welfare of *Vrias*. Neither did the enemie of mankind, let to candie and cloake his perſwaſion to our vnfortunate mother
Gen.3. *Eue*, with an outward ſhew of godlineſſe, *Eritis ſicut Dij, ſcientes bonum & malum*: Ye ſhall be as Gods, knowing good and euill: but what drift he had therein, all her poſteritie feeles. We know, how excellent a vertue obedience is, eſpecially that kind which father *Parſons* would haue vs to practiſe, and which ſpirituall writers call, *Cæcam obedientiam*, blind obedience, for that it cloſeth the eye of our will, and leadeth the iudgement of our vnderſtanding, as the guide leadeth the blind
Li.1 ca.4.in li. 1.Reg. man, agreeable to this ſaying of S. *Gregorie*: *Vera obedientia nec Præpoſitorum intentionem diſcutit, nec præcepta diſcernit, quia qui omne vitæ ſuæ ſtudium maiori ſubdidit, in hoc ſolo gaudet, ſi quod ſibi præcipitur, operatur. Neſcit enim iudicare, quiſquis perfectè didicerit obedire.* True obedience neither diſcuſſeth the intention of his Prepoſitors, neither ſcanneth their commaundements, because he that hath ſubiected the whole courſe of his life to the direction of his ſuperiour, ioyeth only in this, if he do as he is commannded. For he knoweth not to iudge, that hath perfectly learned to obey.

But as we wot the thing that father *Parſons* counſelleth vs too, to be
(y) D.Tho.2.2. q.104.art.3. right good in it ſelfe, being the perfection of the [y] worthieſt of al other morall vertues: ſo do we feare, leaſt he ſecke therein the increaſe of ſoueraigntie, and abſolutely without contradiction to rule in our Country, as already he hath not bluſhed to vaunt himſelfe of the commaund he holdeth in England (we ſpeake from report of an eye and eare witneſſe) as well ouer many of the Laitie, as of the Cleargie, which

vaine bragge he would easily make good with aduantage, could he once bring vs to a blind kind of obedience, neither to discusse the commandements of our Archpriest, whom he directeth in all things, nor the ordinance of any other superiour, vpon what false information soeuer the same was enacted. *Volo vos sapientes esse in bono, & simplices in malo*: I would haue you (sayth the Apostle) to be wise in good, and simple in ill. Which God of his mercies make true in father *Parsons*, and in vs all. *Rom.16.*

Concerning the other part of the charge, *that hauing resolued to be vnquiet, we would not desist, till lastly we fel to contemne our superiours commandement*. Here we haue good cause to aske father *Parsons* how he knew, being no Prophet, nor the sonne of a Prophet, that *we had resolued to be vnquiet*, for so much was neither written in our foreheads, nor manifested in the nature of our actions, doing nothing (as we haue often sayd) more then what the Canons and constitutions of holy Church, and the vniforme consent of all writers allow and direct. But notwithstanding the iustnesse of the cause, we will not trouble him with this demaund, hauing another question of more weight to be assoiled, viz. that he tell vs and the world, vnlesse we and the world must hold him for more then a vaine speaker, wherein and how we *contemned the commandement of our Superiors*, that is (as Diuines and the Summists write) in a thing [z] we were bound to obey them, & did not obey thẽ, for this respect only, because we would not be subiect to their cõmandements. A slander which he nor our aduersaries shal euer be able to proue, & not prouing, we trust he will make cõscience to reuerse the words, as he must needs if he loue his soule: & the sooner if by the gradation and forme of speech he vsed, he intended to giue ayme to the Reader of our nigh approching or perfect arriual to that degree of sin which the holy Ghost mentioned by the pen of *Salomon*. *Impius cum in profundum venerit peccatorum contemnit*: *When the wicked is sunke to the depth of mischiefe, he contemneth* the commaundements of Almightie God, and of his Deputies vpon earth.

(z) D. Tho. 2.2. q.986. art.9. ad 3. Caiet. ibid. & in summa verb. cõtẽptus valẽt. To.3. disp.10. q. 4. punct.5. Siluest. verb. Contemptus nu.1. Archidiaco. in Ca. quicunque dist. 81. Dominicus in Ca. Nullus. dist.55. Viguerius ca.5. §.9 ver.1. Nauar. in Manuali ca.23. nu.42.

Prouerb.18.

Finally, touching the remnant of the obiection vnanswered, to wit, *that our sinne* [in refusing to subiect our selues to the new subordination before it was witnessed or approued by his Holinesse Breue] *can no where else be placed, but in the highest greece of disobedience, seeing it was committed against the supreme Pontifex himselfe, and against the dignitie of the whole Romane Court*: We referre the Reader (the assertion being most ignorant and vncolourable) to that which hath bene said before

*Pag.29.& sequentib. *Pag.85.& 86

* in our second Reason, and * in our answer to our aduersaries third obiection, and to that which God willing, we shall hereafter touch in both the Reasons that follow.

AN eight obiection or shift which our oppositours deuise for maintaining their feeble assertions, and for finding a way out of the straites, which their afterwits saw, would mightily enuiron them, if they should stil hold and maintaine* as they did at first, the subordination to be the act and ordinance of our Cardinal Protector, because to acknowledge this much, did and would euer most hardly rub vpon them, either to shew the rescript of his Holinesse delegation to the Cardinall, or to proue his Holinesse verball Commission vnto him, or driue them to recall (vnles they should shew themselues of worse conscience then they seeme to be) the temerarious and too too vncharitable censures which they had most wrongfully laid vpon vs, and diuulged euery where, for not yeelding our obedience (no law nor rules of conscience binding vs therunto, without proofe first made in that behalfe of the Cardinals authoritie) to M. *Blackwell* vpon view of the *Constitutiue Letter*: to correct this errour, father *Parsons* in the bill of complaint, which M. *Haddocke* and M. *Martin Array* exhibited to Cardinall *Caietane*, and Cardinall *Burghesio* the tenth of Ianuary 1599 against M. *Bishop* and M. *Charnocke*, affirmeth his Holinesse to be the institutor of the subordination, and the Cardinall a witnesse-bearer therof. His words in the foresaid bill are these: [a]*Cum S^mus D.N. hierarchiam quandam Sacerdotum saecularium inter se sub vno Archipraesbytero & duodecim Assistentibus per Ill^mi Cardinalis Protectoris Literas ordinasset:* [b]*statim atque D. Georgius Blackwellus Archipresbyter constitutus, authoritatem suam Ill^mi Cadinalis Caietani literis testatam, Roma transmissam, perhumaniter vocauit ad se duos, ijsq; exposuit quid sua S^tas instituisset, &c.* When his Holinesse had ordained by the letters of the most Illustrious Cardinall Protector, a certaine Hierarchie of Secular Priests among themselues, vnder one Archpriest & twelue Assistants, and assoone as M. *George Blackwell* was made Archpriest, and had receiued his authority frõ *Rome*, testified by the Letters of the most Illustrious Cardinall *Caietane*, he courteously inuited two Priests to come vnto him, & declared what his Holines had instituted, &c. Moreouer, our said aduersarie, as he wrote these words in the names of master D. *Haddocke* and M. *Martin Array*, so keeping his old wont still, to mask and vent his vntruths vnder the persons of other men, commeth in his

* Our Archpriest in his letters in the 8. and 17. of August, see pag 67.

(a) §.1.

(b) §.2.

his Preface to the Appendix (set forth as he gloseth *by the Priests that remaine in due obedience to their lawfull Supeiour,*) to interlace his short notes by way of parenthesises vpō his Holines Breue, being of his own procuring and suggestion of the points. The wordes of the Breue and his parenthesis are these: *Vos filij præsbyteri qui libenter institutum à nobis Archipræsbyterum suscepistis, valdè in Domino commendamus, &c.* You Priests that did receiue willingly the Archpriest appointed by vs (mark how he saith not that he was instituted by the Cardinall, but by himselfe) we do highly commend you.

Which passages, seeming so to auow the subordination to be the act of his Holinesse, as the Cardinall was but a witnes, or at most, a meere Excecutor therof, do, no doubt, if they were true, much weaken part of that which hath bene alleaged before, as shewing it to be spoken besides the matter. But let vs examine the truth of the assertiōs by the tenor and selfe words of the *Constitutiue Letter*, the rule and only touchstone for triall of the premisses. And to cite but one place of many for auoiding tediousnesse.

Cum igitur non parum, &c. Sith therefore some men thinke, that it would not a little auaile to the procuring of peace and concord, if a subordination were constituted among the English Priests, and the reasons yeelded by the Priests themselues for the same matter, were approued by our holy Father: we following the most pious and prudent will of his Holinesse, haue decreed to ordaine the same, and for directing and gouerning the Priests of the English nation that now conuerse in the kingdomes of England or Scotland, or shall hereafter reside there, whiles this our ordination shall continue, we chuse you, to whom for the time we commit our steed and office, induced vpon relation and the publicke fame of your vertue, learning, wisedome, and labours taken for many yeares in the trimming of this vineyard. And the faculties which for this purpose we graunt vnto you, are these: First, that you haue the title and authoritie of an Archpriest ouer all the Seminary secular Priestes, to direct, admonish, reprehend, or also chastise them when neede shall require: and this, either by abridging or taking away their faculties.

Now, let the indifferent iudge whether the *Constitutiue Letter* doth more shew his Holinesse or the Cardinall to be the institutor of the Subordination, or whether it conuinceth not, that the Cardinall had a greater part in the institution thereof, then the part of a witnesse or of an Executor onely.

The Cardinal writeth to M. *Blackwell*: *We chuse and substitute you to be our vicegerent. Ours* (saith the Cardinall) not the Popes. In what?

In directing and gouerning the English Priests. Where? *In the kingdomes of England or Scotland.* How long? *So long as this our ordination shall endure. Ours,* againe, not the Popes. Vpon what cause? *Induced thereunto* (marke who was induced, and consequently who elected the Archpriest,) *by the common bruite of your vertue, erudition, prudence, and the long continuance of your labours, to the splendor of the English Church.* To what end? *To direct, admonish, and correct the seminarie secular Priestes.* In what sort? *By restraining or taking away their faculties.* Who giueth him this power and iurisdiction ouer his brethren? *The faculties which for this purpose, we* (saith the Cardinall, not the Pope) *graunt vnto you, are these. Ergo* the Cardinall was more then a witnesser of the subordination, because a witnesser hath no authoritie to delegate. And as little can the executor call the fact of his superiour his owne ordination, or yeeld the reason why he made choice of such a deputie, as the Cardinall doth both. Because as [c] *Panormitane* writeth, and other [d] authors agree in the same: *Executor est ille, qui habet nudum ministerium facti, in exequendo dispositum per alium.* He is called an Executor that hath the bare ministerie of a fact, in executing things disposed by another, that is, as the same Authour interpreteth in another place, [e] his Superiour.

(c) *2. p. Consil. Cons. 11. nu. 4.*
(d) *Gloss. in ca. super Quæstionum de off. Deleg. Siluest. ver. Executor nu. 1. Fumus eod. ver. nu. 1. & in l. Executorem. c. de exec. rei iud.*
(e) *In ca. super Quæstionum de off. Deleg. nu. 10.*

Againe the Cardinall writeth: *We following the will of his Holinesse, haue decreed to ordaine the subordination. Ergo* if the Cardinal decreed it, as himselfe affirmeth, he was more vndoubtedly then a witnesser or an Executor thereof: and giuing authoritie to the Archpriest *to dispose of secular Priests in our Countrey, to remoue and change them from one residence to another, to heare and determine their doubts,* with other like faculties, which without question are the substance, the principall part, the very sinewes, heart, and life of the Subordination: it followeth of necessitie, that his Grace carried another person in instituting the subordination, then the person of a witnesse or an Executor onely.

Furthermore if his Grace decreed the subordination, as nothing can be plainer spoken by himselfe, then that he did, he either decreed it without authoritie, which we trust our aduersaries will not graunt; or by authoritie from his Holinesse: because neither of his two titles, either of being Cardinall, or of being our Protector, did giue him sufficient iurisdiction to institute so rare, ample, and soueraigne superioritie ouer vs. And if by authoritie from his Holines, then we haue what our aduersaries would seem to flie from, and* all the authorities before quoted do stand in ful force against thẽ, in respect that that which is in this

*Throughout the second Reason, and in the beginning of the third.

this ſort done by the authoritie of another, is a delegatine act, and bindeth the doer to ſhew or proue the commiſſion ere he can compell beleefe or obeyſance in the proceſſe: [f] *verbum [authoritate noſtra] inducit actum delegationis.* The word [*by our authoritie*] induceth an act of delegation. And that the Cardinall did chuſe M. *Blackwell* to be Archprieſt, by authoritie and commiſſion from his Holineſſe, it is witneſſed in the new Breue (euen whence father *Parſons* culled the ſentence in which he inſerted his parẽtheſis aboue mentioned) where the words are theſe, *Habita iam à biennio ſuper hac re, matura deliberatione, bonæ memoriæ Henrico Præſbytero Cardinali Caietano nuncupato nationis Anglorũ Protectori, cõmiſimus, vt virũ aliquẽ probũ, qui hoc onus ad communem Catholicorum vtilitatem poſſet ſuſtinere delegeret, eúmque Archipræſbyterum eiuſdem Regni Angliæ authoritate noſtra conſtitueret.* Hauing had mature deliberation for two yeares ſpace of this matter, we gaue comiſſion to *Henry Preſbyter,* Cardinall *Caietane* of good memory, that he ſhould chuſe ſome honeſt man who might beare this burden to the common profite of Catholickes, and by our authoritie conſtitute him Archprieſt of the ſame kingdome of England.

(f) *Gloſſ. general. in ca. Si eũ de Prebẽd. li. 6.*

Of the 17. of Auguſt. 1601: Note the wreſting ſincerity of the man.

Or why ſtand we to proue this euident truth by the teſtimonie of his Holineſſe Breue, when father *Parſons* the drawer of the foreſaid Bill of complaint againſt our two brethren, and the markeman and inſerter of the parentheſis, acknowledgeth both in the * firſt and in the * eight Chapter of the Apologie, that the Cardinall inſtituted the Archprieſt by commiſſion from his Holineſſe. His wordes in the firſt place are: *his Holineſſe gaue full commiſſion to Cardinall Caietane the Protector to appoint the ſame* (viz. a gouernement) *with conuenient inſtructions, which he preſently did.* And in the ſecond theſe: *his Holineſſe committed the inſtitution of the matter* (that is, of inſtituting an Archprieſt) *by ſpeciall order to the Protector to be done in his name.* Which auowances of father *Parſons*, whether they be true or not true in themſelues (as true they cannot be, if *Signior Acriſio* * the Popes Commiſſarie and Canon of S. *Iohn Laterans*, as he ſtyleth him, be a true man in his word, for he told our two brethren remaining in priſon, that the ſubordination was not the commmaundement of his Holineſſe, as his Holineſſe himſelfe newly affirmed vnto him, adding for reaſon, as it hath bene * before ſpecified, that his Holineſſe durſt not command it for feare of hauing his cenſures contemned by the Prieſtes in England) yet they manifeſt thus much, that euen by his own confeſſion the Cardinall was the inſtitutor of the Subordination.

* *Fol. 7.*
* *Fol. 99.*
* *Fol. 139. &* 121.
* *Pag. 34.*

And now if we adde to these, what it is to delegate, and who is a Delegate, there can (we hope) remaine no doubt, but that the Cardinall was the Popes delegate in the erecting of the subordination, and by consequence not such a bare publisher and witnesser therof, as our aduersaries would faine haue him to be, for ridding themselues out of some narrow straits, by reason of the authorities aforegoing, that otherwise presse exceedingly and ineuitably vpon them, and as clearely excuse vs of all blame for not surrendring our obediēce to M. *Blackwel* vpō view of the Cardinals letters, before either his Holines had ratified the fact, or giuē notice vnto vs of such his pleasure, or the Cardinall proued his cōmission after some authentike or legall maner. Of which, no one was done, so long as we bore off, and so soone, as to our knowledge either was done, we presently submitted our selues. [g] *Delegare est vice sua alium dare*: to delegate (saith *Decius*) is to appoint another in his stead.[h] *Delegatus quoad ecclesiasticos, est is cui à summo Pōtifice vel ordinario, causa committitur, aut ab eo, qui extraordinaria iurisdictione aliquid potest.* A delegate, as the word appertaineth to ecclesiasticall persons, is he, to whom a cause is committed by the Pope or Ordinary, or by him, who through extraordinarie iurisdiction can delegate or appoint that charge to another.

(g) *In rubri. de off. deleg. nu.* 13 *l. delegare ff. de nouationibus.*
(h) *Siluest. verbo Delegatus. nu.* 1.

By which definitions it is very apparant (the tenour of the *Constitutiue Letter*, the wordes of the Breue, and what father *Parsons* himselfe acknowledgeth in the Apologie, considered) that the Cardinall Protector was his Holines delegate in erecting of the subordination, and consequently we not bound (as it hath bene often sayd) to obey his Grace, till such time as he shewed the rescript of the delegation, or proued his Holinesse verball commission, giuing him authority to delegate the like ample and extrauagant iurisdiction to the Archpriest, as is specified in the *Constitutiue Letter*.

(i) *Doct. de rota decis. nou. de off. Dele. decis.* 6. *n.* 2. *& de concess. Preb. decis.* 19. *nu.* 1. *Gloss. in ca. Tibi qui, de rescrip. verbo certo. & Gloss. in ca. Si super de off. Dele. ver. Principalis. l.* 6

Neither are the distresses of our aduersaries releeued a whit, if they should contend (as what vntruth is there, which will & wit cannot in some sort flourish ouer) that the Cardinall was but an Executor in the institutiō of the subordinatiō, because [i] euery Executor is a delegate, & his authoritie delegatine: & therefore not to be obeyed, vnles he proue the cōmission & the tenour. And besides the authorities * before quoted for proofe hereof, this that followeth taken out of [k] the ciuill law, and recorded by [l] *Brunorus*, maketh the case plaine, and confirmeth abundantly. *Executori, dicenti se potestatem habere ad exequendum ex mandato principis, non creditur sine literis, nec sufficit exhibere literarum transumptum*

* *Pag.* 58. *& sequentibus.*
(k) *C. de iure fis. li.* 10. *l. Sancimus. c. de diuer. rescrip.* 25. *quæst. vlt. sancimus.*
(l) *In compend. Resolut. verbo Executor.*

sumptum sed originale exhiberi debet. Beleefe is not to be giuen to an Executor, affirming himself to haue authoritie to execute by the commandement of the Prince, without shewing his letters: nor is it inough to shew the transumpt or copie of the letters, but he ought to shew the originall. Neither is the force of the authorities auoided, in that the Executor was a Cardinall, because in matters of like domage no one is bound to beleeue and subiect himselfe vpon the sole word of a Cardinall, as *Panormitane, Felinus, Alexander de Imola, Antonius de Butrio, Benedictus Valdus*, the Doctors of the *Rota, Nauarre, Siluester, Zecchius, Lancellotus, Conradus, Bartolus, Iason*, with others* before cited do teach, and no author impugnes, that we can learne of. *Pag. 60. 61. 62. 66. 89.

There be other obiections which our aduersaries make, as that none but a few women adhere in opinion vnto vs, * that we cannot pretend ignorance, nor except against the sufficientnesse of the promulgation, and such like, not worth the answering. Neuerthelesse concerning the first, we hope the sentence of the vniuersitie of Paris, giuen in our behalfe will not admit it to be true, if so there were no other at all that did participate in the opinion with vs, as perhaps, if voyces were cast, there would be found as many for vs as against vs. And concerning the iudgement of Priestes, who should best know what they did, we are right sure that we haue 6. for one, if not ten, or rather sixteen that conspire in opinion with vs for one that dissenteth. And as for the two latter and such like, we vtterly disclaime the patronage, standing more assured of the strength and iustnesse of our cause, then to flie to such pretexts for succour. *Father Holtby in his discourse of the last of Iune.

And here to conclude our third Reason, we comfort our selues in the grounds precedent, that howsoeuer the large potencie and aliance of our aduersaries may happen to ouersway, yet that the day of iudgement, if not the seate Apostolicke before, will declare vs guiltlesse of the crimes obiected, and that the measure which hath bene met vnto vs, was and is most oppressing, iniurious, violent, and spiritually hurtfull to manie.

The fourth Reason.

THE fourth Reason of our standing off, was, that admitting there had no surreption appeared in the *Constiutiue Letter*, nor obreption, but that all things had passed by true and full information, and with perfect knowledge of his Holinesse (as the day of iudgement will declare for vs, that at the time of our delay, we did morally assure our selues in both, to the contrarie) and that not onely his Holines commanded the institutiō of the Archpresbytership with the faculties and instructions annexed, but that he himself was indeed the immediate and sole institutor thereof, and that also the Cardinall had certified this much vnto vs in plaine termes, and that finally the preiudices which accompanie the authoritie, did neither licence vs to suspend our beleefe, nor could any way hold vs excused for not beleeuing his Grace on his word, (as how little true all these things were, the reasons aforegoing haue, we trust, sufficiently shewed:) yet we thought our selues secure in conscience, & free from touch of the least disobedience, if his Holinesse promoting M. *Blackwel* to so large, and much more in some respects, then episcopall authoritie, we refused to receiue him to the dignitie and ministration of the office, before such time as he did shew vs the Popes letters for testimonie of his promotion. This we tooke to be lawfull, and the reason why we tooke it to

(a) *De electione ca.* 1. be so, was the [a] extrauagant, *Iniunctæ* of Pope *Bonifacius* the 8. where these words are read: *Præsenti itaque perpetuò valitura constitutione sancimus, vt Episcopi & alij Prælati superiores quocunque nomine censeantur, qui apud sedē Apostolicā promouentur, aut confirmationis munus recipiunt ad commissas eis Ecclesias absque dictæ sedis literis huiusmodi eorum promotionem seu confirmationem continentibus accedere non præsumant: nullique eos absque dictarum literarum ostensione recipiant aut eis pariant vel intēdant. Quicunque verò ipsos absque huiusmodi dictæ sedis literis recipientes vel obedientes eisdem, tam diu sint à beneficiorum suorū perceptione suspensi, donec super hoc eiusdem sedis gratiam meruerint obtinere.* We by this present constitution (saith Pope *Boniface*) continuing for euer, do decree,

cree,that Biſhops and other ſuperiour Prelates, by what name ſoeuer they are intitled,who are promoted by the Sea Apoſtolike,or receiue the benefite of confirmation, do not preſume to take the charge of thoſe churches committed vnto them, without the letters of the ſame Sea, containing ſuch their promotion or confirmation:and that none without ſhewing the foreſaid letters,receiue,obey,or reuerence them for ſuch. And whoſoeuer ſhal receiue or obey them without the teſtimony of ſuch letters from the ſaid Sea,remain ſo long ſuſpended from receiuing the fruites of their benefices, vntill they ſhall deſerue to obtaine the relaxation of the ſaid cenſure from the Sea Apoſtolicke.

That M. *Blackwell* was conſtituted a ſuperiour Prelate, and conſequently in this point,compriſed vnder the words of the Extrauagant, it appeared in that himſelfe had no Eccleſiaſticall ſuperiour in the whole Realme,but was as *Metropolitane*, and all the ſecular Prieſts of our nation reſiding in England or Scotland appointed his ſubiects. A prelate of higher ſuperioritie in this kind then euer England had,were Cardinall *Wolſey* the counter-partie of the compariſon. And that he was alſo contained vnder the other part of the Extrauagant, to wit, *the Church or Churches committed vnto him*,ſeemed moſt plain,hauing our whole Catholicke Church both the Secular Cleargie,and Laitie, committed to his charge, as his Holineſſe two Breues do teſtifie. To auoid that is ſaid,and exempt M. *Blackwell* from being comprehended vnder this latter part of the Extrauagant, vpon pretext that there are no Eccleſiaſticall reuenues (an euaſion of his owne) belonging to the Church or Catholike multitude,whereof he is appointed Superior, is not onely to make the good Pope and prudent Gouernour of Gods Church to regard temporalities,more then he did order and reformation in Gods houſe, but moſt oppoſitely to contradict the Proeme of the ſame Extrauagant,where the holy Pope dilateth of the great perill and ſpirituall preiudice which followeth vpon the admitting of Prelates to the dignity and office they claime,and would aſſume to themſelues before they haue made lawfull proofe of ſuch their promotion, and orderly calling to place of gouernement. For remouing of which inconuenience, the Pope ordained that no Biſhop or ſuperiour Prelate promoted by the Sea Apoſtolike,ſhould [b] be receiued to the dignitie and prelature beſtowed vpon him, before he ſhew the Letters of the ſame Sea, for teſtimonie of ſuch his Eccleſiaſticall preferment.

One of the 6. of Apill 1599. the other of the 17. of August 1601.

(b) *Nauar in c. accepta de reſtitu. ſpoliat. oppoſi. 8. nu. 39.*

Moreouer,if our aduerſaries ſhall denie M. *Blackwell* to be any like superiour Prelate, as is vnderstood in the Extrauagant: we answer, that granting it to be true which they say, although for the Reasons aforegoing, the same may seem somewhat incongruent: neuerthelesse other Popes who haue sithence succeeded, haue in such cases extended the same prohibition and penalties to inferiour Prelates, as writeth [c] *Adzore*, and citeth for instance the constitutions of [d] *Paulus tertius*, and [e] *Iulius tertius*. And certes, we are of opinion, that there is no man of vnderstanding, who shal consider the ample iurisdictiō that our Archpriest carrieth ouer the whole secular Cleargie, but will easily thinke that he may well be included vnder the name of a superiour Prelate, specially if he reflect vpon the wordes immediatly ensuing, *Quocunq; nomine censeantur*, by what title or name soeuer the superiour Prelate be called.

(c) Par. 1. Instit. mor. li. 5 ca. 2. queritur. 5.
(d) Constitut. quæ incipit, Cum nobis.
(e) Const. quæ incipit, Sanctissimis.

Beside, there are many braunches of his authoritie which do either equall or exceede the iurisdiction of a Bishop in the same points. For demonstration, S. *Thomas* writeth [f] that the secular cleargie are not bound to obey their Bishops, but in matters that belong to their Cleargie state, and not in the generall disposition and course of their liues: this being, by the opinion of the same Saint and greatest Clarke, that kind of obedience which the religious vow and ow to their Prelate, and is an ouerplus to that which the Secular owe and are bound to render to their Bishops. But the iurisdiction that the *Constitutiue Letter* giueth to our Archpriest ouer all the Seminarie Priestes of our nation, residing in England or Scotland, is to direct, admonish, reprehend, and chastise them whithout limitation in or for what: yea as him selfe affirmed to me, at the first shewing of the *Constitutiue Letter*, we were bound to obey him in all things. So that in this point his iurisdiction cannot be lesse, and may with facilitie be vnderstood to be more then Episcopall ouer vs.

(f) Quodlibet. 10. art. 10. ad 3 & Tolet. de 7 pecc. mort. c. 21. Ibidem.

Againe, the forme of the *Constitutiue Letter* imparteth iurisdiction to our Archpriest to heare and determine our doubts and controuersies, and may take away our faculties if we impugne or disobey his resolution, or shew our selues vnquiet in any thing he shall commaund. A soueraigntie, which if it doth not surpasse, yet certainly it is not inferiour to the amplest authoritie in this kind, that euer any Bishop or Archbishop had in our countrie: specially, if it be considered, that the hearing and determining of our doubts and controuersies, are like to be and must be (the dangers of the time so enforcing) demeaned without aduocate, without pleading, without legall processe, without tribunall,

bunall, or before any other Iudge then the Archpriest himselfe, who, as matters haue hitherto happened, hath bene a chiefe partie in all the differences.

Further, the *Constitutiue Letter* communicateth iurisdiction to our Archpriest, to remoue vs from the places of our residences being in Lay mens houses, and liuing vpon their charities. And the ninth instruction giueth him authoritie ouer the Catholicke Laity to remoue the Priests they keepe, and assigne them others in their roome. The words of the said instruction are, *Utriq; scilicet Sacerdotes incolæ seu parochi, & Domini laici apud quos viuunt, scire debebunt in potestate vestra esse pro maiori Dei gloria, Sacerdotes ab vna domo vel residentia in aliam mutare, neque ægrè quisquam id ferre debebit, aut obluctari, sed Dei gloriæ, animarumq; saluti suum gustum postponere.* Both the Priests that are resident, and the Lay persons with whom they reside, must know, that for the greater glorie of God, you haue power and iurisdiction to change Priestes from one house or residence to another, and that neither of them ought to take it hardly or striue against it, but to conquer and subordinate his or their liking to the glorie of God and health of soules. A facultie so little second to the authoritie of the highest Archbishop in the world, that it may be a question, or rather no question, whether, circumstances considered, it be not greater then Papall, our own and our benefactors liues depending thereon. Our own liues, for that, put from our acquainted harbour, many of vs vs do not know where next to hide our heads: theirs, in regard that such remoues by authoritie, can hardly, or not hardly be kept secret: and growing to be knowne, our patrons that harboured vs of charitie, become discouered, and by euery base and hungry companion that shall get knowledge of the matter, may informe her Maiesties Officers, and procure their houses to be searched, and their goods to be seazed on, their seruants examined, their children rifled, their wiues throwne out of doores, their lands confiscated, themselues committed to prison, arraigned, conuicted, executed, and their family for euer after vtterly ruined and ouerthrowne.

A pretext soonest deuised, and a readie meane to help the Iesuites or their auowed friends to the best places, & to wreak their displeasure vpon whosoeuer

Arg. D. Tho. 2. 2. q. 104. ar. 5. cor. Et Caiet. ibidē ad secundum dubium. & in Tractatu. 9. de vinculo obedientiæ. q. vnica Grassius p. 1. li. 2. ca. 18. nu. 11. & 12. Innocentius, Abbas, Felinus & alij quos ibi citat.

And here the oportunitie of the place offereth an occasion to speak a word or two, in answer to that which father *Parsons* obiecteth and inculcateth in his bookes and writings against vs, to wit, that we should affirme *that the Pope could not lawfully appoint such a kind of subordination ouer vs:* and likewise that *his Holinesse could not assigne vs a Superiour without our priuity and consent.* Assertions which hitherto I

In the bill of Complaint, of the tenth of Ianuary 1599. In the letter of pious griefe. In the Apologie, and in the Appendix.

cannot find by the ſearch I haue made,in any bookes of ours: neuertheleſſe we do not deny touching the firſt, but that ſome of vs haue ſaid by way of reaſoning, yet ſtill with reſeruation of our dutie to the Sea Apoſtolicke and his Holineſſe, that we did not conceiue how his Holineſſe could giue authoritie to our Archprieſt to place and diſplace Prieſts liuing of temporall almes in Catholike houſes,ſith by the laws of our Countrie,the entertainers muſt and do venter their liues and all that they are worth in the action:and that the Prieſts alſo, who are ſo remoued, cannot but receiue thereby ſome flaw or blemiſh in their credit, as being reputed vnfit or inſufficient for the place they were remoued from,and conſequently much hindred for getting other places,and in the meane,not vnlike to fall into the hands of the enemy for want of conuenient maintenance or harbour to ſhroude themſelues. And now if this doctrine ſeem vnſound or abſurd, or other then moſt conſcionable, we requeſt father *Parſons* and father *Garnet* (whom we no whit doubt to be the deuiſers of the facultie, for that we cannot thinke that euer ſuch a rigour was of his Holineſſe ſetting downe, or euer fully vnderſtood by him with the truth of all circumſtances) to inſtruct vs in the difficultie, and manifeſt the grounds of the contrarie vnto vs, and we promiſe by Gods grace,that their labour ſhall not be loſt, but that they ſhall haue vs forthwith to change our opinion, and to yeeld them thankes for the charitie.

Concerning the other aſſertion, that we ſhould ſay, *His Holineſſe could not aſſigne vs a Superiour without our priuity and conſent*, we take it to be more then all our aduerſaries can proue that we euer ſpake, And as for the citing of the [g] Canons that permit or authorize the Cleargie to chuſe their Superiour, they were not cited by any of vs to the end to proue that his Holineſſe could not appoint vs a Superiour, without asking our voices,or acquainting vs firſt with the deſſigne, but were only alleaged,to ſhew that it was a cuſtome receiued in holy Church,& not yet diſcontinued euery where,that the Cleargy ſhould haue the chuſing of their owne Superiour, and which being a fauour allowed to many by the Sea Apoſtolicke, and by cenſure of common reaſon,a great furtherance to peace and of electing the fitteſt perſon; we could not thinke if his Holineſſe had bene rightfully informed,but that his paſtorall loue and benignitie would haue graunted vs (venturing our liues as we do for the primacy of his ſeate,and oppreſſed with many ſorts of afflictions) the chuſing of our Superiour, or at leaſt not to haue giuen (as the *Conſtitutiue Letter* ſpecifieth) the perpetuall election

(g) *Diſt.61.ca. Nullus inuitis & diſt.63.ca.ſi in plebibus & ca.1.de electione.*

ction of him to the Cardinall Protector, a stranger vnto vs, vnacquainted with the difficulties of our countrey, and distant by more then a thousand miles from vs. To this end were the Canons alleaged, as the circumstances and drift of the places where they are alleaged, do witnesse. And therefore we cannot but feare a sinister intention in father *Parsons*, and in our other aduersaries, that thus adde to and wrest our wordes to the sense and purpose which themselues like best. But to returne.

The *Constitutiue Letter* giueth also authoritie to our Archpriest *to take away faculties granted by whom soeuer*, and he hath *de facto* taken away such faculties from some of vs, as his Holinesse himselfe immediatly gaue to the parties from whom he took them. A larger iurisdiction then any Metropolitane, Patriarke or legate Cardinal in the world hath, as we thinke, adioyned to his person or office. Which supereminencie, together with the reasons aforegoing, seemeth most apparantly to enforce, that M. *Blackwell* cannot be but reputed such a superiour Prelate as is intended by the words of the Extrauagant. *Episcopi & alij Prelati superiores quocunque nomine censeantur*: Bishops and other superiour Prelates by what name soeuer they are called. Or if we should denominate the authoritie according as it is practised, we must needes cal it a high prelacy, because it either dispenseth with the law of God, nature, and man, or violateth the same.

IT either dispenseth with the law of God or violateth the same, because what God commaundeth our Archpriest forbiddeth: for example, God commandeth, *Libera eum qui iniuriam patitur*, deliuer him who suffereth iniurie. Againe, *Liberate vi oppressum de manu calumniatoris*. Deliuer ye the violently oppressed from the hand of the calumniator. And in another place, *Erue illos qui ducuntur ad mortem*. Rescue them who are (vniustly) lead to death. But now our Archpriest prohibiteth vnder heauy penalties, euen when our good names were rather in the act of dying, then in leading to death, and after the Vniuersitie of Paris had giuen sentence for vs; not onely our lay friends, or our fellow Priests, but also our ghostly fathers (who by priuiledge of that office, knew, saw, and were feelingly sure of the wrong and calumniation obiected) to defend vs by word or writing directly or indirectly, although they were bound by the foresaid law of God, and by the right of truth, charitie and [h] iustice, to speake in our purgation. The words of our Archpriests decree and prohibition were these: *Prohibe-*

Eccl. 4. *Ier.* 22. *Prou.* 24.

(h) *Nau. in Manu ca.* 24. *nu.* 17. 18. & 22 & *ca.* 14. *n.* 10. *Decretum* 18. *Octob.* 1600. § 4.

mus in virtute sanctæ obedientiæ omnibus præsbyteris, etiam sub pœna suspensionis atque interdicti, (quorum absolutionem nobisipsis reseruamus) addo etiam amissionis omnium facultatum ipso facto incurrendarum: Laicis verò sub pœna interdicti ipso quoque facto incurrendi, ne quisquam illam præteritam inobedientiam (vnde tanta inter nos extitit pacis perturbatio) quouis modo, verbo vel scripto directè vel indirectè defendere præsumat. We prohibite all Priests in vertue of holy obedience, and vnder paine of suspension & interdict, (the absolution of which we retaine to our selues) I adde also vnder paine of leesing all faculties, to be incurred in the deede it selfe: and the laity vnder paine of interdict to be likewise presently incurred, that no one, any maner of way, in word or in writing, directly or indirectly, presume to defend the foresaid disobedience past, which bred so great contention among vs.

§.3. Which part of our Archpriests decree, may seeme the more seuere, in that he himselfe in the paragraph next before (hauing sentenced and denounced to the whole Realme, that we were truly and really disobedient to the Sea Apostolicke, and rebellious against his office instituted by the same Sea: would immediatly after (the condemnation bearing no more truth then the foregoings haue shewed) forbid vs and all others, in the manner as is set downe, not to defend that disodience by name, *Which bred so great contention among vs*, which as the whole world knows, was for that we would not yeeld our selues guiltie of the crimes, and most grieuous abhominations that were obiected and maintained by the Societie and their adherents against vs. And indeede had not father *Lyster*, father *Garnet*, and father *Iones*, with some other, most dispiteously, and alike vniustly massacred our good names, or our Archpiest not approued and patronized their infinite wrongs done against vs, vndoubtedly all had bene at quiet long since, and neuer growen to the thousand part of that most rufull excesse, to which the violent prosecution of their wrongs, and the vnconscionable seeking to oppresse vs by strong hand, haue caried the contention, and do still alas increase and nourish the flame.

Saint[i] *Antonine*,[k] *Nauar*, and other [l] authors of greatest name, affirme that a man may with safe conscience follow and practise that which one Doctour of fame resolueth to be lawfull, so that it be neither repugnant to the authoritie of expresse Scripture, nor decree of holy Church, as we trow the censure of Paris is not, nor will our aduersaries euer proue it to be.

Againe [m] *Salon*, and all the schoole Diuines write, that to be a probable

(i) *Prima. par. titu. tertio. c.* 10 §. 10. *reg.* 4.
(k) *In ca. cum contingat de rescriptis, remed.* 2. *nu.* 30. *& in manu. ca.* 27. *nu.* 282.
(l) *Albert. Magnus. Panormit. Imola, Felinus, Alexander, Neno, Ioãnes Andreas, Dominicus Perusius,* cited in the places aforesaid.
(m) *Tom. primo q.* 63. *art.* 4. *contro* 2. *conclu.* 4. *vers. est hic. & idem colligitur ex tomo* 2. *in disp. de trib. & vest. ar.* 3. *contro.* 8. *in principio.*

bable and secure opinion, and may boldly be practised, without all scruple, which men of learning, wisedome, vertue, and well experienced in that kind of matter, shall agree vpon, and set downe tobe true. And if two or three men of this sort, make a security in conscience, as none will deny; how much more secure and voide of all feare may our friends and our selues be, in the vngrounded imputation of enormous disobedience and other crimes, when as not onely three or foure of like qualitie, but more then three and foure, the whole selected companie of an ancient and most renowned Vniuersitie, wherof also three of them were the Kings readers, and all the residue of reuerend place and authoritie, chosen by the whole facultie to resolue the difficulties, that come from all partes farre and neare vnto them, did both free vs, and vnder publike testimonie attestate our cleerenesse? The question, the answer of the Vniuersitie, and the decree of our Archpriest follow.

ANno Domini millesimo sexcentessimo, die tertio May, propositum fuit facultati theologiæ Parisiensi, quod literis cuiusdam Illmi Cardinalis, quidam Superior Ecclesiasticus in regno quodam constitutus est, cum titulo & dignitate Archipresbyteri, vt haberet authoritatem & iurisdictionem supra omnes alios presbyteros in eadem regno commorantes. Cardnalis autem in illis suis literis declarauit, se id fecisse iuxta voluntatem & beneplacitum summi Pontificis.

Multi autem ex illis Presbyteris recusarunt subsignare authoritati eiusdem Archipresbyteri, priusquam ipse obtinuisset literas Apostolicas confirmationis suæ tenorem continentes, tum quia nouum omnino erat & in ecclesia Catholica hactenus inauditum, illud genus regiminis, vt Archipresbyter vniuerso regno preesset, & talem iurisdictionem haberet in singulos eius regni Sacerdotes: tum etiam, quia ex quibusdam verbis illarum literarum Illmi Cardinalis visi sunt sibi videre, talem Archipresbyterum & authoritatem eius ex falsa informatione à summo Pontifice fuisse concessam: tum denique, quia in electione eiusdem Archipresbyteri, & consiliariorum eius, magnam aduerterunt extitisse personarum acceptionem. Propter quas & alias nonnullas rationes, Sacerdotes illi miserunt ad summum Pontificem nuntios, qui has suas difficultates ei aperirent, vnaq; significarent, se paratissimos esse in toto hoc negotio, aliisq; omnibus, suæ sanctitati semper obedire.

Archipresbyter vero, & qui ab eius parte stant, alios Sacerdotes schismatis accusant, quod literis Cardinalis quas etiam ex summi Pontificis voluntate exaratas dicit, parere detrectauerint.

Quæstio igitur est, an illi sacerdotes sint schismatici? Et si non sint, an grauiter saltem peccauerint?

Viri Principes facultatis theologiæ Parisiensis selecti à tota facultate, congregati in domo maioris Apparitoris sui, anno & die suprascripto, re maturè considerata, ita censuerunt.

Primò, illos sacerdotes qui distulerunt obedire ob dictas causas, non esse schismaticos.

Secundo censuerunt illos, eo facto in se spectato, non peccasse prorsus.

De mandato dominorum Decani, & Magistrorum nostrorum deputatorum & selectorum sacratissimæ facultatis theologiæ Parisiensis.

Delacourt.

The English.

IN the yeare of our Lord 1600. vpon the third day of May, it was proposed to the facultie of Diuines of the Vniuersitie of Paris, that by the letters of a most illustrious Cardinall, an ecclesiasticall Superiour was constituted in a certaine kingdome, with the title and dignitie of an Archpriest, to haue authoritie and iurisdiction ouer all other priests residing in that kingdome. This Cardinall did also declare in those his letters, that he did it according to the wil and good liking of the Pope.

Notwithstanding many of these Priests refused to subscribe to the authoritie of the said Archpriest, before he had obtained letters from the Sea Apostolicke, containing the tenour of his confirmation, as well because that kind of gouernement was altogether new in Gods Church, and hitherto neuer heard of, that an Archpriest should haue charge ouer a whole kingdome, and such iurisdiction ouer euerie Priest in that Realme: then also for that it seemed to them by certaine wordes of the Cardinals letters, that the Archpriest and his authoritie was graunted by false information: then lastly, because they noted great partialitie in the choise of the Archpriest and of his Counsellors. Vpon which, and some other reasons, these Priests sent messengers to the Pope, for laying open vnto him these their difficulties, and therewithall to signifie their greatest readines, as in this matter, so euermore in all other to obey his Holinesse.

The

The Archpriest and those who are of his side, accuse the other Priests of schisme, in that they deferred to obey the Cardinals letters, which moreouer he said were written according to his Holinesse mind and pleasure.

The question then is, whether these Priests be schismatickes, and if not, whether they did commit at the least some grieuous sinne?

The head & chiefe men of the facultie of diuinitie in Paris, chosen out of the whole companie, assembled together in the house of their seniour Beedle, in the yeare and day aboue written, after full and maturest consideration had of the matter, gaue this censure.

First, that those Priests who vpon the aboue named causes deferred to obey, were no schismatickes.

Secondly, that they commited no sinne at all in that fact, in it selfe considered.

By commaundement of our Deane and Maisters deputed and selected by the whole facultie of diuinitie in Paris.

Delacourt.

The Decree of our Archpriest in prohibition of the foresaid Censure.

IN *Dei nomine amen*: In the name of God Amen. We *George Blackwell* Archpriest of England, and Protonotarie Apostolicall, by the authoritie sufficiently and lawfully committed vnto vs, do strictly commaund in vertue of obedience, and vnder paine of suspension from diuine offices, and losse of all faculties in the fact it selfe to be incurred, all ecclesiasticall persons, and also all lay Catholickes vnder paine of being interdicted semblably in the fact it selfe to be incurred, that neither directly nor indirectly, they maintaine or defend in word or in writing, the censure of the Vniuersitie of Paris, whether it be truly giuen or forged, whether vpon true information or otherwise, as being preiudiciall to the dignitie of the 29. Maij. 1600

Sea Apoſtolicke, and expreſly contrarie to his Holineſſe Breue, and to the ſentence iudicially giuen by the two Cardinals appointed iudges in our cauſe, and to our common peace ſo much wiſhed for by his Holines. And this we inuiolably command to be obſerued vnder the pains afore ſpecified, & greater alſo according to his Holines pleaſure.

In this Decree, there occurre many things that ſeeme very ſtrange: namely, that the ſentence of the Vniuerſitie *is preiudiciall to the dignity of the Sea Apoſtolicke, and expreſly contrarie to his Holineſſe Breue*. O Lord Chriſt! O Sir, our Superiour! who are we, or what may our cauſe be, that not to be adiudged renegates from the Sea Apoſtolike, or traitors to God by ſinne, muſt be accounted *a preiudice to the dignitie of the ſea Apoſtolicke*? ſtrange, and ſo ſtrange as it aſtonieth. You ſay, that the ſentence clearing vs of ſchiſme and ſinne, is *expreſly contrarie to his Holineſſe Breue*. We beſeech you to quote the wordes, to ſhew the place: for if it be *expreſly contrarie*, as you ſay, then the contrarietie muſt needes conſiſt in plaine termes, not in deductions or inferences vpon the tenour or purport of the Breue. Or if this much be not to be ſhewed (as al the labor vnder heauẽ can neuer ſhew it, becauſe neither of the two wordes [ſchiſme, or ſinne] is vſed in the Breue, nor we that prolonged the yeelding of our obedience, any where ſpecified in the ſame:) we then pray you to frame the arguments which conclude and infer ſo much. For verily, we for our parts, do not ſee (as is ſaid before* in the place where we haue diſcourſed of this very point) how any ſuch
Pag. 109. 110 & 111. inferẽce cã with vnderſtãding be made. Or if vnderſtãding be miſ-led to make ſuch an inference: yet we proteſt that we cãnot cõceiue how the authorities that contradict the verity of ſuch an inference, & which we haue alleaged before, cã poſſibly be anſwered or colourably ſhifted
*Pag. 58. & ſequentibus. off. Or were all the Canoniſts deceiued, & their authorities worth nothing, yet if M. *Blackwell* be ſuch a ſuperiour Prelate, as is contained vnder the wordes of the former Extrauagant, and as his former faculties and largeſt iuriſdiction muſt in all reaſon make him: then is it dead ſure, that no ſuch inference can be made, becauſe that cannot be ſchiſme or ſinne, which the Extrauagant decreeth, and commaundeth to be obſerued, vnder the paine of leeſing the fruites of their eccleſiaſticall liuings, that ſhall preſume to tranſgreſſe the precept.

And as we cannot conceiue how the cenſure of the Vniuerſitie could *be preiudiciall to the dignitie of the Sea Apoſtololicke, or expreſly contrary to his Holineſſe Breue*: ſo can we leſſe imagine, how the ſame cenſure can be reckened *preiudiciall to our common peace, ſo much wiſhed*

for

for by his Holinesse, vnlesse our purgation of schisme and sinne, be such a barre or aduerse hinderance of peace, as the one cannot stand or be effected except the other be repealed. Which lacke of charitie, howsoeuer it may sort with the kind of peace, that perhaps some of our aduersaries affect, whose passion of ouerweening of themselues, is so puissant, as they can hardly, if at all, count that peace for peace, wherein our discredit is not proclaimed: yet we are sure that the stiffe seeking of our dishonour cannot sort with that *peace which his Holinesse wisheth to be among vs*. For this being a charitable peace, & charity *not reioycing* 1. Cor. 13.
vpon iniquitie, but reioycing with truth, the fathers of the Societie, especially our Superior, should rather congratulate that we were acquited by publike sentence of a famous vniuersitie, in the crimes obiected vpon errour, then by opinionatiue defending their rash and temerarious iudgement, make *nouissima peiora prioribus*, their last actions worse Math. 12.
then their first against vs.

Concerning the other reason which our Archpriest alleageth also, as part of the cause why he did so seuerely prohibite the defending of the censure of Paris, viz. for that the same was *preiudicial to the sentence iudicially giuen by the two Cardinals appointed iudges in our cause*: we know not where to take the first exception, the whole and euery word thereof lyeth so loose and open. Father *Parsons* in the Apologie, will Fol. 133.
not haue *the said sentence giuen so much by way of a iudiciall sentence, as by way of a letter, vnder the two Cardinals their hands and seales*. So that if we may beleeue father *Parsons*, the sentence was not iudicially giuē. Neither were the two Cardinals appointed iudges to decide whether our deferring (for the causes rehearsed in the question) to receiue M. *Blackwell* our Superiour vpon view of the Cardinals Letter, were schisme or sinne, the matter meerely considered in it selfe, abstracted from all circumstances: nor yet were their Graces appointed iudges in the cause of any one of our whole companie, saue only in the cause of M. *Bishop* and M. *Charnocke*, as the title of the decree, and the decree it selfe doth witnes. Againe, their Graces sentence doth not signifie, that they inflicted the punishment vpon our said two brethren, for refusing to subscribe to the new authoritie, or for comming to Rome; because there is no such thing set downe: nay the contrarie is expressed, in that the causes for which they were restrained from comming into England, or for going into the kingdomes of Scotland and Ireland, were onely (as the words of the decree do testifie) *for maintaining controuersies with other men of their owne order, and for that it appeared in no case*

expedient for the English cause that they should returne into England. Now to mainetaine controuersies with other men of their owne order, and to appeare not to be expedient that they should forthwith returne into England, are things different from deferring their obedience to the Archpriest, and from sending or going to Rome, for fuller knowledge of his Holinesse pleasure, and to lay open our difficulties vnto him. Besides, if the cause, in which the two Cardinals were appointed Iudges, was the refusall to subscribe to the authoritie of the Archpriest instituted by the Letters of Cardinall *Caietane*, and for sending to Rome: then was Cardinall *Caietane* appointed iudge in the cause that most nearely concerned himselfe, a thing against law, and so intollerable in the ministring of iustice, as his Holinesse would neuer haue assigned him iudge therein, nor the Cardinall for edification sake, haue vsed the office, especially in designing the punishment. Or to grant (which is no more so, then a foxe is a fearnebush) that the two Cardinals had giuen sentence in the same cause before, and otherwise, then did the vniuersitie. What then? must the censure of a renowned vniuersitie, one of the most famous in Christendome, be so lightly set by, abandoned, detested, and that in a matter of fact, as whosoeuer shall either defend or maintaine it directly or indirectly, in word or writing, must, if he be a priest, be presently in the fact it self suspended from diuine offices, and leese his faculties? or if such a delinquent be a lay Catholike, he must in like manner be interdicted *ipso facto?* A rigour, as the like whereof all the Annales and records of all the Prelates actions since Christs time hitherto, cannot, as we assure our selues, yeeld one instance or neare example.

See more of this point *pag.* 101. *& sequentibus.*

But that, which of all other points in the decree, seemeth to be most out of rule, is the imposing of so heauy penalties for the direct or indirect maintenance of the censure: *Whether the vniuersitie gaue the same vpon true information or otherwise.* This, this appeared so strange, as we hardly durst beleeue our owne eyes, before we read the wordes ouer and ouer gaine: nor should we so haue beleeued the same, had the decree not come forth in the hand writing of our Superior, and vnder his seale. For, was it euer heard, that one Prelate, and of no higher calling thē an Archpriest & Protonotary Apostolical, being also but a Bachelor of Diuinity, & neuer reader in the facultie, would not only, so ouerrule the cēsure of a whole vniuersitie, but so farfoorth to reiect it, as to bereaue Priests of their faculties, to suspend them from the altar, to interdict the Laitie, man and woman, yong and old, vulgar and noble, whosoeuer

whosoeuer shall maintaine the same so much as indirectly, and this, *Whether the information giuen to the vniuersity were true or false.* Was it euer heard, that Priests, hauing no other meanes to maintaine themselues by, then by vse of their faculties, and liuing euery houre in danger of death for profession of their faith, should be spoiled of their faculties, disabled to do good to others, put from the altar, robbed of their maintenaunce, debarred from Sacraments, and incurre all these spirituall punishments, for defending the censure of a most learned, famous, and Catholike vniuersitie, in a matter neither decided by any decree of holy Church, nor contrarie to any expresse authoritie of holy Scripture? Was it euer heard, that men and women, leesing all their goods, and two third parts of their lands, onely because they will not go to a contrarie Church, and dayly hazarding their liues and the vtter ruine of their whole posterity, for professiõ of the Romane faith, for receiuing Priests, for releeuing their necessities, for the glorie of Gods Church, for preseruation of Religion, for good example to their euenchristen, should be exiled from vse of all sacraments, put from being present at diuine Seruice, and dying not to be interred in Christian manner, and to be thus disgraced, maligned, defamed and spiritually afflicted for adhering to their friends, approued to be honest by long triall, for taking part with their ghostly fathers in a matter of fact, discussed and determined to be lawfull by publicke censure of a renowned vniuersitie? Was it euer heard, that the like measure hath bene met by an Archpriest to Priests, by a Superiour to his subiects, by a father to his children, by a labourer to his brethen coadiutors, by one liuing in persecution, against his fellowes in the same persecution, and this by the counsell and direction of religious persons, who must not be counted *sicut cæteri homines*, as the rest of workemen in the same vineyard? O heauen! O earth! are ye not astonied, or do ye not close your eyes, from beholding the iniustice, the inhumanitie, the vnnaturalnesse, the oppression, the affliction vnspeakeable, enough to stumble any that are not well staied by grace?

The penalties following the censure of interdiction.

But besides these exceptions of our Archpriest against the censure, father *Parsons* as one being inured with the trade of deuising shiftes, descendeth in the Apologie to other particulars, and telleth vs that the *said definition of Paris in very deede very little releeueth our case, and that we might well haue spared to print it. but for making a vaine flourish with ostentation of an Academicall sentence.* And why so? Marie because *the information that was giuen to the Doctours, was wrong and defectuous,*

Fol. 115. & sequentib.

and that there was no man of the Archpriestes side to reply or tell the tale as it ought to be, and tell them how false the information was. Is all this true? then we pray tell vs what man was at Rome, when you laboured and informed the Cardinall and his Holinesse about instituting the subordination, *to reply or tell them how false the information was?* Had not you father *Parsons*, the drawing of the *Constitutiue Letter*, the setting downe of the instructions and additions? The day of iudgement will declare you had, howsoeuer you cloude matters now from the sight of those that will not see light when the Sunne shineth. Were there any Priestes in England which were to liue vnder the subordination that had a part, a voice, or were made priuy to the designe, saue happily some two or three, of whom father *Garnet* your inciter and aduertiser stood wholly possessed, and had the commaunding of their pens, tongues and trauels?

Fol. 98. 99. & 117. & alibi. You write in seuerall places of the Apologie, that both the Laitie and Priestes desired by their letters, and expresly demaunded of his Holinesse a subordination among Priests. Shew their letters, or giue vs some secret notice of their names, that the truth may be knowne, or we shall not beleeue you, but take thi , as we must do innumerable other, for escapes of your pen and memorie. You write likewise, *that if those reuerend learned men had bene indifferently instructed in the case how it passed, they would haue bene of a farre other mind and iudgement then to cleare such a fact.* And we do as verily beleeue, that if his Holinesse *had bene indifferently informed how matters passe* in England betweene the secular Priestes and the fathers of the Societie, he would haue appointed a farre other forme of Subordination, then such as inlisteth but one side of the contenders, and maketh those that were their oppressors before, more potent to exercise their splene, and exempteth them from out the compasse of the iurisdiction appointed ouer the other. Rome, father *Parsons*, cannot perswade vs, that euer his Holinesse pious and tender conscience would suffer you to sit as you do, at sterne, making lawes for vs, chusing our Superiour, directing, gouerning and raigning as a Vice-pope ouer vs, had he bene indifferently giuen to vnderstand of our Princes hatefull auersion from you, and that not for your good deedes, or leauing the world, and the generall auersion likewise, that most of our Priests conceiue of your insinceritie in many matters, and truthlesse dealing. Finally you adde *that they would not haue cleared such a fact as hath caused so many sinfull scandals.* Here we must intreate you to name what kind of cause our action of

delay

delay was, of the ſinfull ſcandals that haue followed. You muſt needs range it (as we thinke) vnder that kind of cauſe, which is called *cauſa ſine qua non*, the cauſe without which the enſuing fact had not bene committed, which as you know, the Philoſophers terme, *ſtolidam cauſam*, a fooliſh cauſe. And ſure, if our bearing off, and ſending to Rome was lawfull in it ſelfe, as beſide the deciſion of Paris, the authorities before going do proue inuincibly: your reaſon, *for that ſuch our fact hath cauſed ſo many ſinfull ſcandals*, is weake & childiſh. For hath not the inſtitution of your owne order, approued by the Sea Apoſtolicke, to be good and holy, bene the cauſe *ſine qua non*, of many ſinfull ſcandals? the world will witneſſe, yea, in that many, ſome by their pens, ſome by their tongues, ſome after another maner, haue ſpoken and done that, which was very ſinfull, and which they would not haue done, had your order neuer bene founded. You know what the Prophet and the Apoſtle writeth, and of whom: *Ecce pono in Sion lapidem offenſionis & petram ſcandali*. Behold I put in Syon a ſtone of ſtumbling and a rocke of ſcandall. And yet we are more then ſure, that you will not inferre any of our Sauiours actions to be vnlawfull, albeit they cauſed many moſt ſinfull ſcandals in the kind of cauſe aboue mentioned. *Eſa.8. Rom.9.*

But now, let vs ſee how you ſhew the information giuen to the *Sorbon* Doctors to be *wrōg, defectuous, falſe & ſiniſtrous*. For euery of theſe is your own *Epitheton*. You make 6. exceptions to this purpoſe. The firſt is, that we in propoſing the queſtion, ſaid only, *that an eccleſiaſticall Superior was cōſtituted by the Letters of a moſt illuſtrious Cardinal, not telling the Doctors that he was Protector of the nation, which doth much increaſe* (as you ſay) *his credit for matters touching the country vnder his protectiō*. The inualidity of this exceptiō is refuted before: & the Cardinal not inſtituting the ſubordinatiō by any vertue of his Protectorſhip, but onely by commiſſion from his Holineſſe, what did the adding, or not adding that the Cardinall, who was his Holineſſe delegate in the action, was alſo Protector of the nation, import? ſith the inſtitution of the ſubordination did not belong to his office of Protectorſhip, and conſequently we not bound to obey his letter vntill he had prooued the commiſſion, becauſe *Literis cuiuſdam credendum eſt, de his quæ facere poteſt vel debet ratione officij ſui*. Beleefe & obedience ſaith *Speculator*, is a tribute due to be giuē to the letters of thoſe that cōmand the things, which appertaine to their office. So that, the ordaining of the ſubordination being a thing not belonging to the office of his Protectorſhip, we held it ſuperfluous to ſet downe in the ſtate of the queſtion, *Pag 66. & 67. De probati. §.3 nu.15.*

that the Cardinall who by his Letters instituted the subordination, was also the Protector of our nation. And whereas you say, that the adding of *being Protectour of the nation doth much increase his credit for matters touching the Country vnder his protection*: we say the same, if either you meane [by matters] such as belōg to the office of Protectorship, or do meane that the title of being Protector doth much increase his credit, though not so much as we were bound to beleeue and take his Graces word for warrantize of his Holines commission vnto him. But if you meane another, or greater increase of his credit then either of these, then we discent from you in opinion, and assure our selues, that ye can neuer make good by reason or authoritie that which you say herein.

Your second exceptiō. That we putting down the questiō, did but onely signifie that the Cardinall *did it according to the will and good liking of the Pope, but did not tell them that it was, expresso mandato, by his Holinesse expresse commandement, which the Cardinall setteth down clearly in his Letters.* Father, your little sincerity, or rather boldest audacitie amateth. For, where doth *the Cardinall cleerely set downe in his Letters,* that he receiued an expresse commaundement to erect a subordination? Certes, either your ignorance appeareth grosse and verie faultie, that would not ouerview the letter before you affirmed out of it a matter of such weight: or your audacitie in the affirmance: there being no such commandement. We graunt that the Cardinall in the beginning of his Letter maketh mention of an expresse commaundement receiued from his Holinesse to make peace in our countrey, to the example of the peace in the English Colledge, but what is this to an expresse commandement of erecting a subordination, especially so afflictiue & burdenous in our whole church? How litle these two do folow one another, and how the expresse commandement of doing the one, is not nor cannot be the expresse or tacitiue commandement of doing the other, the three first Propositions with sundry other places in our second Reason, do manifest and confirme aboundantly. When the Cardinall came in his Letter to appoint the Subordination, he made this entrance: *For so much as some men thinke it would not a little auaile to the making of peace, if a subordination were constituted among the English Priests, and the reasons yeelded by the Priests themselues* (which was but M. *Standish* onely, so farre as yet we know) *for the same, were approued by our holy Father: we following the most godly and most prudent will of his Holinesse, haue decreed to ordaine a subordination.* Where is the expresse commandement

Pag. 23 & 24.

commandement you talke of, and which, as you say, the Cardinall setteth downe clearely in his Letter, we meane, an expresse commandement of instituting a subordination? Verily we must answer you with a *Non est inuentus*, except you can lend vs a spirit to find that which is not. We propounded the question in as full or more large termes then the Cardinall vsed: for his Grace wrote *sequentes voluntatem, we following the most godly and prudent will of his Holinesse, haue decreed to ordaine a subordination.* And we, in the state of our question wrote, *that the Cardinal did also declare in his letters vnto us, that he decreed the subordinatiō iuxta voluntatem & beneplacitum, according to the will and good liking of his Holinesse.* So that where the Cardinall said, he did *institute the subordination following the will of his Holinesse*, we added that not onely he did it, *following his will*, but that also he did it *according to his Holinesse good will and pleasure*, which is somewhat more ample, or of greater emphasis.

Your third exception. *We concealed another thing vttered also in the Cardinals Letters, to wit, that a subordination was demaunded by Priests letters to his Holinesse.* What? did you dreame when you wrote this? for where, we pray, is it *vttered in the Cardinals letters, that Priests in their Letters to his Holinesse did demaund a Subordination?* Fie, what failings are these? must we thinke the cause you pleade, no better, but that it requireth to be vpholden with such apparant falsities? The Prophet saith, in detestation of idols, *Lingua ipsorum polita à fabro, ipsa etiam inaurata & inargentata, falsa sunt, & non possunt loqui.* Their tongue is polished by the Carpenter, and themselues being gilded and siluered ouer, are (notwithstanding) counterfeit and cannot speake. We know not what Art hath polished your pen, but certaine we are, that howsoeuer, the counterfeits she draws, shew faire to the outward view, yet looked into and examined, they are false, and, as idols, speake little truth. Againe, how shall we know, that *his Holinesse allowed of the reasons?* You set it so downe indeede, in the Cardinals Letter, and we beleeue it so farre, as it is meant by the reasons touched in M. *Standish* his oration to his Holinesse, a bird (as all men thinke) of your owne hatching: but if you vnderstand by the words, the reasons that the Priests yeelded in their Letters to his Holinesse, when they demanded a subordination of him, as the words themselues must needes inferre: then we do not beleeue it, because we cannot thinke, that any of our fellow Priests did euer write such letters to his Holinesse. But let it be true, that *his Holinesse allowed of the reasons which the Priestes made in their*

Baruc. 6.

Letters vnto him for a ſubordination: yet we know,and not onely by his Holineſſe words to ſome of our brethren, but euen by the record of your owne reports, that his Holineſſe yeelding to graunt a ſubordination, would not aſſigne the particular ſubordination till he had receiued ſignification from the prieſts in Englãd,what kind of ſubordination we liked, and beſt agreed with the ſtate of our countrey. And thus hauing his Holineſſe word for warrant, related alſo by your ſelfe to ſome of our companie: had we not good reaſon (we aske the indifferent and all of iudgement) to thinke (we not aduertiſing his Holineſſe of the kind of gouernement we thought fitteſt) that ſurreption was vſed in the information, and conſequently to delay as all lawes permit,the ſubmiſſion of our obedience, vntill the truth and ſtate of matters were better knowne? Vndoubtedly theſe,howſoeuer they appeare to other, conuinced our vnderſtanding, and bid vs not to feare ſinne, neither to doubt but that his Holineſſe would take in good part,if not thankefully,our ſending vnto him about the premiſſes.

An holy prudence, that thoſe who were to obey and bore the heate and burden of the day ſhould make choiſe of the ſubordination and ſuperiour.

Your fourth exception: *We ſaid* (in putting downe the ſtate of the queſtion vnto the Vniuerſitie) *that many of vs refuſed to ſubſcribe to the authoritie as though we had bene a great multitude, or the maior part.* Good ſir where do you reade that this word [*multi many*] muſt be taken for *a great multitude or for the maior part of that companie whereof it was ſpoken?* The Canon hath [a] *Pluralis locutio duorum numero contenta eſt*:the ſpeaking in the plurall number, is verified in the number of two. And *Panormitane* writeth,that [b] *Duo dicuntur multi*,two are called many. And although the words [*many & few*] do take [c] their moſt proper and relatiue denomination of the number whereof they are auerred to be *many or few*: yet no doubt, fewer after this account would beare the name of *many*, then *ſo great a multitude or maior part* as you require, and ſeeme to inferre that the Doctours vnderſtood by our words in the propoſing of the queſtion, and that they made it one of the cauſes why they cleered vs from all ſinne in the nature of our fact.

(a) 4 q. 3. § *ſi teſtes.*

(b) *In ca. ad noſtram de reb. ec. alienat. nu. 5.*

(c) *Gloſſ. in ca. Latores de Cler. excõ. vel depoſ. verb. Multitudinem.*

Vndoubtedly ſir,to make that this your fourth exception ſhould cary any weight,it is of neceſſity that you firſt proue(and yet it is a thing which you can neuer proue) the ſmall or great number of the refuſers to ſubſcribe,to be of that intrinſecal aliance or eſſence with our fact,as it made the ſame in his owne nature ſinne or no ſinne. For if the nature of our fact in delaying our obedience,and ſending to Rome,were not changed by the ſmall or great number of vs, who in ſuch ſort prolon-

ged

ged to receiue the authoritie : what skilleth it, or what difference can it put, the fact considered in it selfe, (for with that limitation the vniuersitie deliuered their censure) whether the doers were many or few, one or a thousand, this being but an accident and a circumstance, and of no such omnipotencie, as could possibly change the nature of the fact in it selfe considered? Further, if notwithstanding that which we haue said, the exception must still appeare of force (as all that are of iudgement do wel see, it cannot) yet the same is doubly satisfied in our answere to the fourth obiection of our aduersaries, to which place for auoiding of vnnecessarie repetition we referre the Reader. *Pag. 92.*

Now that which you adde for explication or better proofe of the exception, bewraieth a worse conscience. Your words be these: *That not being the twentieth part at the beginning of those that admitted the gouernement, if we haue increased our number since, it hath bene by as false information as this was to the Doctors of Paris, and by perswading them to the participation of our libertie and freedome from all gouernement, which is a sore baite for yong men, as all the world knoweth.* Is this your charitable iudgement father, that neither we, nor our brethren had better ends in our actions then you specifie, and which you recken by verdite of the whole world, a *sore baite for yong men?* But let vs see, now you haue passed your censure ouer vs, how true the same is. The censure consisteth of these three points : first, that we seduced our brethren by *false information:* then, that we perswaded them *to the participation of our libertie:* thirdly, that *this libertie and freedome from all gouernement, was a sore baite for yong men, as all the world knoweth.* So that you make the meanes, by which we drue our brethren to our side, to be sleights and leasings: and our end, why we drew them, no other then to haue them our fellowes in libertie, and in such a libertie *as all the world knowes, to be a sore temptation to yong men.*

Touching the first, what *false information* could this be in particular by which you say we beguiled our brethen? were not all our brethren who haue since turned for vs, or manifested themselues to be of our mind, both eye and eare witnesses of all matters as well as our selues? were they not euermore lookers on, & priuier to our aduersaries proceedings, then any of vs, from whom they were more auerted? Surely if you know what the particular information was, by which we won thē to our part, you may do well to set the same downe: or if in case you do not know the information in particular, then we aske you with what conscience do you so confidently auerre it to be false? not knowing it what it was? When you shall open this much, we doubt not, but that we shall be also able to giue you and the world satisfaction to the contrarie. In the meane, we deny your speeches to be true. But what say we? do we deny them to be true, sith you affirme no more, but *that we increased our number by as false information, as was the information which we gaue to the vniuersitie*, and which being true, as we maintaine, and the other information to our brethren, by your owne wordes, *but as false*, we are content if this much do please, to allow the comparison? Neuerthelesse the truth is, that the information and motiues which inuited some of our brethren to manifest themselues, and drew others to amend their former hastie errour in receiuing so fruitlesse an authoritie, vpon the sole warrantize of the Cardinals Letter, was times deciphering of matters, the loue of truth, the direction of their owne consciences, the inward working of their compassion, the sorrow & griefe their hearts felt, by seeing how vniustly we their brethren were slandered, and how violently beyond all measure, extremities were caried & prosecuted against vs: and this vpon no colour or inducement more then because we were few. So that compassion of our miseries, and loue of lessening the burden by diuiding it among more, were the meanes and information that increased our number, and not *the participation of our libertie, and the sore baite thereof.* Neither is there scarce any one Catholicke or Protestant in our countrey, that markes how matters passe, but can tell, that we onely, and none but our partie are punished by the Archpriest. Which thing whether it be true or no, or not more then our words import, let the taking away of faculties from seuerall of the Appellants since the making of the appeale: let the suspending and interdicting of vs: let the solemne declaration which he made by his letters addressed to that end, *Vniuerso clero Anglicano, caterisq; Christi fidelibus in Angliæ regno commorantibus*: to the vniuersall English Cleargie, and other faithfull people of Christ, abiding in the kingdome of England: let his refusing of our appeale, *let his strange inuerting of our words: let the contumelies in calling one of vs, *Erraticus & per saltũ ascendens Doctor*, a wandring Doctor & ascending by iumpes: and another, *the sonne of Belial*: let the exempting of vs from hauing part of the common diuidents, if we be prisoners, or if we be at libertie: let their excluding of vs from all places and fauors where the aduerse part can preuaile: let the disgraces, the obloquies, the slanders that are euerie where in citie and countrey spread, tennised and maintained against vs, and the freedome, and rich friendship which our brethren

The true causes of the increase of our numbers.

In his letter of the 21. of February, 1601.

*In the same Letter.

In his letter of the 16. of May 1601. D. Bagshaw.

In his Letter the 18 of March 1601. M. Colleton.

thren of the other side find, beare witnesse and decide, whether *the participation of our libertie, and the freedome we enioy*, aboue our fellowes of the other partie, *be a sore baite for yong men*: or not rather most potent meanes to deterre both yong and old from taking part with vs.

Moreouer there be some Priests in our countrey, who for that they be destitute of friendes, and know not how possibly to liue, if they should openly appeale, or otherwise manifest their conscience in matters, haue written and protested to his Holinesse that they dare not appeale, by reason of the foresaid extremities. Againe, our Archpriest *warneth and exhorteth in our Lord all Catholickes, Vt omnibus modis quibus possunt, nos vitent*: that by all meanes possible they should shunne our companie: and taking vs to be breakers of peace, he *wisheth them as they do shew themselues patrons and foster-fathers of the Church of Christ, Omni ope atq; opera iuxta Apostoli præceptũ etiam confundere nitãtur*: that they would labor by all helpes and furtherances to confound vs according to the precept of the Apostle. Likewise one of the Assistants said, that he wold no more frõ henceforth account the Appellãts his brethrẽ, nor otherwise esteem of thẽ, thẽ of *Bel* & *Topclif*. Also another Priest of like forwardnes aduiseth *that our cõpany should be shũned as his, who hath a plague sore running vpõ him*. And some Priests that are not known to adhere vnto vs, haue told vs, that if their benefactors did know they were in our cõpany, they would discontinue their charities, & withdraw their good affectiõ from them. All which, to our seeming do conuince, that *the benefite and libertie we enioy*, by appealing *is not so sweete a baite for misleading young men*, as the matter is made, but rather, most sower auersions, and such as he that is a young man, and not a senior in vertue and in contempt of worldly fauours, will beware as of his vndoing, how he appeales, or haue commerce with vs in the cause.

The rigor of the gouernement.

In his Letter of the 21. of Febr. 1601. *Stilo Romano.*

M. Standish words to M. Drewrie.

M. G.

And albeit we haue staid long about the confutation of this reason, yet here we cannot omit to note one thing more, viz. that you hauing otherwhere affirmed that we were not aboue ten, or not so many, and repeating also in this very place *that we were not the twentieth part, at the beginning, of those that admitted the gouernement*, would neuerthelesse after the reading of our appeale, and seeing thirtie of our names therunto, make a doubt by an *if*, whether *we haue increased our number since*. Certes how slow of beleefe soeuer you would make your selfe to appeare in this point, yet our Archpriest is not so incredulous: for he said not long since, by credible relation, that *the Laitie had neede to sticke vnto him, for the Priests were fallen away*. Neither do we doubt, if

In the libell the 10. of January 1599. In your letter to M. Bishop the 9. of October 1599.

there were a commission graunted to examine euery Priest on his oth how he liketh the gouernement, but that the number of those which would depose for it, would be very small, and hardly twentie besides the Assistants in all England, if al the Assistants should take theis othes for the allowance thereof, as we doubt they will not.

Your fifth exception: that we pretended *onely to refuse to subscribe to the authoritie of the Archpriest before he had obtained letters from the Sea Apostolicke for confirmation, as who would say that this being done, we meant to be quiet.* Sir, how highly you esteeme of your owne credit, yet deedes being euer of more power to perswade then wordes, we hope, especially hauing thousands of witnesses on our side, that our deedes will be credited before your wordes. Did we not all presently vpon the arriuall of his Holinesse Breue, receiue the authoritie, and subiect our obedience to M. *Blackwell?* the matter is plainer then can be denied, and it is acknowledged by our Archpriest, and fuller by father *Garnet* in their letters which are set down in the tenth Chapter of the
Fol. 146. & 147. Apologie, yea your selfe intitleth that Chapter in this manner: *of the ending of all controuersies vpon the publication of his Holinesse Breue.* But
Fol. 148. you call in doubt whether the peace that was made, and *our accepting of the authoritie were inwardly and sincere, or outwardly onely for a shew to satisfie the world for a time.* What shall we answere? you know those
Eccle. 3 words of *Salomon: Multos supplantauit suspitio illorum, & in vanitate detinuit sensus illorum.* Suspition hath deceiued many and detained their iudgement in vanitie of errour. And you know also, from what bad
2. 2. q. 60. art. 3. c. rootes S. *Thomas* teacheth the sinne of suspition to grow, and chiefly from this, that being culpable our selues, we become easily inclined therby to deem others guilty of the same faults, according to that say-
Eccle. 10. ing of Scripture cited by the said Doctour for proofe of his words, *In via stultus ambulans, cùm ipse sit insipiens omnes stultos æstimat.* The dissembler or fraile person esteemeth all others to be like himselfe.

Let vs now see the grounds vpon which you build so sinister a conceit, as that neither our admitting of the authoritie vpon sight of the Breue, was more then a pretext, nor the peace which some of vs made,
Fol. 148. other then counterfeit, concluded *onely in externall shew for the time,*
A charitable surmise of a religious mã. *vpon assurance that there would not want some probable occasion afterward to breake againe, and to lay the cause of breach vpon the other side.* The onely coniecture you alleage of so hard a surmise, is part of an appeale
Fol. 149. which you cite in this manner. *We whose names are vnderwritten do contest that we do appeale, and to haue appealed by our former writing, from*

you

you to the Sea Apostolike, as well for our selues as for all our brethren, who haue adioyned themselues vnto vs in this cause, or shall adioyne themselues hereafter. 6. May 1599.

And hauing rehearsed this whole passage, you adde immediatly: *By this Appeale not only for themselues but for all others in like maner that shall ioyne themselues vnto them (which is against the nature of all iust appeales) is easily perceiued that an egregious faction was meant.* O Lord! who did euer heare a weaker presumption of so grieuous a charge? we did appeale for our selues and others, which is against the nature of all iust appeales. *Ergo* we dissembled the peace we made after: *Ergo* an egregious faction was meant before. Good consequences. *Abel* offered to God a pleasing sacrifice: *Ergo* his brother *Cain* iustly killed him. As good a sequele. The AEgyptians oppressed and miserably afflicted the children of Israell: *Ergo* the children of Israell committed sinne in resigning themselues to the conduction of *Moses*, whom God had appointed to deliuer them out of the bondage. *Mary Magdalē* wrought a good worke in powring the boxe of precious ointment vpon the head of our Sauiour: *Ergo Iudas* taxed her worthily: which followeth as well, as your argument or presumption against vs, that therefore we doubled in the making of peace, as hauing an intention afterwards *to breake againe, and to lay the cause of breach vpon the other side*, because we appealed for our selues and others adhearing vnto vs. And where we pray you, do you find it written, that to appeale for others, who haue or shall ioyne themselues vnto vs in the same cause, is *against the nature of all iust appeales? Panormitane*, the approuedst Author of all the expositors of the law, calleth this manner of appealing, common and vsuall. *Nota [adhærentes eisdem] pro communi consuetudine appellantium, qui appellāt pro se, & sibi adhærentibus*. Note, saith he, by the words of the law [*adhærentes eisdem*] for the common custome of Appellants, who appeale for themselues and for those that adhere vnto them: which forme also of appealing, he proueth to be lawfull by the first Chapter, *De officio Iudicis delegati*, and by the Chapter, *Olim de accusationibus, inquisitionibus, & denunciationibus*. Or be it that the forme of our appeale made it doubtfull whether we intended thereby to make an *egregious faction*, and to that end *dissembled the peace* (as how little these things could be doubted of by the nature of the appeale and our actions, there are none, who are not disposed to picke quarrels but do see:) yet those that are brought vp in the schoole of charitie, know that *dubia in meliorem partem sunt interpretanda*. Things doubtful are to be interpre-

Gen. 4.

Exod. 1. 3. 4.

Mark. 14.

In ca. Olim de accusat. nu. 2.

D. Aug. li. 2. de Sermone Domini. ca. 28.

D.Tho.2.2.q. 60.art.4.

ted to the better sence, and that we ought not without manifest coniectures to suspect ill of another, and lesse, make knowne and publish our suspition.

And touching the beadroll of defamations, which you say *might haue bene laid downe against vs, if there had bene any man there present of the superiours side to informe the good Doctors: as of pride and arrogancie, of our disobediēt & tumultuous behauiors, of the reuell we kept throughout England, by writing, sending, and perswading against the Popes ordination; what reasons we inuented to discredite the Protectours letters and person, as also the Archpriest our immediate superiour appointed: what terrours we cast into lay mens heads of admitting forraine authoritie from the Pope: which tendeth to a worse consequence then al the rest.* Sir we hope that neither God nor good man gaue you the dispensation you take in deprauing vs, and that in points most open to disproofe. For first concerning the *pride and arrogancie* you impute vnto vs, in that being *scarce ten against 300. we durst make so dangerous a diuision among Catholickes in the sight of the common enemy, and in time of persecution.* What was the *dangerous diuision* you thus exaggerate? was it more then a suppliant intreatie we made to M. *Blackwell*, that he would not enforce vs to take him for our superior, before such time as we should receiue more certaine and particular proofe, then yet we did of his Holinesse commission to the Cardinal Protector, for instituting the subordination? Neither did we barely intreate him to this, but to the end we might the sooner win him thereunto, we offered and promised to obey him in the meane space, albeit we would not admit him to the authoritie he claimed. And that this was our petition and offer, and consequently the whole diuision at first, M. *Blackwell* himselfe cannot denie, who in his reioynder to the said petition termed the same *an insolent request*, adding, that for him *to yeeld thereunto, was nothing else but to yeeld vnto vndutifulnesse, and to giue a preferment to our priuate inuentions*. And for the more cleerenesse of this point, because it is of moment, we will here put downe two seuerall writings of others, whom our Archpriest counteth the chiefe of the faction, and which do most apparantly witnesse so much as is affirmed.

In his Letter to M.Heburne the 2. of March.

Anno 1599. 8. Martij.

Quæritur an acceptare velim pro meo superiore Archipresbyterum, eidemq; me subijcere, quem alij dicunt iussu suæ S^tis alij vero narrant eius

eius iniussu & per solum Illm Cardinalem Protectorem super vniuersum Clerum Anglicanum constitutum esse Superiorem.

Dico, cum ex huius authoritatis occasione, & eius prima promulgatione, grauissima scandala & contentiones in Ecclesia Anglicana oborta sint, & inde adhuc magis quotidiè eadem ingrauescant, asseraturq́; à multis præsbyteris hanc potestatem non ex iussu vel mandato Smi D. N. institutam, sed ad quorundam priuatorum instantiam, absque aut omnium, aut plurimorum certè sacerdotum consensu, vel notitia esse surreptam: interea dum communibus eiusdem Cleri suffragiis & votis ageretur de quibusdam mittendis Romam, qui à sua Ste Episcopos peterent, vel suffraganeos in variis regni prouinciis constitui, & nobis præfici pro maximis Ecclesiæ Anglicanæ necessitatibus subleuandis: cū deniq́; præsbyteri aliqui iam Romā profecti sint, qui Sm D. N. de omnibus reddant certiorem, atque ad nos referant quid in quaque re sua Stas statuere velit, ac iubeat obseruari: num videlicet Episcopos nobis præficiendos vel Archipræsbyterum decernat: dico inquam me nihil ad quæsitum iam posse respondere donec plenius constiterit quid sua Stas in hac controuersia decernere & statuere velit. Sed cum primum Smi D. N. sententia & decretum nobis innotuerit; eidem libentissimè & promptissimo animo in omnibus me pariturum profiteor. Interea autem dum hæc sciantur, Archipræsbytero, quem narrant nobis superiorem iam esse constitutum, in nulla re contradicam, aut eius authoritati (qualis qualis fuerit) refragabor, vt Christiana pax, & charitas integra inter nos, & illæsa in omnibus permaneant.

Ita ego Ioannes Musheus Præsbyter mea manu.

The English.

The yeare of our Lord 1599. the 8. of March.

I Am demaunded whether I will accept the Archpriest for my Superiour, and submit my selfe vnto him, whom some affirme to haue bene appointed Superiour ouer all the English Cleargie by commandement of his Holines, some others say without his commandement, by the most illustrious Cardinall Protector onely.

I say, that whereas by occasion of this authority, and by the first promulgation thereof, many grieuous scandals and contentions haue growne in the English Church, and more do grow dayly vpon that occasion, and wheras it is affirmed by many Priests, that this authority was not instituted by the commandement or mandate of his Holines, but procured by surreption at the instance of some particular men, without the consent or notice either of all, or the most part of Priests: in the meane while, sith there is order taken by common suffrage and request of the same Cleargie of sending certaine to Rome, to the end to craue of his Holinesse the constitution either of Bishops or suffragans in sundrie Prouinces of the kingdome, and to appoint them our gouernours for releeuing the great necessities of the English Church: and lastly whereas certaine Priests are alreadie gone to Rome to certifie his Holinesse of all these affaires, and to aduertise what his Holinesse shall in euery thing determine and commaund to be obserued: to wit, whether he will ordaine Bishops or an Archpriest ouer vs: I do therefore say, that I can make no answer to this demaund, till such time as it shall more fully appeare, what his Holinesse will decree and establish touching this controuersie. But so soone as euer the sentence and decree of his Holinesse shal be made knowne vnto vs, I protest I will be readie most promptly, and willingly, to obey the same in all things. In the meane, till the things be knowne, I will in nothing contradict the Archpriest, whom they report to be constituted Superiour ouer vs, neither resist his authoritie of what nature soeuer it be, to the end that Christian peace and charitie may remaine sound and vnblemished in all respects among vs.

This much I Iohn Mush *Priest do attest vnder mine owne hand.*

Verie reuerend Sir,

ALthough some be pleased to passe their hard censures of me, yet by the record of my owne conscience, I both feare and am loath to offend, and do no way affect ignorance: I requested you once heretofore, and now againe with all instance and like humilitie do redouble the petition, that I may receiue from you perfit notice of all such particulars wherein your authoritie bindeth me to obey. Suffer not (good sir) an vnwilling mind to erre, I hope I aske no other thing, then what of right to me belongeth, nor after an vndue manner. Verily, if I see my selfe, I dare affirme my wil and care for such, as I would not for ought aduisedly disobey in any commaund whereto the most of your authority stretcheth, or may iustly be extended. In other points wherin my vnderstanding holds me not tied, I must confesse that the maner of

vsage

vsage I haue receiued from you,and the hard conceits which you cary of me diuulged and brought by many waies to my hearing,haue made me much lesse respectiue and of more vnfriendly demeanour then otherwise I should haue bene, or by nature am inclined to. Fare you well.11.of August.1598.

By him who desireth to see and amend
that is or hath bene amisse.

I. Colleton.

These shew how *daungerous the diuision was* which we made *among Catholickes in the sight of the common enemie, and in time of persecution*, as you describe & amplifie the matter. Neither was the diuision greater betweene vs, nor otherwise knowne but by their own publishing, til such time as father *Lister* diuulged his discourse,and our Archpriest decided our disobedience to be alike enormious, as we could not defend the same without mortall sinne. And now also after the increase of so many wrongs,what haue we done?Mary we made sute to dispute the case with the fathers of the Societie, and refused to graunt our selues to be so desperately fallen from grace, and the vnitie of Gods Church,as they would needes make the world and our selues beleeue that we were. Againe being denied this, we sent to the vniuersitie of Paris for their censure in the difference. Further, being debarred also vnder heauiest penalty to maintain euen indirectly the sentence which the vniuersitie gaue for vs,we appealed, hauing no other refuge,to his Holinesse,for redresse of the oppressions.And here loe,was the beginning,progresse and qualitie of the diuision.

Now we must demand of you father *Parsons*,that knowes thus perfectly how to aggrauate the matters you take against, whether our delay and sending to Rome,and our promise to obey M.*Blackwell* in the meane,were like to *make so dangerous a diuision, &c.* as was the treatise of father *Lyster*, specially approued and praised in the rate it was, and highly commended by your selfe? Sure if our disunion in not consenting to our other brethren, wherein all learning was with vs, and the ordinances of holy Church against them, and we not knowing when we first dissented, but that they would demur as we did, about the absolute admittance of the authoritie,were a thing so dangerous (as you relate)to be attempted among Catholickes *in sight of the enemy, and in time of persecution*: the other diuision which father *Lyster* and other of

To M. Charnocke whiles he was prisoner in Rome.

the Iesuits made, was beyond all proportion more daungerous, as wherein so many failes of modestie, learning, iudgement, ciuilitie and charitie hudled together. But as our prouerbe is, some may better steale a horse, then some others looke ouer the hedge.

For our *tumultuous behauiours, for the reuell we kept in writing, sending and perswading against the Popes ordination, for the conuenticles and tumults we made to draw men into faction*, because you barely affirme them without making any proofe, or descending to any one instance, we will leaue those that know vs and our actions, to iudge of the truth of the accusations, and to take you for such a one herafter, as the libertie of your pen deciphereth you to be. But touching *the reasons we inuented* (as you say) *to discredit the Protectors Letters and person*: because you set them downe in another place what they were in particular, we will answer vnto them. You affirm, that *to diminish his Graces estimation with the Catholickes, we wrote he was Protector of the English Colledge*
Pag. 17. *at Rome, and afterward honoured by the title of Protector of England, but we did not graunt* (say you) *that he was so indeed*: was not this a high point in a low house trow ye, and worthy to be taxed by a religious pen? Could his Graces estimation, especially being more then a twelue-moneth dead before the writing of the words, be diminished with the Catholickes of England thereby, who neuer knew him, nor scarce euer heard whether there was such a man or no? or was our acknowledging of him to be Protector of the English Colledge at Rome, and our graunting that he was afterwards honoured by the title of Protector of England, a deniall *that he was so indeede*? who would thus infer that had his wits about him? But you go onward, and make another reason of our discrediting his Grace, because (forsooth) we no plainer acknowledging him to be Protector of England then is said, did adde *that we were not bound to beleeue him in a matter of so large a consequence as the institution of the Archpriest, without Bull or Breue*. A reason much
Pag. 62 & 88. like to the former. For it hath bene shewed before, that it is no discredite to a Cardinall not to be beleeued on his word, in matters greatly
Decius in ca. Causam quæ. de offic. Deleg. nu. 26. preiudiciall to others, because according to the *Maxime, Non attenditur illa præsumptio, quòd quis præsumatur bonus, vbi agitur de præiudicio tertij*: for a man to be holden good, is no presumption to be regarded, where the matter concernes the preiudice of a third person. You fashion a third argument for proofe that we laboured to discredite our Protector, because *we wrote* (you say) *that he was knowne to be allied to father Claudius Aquauina Generall of the Iesuits, and said to be ruled al-*

together

together against the English schollers and Priests, whose Protector he pretended to be. Are not these weightie exceptions? Will you inferre it a discredite to the Cardinall to be allied to your Generall? or if not, why do you alleage it? And touching the other part of the reason, are we the first, or onely men who report that the Cardinall was said to be ruled by persons of your Order, against the schollers and Priests? You would be loth to feed all those that haue, and do make this report besides vs. Did his Holinesse himselfe allow the schollers appellations from the Cardinal Protector, as reputed partial on the Iesuits side, and gaue them other visitors, namely Cardinall *Sega* and Senior *Moro* at one time; and at another time, Cardinall *Burghesio* and the same Senior *Moro?* It is straunge to see how fondly you reason and leese your selfe. A fourth reason of yours consisteth in that we wrote *that his Graces Letters drew on a generall and extreme persecution vpon our necks, and consequently were not to be allowed by vs.* Sir, here we must tell you that you clippe our words, and maime or inuert the sense: for these are our words in the place you quote: [What reason is there that his Graces bare Letters, the contents whereof drew on so great and extreme persecution vpon our neckes should be allowed of by vs as a sufficient proofe of the delegation?] Now marke how you chaunge them. We made them a demaund, and you make them positiue, without asking the question. We said, the contents thereof drew on so generall and extreme persecution; pointing by the word [so] to the meere punishing iurisdiction, which the Cardinall gaue to the Archpriest, without counterpoise of anie commoditie at all, and to the increase of our daunger and our Princesse disfauour through the institution thereof: and you turne the word [so] into [a] which cutteth away the reference. And in stead of our demaund, whether his Graces bare letters, so preiudiciall vnto vs, ought without anie further euidence, to be allowed by vs, as a sufficient proofe of the delegation: you come in with a *consequently they were not to be allowed by vs*, omitting that addition of ours, *as a sufficient proofe of the delegation*. And if doubt be made, whether the contents of the Constitutiue Letter can be said to drawe on a persecution, let the Iurisdiction graunted to the Archpriest, of remouing vs from the places of our residences: of binding vs to stand to his decision and arbitrement, in the doubts and controuersies that shall arise: of prescribing what he listeth, and of forcing vs to obey the same vnder losse of our faculties: Let these and other of like qualitie declare, whether the contents of the Cardinals Letter may not beare the name of mouing a perſecution, when the perſon to whom the like ample authoritie was committed, was promoted to the office, and directed in the execution thereof, by thoſe that are the chiefeſt and moſt potent parties of the other ſide of the difference: yea, the verie ſetters downe of the ordinances. Verily whatſoeuer others may think in this point, yet we that are the ſufferers, and againſt whom the ſpleene is borne, do feele more aggrieuances, and a heauier weight of perſecution by the vſe or abuſe of the iuriſdiction graunted, then we doe by the ſtraite condition of the lawes of our countrey. In briefe, for concluſion of the premiſes, and for binding vp all to our greater reproch, you ſay, *It is ſufficient to ſhew our paſſionate and diſcompoſed minds, for that, the Cardinall protector now gone to God, hauing bene to all our nation a moſt deare patrone and father in all occaſions, we* notwithſtanding, *in all ſpeeches and writings do ſpeake euery where very vnkindly and vnreuerently of him.* Sir, if we ſhould aske you, what theſe vnreuerent ſpeeches & writings were, the inſtances would be to ſeeke, vnleſſe you deuiſed matter of your own coining Or to let this paſſe, whom ſhould we beleeue, you, or the famous Cardinall *Allen* gone alſo to God? who told *M. Muſh*, that the ſaid Protector neuer did, nor euer would, as he feared, do good to our countrey. And we are ſure, that fewe or none taſted anie part of that you report, except *M. Haddocke* (who left our campe, without any great loſſe to our cauſe) and perchance ſome other deuoted perſons whom you recommẽded. And here we humbly requeſt, that we may not be thought to write this (being more then anie of vs wrote before) either vpon another motiue, or to other end, then we did; that is, to purge our ſelues of the note of hatefull ingratitude, which you impute vnto vs, and to ſhew how litle beleefe you deſerue in many of your writings.

Fol.117. Touching the laſt calumne in the beadrole, vz. *the terrours we caſt into lay mens heads, of admitting forreine authoritie from the Pope, which tendeth* (you ſay) *to a worſe conſequence then all the reſt,* and *by which* (as *Fol.14.15.& 16.* you write in another place) *his Holineſſe and all other godly and learned men may ſee and pitie vs, but eſpecially our ſpirit of vindicatiue and maleuolous proceeding, &c.* We anſwer; that you ſeeme by this courſe conſtruction of our wordes, to carrie a verie ſharpe diſpoſition of wounding vs in the ſpeedingeſt place you can. Is your religious charitie no more? *In the copie of Diſcourſes. pag.6.* That which was affirmed, was onely *that by the opinions of diuerſe men of iudgement in the lawes of our countrey, this our admitting of the Archpreſbyteriall iuriſdiction, may* (by law) *and will* (by likelihood) *be drawne*

within

within the compasse of an old law of Premunire made in a Catholike time, because it is an externall iurisdiction, brought into our Realme against the will and notice of our Prince and countrey. This was the summe, and the worst of all that was written: and the cause of the writing was to yeeld a reason why we deferred to receiue the Subordination vpon view of the Cardinals Letter; namely, because the preiudice it might this way turne vs vnto, was great, and great by an auncient law of the Realme. Which brought vs into a most certaine opinion, that we were no wayes obliged in conscience (notwithstanding the contrarie position of the Iesuites and our Archpriest) to admit the Subordination vpon the sole credence of the Cardinals Letter, the preiudice we should incurre by the admitting thereof, being as we haue said, so great to our selues, and profitable to none; and consequently, that which most of anie other thing did iustifie our delay. Because no writer, who is largest in the prerogatiues of Cardinals, but doth hold, that in matters of verie great preiudice, a Cardinall is not to be beleeued vpon his word, in things that he relateth to haue receiued from another. So that the cause which enforced vs to mention the said law of *Premunire*, being no other then to iustifie our bearing off, or to free our selues in the crimes obiected against vs by father *Lyster* and others, and our words also which ensued in the verie next page, witnessing *that his Holinesse least commaund should euer bind vs, though with hazard and losse of our liues, to accept of any Ecclesiasticall iurisdiction which he should appoint & make known vnto vs, after a Canonicall maner:* we cannot but maruel, what passion guided or rather blinded your pen, in running thus eagerly vpon vs without iust or colourable cause giuen, if you had bene pleased to vnderstand our intention and words aright. And we maruell the more hereat, in respect you fall into this inuectiue humour, after our deeds had verified our words, and we really admitted the subordination, according to our promise, vpon the first appearance of his Holinesse Breue, notwithstanding the danger of the foresaid lawe of *Premunire*, standing in force and inlisting vs within the penalties thereof for so doing. A fact, wherein we litle doubt whether the clergie of Fraunce or Spaine would haue followed vs, if the case had bene theirs, but would haue respited their acceptance, notwithstanding the Breue, till his Holinesse had bene otherwise and fuller aduertised, and the mischiefe prouided for.

See the Authors quoted pag 61. 62. & 69.

But now we *being so few, that is to say, some fiue or sixe, and such as we were;* (for so scornefully do you terme vs) small account perchaunce is

Fol. 15 & 119

to be made of our right, ſpecially ſtanding againſt the deſigne of a Ieſuite: we haue to alleage, *Nulla erit diſtantia perſonarum, ita paruum* Deut.1. *audietis vt magnum.* That in diſcuſſing of rights, there is no difference of perſons or number to be reſpected, but the caſe of the few & ſmall is to be tendred as well as the caſe of the many and great.

Your other aſſertions that we by our foreſaid naming of the Statute of *Premunire* laboured *to caſt terrors into lay mens heads of admitting foreine authoritie from the Pope, and that we would haue the Princes conſent to be needfull for the legitimatiō of the* new *authoritie,&* denominate *our ſelues, being but ſome fiue or ſixe, to be the Countrey, and that we alſo oppoſed our ſelues againſt the Subordination, for that his Holineſſe had not asked our conſents.* Theſe are ſo ill deductions, ſo farre fetcht, and ſauouring ſo ſtrongly of the old leuen, that whoſoeuer reades them muſt hold you farre gone in paſſion, or drowned in indignation againſt vs. Did the Subordination concerne anie lay man at all, when we mentioned the Statute of *Premunire?* The Conſtitutiue letter is as flat, as flat may be, againſt anie ſuch inference or interpretation. For it onely inſtituteth *M. Blackwell* Archprieſt ouer the Seminarie prieſtes abiding in England or Scotland, and giueth him not the leaſt authoritie in the world ouer the Laitie, or ſo much as once toucheth anie ſuch matter. How ſhamefully therefore do you wreſt our words, ſith when we firſt wrote them, the Subordination implied none of the Laitie, and were onely printed to ſhew, by reaſon, that we were no ſuch lewd perſons, nor intangled in the cenſures of holy Church, as father *Lyſter* with his adherents did moſt ignorantly or moſt vncharitably cenſure and diuulge vs to be. We aſſure our ſelues father *Parſons*, that your reſtleſſe ſpirit and pen, your enterpriſing and buſie actions haue turned heretofore our Catholike Profeſſants to infinite preiudice; for to no knowne cauſe can we impute ſo much the making of the ſeuere lawes of our countrey, as to your edging attempts and prouocations. And as we aſſure our ſelues of this: ſo do we feare leaſt this your notorious play- Fol.15.110. 117.& 132. ing and deſcanting vpon our wordes, and your forward endeuours to draw all things after your owne byas, may more endomage their hard ſtate, then they wil be readie or haue cauſe to thanke you for. Did you meane to bid all truth and modeſtie farewell, when you determined Fol.15. to put downe in print that *here is nothing but maleuolence and diſobedience diſcouered, with deſire to bring the Archprieſt and all thoſe which obey him within the compaſſe of temporall lawes and treaſon.* Hath our mention of *Premunire* ſo ſoone hatched treaſon? And are you ſure that ſo

wicked

wicked a desire did possesse vs? Fie, fie, the libertie of your penne and conscience appalleth.

To end our answer to this your sifth exception against the Censure of Paris, we would know what decision others do thinke that the said Doctors would haue giuen in our case, if we had layed downe in the state of the question, that the chiefe plotters, and procurers of the Subordination were some of the fathers of the Society, and none their cooperators or vnder-workmen in the action, but such onely as were suborned or set on by them: that those who defined our bearing off and sending to Rome to be the sinne obiected, were some of the Societie: that those who reported vs to be excommunicate, irregular, without faculties, infamous persons, sacrificers in mortall sinne, and the giuers of poison in lieu of medicine, were some of the Societie: that those who most precisely abandoned our companie, and would not execute anie diuine office in our presence, nor in the presence of our lay-adherents, were some of the Societie: that those who broched our troubles, reared the tumults, reuiued the contention, disquieted our Catholike communion, made parties or faction among Priestes, kindled dissention betweene the laitie and clergie, made dislike and diuision betwixt nearest friends, and blew the coles to all our stirres, were some of the Societie, acknowledged in the Epistle of *Pius Greil* fol. 7. who first entring into our labours, we welcomed with all honor, we gaue them the preheminence, we acquainted them with our friends and places, we extolled their order, and in a sort receiued them as the Galathians did S. Paule, that is, *as Angels of God,* and with like tender affection, *as if it could haue bene, we would haue plucked out our owne eyes to haue giuen them vnto them.* We say, if we had particularized these things in the bodie of the question as we did conceale them, and did not so much as insinuate that anie father of the Societie had a finger or his assent in the accusations: what would the learned Doctors haue said, how would they haue blushed and blessed themselues at the demonstration of the ingratitude?

Your sixt and last exception: *That no man was present in Paris to tell the Doctors how falsely we put downe in the question, that it seemed to vs by certaine words of the Cardinals letters, that the Archpriest his authority was graunted by false information, and that partialitie was vsed in the choise of him, and his assistants, and that our messengers to Rome, were not sent to lay open our difficulties to his Holinesse, but rather to contradict and make a broyle in Rome.* Sir, we pray you to tell vs whom you take your ſelfe to be? Muſt theſe be falſe becauſe you affirme them ſo, without making any proofe at all of their falſitie? Verily we repute you for no ſuch man as yet: and how litle theſe your words do deſerue ſuch a reſpect, let the inſtances ſet downe in our firſt Reaſon declare, which do manifeſt falſe information moſt apparantly. Yeã good nature would rather haue commended the temper of our information, then reproued it, wee ſaying no more but *it ſeemed to vs by certaine wordes of the Cardinals Letters, that the Archprieſt his authoritie was graunted by falſe information &c.* when the matter we auerred, was moſt euident by the teſtimonie of the whole Realme. For who is ſo ſhameleſſe as will affirme, either that the Catholike Laitie were at diſſention amongſt themſelues, or the ſecular Prieſts amongſt themſelues, or that both of theſe two were at variance one againſt the other? Auowances expreſſed in the Cardinals letter, and alleaged as the ſole cauſe of inſtituting the Subordination. Sure, how worldly wiſe ſoeuer you are in other points, yet in this you ſhew litle: that would iterate and contend to beare down a matter with the ſole waight of your own denial, wherin there be thouſands that know and can conuince the contrarie. Saint *Thomas*, and common reaſon teach, that *peccare mente obſtinata aggrauat peccatum*, to maintaine an vntruth with a wilfull minde, increaſeth the malice of the ſinne.

Pag. 16 & ſequentem.

2.2.q.88. art. 6.c.

And whether *partialitie was vſed in the choiſe of the Archprieſt and his counſellers*, or no: we leaue it to the common voice of our brethren to determine, and to the wofull effects which haue meerely proceeded from the imperfection and diſtemperature of the maner of gouerning: hoping that there are none of right iudgement, but will ſee by the peeces of letters and other writings which follow, that we had reaſon *to note partialitie in the choiſe of the Archprieſt and his counſellers.* *Tantum abſunt illi pij patres ab omni appetitu dominij, vt nobis in omni loco inſignis humilitatis, manſuetudinis, patientiæ, pietatis & charitatis exemplar præformarint. Valde certè ingrati eſſemus ſi non illos honore proſequeremur vt patres; amore complecteremur vt amicos; officio coleremus vt beneficos; ſtudio imitaremur vt magiſtratos; pietatis affectu agnoſceremus vt patriæ ſalutis, & Eccleſiæ apud nos varijs tempeſtatibus iactatæ, præcipuos adiutores & acerrimos propugnatores. Qui illis detrahunt nec ſeipſos, nec illos norunt: nam qui ſunt apud nos, qui aduenientibus præſbyteris ex tranſmarinis partibus auxilio ſunt, niſi patres Societatis Ieſu? Domi excluſi, ab illis excipimur, indumento latera ab illis commodè & comptè veſtiuntur, victu deſtituti & pecunia ab illis ſuſtentantur, & neſcientes vbi commorarentur,*

A part of M. Blackwelles Letter to the Cardinal protector of the 10. of Ianuary 1596.

tur, quia ignoti, ab illis equos & alia ad iter necessaria habent paratissima, & loca etiam prudentissimè designata, vbi in lapsis recuperandis, Catholicis confirmandis, & in Dei cultu propagando laudabiliter laborare possunt. Neque hisce finibus concluditur eorum charitas. Nos enim ipsi qui pondus diei & æstus per plurimos annos sustinuimus, ex eorum fontibus in nostra necessitate plurimum alleuamenti & consolationis habuisse nos liberè profitemur. Si sciret amplitudo vestra quantum pecuniarum ex proprijs suis patrimonijs (nam minima sunt quæ ex eleemosinis illis obueniunt) in talibus & in alijs pietatis officijs patres insumpserint, & quàm promptè ad Sanctos refocillandos in carcere detentos, & alios varijs rerum & temporum difficultatibus implicatos & oppressos illi semper occurrerint, non dubito quin actutū coerceret effrænatam audaciam illorum qui inuidiæ stimulis agitati de patrum existimatione & charitate quicquam imminuerint.

The English.

So farre are these holy fathers estraunged from all appetite of seeking to beare rule, as in euery place they prefashion vnto vs an exemplar of rare humilitie, mildnesse, patience, pietie and charitie. Certes we should be verie vngratefull if we should not honour them as our fathers, embrace them with loue as friends, reuerence them with dutie as liberall benefactors, with studie to imitate them as maisters, acknowledge them with affection of pietie, as the chiefest adiutors and most earnest mainntainers of the safetie of our countrey, and the good state of our Church tossed wirh sundrie tempests. Those that diminish their praises, neither know themselues nor them. For who are they amongst vs that furnish Priests at their first comming from beyond the seas, but the Fathers of the Societie? The harbourlesse are receiued by them, those that want apparell are fitly and neatly clothed by them, those that are destitute of meate, drinke and money, are maintained by them, and those that cannot tell where to abide, because they are vnknowne, haue horses and other things necessarie for their iourneys most readily of them, and places also most prudently designed where they may commendably apply their labours in recouering the lapsed, in strengthening Catholikes, and in propagating the seruice of God. Neither is their charitie contained in these bounds: for we our selues who haue for many yeres born the burdē & heate of the day, do freely confesse to haue had from their fountaines in our necessitie, greatest succour and consolation. If your Grace did knowe what summes of

Priests that are now most defamed.

money the Fathers of their proper patrimonies haue consumed (for it is litle that cometh to them of almes) in such and other deeds of charitie, and how promptly they haue alwayes shewed them selues in releeuing prisoners, and others incombred and oppressed with diuerse difficulties of things and times: I doubt not but you would by and by restraine the vnbridled boldnesse of those who gored with the pricks of enuie, haue any whit dimmed the estimation and charitie of the Fathers Thus farre *M. Blackwell* in his Letter to Cardinall *Caietane*, before he was constituted Archpriest, and to which dignitie the writing of this Letter, as it is generally reported, was his greatest furtherance. And since his promoting thereunto, *M. Bishop* made request vnto him that for peace sake and contentment to all parties, he would choose some one or moe of the Assistants that were left to him to nominate, out of the number of those of the other side, but he answered him and others as followeth.

A part of our Archpriestes Letter to M. Bishop, M. Colleton and others, the 17. of August 1598.

Petitis vt aliqui ex vestris ad communionem nostræ authoritatis admissi, saltem in numerum consultorum referri possint. Cæterùm quid aliud inde consequeretur, nisi monstrum ex contrarijs, diuersisq; atque inter se repugnantibus animorum studijs conflatum? Hoc non erit pacem constituere, sed quasi nubium conflictu, fulmen dissentionis emittere, cuius vi nos omnes conciderimus, ardoreq; flammæ conflagaremus. Ne quid tale accideret, prudentissimè prouidit Ill^mus D. Protector, vt qui authores prœlij faciendi & cum Patribus confligendi fuerunt, illi ab omni curatione rerum apud nos & administratione remouerentur. Non enim vuæ ex spinis colligi possunt, nec ex tribulis ficus. That is: Ye desire that some of yours, admitted to the communion of our authoritie, may be chosen into the number of the counsellers. But what other thing would ensue thereof but a monster, composed of contrarie and diuerse dispositions of minde, repugning one the other? This will not be to make peace, but after the maner of fighting clouds, to send foorth the lightning of dissention, by whose force we all should be slaine, and burnt with the heate of the flame. That no such thing might happen, our most Illustrious Lord Protector hath most prudently prouided, that those who were the authors of making warre and bickerings with the Fathers, should be remoued from all charge and gouernment of matters among vs. For grapes cannot be gathered of thornes, nor figges of thistles.

Moreouer the said Cardinal Protector, or to speake as the truth is, father *Parsons* in his name, vsed these words in the sixth Instruction annexed to the Subordination: *Licet Superior ille ex consultoribus Archipræsbyteri*

chipræsbyteri non sit, qui a tamen summoperè expedit suáque Sanctitatis id omnino cupit, atque præcipit, vt inter Patres & Sacerdotes summa sit animorum vnio, ac consensio, & quia dictus Superior pro sua in rebus Angliæ experientia, pro eaq; quam apud Catholicos habet, authoritate plurimum poterit, ad omnes Sacerdotum consultationes adiumenti adferre, curabit Archipræsbyter in rebus maioribus iudicium quoque eius consiliumq; acquirere, vt omnia ordinatius ac maiori luce ac pace ad diuinam gloriam dirigantur. That is: Although the Superiour of the Iesuites be not one of the Archpriests Assistants, yet because it is verie greatly expedient, and his Holinesse doth wholly desire and command, that there should be nearest vnion of minds and consent betweene the Fathers and the Priests, and because the said Superiour, for his experience in English affaires, and for the authoritie which he hath with the Catholikes, can most benefit and further all the consultations of the Priests, the Archpriest in greatest matters shall take care to seeke his iudgement and counsell, to the end that all things may the more orderly & with greater light and peace be directed to the glorie of God.

Now we appeale to the iudgemēt of the wise, whether these things do not seeme (and this was all that we said) *to bewray partialitie in the choise of the Archpriest and his counsellers.* Or whether the contention now on foote among vs, (and for appeasing whereof the Subordination is said to be instituted) being betwixt the Iesuites and the Secular Priests, were like by this choise to take an happie or a peaccable end, when the Superiour appointed, had before so engaged him selfe in the false praises of the one side, and alike vntruly derogated from the due deserts of the other: when all the Assistants must be of the Iesuits partie, and none for vs whom they impugned: when father *Garnet* our capitall aduersarie, by expresse order must be called to consultation in all matters of moment, and nothing passe without his aduice: when his calling also to consultation must be holden for a supreme benefite and furtherance of matters, and for a greater increase of order, light, peace, and the glorie of God; and yet the admitting of any of our side to the same consultation, must be deemed as litle consonant to peace and reason, as for men to seeke grapes vpon thornes, or figges vpon thistles: when finally some of those that were chosen Assistants, and perchaunce chosen for so kinde a part, had testified to the Cardinall vnder their handes in the behalfe of the Iesuites, that they knewe the accusations which were exhibited or giuen out to be exhibited in a memoriall against them to be false: (a testimonie which they could not poſſibly geue in the maner they did, vnleſſe they had bene their gardian Angels, and preſent at all times, and euery where with them:) vndoubtedly if theſe and other perticulers we could recite beare no note or badge of partiality; then ſurely neither heate is a qualitie of fire, nor moyſture of water, nor the noſe a viſible thing in a mans face.

Now then if you father *Parſons* ſtriue to inualidate the cenſure of *Paris*, and would make it of no force, becauſe no man was there preſent to ſpeake of the Archprieſts ſide, nor to reproue the reaſons of our Information; how infinitely more may we returne the ſame arguments backe vpon you, for weakening, or auoyding the force of the Conſtitutiue letter, and his Holines two Breues? For who was there in *Rome* that aduertiſed either the Cardinall or his holines of the ſtate of matters in our country, but your ſelfe, and ſuch trunks as you ſpake through? Who was there that informed either of them how ill and iealouſly our Prince and the State would conſter any forme of gouernement your ſelfe ſhould erect or procure? Who was there to controwle the falſities of your reaſons, to check your ſlaunderous reports, to diſcouer the end of your drifts, or to acquaint them with your vnconſcionable trade of dealing? Who was there, to geue them to vnderſtand how contentious you haue bin euer counted, and how ouerlong and troubleſomely you haue marchandized the Crowne and Kingdome? Who was there to ſhew his Holines the contrarieties of the firſt Breue to the Cardinals Letters, and of the ſecond Breue to them both, and how groſſely you caried your ſelf, eſpecially in ſetting downe the points of the later Breue, in which the demonſtrations of ſurreption are ſo plentie, and palpable, as the meaneſt capacitie may feele and handle them? Briefly, who was there in *Rome*, to informe his Holines or that higheſt Court, how deepely, ſeuerall of your actions haue derogated from the moſt venerable reputation of that diuine humane Conſiſtory, and how your oppreſſions and crafty ſtoppings of iuſtice hath ſcandalized infinite in our country, as well Catholike as Proteſtant, that we ſay nothing of forraine Potentates? Verily we aſſure our ſelues, that if theſe things had bene deliuered to his Holines, and all matters, how they paſſed, vprightly vnfolded, his holy zeale of iuſtice and moſt compaſſionable hart, would neuer haue ſuffred you ſo long to ſway matters as you haue done, and much leſſe would his bleſſed fatherhood haue refuſed our appeale without plainer deciſion of our caſe in the accuſation and iniuries obiected, and without reſtoring vs to the vſe of our faculties, or commaunding the

leaſt

least satisfaction for the damages susteined being innumerable and most great,yea and that without making mention at all of the Iesuits, or comprizing them vnder the censure of the Breue, notwithstanding they were the only authors of the calumniation imputed, and the most stiffe and continuall maintainers thereof.

Albeit we haue bene long in our reply to these exceptions, neuerthelesse we must craue the Readers patience, to touch a by-point or two which the father interlaceth in the treaty of the said exceptions. The first is, that whereas the Sorbone Doctors, did according to custome obserued in all other the like resolutions, set downe the persons, day, yeare, and place, where, when, and by whom, the case was decided; Father *Parsons*, for that we should know, he keepeth his old wont of gibing, giueth a prety frumpe by clipping their words, and adding of a parenthesis. Their words were these: *Viri principes &c.* The chiefe and principall men of the facultie of Diuinitie in *Paris*, selected out of the whole facultie assembled together in the house of the Senior Beadle &c. Which passage father *Parsons* curtalleth and carpeth at in this maner: *No maruell if these Doctors that were chosen to meet in the Senior Beadles house about this matter (for so it is set downe also in this printed booke) did lightly ouerpasse the matter &c.* Where it is to be noted that in stead of [*chosen or selected out of the whole faculty of Diuinity, and assembled together in the house of the Senior Beadle*] he loppeth the words and saith, *were chosen out to meete in the Senior Beadles house*: as who would ieast, that these famous clarks were chosen out to meete in the Beadles house, and not selected out of the whole facultie to resolue all doubts which should happen to be sent to the Vniuersitie for their resolution. Or if father *Parsons* had no intention to gibe by contracting the words, then let him tell the reason why he added the parenthesis [*for so it is set downe in this printed booke*] the words being the words of the Doctors themselues,and put downe for the causes aboue mentioned. Fol.116.

The second thing we will touch, is, the fauour that father *Parsons* pretendeth to shew vs, in that he will not impugne the censure of *Paris* further, then for that it cleared vs from all sinne, *for of the other point of schisme*, he saith, *he will not talke at all*. Are we not greatly beholden vnto him? His holines second Breue was not extant when he wrote the Apologie, as himselfe giueth notice in the Appendix, and therfore that was no cause why he omitted to vrge this point against vs. What then might it be,that caused this fauour in him towards vs? Fol.115.

Was it in respect he misliked the imputation of that crime? No, for he commended the Treatise of father *Lister* to *M. Charnocke*; and said to *M. Barnby* in approuance thereof, that if we should reconcile any body, we did no more then if we should reclaime one from Atheisme to heresie. Or did he befriend vs thus far, in regard that by conniuence of the fault, he might the sooner attone the difference, or for that he would not taint our good names? Let his deprauing termes, let his exaggerations, his fetching of matters a far off, his bewayling our state, his winding of himselfe into narrowest creekes for small aduantage against vs, his feare of our reuolt, his doubtfull and halfe speeches wounding vs deeper with the reader, then if he had spoken all he could and plainely. Let the inuectiues and bitternes he vseth throughout the Apologie and the Appendix, beare witnesse whether he omitted to handle that point for benefit of the common cause, peace, or our good names; or for that the assertion was so absurd, so childish, so contrarie to all learning, iudgement and common
Fa. Magio and others. sense, and for such condemned also by some of the best in his religion, as without vtter wracke of his credit, he could not occupie his pen in defence of the paradoxe. What others will thinke in this point, we know not, but our selues seeme most sure hereof.

The other points that we would haue the reader to note in the de-
Fol. 115. lating and proofe of the exceptions, are the words he vseth, *that he will not presume to determine any degree of sinne touching the deferring of our obedience to the Archpriest, but will leaue that to God and to the offenders*
Fol. 118. *consciences:* and likewise his declaration, that *well we might haue spared to print the Censure of Paris, but that M. Champney would make a vaine flourish with the ostentation of an Academicall sentence.* Of like he wrote the former without any deliberation, or did not afterwards remember what he had written, because in the eleuenth chapter he defineth re-
Fol. 172. solutely, *that we were bound vnder grieuous sinne by all rules of true diuinity to haue obeyed with far lesse euidence then was shewed vnto vs.* Which doubtlesse seemeth to be written when his iudgement was asleepe,
*Pag. 61. & 62. as may appeare by that which is said before, * and by the text of holy scripture: *In ore duorum vel trium testium stabit omne verbum.* In the
Deuteron. 19. mouth of two or three witnesses euery word shal stand. And touching his opinion, that we might well haue spared the printing of the Censure of *Paris*, we neede say no more but that such outfacing words do way little with the wise, who know, that where shame is not, the like words may be spoken of any truth in the world. And likewise know,

that

that put case all the exceptions were true which are alleaged against the Censure, yet the same Censure doth cleere vs of father *Listers* imputation, and of enormious disobedience: because if it were either of these crimes, our deferring could not be but sinne in the fact considered in it selfe, which the censure denieth, and that we had so wicked and diuellish intention as to cut our selues from holy church, or rebell against any lawfull superior, in a deede lawfull in it selfe, as the Vniuersitie defined our deferring to be, we thinke our aduersaries will not say it, and we are sure they cannot say it without guilt of vsurped iudgement, and most grieuous sinne to their soules, and so leauing these matters, we will returne and proue that the aucthoritie as it hath bin practised, infringeth, or dispenseth with the law of nature. Math.7. Rom.14. Iac. 4. *D.Tho.22.q.60.art.2. & 6. & q.67.art.1.*

THe aucthoritie as *M.Blackwell* hath hitherto demeaned it, either dispenseth with the law of nature, or violateth the same, in that he, by vertue of the aucthoritie, prohibited the accused to defend themselues. A right (if any other) taught by nature her selfe. And that he hath thus done, the proues be many, and vndeniable. Father *Lister* accused vs of a foule crime: the infamie was diuulged in all parts of the Realme, and in many places beyond the seas: our company grew thereon to be shunned: our benefactors were put in feare that their soules would finde smart in the next world, for harboring of vs in their houses: seuerall meanes were practised, and attempts giuen to remoue vs, * and not to leaue vs where to hide our heads. * Father *Garnet* the superiour of the Iesuites affirmed that we ministred, and receiued sacraments in deadly sinne, that we gaue poyson in liew of medicine, that we were such, by the opinion of all the learned, as his brother *Lister* had censured vs to be, that our criminous, sinfull, irregular, and excommunicate state, was so plaine and notorious, as none vnder sinne could forward, or assist vs in the exercise of our functions: Priests were dealt withall, and fauors promised, so as they would affirme or report vs guiltie of the crimes obiected. To make our oppressions great enough, a Roman resolution without name of the author was published against vs by our Archpriest, and direction giuen by him, that none should absolue vs in confession, before we would acknowledge and make satisfaction for the enormities wherewith we were charged. Likewise, to increase our burthen, father *Iones* gaue foorth, and our superior said the position was true, that whosoeuer mainteined vs not to be the abandoned creatures which father *Lister*

Clem.ca.pastoralis de re iud. § cæterũ.

In his letter the tenth of Nouember.

iudged vs to be, incurred *ipso facto* for such their defending of vs, the censures of holie church. What shall we say? Our Archpriest himselfe charged vs *with enormious disobedience & to liue a gracelesse state*: and in the letters wherein his Reuerence thus censured vs, (which were also made common ouer the Realme) he forbad vs (being no otherwise condemned) vnder threate *of suspending vs presently from the vse of our function either by word, or writing, to defend the disobedience imputed.* Againe, there was neither meane, nor measure obserued, in multiplying of afflictions vpon vs: *M. Blackwell* in his decree of the 18. of October 1600. *denounceth, and declareth vs to haue bin truly disobedient to the Sea Apostolike, and rebellious against his office:* and in the next paragraffe of the same decree *prohibiteth all of vs in vertue of holie obedience, and vnder paine of suspension and interdict, and vnder losse of all our faculties* ipso facto *to be incurred, not any maner of way, by word or writing, directly, or indirectly, to presume to defend the disobedience whereof he immediatly before condemned vs.* Was there euer greater iniustice heard of vpon earth? Can that ecclesiasticall, secular, or prophane Iudge be named, who before Iuridicall condemnation forbad vnder like, or so grieuous penalties, any offendor guilty of what crime soeuer to defend his reputation? Pope *Clement* the fift affirmeth, that *facultas defensionis quæ à iure prouenit naturali adimi non valet*, libertie of defending our selfe proceeding from the lawe of Nature cannot be forbidden. And what is more ingraffed in nature, or a deeper instinct thereof, then not being conuicted, nor cōdemned, to defend our good names?

* In his letters of the 21. and 27. of February, and of the 14. of March 1600.

Clem. ca. pastoralis de re iud.

We do not denye that the deferring of our obedience to the *Constitutiue Letter* and Archpriest, was notorious, we meane publikely knowne, but that this deferring and protracting of our subiection till the comming of his Holines Breue, was either enormious disobedience, or any of the other crimes pretended, this we denye to be notorious, or to be true at all. That kinde of defence which consisteth in denying the vnlawfulnes of a fact acknowledged to be done, cannot be taken away by the prerogatiue of the Prince, or by any law. *Sum accusatus de homicidio, fateor, sed volo me defendere quia feci me defendendo, ista defensio tolli non potest*: I am (*a*) sayth *Felinus* accused of Homicide, I confesse the fact, but I will defend that I did it in my owne defence, or vpon some other lawfull cause, this defence cannot be impeached. The like hath (*b*) *Panormitan*, (*c*) *Benedictus Vadus*, and others. And if this kind of defence, so intrinsecall a right of nature and iustice could be, or were once imbarred, alas, what oppressions

(a) *In ca. ex parte 2 de offi. delegat. nu. 4.*
(b) *In ca. dilecti de except. nu. 13.*
(c) *In repert. verb. defensio.*

pressions would there presently appeare in the world, what villanies swarme euery where? For would not euery charge, euen against innocencie it selfe be a condemnation, when the partie charged, and not condemned by lawe, must not be permitted to speake in his owne defence, nor in purgation of the sclaunder obiected? *Non sufficit quod factum sit notorium nisi etiam sint notoriæ qualitates ipsius facti, scilicet quod nulla defensio, siue excusatio competat.* The notoriousnes of the fact is not sufficient, as (*d*) *Alfonsus Vilagut* writeth, for the Iudge to proceede to the condemnation of any one, vnlesse the qualities, and all the circumstances of the same fact be likewise so notoriously ill, as no defence, excuse, or tergiuersation can be pretēded to the cōtrary: which if it be so, how much more doth the same hold true, ere the Iudge or ecclesiasticall superiour can forbid the accused to defend their vnguiltines, especially before triall & iuridicall condemnation?

The (*e*) excommunicate, the (*f*) bandite, the (*g*) hopelesse and deepest sunke person in all wickednes, are allowed to speake in their own defence, yea, the Diuell himselfe, if he should contend with another in iudgement, is not as (*h*) *Panormitan* and (*i*) *Durandus* write, to be put from this rite, and due of iustice. Againe (*k*) *Panormitan* affirmeth, & the like doth (*l*) *Felinus* with all (*m*) other of account; that a statute or decree which prohibiteth the accused to defend themselues, is of no validitie: by reason it impugneth the very instinct of nature, and of that kind of intrinsecall instinct of nature which most properly belongeth and proceedeth from reason. Alas (*n*) must now the ministers of Christ, and the dispensators of the mysteries of God, be inferiour to the Bandite or outcast of the world, in so conscionable a dutie? Must Priests being called the (*o*) Angels of the Lord of hosts, the children (*p*) of *S. Peter*, and the vicars of the Apostles, not receiue that tribute of iustice which cannot be denied to the Deuill? Vndoubtedly if this, being the practice of the aucthoritie and our case, be not to breake the law of nature, or to dispence therein, our wits, iudgement, and common reason are cleane extinguished, and all the learned must needes go to schoole againe; but to the third breach.

AS the authoritie is practised, it either transgresseth the law of man, and holie church, or else maketh our Archpriest a dispensor with himselfe in the same. And to begin our prooues hereof with his transgressings of the *Constitutiue Letter*. The said letter, only maketh him Archpriest ouer the secular priests, and giueth him no iuris-

(d) *In sua prac. cano. li. 3. de modo procedendi in criminibus notorijs conclu. 1.*
(e) *Ca. cum inter de except.*
(f) *Panor. in ca. Dilecti de except. nu. 13.*
(g) *Ibidem.*
(h) *In ca. Cum contingunt de foro compet. nu. 27. & in pract. ca. 3. nu. 2.*
(i) *Li. 3. de inquisitione § 5. nu. 6.*
(k) *In ca. Dilecti vbi supra.*
(l) *In eodem ca. nu. 6.*
(m) *Bartolus in l. cum mulier ff. sol. mat. Petr. de anchorano in reg. accessoriū in verb. 70. quæro de reg. iuris in 6. Baldus in ca. 2. de rescript. in fine, & alij.*
(n) 1. Cor. 4.
(o) Malach. 2.
(p) *S. Ambr.*

diction at all ouer the Laytie, especially to interdict thē. Also the letter giueth him authoritie to restraine, & take away priests their faculties, but granteth him no iurisdiction to impose any ecclesiasticall censure either suspension, interdict, or excōmunication vpon them. These things are all apparāt in the letter, saue that only about the censure of suspension, there may some vaine cauill, but no substantiall doubt be made, if places be conferred together, and no words oueruiolently diuorsed from their fellowes in the same clause. The words which can only make for shew of aucthority to suspend are these, *Si quis his in rebus inobedientem se, aut inquietum, aut contumacem ostenderit, hunc, post debitum admonitionē ac reprehensiones fraterna charitate præmissas, liceat etiam pænis coercere ecclesiasticis: ablatione nimirum facultum, vel suspensione,* If any one in these matters, shall shew himselfe disobedient, vnquiet, or stubborne, it is lawfull after due admonition and reprehensions, first vsed in brotherlie charitie, to correct this partie by ecclesiasticall penalties, *viz.* by ablation of faculties or suspending. Our Archpriest, and the maintainers of his clayme of hauing authoritie to suspend vs from the Aultar, and other diuine offices, do separate and abstract the word [*Suspending*] from the word [*Faculties*] and would haue it to signifie the generall Censure of suspension, and not the penaltie of suspending faculties only. To which we answere, that the said separation, and vnderstanding of the word, cannot be true, because the Cardinal particularising the faculties he giueth to the Archpriest, maketh no mention of suspending from the Aultar or other deuine offices, but only rehearseth these two, *facultatum restrictio, aut etiam reuocatio, si id necessitas postulauerit,* the restraining of faculties, or also the reuoking of them if necessity shall require it. So that in the first place, the Cardinall declareth the faculties he giueth to the Archpriest for him to chastice vs, if neede be. And in the second he directeth him when, how, and vpon what cause, he should vse the said punishing faculties.

In the constitutiue letter pag. 2.

And thus hauing shewed the reason, and our owne grounds, why we assure our selues that our Archpriest hath not aucthoritie to suspend vs from the Aultar, or from any other diuine office, saue only from the vsing of our faculties, let vs see the proofes by which he practiseth and iustifieth the contrarie.

After that *M. Blackwell* had suspended and interdicted me and diuers others, I addressed this Letter following vnto him.

Sir,

SIr, *M. Iackson* hath shewed me the * writing that Maister *N.* deliuered him frõ you. These are (as much as I may without preiudice to my appeale) to request you, first to giue me to vnderstand by what aucthoritie, you interdicted me, in respect that neither the letters patent, nor his Holines Breue, nor any addition that I euer heard of, giueth you any show of the like iurisdiction. Secondly, if you haue more aucthoritie then the *Constitutiue Letter*, the Additions, Instructions, and the Breue import, yet to vouchsafe to let me know the ground & warrantize you proceed vpon, in suspending and * declaring me to be interdicted without citing me before. Thirdly, that being the imposer of these heauie censures, you would not refuse to acquaint me by what lawe or right you can (hauing admitted my appeale) take this seuere course, so infinitely both to my owne hurt, and to the temporall, and spirituall domage of many others. Fourthly, to instruct me, by what rule of conscience you charge me with fraude, and so grieuouslie punish me for the same, making it a cause of inflicting the censures, for that * three names were put to the appeale, which the parties themselues, whose names they were, do now deny to haue yeelded their consents thereunto, wherein I am as free, be it true, or be it otherwise, from all fault, (the setting downe of their names being no acte of mine) as your selfe, or any man in the world. You say, because I sent you the appeale, a weaker colour could not be set out: I expect a better reason, or else I must thinke the iniurie to be most great. That *M. Trensham* was put downe in the appeale by the name of *Potter*, (this being the name whereby he was vsually called both in *Rome* and *Wisbich*, and taken to be his right name) is so light an errour, as amongst the wise, not worth the reckning of. I desire to receiue your answere and satisfaction to these, and in writing, as you deliuered my rebukes. Or if you meane not to deale so charitably with me, I would by these aduertise you, that there is small reason why I should make scruple to serue God in wonted manner. Our Lord forgiue you and father *Garnet*, if his aduise be to these afflictions, as without his aduise, one of the Instructions directeth you not to do any thing of waight: I leaue, not mistrusting but when the extremities are truly knowne, a good part of Christendome will cry shame vpon the iniustice and measure. Tenth of March when I receiued yours 1600.

Your Reuerences

Iohn Colleton.

*By which he suspended & interdicted eight of the prisoners in Framingham and my selfe.

* Because as *Nauar* writeth *li. 5. cons. de sent. exco cons. 65. nu. 5.* that no one can be declared excommunicated, suspended, or interdicted without summõs, and being heard before: and if without these he be declared, the declaration is none by the law it selfe.

*M. Thrensham, maister Cope, and M. Button, who sithence haue renewed, and sent their seuerall appeales to maister Blackwell.

M. Blackwell either disdaining, or not thinking it meete, notwithstanding the iust petitions of my letter to returne me answere, wrote a letter to *M. Iackson* for him to shew vnto me, which was also diuulged in the North, & God knoweth in what other parts of our realme, if not euery where. In which letter after it had phansied his reuenge to call me *the sonne of Beliall*, and to apply these places of scripture vnto

Eccle. 34. & 14.

me, *ab immundo quid mundabitur, & a mendace quid verum dicetur? Et, qui sibi nequam est, cui alij bonus erit?* What shall be clensed by the vncleane, and what truth can be spoken by a lyer? And he that is wicked vnto himselfe, to whom will he be good? He goeth on, and vseth these

His letter to M. Iackson the 18 of March 1600.

words, *But my authority in interdicting is denyed, when it is euident both by the letters of mine institution, and also by the Breue, that I may, inquietos pœnis coercere ecclesiasticis: and that I am appointed Archipresbyter Catholicorum Anglorum pro fœlici gubernio & regimine, ac mutua dilectione catholicorum &c. The wayward man is to know that the Canonists agree herein, that, qui habet iurisdictionem in foro externo, potest infligere censuras: yea he may reade that, Prælatus inferior Episcopo, potest facere statuta pœnalia contra subditos, statuendo pœnam ad eius arbitrium. Zab. in Clem. Cupientes § quod si, de pœnis.* Againe, that *Prælatus singularis habens iurisdictionem potest ponere interdictum &c. Zab. in Clem. ex frequentibus § quod etiam de sent. excom.* Moreouer, *Prælati inferiores Episcopo possunt præscribere iura quasi Episcopalia in sibi subiectos &c. Zecch. de Repub. ecclesiast. de prælatis in genere ca. 1. nu. 6. His bookes may teach him what I may do ex iure communi, if other sufficient warrant wanted. My ground I rest vpon, in declaring him to be interdicted without Citation before, is to be fōud out of Siluester verb. Citatio nu. 5. Write to him and to M. Clarke, I mind not, vntill I write to punish them farther &c.* Hitherto the words of *M. Blackwell*, and for more perspicuitie we will accommodate, and distinguish our answere by parts, according to the parcels of his proofes and allegations.

First where as his Reuerence affirmeth *that both by the letters of his institution and by the Breue he may correct the vnquiet by ecclesiasticall penalties*; we graunt it to be true. Neuerthelesse, if he will infer hereby (as he must, or else what he saith is to no purpose) that therefore he hath authority to suspend from the Aultar and to interdict, we deny the consequence. And the words immediatly following in the Cardinals letter do vtterly contradict any such illation, in that they limite and specify, what penalties these should be, namely, *ablatione facultatum vel suspensione*, either by taking away of faculties, or by suspen-

ding

ding the vse of them, as it hath bin proued before. Neither is there any one word of suspending from the Aultar, or interdicting, either in the Constitutiue Letter, or his Holines Breue.

Againe, let the word [*suspending*] be extended, contrarie to the tenor of the Cardinals letter, and the circumstances of the place, to signifie the ecclesiasticall censure of suspending from the practise of all diuine functions, as our Archpriest would enlarge it vnto: yet neuerthelesse how can the censure of interdict (which he hath imposed vpon certaine of our company by name, aswell as the censure of suspension) be vnderstood, to be contained vnder the limits of his authority, when neither the letters of his institution, nor his Holines Breue do expresse, or imply in generall or particular termes any such iurisdiction, as may be seene by euery one who will but reade the said letters and Breue? And here we can but note the indirect or deceitfull dealing, which is offered in citing places so by halfes, for proofe of the things they would prooue against vs, as if they did not maime or diuide the sentence, by leauing out words which immediatlie follow in the place, the very same authorities which they alleage for proofe of matters against vs, would most disproue their owne sayings. For example: After that our Archpriest had interdicted some nine of vs by name, I wrote vnto him the aforesaid letter, requesting his Reuerence to aduertise (if he would haue vs to obey him therein) by what authority he inflicted the like Censures vpon vs, because neither the Constitutiue letter, nor the additiōs annexed thereunto, did giue him any such kind of iurisdiction ouer vs: who to proue that he had authoritie to interdict vs, affirmeth that *by the letters of his institution, and also by the Breue, he may inquietos pœnis coercere ecclesiasticis, correct the vnquiet with ecclesiasticall penalties*, leauing forth the words which immediatlie followed, and which specified with what ecclesiasticall penalties he should correct, *ablatione nimirum facultatum vel suspensione*, namely, *by taking away their faculties or suspending*. Which words, and part of the sentence, if *M. Blackwell* had not left out, the very place he alleaged for proofe of his authoritie, did most clearely demonstrate and conuince the contrarie. Neither is this the first time, that such kind of foule play hath bin offered vs: for in the third of the twelue questions (which our Archpriest, or father *Garnet* in his name proposed vnto vs to be answered, in stead of graunting the dispute we intreated, for ending of the controuersie) the like pranck is practised, the propoūder alleaging *Zecchius* to affirme that, against vs for

In sua eccle. rep. de statu Ill. Cardinal. nu. 9.

them, which if the whole ſentence had bin taken, & not cut off guilefully in the mids, it had made moſt ſtronglie for vs againſt them. *Zecchius* words are theſe, (*Cardinali creditur teſtanti ſibi aliquid à Papa vinæ vocis oraculo mandatum, vt quod reſtituat aliquem natalibus, ſi tamen de magno alicuius præiudicio agatur, ei non creditur.* A Cardinall is to be credited on his word, affirming that he receiued a Mandate from the Pope by word of mouth, namely, that he ſhould make ſuch an one a Gentleman, who was of baſe bloud before: but if the matter whereof the Cardinall giueth teſtimony, concerne greatly the preiudice of an other, then is his ſole word of no ſufficient power, to bind any to belieue him. Now the propoſer of the twelue queſtions (were he father *Garnet*, or *M. Blackwell*) aſſumed only one part of the ſentence, as euery one may ſee, where the difficultie lay not, and which made for them, and omitted the other part, that belonged to the ſtate of the difference, and which made moſt ſtrongly againſt them. But can theſe odde ſhifts and paring of ſentences proclaime other then a bad cauſe, and lacke of ſinceritie in the mainteiners? No, no, the wiſe do note it.

Secondly, whereas our Superior affirmeth in his letter, *that he was appointed Archprieſt of the Engliſh Catholikes, for the happie rule and regiment and mutuall loue of Catholikes &c.* we pray him to ſhew vs whē, and by whom he was appointed Archprieſt of the lay Catholikes. The Conſtitutiue Letter maketh him Archprieſt but only ouer all the ſecular Engliſh Prieſts reſiding in *England* or *Scotland*. And though his Holines firſt Breue (for his ſecond was not extant long after *M. Blackwell* wrote theſe) ſignified *that the Cardinall had by his commaundement for the happie rule and gouernement, and mutuall loue, peace, and vnion, of the Catholikes of the kingdomes of England and Scotland, and for conſeruing and augmenting eccleſiaſticall diſcipline, deputed M. Blackwell Archprieſt by his Letters patents ouer the Engliſh Catholikes:* Yet no ſuch thing appearing in the ſaid Letters, *M. Blackwell* can no more rightfully ſtile himſelfe *the Archprieſt of Engliſh Catholikes*, (becauſe *per confirmationem Papæ, nihil noui iuris datur.* No new right is giuen by the Popes confirmation) then *Iohn Aſtile* can write himſelfe the Lieutenant of the Shire, becauſe the Queene commaunded the Lord Keeper to appoint him ſo, who neuertheleſſe in the commiſſion he ſent him, made him but Iuſtice of peace. And whether *Iohn Aſtile* be Lieutenant in this caſe or no, there is none of iudgement, eſpecially of knowledge in the lawes, but will ſay he is not, becauſe

Gloſ. in ca. Quis neſciat. diſt. 11. verb. Autoritate. & Gloſ. in ca. quia diuerſitatem de conceſ. Præbend. verb. forma cōmuni.

cause he is no more, nor can be taken for other, then the writ of Commission ordaineth him.

Thirdly, to that *M.Blackwell* saith, *that the wayward man is to know, that the Canonists agree that he which hath iurisdiction in the exteriour court, can inflict censures:* we answere, that it is true in any who hath iurisdiction in the exterior court by vertue of any ordinarie office or delegatine, vnlesse there be a forme prescribed together with the graunt of the delegatine authoritie, how he shall punish and proceede with the contumacious or delinquents. For if there be such a specification or limitation added to the authority, then that forme is most strictly to be obserued, and any thing done beyond it, is of no obligation: *Vbi datur certa forma procedendi, processus corruit non solum si aliquid attentatur directè contra formam, sed etiam citra vel præter formam.* Where there is a certaine forme giuen of proceeding, the processe falleth, and is of no effect, not only if an attentatiue be made directly contrary to the forme, but also if any thing be enterprised beside or out of the compasse of the forme. Againe, *Subdelegatus delegati Papæ si excesserit formam rescripti, processus est nullus.* The Subdelegate of the Popes delegate, if he shall exceede the forme of his commission, the thing that he doth therein, is of no force. And that *M.Blackwell* was the Cardinals Subdelegate, none can deny who shall reade the Constitutiue Letter.

Panorm. in ca. Prudentiam de offic. deleg. nu. 5.

Idem in Can. venerabili de off. deleg. nu. 1.

Now the ordinarie authority that *M. Blackwell* hath, being the only authority of an Archpriest, which giueth him no iurisdiction at all in the exterior court, because as the Canonists yeeld the reason, the (*a*) Archpriest supplieth the stead of the Bishop in celebration of certaine spirituall things, as the Archdeacon doth in matters belonging to iurisdiction: and therefore the Archpriest hath no power in the exterior court, as the authorities ensuing do proue. (*b*) *Archipresbyter iurisdictionem habet voluntariam, non tamen contentiosam.* An Archpresbyter hath a voluntarie but no litigious iurisdiction, that is, (*c*) he can exercise no authority by compulsion, but only where the parties are willing. (*d*) *Archpræsbyter punire aliquem non potest authoritate sua, sed de præcepto sui Episcopi.* An Archpriest cannot punish any body by his owne authority, but vpon commaundement of his Bishop.

(a) *Ioannes Andreas in ca. 1. de Archip. nu. 3. Lancelottus in Insti. nu. Ca li. 1. tit. 14. Hostiensis in summa, de offi. Archipræsb. nu. 2.*

(b) *Zecchius de Eccl. rep. ca. 24. nu. 14.*

(c) *Schardius in suo Lexicon. verbo Iurisdictio.*

(d) *Ioannes Andreas in ca. ministrum de Archipræsb. nu. 3.*

Of the other side, touching his delegatine authority, the particulars and the forme thereof are set downe, and therefore not to be extended to any thing that is beyond the limits of the said forme: or if in case it be further extended, neuerthelesse the like extension is of no validity nor bindeth any to obey, as the first, third, fourth and fift Propositions laid downe in the second Reason do most euidently teach & conuince. So that the vttermost of the authoritie concerning the inflicting of penalties vpon the disobedient, being (as hath bin before proued by the expresse words of the Constitutiue Letter) only to abridge, suspend the vse, or wholy depriue vs of our faculties, and neither to suspend vs frō the Aultar, interdict or excommunicate: it followeth directly that he can do none of these. Or if the words in the Constitutiue Letter [*vel suspensione*, or suspending] must be taken for the generall censure of suspending from what our Archpriest listeth, and not for suspending frō the practise of our faculties only, as the circumstance of the place, but especially the Cardinals rehearsing of the faculties, which he graunted to the Archpriest, doth most apparantly gainesay, and vtterly contradict any such ample signification of the word *suspending*: yet is it most certaine that he can not interdict, for this authoritie is no where specified either in the Constitutiue letter, additions, instructions, or his Holines Breue. Againe, it appeareth by an other reason, that notwithstanding the generall signification which the word *suspending* may beare, yet for that the matter is penall which is imported, the said word ought to be taken in a strict sense, because as *Siluester* writeth (e) *Cum verba sint ambigua & generalia, & factū odiosum, & alteri parti praeiudicatiuum, debet fieri interpretatio stricta.* Whē the words are doubtfull and generall (as in our case) and the fact displeasant, and preiudiciall to an other, there ought to be made a strict interpretation, and the words not to be trained to the largest sence.

Pag.23.24. & 25.

(e) *Verb. Excommunicatio 1. nu.6.*

Fourthly, touching the authorities, his reuerēce citeth out of *Zabarella* and *Zecchius*, *that an inferior Prelate to a Bishop, may ordaine penall statutes against his subiects, and assigne the penalties as he will himselfe: and that a single prelate hauing iurisdiction, may interdict: and that also lower prelates then Bishops, may prescribe lawes in a maner episcopall to their subiects.* We answere. Let it be so, that a lower prelate then a Bishop can do these things, yet how doth it appeare that himself is such a Prelate? Iwis whē this is proued, he being but an Archpriest, we shall see greater wonders, then euer any Canonist read or heard of. For if he can do these things by the authority and title of an Archpriest (as it is most sure by the places alleaged before, and by the vniforme consent of all writers that he can not:) then these and other like particulars, which his Reuerence hath aduentured vpon, being more, and beyond the

forme

forme of the Constitutiue Letter; it followeth most certainely, both, that he could not do them, or if he should do them, yet that they are of no obligation. First that he could not do them, is very cleare, because he could do no more in matters not belóging to the office of an Archpresbiter (which are all things requiring iurisdiction in the exterior court, as it hath bin proued before) then was expressed in the commission or instrument of his authority: And secondly that if he should do them, they are of no obligation, is also cleare, because whatsoeuer is done without authority *(f)* ne doth by law, nor can bind in cóscience: and therefore I can but maruell what moued his iudgement to write *that my books may teach me what he may do ex lege communi by right of the generall Law, if other sufficient warrants wanted*; when hauing but a delegatiue authority in all matters appertaining to the exterior court, and this also in a set forme prescribed vnto him, (which he could not exceede without the vsurping of authority, a *(g)* mortall sinne of his owne nature) would notwithstanding clayme, or seeme to clayme an increase of his punishing iurisdiction *ex iure communi*, from the generall law, sith the amplenesse thereof was particularised in the same Instrument, in which the office and prelature were graunted vnto him.

(f) *D.Tho.1.2.q.96.ar.4.c.& 2.2.q.60.ar.2.& 6.*

(g) *Idem, ibidem, & Nauar in man. ca.27.nu.8.*

Lastly concerning his *ground in declaring me to be interdicted without citation before*, I little doubt, but that vnder his leaue, he is greatly mistaken in the matter. For *Siluester* in that place only saith: *In facto notorio potest ferri sententia contra absentem non citatum, quando certum est absenti nullam competere defensionem.* Sentence may be giuen in a notorious fact against a party absent, and not summoned, when it is certaine that he can alleage no pretence for iustification or excuse of the fact. Our Archpriest in the letter or instrument, in which he suspended and interdicted me, and redoubled the taking away of all my faculties, layeth downe three causes of such his processe against me. First, for that I confessed to haue giuen consent to the prefixing of the reasons set before the Appeale: whereby, the same being the breaking of his decrees, I incurred, as he saith, the censure of suspension, interdict, and the losse of all my faculties. Secondly, for that I wrote other Letters not vnlike to those which the Appellants of *Wisbich* had addressed. Thirdly, for that I sent him the Appeale, wherein three of the Appellants, whose names were subscribed thereunto, had seriouslie or by other protested their vnwittingnes to the said Letters prefixed before the Apeale. These were the causes, which our Archpriest yeelded for inflicting the abouenamed censures and penalties vpon me, as the words of the Instrument it selfe do shew, which follow.

21. Febr. 1601 stylo Romano.

Quoniam autem D. Ioannes Colletonus non solum ob priores illas literas prætensæ Appellationi præfixas (quæ verius titulum libelli famosi sustinerent) quibus ipse fatetur se consensisse: sed ob recentes etiam 29. Ianuarij emissas, harum posteriorum W:sbicensium non dissimiles, in pœnas easdem incidit: eum quoque declaramus similibus censuris ac pœnis innodatum, sicuti per præsentes eum innodamus. Quod profectò vel eam solam ob causam facere necessariò deberemus, quod D. Doctori Georgius Trenshamus (quē illius libelli fabricatores Potterum nominant) Iacobus Copus, Richardus Buttonus, partim sub proprio chirographo ac iuramento, partim (sicut audiuimus) sub grauibus protestationib. negant se illis Literis consensisse. Cuius fraudis culpam, nos sanè nescimus in quem potius conyciamus, quam in D. Colletonum, à quo illæ Literæ ad nos transmissæ sunt: that is, And because Maister *Iohn Colleton* not only for those former Letters prefixed before the pretended Appeale, (which may truer beare the title of an infamous Libell) whereunto himselfe doth acknowledge to haue giuen his consent: but also in respect of his Letters lately sent the 29. of Ianuary, not vnlike to these later which came from *Wisbich*, hath fallen into the same penalties: him likewise we declare to haue incurred the like censures and penalties, *namely suspension, interdict, and the losse of all faculties,* as we by these presents do impose vpon him. Which truly we ought necessarily to haue done, though it had bin but for this only cause, that Maister *George Strensham* (whom the framers of that Libell call by the name of *Potter*) *Iames Cope, Richard Button,* partly by their owne hand-writing and othe, and partly (as we haue heard) by serious protestations, do deny euer to haue giuen their consent to those Letters. The blame of which fraude we trulie know, not to whom we should rather impute it, then to *M. Colleton,* who sent vs the Letters.

Now, that neither of these three imputed offences were so notorious as our Archpriest by law or conscience could declare me to be suspended and interdicted, or could suspend, interdict, or reduplicate the taking away of my faculties without citation before, or hearing what I could say in the matter, I lay this ground: That a fact be so notorious as the ecclesiasticall iudge may declare the doer to haue fallen into censures, or to impose censures vpon him for the same without summons, it is not only of necessity (as it hath bene aboue prooued out of *Alphonsus Vilagut, Panormitane,* and *Felinus*) that the fact it

selfe

selfe be notorious, but that also the nature and the circumstances of the said fact be likewise notorious, that is, so manifestly and palpably faulty, as no colour or tergiuersation can be pretended. For then only (as the (h) Canons teach) may the iudiciary order of citing be omitted, when the fact which is to be punished is apparant, knowne to many, and can neither be denied, nor iustified by any shift or pretext soeuer. Qualities, which can not fall in, or sort with any of the foresaid three offences obiected. And to shew that they can no way agree with the imputed offence of subscribing my name to the Appeale, or with yeelding my consent to the reasons prefixed before the same, we will first set downe the two braunches of the decree, for breaking of which, our * Archpriest affirmeth that we incurred the censures of suspension and interdict, and the losse of our faculties, and then after prooue that our default therein was not so notorious, that he could without citation declare vs to haue incurred the said censures and penalties.

(h) 2.q.1 *Prohibentur part. 2. & sequenti. & ca. Tua. de cohab. Cler. & ca. Vestra eod. tit.*

*In his Letter to the Assistents of the 28. of Nouemb. 1600.

Decretum 18. Octob. 1600. § 4.

Prohibemus in virtute sanctæ obedientiæ omnibus præsbyteris & sub pœna suspensionis atque interdicti, addo etiam amissionis omnium facultatum ipso facto incurrendarum ne quisquam præteritam inobedientiam quouis modo, verbo vel scripto, directè vel indirectè defendere præsumat.

§ 5. *Prohibemus sub pœna suspensionis à diuinis & amissionis omnium facultatum ne quis sacerdos vllo modo suffragia vel scripto, vel verbo, danda ambiat, vel det ad quamcunque causam, quam antea nobiscum vel cum duobus Assistentibus nostris non constat fuisse communicatam:* that is:

We prohibite all Priests in vertue of holie obedience, and vnder paine of suspension and interdict, I adde also of leesing all their faculties, to be incurred in the fact it selfe, that none presume any maner of way, by word or writing, directly or indirectly, to defend the former disobedience.

We prohibite vnder paine of suspension from diuine offices and losse of all faculties, that no Priest in any sort, either by writing or word of mouth, seeke or giue voyces in any cause soeuer, not knowne to haue bin communicated before to vs, or to two of our Assistants.

Now, though by the setting downe of our reasons why we did appeale, and the giuing of our names to the appeale, were a notorious or publike fact, which had many witnesses and could not be denied: neuerthelesse the nature and qualities of the fact were not so certainly and openly knowne to be criminous or ill, as that no circumstances or causes might occurre to make the same both lawfull and commendable. To defend our good names, being priests, and tootoo wrongfully assailed, and to seeke redresse by appellation to *S. Peters* chaire, of most vnworthy oppressions heaped on vs and the Catholike Laity, euen to the scandall and iniury of religion, are circumstances, and such approuing qualities of our fact, as do make our breach of the decree not only no apparant offence, but most euidently free it from all blame, or rather highly commend it. And to the end that the vnskilfull in the Latine tongue may see how vniustly our Archpriest hath proceeded against vs, as well in calling our reasons a (o) libelling, and * seditious letter, as in suspending, interdicting and taking away our faculties for putting our names to the Appeale, we will here set downe the whole Appeale it selfe in English truly translated, omitting the Latine, because that is already printed in our booke to his Holines.

(o) In his letter to Master Mush the first of March 1600.

* In his letter to M. Iackson the 18. of March 1600.

To the very Reuerend, Maister George Blackwell Archpriest of the Seminarie Priests in England.

VEry many, and most vnworthie are those things, which for these two yeares last past, we haue indured at the hands of the fathers of the societie of *Iesus*, and of your Reuerence, both approuing and multiplying their iniuries done against vs.

Among the reasons, why hitherto we haue borne with silence so vniust burdens, our affiance was not the least, that the equitie of our cause by little and little deeper seene into, some ease or tolleration of our said burdens, would in short time growe vnto vs. But hauing now by more then long tryall found, both our selues to be deceiued in our hopes, and also the weight of our afflictions so excessiuely increased by reason of such our qualited patience; that not only we our selues, but a great number of lay Catholikes, most deseruedly deare vnto vs, are thereby also maruellously oppressed, so that we are enforced by appealing to flee to the sea Apostolicke in most humble manner for succour. The reasons of which Appeale, are these that ensue.

The first cause.

First, for that your Reuerence hath often approoued the too great iniuries and reproch, which the Fathers of the Societie in word and deede, most wrongfully laid vpon vs: as namely when father *Lister* Iesuite composed, and had set forth a treatise of Schisme against vs (who vpon iust causes, deferred for a while, to subiect our selues to your authoritie, till either by view of Apostolicall letters, or other canonicall

nonicall proofe, the same were shewed to be instituted by his Holines commaund, and inioyned vnto vs) in which beside other vnseemely speeches, he hath these slaunders in the fifth paragraph.

These factious persons are striken downe with the dolour of their owne ruine, in that they haue resisted the Popes decrees: they haue lost their place among Priests: they are debarred the practise of their holie function: their iudgement is to be contemned, and alreadie they are condemned by the holie Apostolick Church.

And in the conclusion or seuenth paragraph, these.

1 *Ye are rebels.*

2 *Ye are schismatiques, and are fallen from the Church and spouse of Christ.*

3 *Ye haue troden vnder foote the obedience you ow to the Pope.*

4 *Ye haue offended against all humaine faith and authoritie, by reiecting a morall certaintie, in a morall matter.*

5 *Ye haue runne headlong into excommunication and irregularitie.*

6 *Ye haue lost the faculties by which you should haue gained soules to Christ.*

7 *Ye haue raysed vp so great scandall in the minds of all the godly, that as infamous persons, you are tensed in euery mans mouth.*

8 *Ye are no better then soothsayers and Idolaters, and in regard ye haue not obeyed the Church, speaking vnto you by the highest Bishop, you are as ethnicks and publicanes.*

When after the publishing of these detestable vntruthes, we made petition to your Reuerence, to know whether you did approue these defamations against vs, you answered vnder your owne hand-writing as followeth, 26. of March 1599. To Master I. C.

I allow of the said discourse and censure.

George Blackwell Archpriest.

Furthermore, when at an other time we made humble request to your Reuerence, for the reuoking of the said slaunderous treatise: you wrote backe this answere. April. 1599. To Master I. M. I. C. and A. H.

Your request is, that we should call in the treatise against your schisme, and this is vnreasonable, because the medicine ought not to be remoued, before the sore be throughlie cured; if it grieue you, I am not grieued thereat. *George Blackwell Archpriest.*

Also in your letters of the foureteenth of March, in the yere following, we hauing then written againe to your Reuerence about the seuerall infamies wherewith three of the Fathers of the Societie had To Master I. C. Th. M. Ro. D. A. H.

charged vs, and ſpecifying ſome of them in particular, you gaue this anſwere.

You note in theſe tearmes condemning vntruthes, not ſeeing how trulie and iuſtlie your condemned deſerts did draw ſuch names vpon you before your ſubmiſſion, and theſe names might haue taught you, how each mans iniquitie euermore hurteth himſelfe, neuer profiteth.

George Blackwell Archpriest, and Protonotarie Apoſtolicall.

In briefe, when father *Henry Garnet* prouinciall of the Ieſuites in *England*, writing to one of our auncient Prieſts, auowed among other indignities, this ouerbold aſſertion.

To Maſter I. C.

Ye haue in the iudgement of all the learned, incurred the moſt ſhamefull note of ſchiſme.

And turning his ſpeech to the Prieſt himſelfe, thus.

You haue ſo intangled them whom you haue brought to Christ, or whoſe paſtor and father you haue bene, as if they ſhall receiue Sacraments of you, if they ſhall induce you to ſay Maſſe, or ſhall aſſiſt you in celebrating, they ſeeme to partake with you in the crime of exerciſing your function vnworthilie, and in liew of a medicine, cary away poyſon 7. March. 1599.

And when the Prieſt to whom the foreſaid Letters were written, had reioyned, complayning of the iniurie, your Reuerence in behalfe of father *Garnet*, thus by letter anſwered him againe.

You ought for their writings and admonitions to haue thanked them in moſt dutifull and humble maner. And after a few lines: *I will defer to chaſten you for a while, in hope of your recouerie, and therefore this ſhall be to you, but as a meſſenger of puniſhment for your diſobedience, and as an aduertiſement for you to view aduiſedlie, how ignorance, errour, pride, and obſtinacie, haue drawne you within the compaſſe of ſchiſme.*

The ſecond cauſe.

The ſecond cauſe is, becauſe notwithſtanding we euer by word and writing, proteſted our ready obedience, to all and euery commaundement of his Holines, and that neither Breue nor other binding teſtimonie, ſhould ſooner at any time be ſhewed vnto vs, but it ſhould finde vs ſubmiſſiuely obedient in whatſoeuer: neither was this more or otherwiſe, then what our deedes themſelues made good. For as very many can witnes, no moment paſſed betweene the ſhewing of his Holines Breue, and our acceptance or abſolute ſubmiſſion to your authoritie: yea further, we were then alſo content meerely for peace ſake to remit all the reproch, infamie, calumniation, all and ſingular iniuries that were moſt riotouſly ſpent, in the interim, aſwell

againſt

against our selues, as our best friends: we say, that notwithstanding all this our pressed readines and submission, your reuerence diuulged the resolution following; which tootoo vnlucky fact, was the totall cause of these our new debates.

We haue receiued a resolution from our mother Citie, that the refusers of the appointed authoritie, were schismatiques. And surely I would not giue absolution to any that should make no conscience thereof. And a few words betweene. *And therefore my direction is, that they make accompt thereof, and do make satisfaction before they receiue the benefite of Absolution.*

And according to the purport of this dispersed resolution (which albeit by your owne affirmance, you receiued it either from father *Warford*, or father *Tichburne*, two English Iesuites resident at *Rome*: yet your reuerence did so propose and grace the same, as many then did, and as yet some do beleeue, that the said resolution came as a definitiue sentence, from the see Apostollke) your selfe would not restore *M. Benson* to the vse of his faculties, neither vpon his owne humble sute, nor mediation of his felow prisoners, who also had, and then did, suffer very hard imprisonment with great constancie, vnlesse he would first agnize and testifie vnder his hand, that he was grieued for his adherence to the schismaticall conuenticle, your reuerence being pleased, to dubbe our companie with so hatefull a name.

Also in your Letters to an other Priest, bearing date the 22. of February 1600. thus you write. To Master I. M.

I determined that hereafter, whosoeuer had faculties of me, he should first be content to recall his peeuish opinion (tearming the opinion peeuish, that doth not hold vs for schismatiques.)

Furthermore your reuerence affirmed (which shooke and galled the new peace not a little) that assertion of father *Iones*, a Priest of the Societie, to be true, auowing all those to incurre presently, the censures of holie Church, who should stiffely defend, that we were no schismatiques: which position you againe ratified in your Letters giuen the 14. of March 1600. To Master I. C. To Master R. D. Tho. M. A. H. &c.

The third cause is, because that after the contentions thus reuiued by your reuerence and the Fathers of the Societie, we, who euermore most desired peace, did neuer but finde you partiall on our aduersaries side, and towards vs and the cause in controuersie, a hard superiour, and so exceeding proane to haue vs generally condemned, that you spared not to forbid vs to defend our owne good names, vnder threat The third cause.

of grieuous punishment, as is manifest by your Letters of the 12. and 17. of February, and the 14. of March, where these words are read.

If euer I can finde hereafter, that either by word or writing you iustifie your enormous disobedience(*viz.* in delaying to yeeld your selues absolutely to our authoritie, before the comming of his Holines Breue) *as voide of sinne, this being a signe of want of grace, and the maintenance of sinne, which is a high pride: I will suspend you from your function, as vnworthie to exercise the same.*

Likewise when we, to take away the scandall, which by reason of this our imputatiue schisme, was rise euerie where, and to make peace againe in our Church now a long while most miserablie rent through this mutuall discord, besought most earnestlie your Reuerence, and the Fathers of the Societie, that it would either please you to leaue off to renue the calumnie of schisme against vs, or affoord your assistance and furtherance, that the question might quietlie be conferred of or disputed, by some of either side, before three or foure of the seniour Assistants, and one auncient Priest of our part, as vmpieres and determiners of the whole controuersie: your Reuerence vtterlie reiected the petition: in what sort, the words of your owne letters do best testifie, 14. and 16. of March.

To Maister I. C. F. C. I. M. &c.

Your petition is a tumultuous complaint.

Your prescriptions (so tearming our supplication) *are as emptie of due consideration, as they be blowne out with the spirit of a tumultuous presumption.*

Your supplication cauilleth against my proceedings, and the speeches of my best friends. I shall much muse, if ye shall not be abashed of this your attempt.

Moreouer, when seuerall detractiue letters written by Father *Parsons* and others, and made common in our countrie, did dailie more and more wound in credit both our selues and our dearest friends: and when for this cause our ghostly children (who together with vs, were both reputed and shunned by you, as schismatiques, or at the least as very grieuous sinners, and for none other fault, saue only for that they tooke our part, and relieued our miseries) very instantly delt with vs, that now without any further delay, we would addresse our selues, to free both their and our owne innocency from the crimes and calumniations imputed: Wherefore as men thereunto obliged in conscience, we determined as well for the remouing of infamie frõ

As that to Master A. G. the 13. of Iuly 1598. and to his friend the 20. of Febr. 1599. and to M. Bish. the 9. of Octob. 1599. and others.

our

our priesthoode, as to bring quietnes of conscience to such as are vnder our charge, to diuulge a temperate apologie: which intention and designe of ours being vnderstood, your Reuerence anon prohibited vnder heauy censure and forfet of faculties, the diuulging of such a defence, & to this purpose vsed a smooth pretence of godlines & peace, *viz. least the lawfull state might be troubled, or any mans good name receiue blemish,* as is apparant by the specialties that follow.

I George Blackwell *Archpriest in England, in vertue of holie obedience, and vnder paine of suspension from your office, and losse of all faculties in the deede it selfe to be incurred, do prohibit all Priests, to diuulge any booke set out within these two yeres, or hereafter to be set out, by which the lawfull state may be disturbed, or the fame of any clergy Catholick person, of our English nation may be hurt by name: and the same commaundement is giuen to the laitie vnder paine of being interdicted, 17. January 1599.*

George Blackwell *Arch-priest.*

The seueritie of which edict appeareth so much the greater, in that your Reuerence afterward declared, that you tooke the word [*booke*] in the signification which it carrieth in *Bulla cœnæ domini*, where hereticall bookes are forbidden, so as now we fall into the aboue-mentioned penalties, if we but diuulge the least writing or defence, whereby any english catholick Clergie-man (such as all our hard friends be) shall or may receiue blot or hurt in his good name; neither skilleth it whether iustlie, or vniustlie, vpon desert or without, the edict containing no such limitation or prouiso at all. And being after this maner suspended and depriued of faculties, we are therewith bereft of all the meanes, of getting sustenance, harbour, or other temporall succour, these euery way depending on the practise of our priestly function and vse of faculties.

Finally, seeing that there was neither meane nor measure kept in opprobrious speeches against vs, nor that we might any way obtaine a friendly discussing and ending of the matter betweene our selues, no, nor as much as to be licenced to defend our cause or good name, either by word or writing: we especially for the greater safetie of our conscience, held it our bounden dutie to propose the whole difficultie and state of the controuersie, to the Diuines of the Vniuersitie of *Paris,* to the end, that they taking pitie of the calamitie of our Church, and the sooner, through the mediation of our humble sute, would vouchsafe to deliuer their censure & opinion, in the difference.

Which good and charitable office, they no ſooner performed, but your reuerence enacted a decree, that no one vpon paine of heauieſt forfeitures, ſhould any way maintaine the cenſures of ſo great and famous Clarks. The ſtate of the queſtion, the reſolution of the Vniuerſitie, and the edict of your reuerence, follow word by word.

In the yere of our Lord 1600. vpon the third day of May &c. as it is verbatim ſet downe in the page 146.

The fourth cauſe.

The fourth cauſe is, becauſe your Reuerence doth very earneſtly defend whatſoeuer the fathers of the Society either ſpeake or do againſt vs, in ſo much that when we refuſed to obey them in that counterfet imputation of ſchiſme, and required a retractation of that foreſaid infamous Libell, your Reuerence ſtood ſo mightily againſt vs, that for this cauſe the 17. of October 1600. it pleaſed you to reuoke and wholy to take away all faculties from two of our moſt auncient and reuerend Prieſts. By which fact, very many of good place and account, were touched with ſo great griefe, ſcandall, and offence, that euery where they bewayled and complained of this calamitie, and ſo much the more, for that theſe were the ſpeciall men, that had longeſt and beſt deſerued of our Church, and being greatly loued of Cardinall *Allen* of pious memory, were by him honored with ſpeciall and extraordinary faculties aboue the reſt.

Furthermore, although your Reuerence could not but ſee, that all theſe perturbations of peace and concord which are now in our Church, tooke their beginning at firſt, and continued afterwards vpō no other cauſe or motiue, but the defence of father *Garnet* and father *Liſters* paradoxe of the imaginatiue ſchiſme, and the patronage of that more improbable aſſertion of father *Iones* aboueſaid; and albeit likewiſe, that your Reuerence very well knowes, that all theſe miſchiefes or home-diſſentions might at the beginning, and may yet without any difficultie, be quenched by the retractation of theſe opinions: yet for all this, your reuerence had rather that all places ſhould be diſquieted with the trouble of theſe variances, and that maſters and ſeruants, parents and children, husbands and wiues, paſtors and ſheepe, Prieſts and lay people, ſhould grow to a hurly burly and mutuall contention, yea and that Prieſts themſelues ſhould fall at iarres by meanes of this controuerſy, then that thoſe three fathers of the Society ſhould reuoke their errors, or by acknowledging their temeritie, make ſatisfaction to thoſe whom they had offended by ſuch, and ſo great an iniury.

The

The fift cause is, that seeing the holy Canons do ordaine, and the lawes of nature it selfe and of all Nations do require, that no man being accused, ought to be condemned of the crime, or endomaged in his goods or fame, or suffer any punishment in his person, till he be first in some sort cited, and permitted to answere vnto the crimes obiected: yet your Reuerence doth testifie by your owne writing, that you in no sort are bound to any of all these rules, either in iudging or punishing, and this also, by the will of his Holines himselfe. By which new kind of iudgement and authority neuer heard of since the world begun, your Reuerence hath lately taken away all the faculties from our two Priests as is said before, and there is none of vs, but may iustly feare, least that ours likewise be taken from vs, how much soeuer this course of proceeding seeme to violate the expresse tenor of the Letters patents of the most illustrious Cardinall *Caietane*, Protector of good memory, by the which, your authority was delegated vnto you, as doth manifestly appeare to him that reades the same, your R. owne writing we will heere set downe word for word.

The fifth cause.

From Master I. M. and I. C.

§ *It is not his Holines intention, nor neuer was, that in exercising of my authority for correction of manners, and conseruing of our ecclesiasticall discipline and peace in this time and in these difficulties, that we should be bound in any wise to the forme of contentious or Court trials, especially in the reuocation of faculties, the graunt whereof, as also the continuance is to be deemed meerely voluntary, whereas delegated faculties do cease, without any crime committed, at the only pleasure of the graunter, or of one that hath authoritie from him. Iune* 17. 1600.

G. B. Archpriest of the Cath. of England.

To Master R. Ch.

The last cause is, for that your Reuerence hath by ordayning decreed (we will vse your owne very words) and promulgated a degree, wherein you haue pronounced and declared all vs, who before the comming of the Apostolike Breue, made stay of submitting our selues, for many causes, vnto your authority, to be in very deede disobedient to the See Apostolike, and rebellious to your office instituted by the same See; and haue moreouer, vnder paine of suspension, interdiction, and losse of all faculties to be incurred *ipso facto*, prohibited vs, that by no meanes we should presume either by word or writing, directly, or indirectly, to defend that our delay; wherein your Reuerence and the Prouinciall father of the Society of Iesus, with others your complices, do affirme and boldly maintaine the nature of deadly

The sixt cause.

ſinne, and very ſchiſme it ſelfe to be included: and many mo through your authority and perſwaſion, haue commonly holden vs, and do ſtill repute vs as men guilty of the ſaid enormities. Whereupon we cannot but wonderfully admire the too too great ſeueritie of this decree, both depriuing vs of the reputation of our good names, and bringing burden intollerable for many reſpects vpon vs. For ſeeing we are commaunded, both by Gods law and mans, yea by the very inſtinct of nature it ſelfe, and laſtly by the reaſon of our office, to defend our fame, and ſo neere as we can to preſerue it from touch or blemiſh; your Reuerence hath expreſſely forbidden vs this duty, vnder moſt grieuous eccleſiaſticall penalties and cenſures. And whereas beſide, we tooke our orders of Prieſthood (by which inſtitution of life we fell into the heauy diſpleaſure of our Prince, and are made incapable of all temporall commodities, and are euery minute in continuall danger to looſe our liues) only for the recouery of ſoules, and for propagating the Catholike faith: your Reuerence hath bereaued vs of that ſpeciall thing, which before others, was moſt neceſſary to the attayning of the ſame, *viz.* the vſe of our faculties, for this only cauſe, that we labored to free our good names from infaming calumniations, as we are bound to do. Whereof it muſt needs follow, that we ſhall in ſhort ſpace be brought to vnſeemely beggery and want of all neceſſaries, and ſoone after, to moſt certaine deſtruction of life. We purpoſely omit here to make any mention of that prohibition of yours, to wit, *that no man goe about to ſeeke or giue any voyces, or make any meetings or aſſemblies.* Which reſtraint is thought to bee ordayned by your Reuerence to this end, that all courſes may be debarred vs by theſe meanes, both of repelling vniuſt oppreſſions by mutuall connexion of voyces and wils, and likewiſe of appealing to *Peters* Chaire.

With the like ſeuerity, your Reuerence in the ſame decree, doth alſo thunder the penaltie of interdiction to be incurred *ipſo facto*, againſt all the laiety that ſubmit not themſelues to your ſentence or iudgement in this controuerſy. The ſharpnes of which hard dealing, may iuſtly ſeeme to them for this cauſe the more violent, in reſpect that the penalties which they are charged by the lawes of our country, become ſo much the heauier and more burdenſome vnto them. For thoſe that are of ability, pay twenty pound a moneth to the Queenes Eſchequer, and thoſe that pay not the former ſumme, forfet all their goods, and two third parts of their lands: and if it can be

prooued

prooued that they haue heard Maſſe, they pay one hundred marks. Likewiſe if they receiue any prieſt into their houſe, or otherwiſe releeue his wants, they looſe all their goods, lands, and life. Which being ſo, they thinke your Reuerence dealeth too ſeuerely and vniuſtly with them, by inflicting this cenſure of Interdict, whereby they neither can receiue Sacraments, nor be preſent at diuine Seruice, nor yet be buryed after. chriſtian maner, if either they defend the ſentence of the moſt famous Vniuerſity of *Paris* (as appeareth by the Decree of your Reuerence before alleaged) or take vpon them in any ſort to defend the good names of their ghoſtly fathers, or any way cleare thoſe from the imputation of ſchiſme, by whoſe good meanes they were either firſt brought to the obedience of the See Apoſtolike, or continued in the ſame, and do well know by their long conuerſing with them, the ſincere integritie of their liues. The Decree is, as followeth.

We by our authority receiued from his Holineſſe, do pronounce and declare, that thoſe firſt letters of our Inſtitution, did truly bind all the Catholicks in England, and that thoſe who haue any wayes wittingly impugned our authority, were truly diſobedient to the See Apoſtolike, and rebellious againſt our office inſtituted by the ſame See. And a little after.

We forbid all Prieſts in vertue of holie obedience, and vnder paine of ſuſpenſion and interdict (the abſolution whereof we reſerue to our ſelues) I adde alſo, the loſſe of all their faculties to be incurred ipſo facto : *the Laiety likewiſe, vnder paine of interdict to be incurred* ipſo facto, *that none of them preſume in any wiſe by word or writing, directly or indirectly, to defend that former diſobedience, the cauſe of ſo great perturbation of peace amongſt vs.*

Instructed by long experience, what great inconueniences haue growne to the vpholding of diſcord by thoſe priuie meetings, which in former yeares we haue prohibited, ſo farre as they haue bin the nouriſhments of ſchiſmes: do therefore once againe ſtrictly forbid all ſuch aſſemblies, commaunding all our aſſiſtents, and other reuerend Prieſts, that they aduertiſe vs of all ſuch meetings and aſſemblies, which tend not to the furtherance of piety and hoſpitality, or of ciuility and peace. And we prohibit vnder paine of ſuſpenſion from diuine functions, and loſſe of all faculties, that no Prieſt, in any wiſe by word or writing, goe about either to ſeeke or giue any voyces for what cauſe ſoeuer, before the ſame be knowne to be communicated with vs, or with two of our aſſiſtents. Theſe things are in the aforeſaid Decree.

For which intollerable wrongs and oppreſſions, and many other indignities which we haue indured theſe two yeares ſpace and more, and for that likewise we do not know, whether your Reuerence hath any authority at all to make Decrees, seeing no such facultie appeareth in the Constitutiue Letter.

In the name of God Amen. In the yeare of our Lord 1600. 13. Indiction, the 17. day of the moneth of Nouember, and in the 9. yeare of the Papacy of our most holy Father *Clement* by the prouidence of God the eight of that name. We English Priests, whose names are vnder-written, finding our selues agrieued in the premisses, and fearing more grieuous oppressions in time to come, do make our appeale and prouocation to the Sea Apostolike, and aske of you Maister *George Blackwell*, the first, second, and third time, instantly, more instantly, and most instantly our Apostles or dimissory letters, submitting our selues, and all we haue, persons, faculties, goods, and rights, to the tuition, protection, and defence of our most holy Father *Clement* the eight, and to the See Apostolike. And we make this our appeale in our owne names, and in the names both of the Cleargie and Laiety, of which later, there are many hundreds, whose names for iust causes are concealed, that adhere vnto vs by meanes of the controuersie of schisme, or in any of the aforesaid matters, or dependance, or prosecution thereof, or after any other sort: desiring, if there be any thing to be added, taken away or changed for the more validitie of these presents, that the same may be added, taken away, or changed, as the forme of lawe shall require.

Giuen at Wisbich, the yeare and day of the moneth, Indiction, and the yeare of the Papacy, as aboue.

Thomas Blewet.
Christopher Bagshaw.
Christopher Thules.
Iames Tayler.
Iohn Thules.
Edmund Caluerley.
William Coxe.
Iames Cope.
Iohn Colleton.
George Potter.
Iohn Mush.
William Watson.
William Clarke.
Iohn Clinsh.
Oswell Needem.

Roger Strickland.
Robert Drury.
Francis Momford.
Anthony Hebbourne.
Anthony Champney.
Iohn Bingley.
Iohn Boswell.
Robert Thules.
Cuthbert Troolop.
Robert Benson.
Richard Button.
Francis Foster.

Edward Bennet.
Iohn Bennet.
William Mush.

Since

Since the making of this Appeale, there are others who haue subscribed thereunto, and giuen their names, as Maister Doctor *Norris*, Maister *Roger Cadwalader*, and Maister *Iasper Lobery*, beside some other, who for feare of the extremitie vsed against the Appellants, durst not (their friends being few, and their state meane) manifest themselues to our Arch-priest, but sent their Appeales by our bretheren that are gone to *Rome*. The Letter following was sent, together with the Appeale.

VEry Reuerend Sir, we send you our Appeale herein inclosed, and haue prefixed the reasons:to the end,your self denying to mitigate the rigour on foote against vs, our countrie may see, till further satisfaction come foorth,whereupon the discreete may suspend their condemnation of vs. Another cause that alike moueth vs thereunto, was, the affiance we hold, that your Reuerence vnderstanding our grounds in this full maner, would neither reiect the appeale, nor blame vs for the making, and lesse punish vs for a necessitie so many wayes behoouable. Againe, our pouertie, want of meanes, skill, and friends, to prosecute the matter, did not a little perswade the particularizing of some of our pressures; in regard the persons, whose helps we are to solicite in the managing of the busines, may the more willingly, viewing the measure of our oppressions, yeeld vs their most furtherance. How long, and with what discontentment of my fellowes,I haue prolonged the sending of the appeale,in hope of a more quiet issue in the difference; none almost that are of our side but can witnes. And now being brought in dispaire of expecting any such good end, by the tenour of your yesterdayes Letter, I can but grieue, and commend the successe to God. Concerning that part of your last Edict, which forbiddeth vnder heauiest penalties, either to giue, or collect suffrages vpon any cause soeuer, before the same be communicated to your selfe, or to two of your reuerend assistants, how hard soeuer the Iniunction appeareth, yet for obedience, we acquaint you by these, with our determination of procuring other our bretheren to subscribe to the appeale; and as their names shall come to our hands, so to send them vnto your Reuerence. Thus beseeching the goodnes of almightie God, euer to guide you, to the doing of his holie will, I take my leaue. Nouember. 25. 1600.

Dutifully yours,
I. Colleton.

Now our precedent appeale being *à grauamine* from aggreuances, we were consequently bound to *(a)* expresse particularly the causes of our appellation, *(b)* nor could we by law alleage any other causes though neuer so notorious in the prosecution of the appeale, then such only as we had before set downe in the same. Which plainely sheweth the necessity we had to particulate and prefixe them in the maner we did. And to the end they might appeare not to be feigned, we quoted the letters, annexed the date, and cited the words which deliuer the aggreuances. Againe, it seemeth most strange how this orderly course (the Canons *(c)* licensing euery one to appeale vpon reasonable cause, & none of the causes rehearsed, carying with them but sufficient matter of appellation) can be called either a seditious pamphlet, or a libelling letter (as our Arch-priest vseth them both) when the substance of all that we auerred was wholy taken out either of his owne letters, or out of their writings * *whose counsaile* (by his owne affirmance) *is the stay, and their friendship the continuance of our whole catholicke state, and whome to follow is his comfort,* except we must be intreated as our Sauiour was by the high Priest, who for repeating the high Priests words, was said to blaspheme; And so we alleaging what our Arch-priest and some of the Fathers wrote and maintained against vs, the allegations must be termed libelling and seditious, whereas we rehearsed but their owne words, and such as themselues diuulged, iustified, and seemed to take pleasure in. Yea further, our repeating of their words, and this also by way of appeale to his Holines, must be so notorious and hainous a crime in vs, that for the same we must be euen after appellation suspended, interdicted, bereaued of our faculties, and publiquely declared without citation before to be such, and the subscribing likewise to the foresaid repetition defined *a breach of wholesome decrees.* Vndoubtedly, if this manner of proceeding be not to infringe or dispence in the lawes of holy Church, or not rather to turne vpside downe the hierarchy of all ecclesiasticall discipline, there was neuer hitherto disorder in the christian world. *(d) Nemo Episcoporum quemlibet sine certa & manifesta peccata causa communione priuet ecclesiastica:* Let no Bishop saith the Cannon, depriue any other from ecclesiasticall communion, without certaine and manifest cause of sinne. And which cause also by the *(e)* constitution of Pope *Nicholas*, ought to be proued before the censure be inflicted: or else the Prelate so vndiscretly offending is to be punished

(a) *Pan. in ca. vt debitus de appel. nu. 38. & in Clement ca. appellanti de appel. nu. 1. Decius in ca. vt debitus de appel. nu 83. & alij.*

(b) *Clement. ca. appellanti de appel.*

(c) *Ca. super eo secundo de appel.*

In his letter to Maister *T. B.* and in his letter to M. *Mush* the 1. of March 1600.

* In his letter to M. *Mush* the 21. of Febr. 1600.

Math. 26.

(d) 11. *q.* 3. *nemo.* 2.

(e) 1. *q.* 6. *ca. Nono.*

punished with the same penaltie, and to make *(f)* satisfaction for the domages sustained.

(f) *Ca. sacro. de sent. exco. & ca. Cum medicinalis eod. tit*

The second cause that our Archpriest alleageth for suspending, interdicting, and reduplicating the taking away of my faculties, is for writing a letter the 29. of Ianuary, which as he saith, *is like to those which the Appellants of Wisbich addressed vnto him.* And what those were I know not: but the letter for which he punisheth me in so rigorous sort, is the letter that followeth, and which I wrote to a lay Gentleman, taxing me of seuerall faults, and in reply to one of his, as the tenor sheweth.

Sir, I wrote to know whether you spake the words, not whether you spake them lately, or long since; neither did I auerre more then that only the notice of the speeches was giuen me the night before the date of my letter.

You say, *you know not wherein you haue charged me with ambition, spite, and reuenge.* Sir, reade but ouer my letter againe, and consider of the words you are sayd to haue reported of me, and you may easily see wherein, and how, you charge me with the sayd enormities, for reckning me (as you do) the chiefe of those whom you call contentious, what followeth more directlie (if I be chiefe of the sayd companie, and that also the totall cause of the stirres, another affirmance of yours, is or was no other, but because my selfe was not appointed Arch-priest) then that I am through this my continuall maintenance of the controuersie vpon the foresaid wicked ground, both ambitious, spitefull, and euen great with reuenge, yea and enuy too.

You also affirme, *that you tooke a great dislike at the last time you talked with me, by reason of certaine words I then vsed of spite and reuenge against a religious person, that beholding as in a glasse such imperfections in a man of my sort, it hath made you euer since the more heedfull to shunne the fault.* Sir, I am glad that my frailties are steps to your vprising in vertue. But touching the truth of your affirmations, what might the words be that I then vsed, and which so mightily disliked you? I remember that when you extolled father *Parsons*, auowing him to haue procured, & done more good to our country, then any other that liued these many yeres: I answered, that I could so litle be of that opinion, as I verily thought him of meaner deserts in that point, then any other that was a Catholick & loued his country-men. And thus much I hope I shall be able to make good by euidence of moe particulars, then your ſelf or any other ſhall be able to diſproue. Further I recall, that when you would free father *Parſons* from writing any vntruths, I replyed and ſaid, I could reprooue his pen of many, which now againe I ſhould haue no ſcruple to double ſpeake it, might not the ſame miniſter an occaſion of a new diſlike vnto you; yea and to all too that he hath ſhewed in ſome number of his actions as little ſinceritie, as truth in his writings. No doubt you will heere cry fye on paſſion. But patient your ſelfe, and thinke if I be put to prooue it, I may perchance ſhew it to be rather the iſſue of true charitie, then of choler or paſſion. For father *Parſons* being but one, and one who alreadie in many places carrieth but a hard report; and thoſe of whom he taketh his pleaſure being many, and ſuch as euery where moſt men ſpeake well of, and the matters wherein they are accuſed by him very foule: reaſon and conſcience tell, if proofes were alike of both ſides (as I take them to be much vnlike) yet that it were a point of greater charitie rather to thinke that father *Parſons* ſtrained a point in the accuſations, then to condemne ſo many as ſtand accuſed, and of like offences.

Moreouer where you ſay *I exacted an oath of you for concealing my ſpeeches,* I verily thinke you are miſtaken. My reaſon is, becauſe I do not remember that for theſe many yeares ſpace, I euer exacted an oath of any in what ſecreſie ſoeuer, but only contented my ſelfe with an aſſured promiſe. Or be it as you ſay, I do now free you of the bond, and giue you moſt franke leaue to diuulge it to whome, and how many, you pleaſe.

You notifie in your Letter, *that you neuer regarded to put your ſelfe in my companie ſince you heard me ſpeake ſuch vncharitable words* (as you terme them) *againſt a religious perſon.* Well, I hope as good men as your ſelfe will make no conſcience to be in my companie.

But why I pray you do you ſpecifie thus much of your diſpoſition vnto me, the knowledge thereof no more auailing? Is it for that my ſelfe and the world ſhould ſee how exactlie you obey the commaundement of holie ſcripture, *Cum detractoribus non commiſcearis,* Companie not with detractours? I do not beleeue it, becauſe I can not beleeue that you are alike ignorant, as to take that to be detraction which is ſpoken in refutation of defaming vntruths, in defence of innocency, and in preſeruing the odour of our good names, as alſo in diſcharging the bond that God, nature, & the duties of our function lay vpon vs, being Prieſts as well as father *Parſons,* and hauing the

particular

particular charge of more ſoules then (I thinke) he hath, and abiding within the reach of our countrie-perils, from which he long ſince forſaking our campe, hath reſcued himſelfe. Or if you be ſo ignorant, that you know not to put difference betweene chalke and cheeſe, yet why are you more nice to come into my companie, then you are to conuerſe (and moſt affectionately) with others, who by toong and pen, in ſecret and in publick, and with diſcouerie of infinite more paſſion, haue at once ranſacked the good name and eſtimation of many Prieſts, whereof ſome alſo (how vile a wretch ſoeuer my ſelfe am) are imputed no whit their inferiours, either for vertue, iudgement, experience, ſufferance, or learning, except in the glorie of a religious name, or title of authoritie. I ſay ranſacked their good names and eſtimation, by denouncing them to be ſchiſmatikes, to be fallen from Gods Church, to be excommunicate, irregular, without faculties, to miniſter Sacraments vnworthily, to continue in a damnable ſtate, to bring mortall ſinne vpon thoſe that partake with vs in Sacraments, or ſerue vs at Maſſe, and deliuering the precious body of our Sauiour to our penitents, to deliuer poyſon. But I will leaue you to your partiall ſcruples, and ſtirre this puddle no further, nor aske you moe queſtions, but deſcend to another point.

Whether the Letter you wrote right before the comming ouer of his Holines Breue, were fulleſt of moſt vnſeeming and bad termes, let the by-words and aſſertions folowing taken out of the ſaid Letter, and by you imputed vnto me, beare witnes for me: namely, *diſobedient, factious, directlie againſt the authoritie of his Holines, as all but wilfull blind men may eaſily diſcerne: obſtinate, reſiſting lawfull autheritie: wilfulneſſe, obſtinacie, diſobedient diſpoſition: my credit to be in the waine: my preſent ſtate is adiudged ſchiſme; and my perſiſting therein feared a reuolt.* Now Sir be iudge your ſelfe, whether theſe termes (and yet theſe were not all that your Letter contained) be not in number ſufficient, and of that qualitie, as may well verifie that your Letter was fulleſt of vnſeeming and bad termes? Certes whatſoeuer you thinke, my ſelfe made alwayes conſcience to ſhew your Letter to any Lay perſon, nor did the partie either reade the ſame, or heard it read to my knowledge, what intelligence ſoeuer was aduertiſed of her ſpeeches thereupon vnto you. And for Prieſts, I neuer ſhewed it to any, who did not condemne it for a moſt bold and vncomely kind of writing, that I ſay no worſe.

You aduertiſe, *that one who indured the authoritie as impatientlie as my selfe, is become an Apostata, and that other of our companie liue so scandalouslie, as good men thinke them nighest to ruine.* Sir, if by the Apostata you meane M. *Butler* (as I thinke you can meane none other) then must I say you do vs iniurie, for Maister *Butler* neuer tooke part with vs, for ought that euer I knew or heard, but was alwayes of our Arch-priest his side, and now since his fall, hath not letted to insult and preferre his case before ours, in respect his faculties were neuer taken from him, as Maister *Mushes* and mine were, and still are. And by whom you meane the other part of your speeches, I neither know nor can coniecture. But if you vnderstand them by any of those that subscribed to the Appeale, or that refused to giue their names to the cunning drift of *olim dicebamur*, I am the more sorie, but shall not beleeue you, till I see it true in the effect.

Moreouer you auouch, *that those men which now are most obstinate to obey, laboured all they could at Rome to make me and other their friends Archbishops and Bishops.* Surely, hardnes of beliefe in the reports that make against vs, is not your fault, God graunt your facilitie or rashnes therein be no greater. What were their names Sir, that so mightily laboured our promotion at *Rome?* My selfe knoweth none that were there to labour it, saue only Doctor *Bishop*, and Maister *Charnock*, and the one of them liuing out of the Realme, is no way subiect to Maister *Blackwels* authoritie, and therefore neither *most obstinate*, nor obstinate at all *to obey* as you affirme. But did these two or either of them labour to make me, or any others within our Realme, I say not Archbishops, for that is too fabulous, but Bishops? Let the records of their examination be reueiwed, and it will euidentlie appeare that neither of them euer named other for Bishops, but only Doctor *Elie*, and Doctor *Barret*. And how did they also labour this preferment? You say, *that they laboured it all they could.* And what possiblie could that all be, when they were committed close prisoners, and apart, ere they had entred into any course of dealing, or throughlie mentioned their intentions, and so continued in that kind of indurance, till father *Parsons* had made all sure by getting forth a Breue for confirmation of his plotted authoritie. Me thinks you should do well, for so much as you write, that *some are most obstinate to obey*, to particularize their names, and let vs and others know them. But I dare say, you can not name the Priest in our companie, who hath refused to obey Maister *Blackwell* since the confirmation of his authoritie, in any point, or iot soeuer, that our reason, reading, and the counsell of the learned, hath thought vs bound vnto, or not clearely resolued the contrary.

You say, *you will prooue where one at least of my friends said, that for certaine I should be a Bishop.* Sir, I could wish I did know whether the intelligencer did here my friend to appoint the time, when, or within which, I should be made a Bishop; for if he did, and the time be past, he, or you, or both, may boldly tell my friend (vnlesse difference in your states do make it ill nurture) that his certaintie did greatlie deceiue him. But let this be as it may be, yet what worthie exception can the report bring against me, vnlesse I had all the toongs of my friends tyed in a string, as they can not speake ought belonging vnto me, but by my assent or prompting? Can you, or your intelligencer, or any other prooue, or wil say, that I soothed my friend in the speech, or that I heard it, and did not reprehend him, or her, whatsoeuer the speaker was, for the same? If you can prooue thus much, you say somewhat, otherwise prouing what you can, you say nothing that is materiall against me in this point.

Finally, *to that you say, that if at the first the authoritie had bin cast vpon me, as it was vpon Maister* Blackwell, *I would vpon such good grounds as he did, haue accepted and exercised the same, without testimonie of a Breue to confirme it*; I thus answere in few words: I confesse I knew not of certaintie what I should haue done if the accident had so fallen out; but if you will haue my coniecture, and what my thoughts now giue me, I do verily perswade my selfe, that if I had made, and set downe in writing the like reasons in the disallowance & reproofe of the other kind of gouernment before intended, as Maister *Blackwell* did, and so greatly to his owne liking, I should not doubtlesse so at the first and with like applause, haue admired and congratulated the authoritie. For what one reason did his Reuerence alleage in mislike of the gouernment he impugned and went against, which did not conclude as much and as directlie against this subordination, which, his complying with the Iesuites, and actioning for them, (as beside other testimonie, his letter of the first of Ianuary beareth witnes) haue solicited and procured to himselfe? The chiefe reason he vsed, and which carried most weight was, that we Seminarie priests hauing liued now in *England*, more then twentie yeares in great peace, and with like fruit of our labours, without any superioritie constituted among vs, it could not be thought either wisedome, or pollicie, or other then extreme follie, if after so long experience of a happie state, we should goe about to ordeine a subordination; and therefore he for his part

To the Cardinall Protector.

did condemne, and would euer be againſt any ſuch innouation, during the preſent ſuite and afflictions of our Countrie. Againe, when Maiſter *Blackwell* reaſoned with me in this matter, among other exceptions, he inſiſted moſt in this, that the kind of gouernment purpoſed was very defectiue, preiudiciall, and faultie, in that it did aſſigne but one onely Superiour ouer all the Prieſts throughout the whole Realme; adding, that if he ſhould liue to the conuerſion of our countrie, he would for ſo much as ſhould lye in him, ſolicite that the Biſhopricks might be deuided into moe Sees: for that as he then affirmed, the Dioces were greater, and the vnder-paſtors moe in number then the trauels of one man could well gouerne: And therefore admit (quoth he) that we ſhould haue a Superiour appointed, yet it were moſt vnmeete, that there ſhould be but one made in the whole Realme.

By that which is ſaid I would ſay, that how deſirous ſoeuer you or others thinke me of authoritie (a fault of which mine owne conſcience doth not much reprehend me, and I thanke my Lord Ieſu for the grace) I ſhould not, hauing before vſed the like reaſons, and ſpeeches, haue accepted of the authoritie in the manner that Maiſter *Blackwell* did, or if ſo I had with moſt ioy accepted thereof, yet without all peraduenture I ſhould not before the receipt of a Breue or other Apoſtolicall inſtrument, alike violently haue inforced the ſubmiſſion of my bretheren thereunto, with like ſpeede, with like conſtraint, with like condemnation, and wrack of their good names, and trouble of no fewer (as I thinke) then of a thouſand ſoules.

To make an end, I let paſſe vnanſwered the exception you amplifie againſt me, for writing, that you were in times paſt beholding vnto me, and that you ſpared not to interpret the words in the ſence that was furtheſt from my meaning, and thereupon alſo to inferre, that moſt pleaſed your ſelfe. For my leaue-taking I pray you if you write againe (which I do not deſire) that you would write more to the purpoſe, and with fewer failes, or not to miſlike if I omit to aunſwere you. Fare you well, Ianuary 29. 1600.

Yours in charitie
I. Colleton.

I Hope the truth of the contents, but eſpecially the nature of the occaſions which inforced me to write, being the defence of my vnguiltines, do ſufficientlie of themſelues without other iuſtification, cleere me from blame, or vndoubtedly from that manifeſt kind of blame,

blame, as might iustly, or colourably induce our Arch-priest to lay so heauie censures vpon me, without so much as citing me before, or examining the particulars and such proofes as I could make of that I had written. This I trust is so euident to common sense, and palpable to the dullest vnderstanding, that it were wast labour to dilate thereof, and greater idlenes to stand to confirme it by authorities. For against whom should the imputatiue offence be cōmitted? Not against the lay Gentleman to whom I wrote, for I did but aunswere to what he obiected, and (if I may be my owne iudge) in no degree of like quicknes, as his accusations, or truer, his egging slaunders did patterne vnto me: not against father *Parsons*, vnlesse the man must be alike priuiledged, that what soeuer he say, or do, and how vsurpingly soeuer he shall prosecute and inlarge the same, all notwithstanding must be bound, vnder the present clapping on of Censures, not to touch, no not in a priuate letter, his least imperfections, albeit they smart neuer so deepely through his intemperate humor: not against father *Lyster*, and his soothers, because I repeated but their owne words, and such as themselues diuulged both here, and in other places beyond the seas, with great applause of their ignorant fauorites. And if against Maister *Blackwell* (as I do not see how it can be so taken, because in one point I wrote no more then his Reuerence affirmed vnto me: and in the other, I sayd only what my selfe should not haue done, as my thoughts then gaue me, if so I had bin in his place) yet the iniury I did him, being properly against himselfe, he could not by the (*a*) Cannons of holie Church be iudge in his owne cause, and inflict the punishment. A transgression whereof Saint *Gregory* reprehended the Bishop *Ianuarius* with no lesse words then these: *Nihil te ostendas de cælestibus cogitare, sed terrenam te conuersationem habere significas, dum pro vindicta propriæ iniuriæ (quod sacris regulis prohibetur) maledictionem anathematis inuexisti. Si tale aliquid denuo feceris, in te scias postea vindicandum.* You shew that you haue no thought of heauenly things, but signifyes an earthlie conuersation, whilest for reuengement of your owne peculiar iniurie (which holie rules forbid) you impose the curse of excommunication. If you shall do the like againe, know that punishment must be done vpon you. And thus hauing briefely shewed that my letter could not be iustly a cause of the censures and penalties inflicted, for that it neither wrought, nor inferred a correspondent iniury to any person therein

(a) 4.q.4.Ca. 1. & 23.q. *inter querelas.* *Epist.*34.

ſpecified; I will diſcend to the other cauſe which as yet remayneth vnexamined.

The third and laſt cauſe which our Arch-prieſt alleageth for ſuſpending, interdicting, and redoubling the reuocation of my faculties, is: *for that there were three names ſubſcribed to the Appeale, and the Prieſts whoſe names they were, denyed to haue conſented to the letter, or cauſes prefixed before the Appeale. The blame of which fraude, his Reuerence knew not* (as he writeth) *to whome ſooner to impute it, then to me the ſender of the Appeale vnto him.* When the will is vehementlie bent vnto a thing, ſhe occupieth eftſoone the vnderſtanding in deuiſing reaſons to make it lawfull, wherein often ſhe ſheweth her ſelfe ſo powreable, that inchanting the vnderſtanding, ſhe maketh it to receiue in groſſe error, in ſtead of truth. What could be written with leſſe reaſon, or more contrary to the ordinances of the Catholick Church, then for our Arch-prieſt to declare by a publick inſtrument, addreſſed to the whole Clergie, and Catholick laytie, that I had fallen into the Cenſures of ſuſpenſion, and interdict, and incurred the loſſe of all my faculties, hauing taken them from me almoſt halfe a yeare before, and at that preſent to impoſe a new the taking away of them againe *for a fault* (to vſe his owne words) *which indeede he knew not, on whom rather to lay it, then on me?* Yea and to adde, that *he ought of neceſſitie ſo to do,* hauing neither cited me before, nor any way heard or demaunded, what I could ſay to the contrarie.
Hebr.4. God, who is the viewer of all ſecrets, and to whoſe eyes (as the Apoſtle writeth) all things are naked and open, would not condemne our Protoparents *Adam,* and *Eue,* notwithſtanding his diuine Ma-
Geneſis 3. ieſtie moſt thoroughlie knew, they had tranſgreſſed his commaundement, before he had both ſummoned *Adam* to appeare, and heard his and *Eues* defence in the matter. And if almighty God knowing not only what we can ſay, but what we will ſay in defence, would for example to man, ſpecially to ſuperiours, vouchſafe notwithſtanding to cite and heare the offendor before he proceeded to condemnation, and the inflicting of puniſhment: how much more meete, and neceſſary is it, that inferiour Iudges, who know nothing but by receipt of their eye, and eare, ſhould not without ſummons and examination before, puniſh or condemne any, but where the fault and circumſtances are moſt certaine, alike apparant, and altogether incapable of any defence or tergiuerſation? Of which kind we are very ſure that none

of

of our actions: were, which our Arch-priest hath hitherto censured, and sore punished in vs without citation, without triall, without any legall processe or inquirie, what we could say for our selues: and this only, vpon pretence that our offences be notorius, or manifest, and therefore no neede of citation or triall. A thread-bare shift, and which cannot couer the iniustice, because that may only be called (*b*) notorious or manifest in this matter, as all the Canonists teach, which is by the nature and euidence of the fact so apparant, as it can neither probably, or without blushing be denyed, nor any defence, or tergiuersation pretended, (*c*) *vbi factum est adeo notorium, quod nulla defensio potest parti absenti competere, tunc non requiritur citatio: sed vbi factum non est ita notorium, tunc requiritur citatio, alias sententia siue processus factus est nullus*, where the fact is so notorious that no defence can appeare to be made by the party absent, then citation is not required: but where the fact is not in such sort notorious, then summons must be made, otherwise the sentence or processe is of no validitie. Now that the fraude which our Archpriest imputeth vnto me, is not so notorious or manifest; his owne words in the same place do apparantly declare, in that his Reuerence saith, *that he knew not on whom rather to lay the same fault then on me*. Which words cannot but imply an vncertainty, and consequently not possible that the fact could be notorious in relation to M. *Blackwell*, to whom it ought of necessitie to haue bin notorious, if so his Reuerence, in the sentence & declaration which he made of me without citing, would not haue broken the (*d*) law of God, (*e*) Nature, and (*f*) all Nations.

(b) *Gloss. in 1. q. 2. Ca. manifesta. Anto. Fran. in ca. item cum quis de restit. spol. sub nu. 1. Innocent. in ca. tua nos de cohabit. cler. Panor. in ca. cum olim de senten. & re iud. nu. 10. Nauar consil. lib. 5. de pœnit. & remis. consil. 15 nu. 7. & aly.*

(c) *Panor. in ca. bonæ memoriæ de elect. nu. 5.*

(d) *2. q. 1. Deus omnipotens.*

(e) *In Clem. pastoralis de re iud.*

(f) *Bartola. in L. filius familias ff. de don.*

Touching the suspicion cõceiued, I am as cleere of the fraud his Reuerence obiecteth, as any man in the world, for I was neither the setter downe of any of the three names, nor the motioner, as M. *Clarke*, M. *Mush*, & M. *Hebborne*, with some other can witnes. And to infer as M. *Blackwel* doth, that I was guilty of the fraud, because I sent him the Apeale, is so weake a proofe, as there needeth no disproofe. But what might this notable fraud be, which at least in the punishmẽt is so exaggerated? forsooth 3. of the apelãts who haue since renued their apeale, *denied to haue giuẽ their cõsent to those letters, which indeed are the causes which were prefixed before the Apeale*. A capitall offence, Priests giuing their assent & voices to the making of an appeale, for relieuing such & such oppressions, & leauing the forme & causes therof to be drawn by others, they after protested, that they were not consenting to the said causes which were yeelded in particular for proofe of the agreeuãces.

A Second principall point wherein our Arch-prieſt ſeemeth to transgreſſe his Commiſſion, is, if not in making Decrees, yet vndoubtedly in annexing ſuch cenſures and penalties as he doth vnto his Decrees. It hath bin ſhewed before, that in all probabilitie our Arch-prieſt hath no authoritie to ſuſpend from the Altar; and for moſt certaine, he hath no authoritie to interdict Prieſts or any Catholick: therefore theſe Cenſures annexed to his Decrees, neither is nor can be leſſe then an vnlawfull exceſſe of the authoritie graunted. But let vs ſuppoſe that the word [*suſpending*] in the Conſtitutiue Letter, giueth authoritie to the Arch-prieſt to ſuſpend from the Altar, and miniſtration of all Sacraments: and let vs alſo ſuppoſe that the words [*eccleſiaſticall penalties*] do giue him authoritie to interdict, whereof there is no colour at all, as we haue proued before: yet becauſe the Cardinals letter ſo cōſtrued, doth not giue our Arch-prieſt authoritie to vſe theſe cenſures how and when he liſteth, but onely that he may inflict theſe cenſures, *if we after due admonitions and reprehenſions firſt vſed in brotherly charitie, ſhall ſhew our ſelues diſobedient, vnquiet, or contumacious in the things he commaundeth to be obſerued*. So likewiſe the authoritie of reſtraining, or reuoking faculties, is not graunted him abſolutely to exerciſe at his pleaſure (as he ſeemeth to pretend in his Letter to Maiſter *Charnock*) but only when *nee*[illegible] *ſhall require the one, or neceſſitie conſtraine the other*: that is, as the Cardinall himſelfe explaineth the particulars, when we *after the foreſaid admonitions and reprehenſions ſhall demaine our ſelues diſobediently, vnquietly, or contumaciouſly againſt his commaundements.*

Pag. 182. ex ſequ. — *Pag. 185.* — The words of the Conſtitutiue letter pag. 2.

From theſe premiſſes we inferre, that albeit our Arch-prieſt hath authoritie to make Decrees, which we neither denye nor affirme, though we rather thinke he can not, vnleſſe he firſt ſummon vs, and propoſe (as the Conſtitutiue letter directeth) the things he intendeth to decree: yet we aſſuredly beleeue that his Reuerence hath no authoritie nor iuriſdiction at all, to annexe the cenſures of ſuſpenſion, or interdict, or the penaltie of leeſing our faculties to be incurred *ipſo facto*, if we diſobey and breake his Decrees. And the reaſons why we be thus perſwaded, are, firſt becauſe this were preſently, before any fact done by vs, to paſſe and impoſe the ſaid cenſures, and eccleſiaſticall penaltie, and to lay them in the Decree, for it, to execute them, without any his further concurrance, when the offence is committed. But our Arch-prieſt hath no authoritie to paſſe and inflict a Cenſure, or to reſtraine and reuoke faculties (as appeareth by the tenour

Pag. 6. § 3. — *Vgolinus ta. 1. ca. 9. § 6 nu. 3.*

nour of the Cardinals letter) saue only after the committing of an offence, and after charitable admonitions and reprehensions for the same: and therefore till the offence be committed, and the reprehensions first vsed, he can not passe and impose any censure or penaltie. And although the publishing of a Decree be a sufficient admonition, yet the publishing thereof doth not nor can not supplie (as we thinke) the reprehensions, which by the prescript forme of the Constitutiue Letter is to be vsed before the inflicting of the said penalties.

Againe, the edition of a Decree is *(g)* a thing of greater authoritie, and distinguished from the exercise of bare iurisdiction, because one may appeale from the sentence or iudgement of his superiour, but not from *(h)* the penaltie or mulcte of a statute: and also because Decrees be certaine and perpetuall, but the exercise of iurisdiction variable, according to the conditions of persons. Wherefore it seemeth that he, who hath but only authority to impose Censures, or other ecclesiasticall penalties, as time, place, the condition of the offender, and the nature of his offence shall require, as the Cardinals letter giueth our Arch-priest no more, can not by vertue of the same authoritie make Decrees, and adioyne those penalties vnto them, which he may impose vpon the offender after the offence committed: because as *Panormitane* writeth: *(i) potestas habens arbitrium imponendi pænam, non potest à principio per sua statuta declarare pænas.* He that hath authoritie to inflict punishment according as he shall thinke good, can not by his statutes before the trespasse be committed, declare the penalties he intendeth to impose. Briefely the Arch-priests authoritie in the exteriour court being whollie delegantine, and in a set forme, and no part thereof containing like iurisdiction as to make Decrees, and annexe such penalties, the fift Proposition in the second Reason teacheth, that what he doth therein, is of no obligation, because *(k) statutum excedens fines potestatis statuendum est ipso iure nullum*, the Decree that exceedeth the decreers authoritie, is absolutelie none at all.

(g) *Panor. in ca. cum à consuetudinis de eod. tit. nu. 6.*

(h) *Panorm. in ca. ex literis de constit. nu. 9 & Silu. verb. Appell. nu 6.*

(i) *In ca. cum consuetudinis eod. tit. nu. 6.*

Pag. 25.

(k) *Panorm. in ca. quæ in de constit n. 1.*

A Third principall thing wherein our Arch-priest seemeth to transgresse the lawes of holie Church, is, that the sacred Canons *(l)* giuing all men leaue to appeale *(m)* euen for the smallest iniustice, and commaunding the Superiour *(n)* to admit euery such Appeale, his Reuerence notwithstāding imbarreth vs to appeale by collection of names, vnlesse we haue first his licence thereunto. Againe, thirtie of vs hauing ioyned in one Appeale, and some moe since, all alleaging

(l) *Ca. super eo 2. de appel.*

(m) *Ca. de appel. eod. tit.*

(n) *Ibid. & ca. vt debitus eod. tit.*

the ſame cauſes, and prouing them to be moſt weightie and true, neuertheleſſe his Reuerence refuſed to admit the Appeale, ſaue onely for one of the whole number. Courſes which moſt directly croſſe both the rules of law and conſcience. And to prooue the particulars.

First, that his Reuerence hath in the foreſaid manner debarred vs to appeale, and that he hath alſo (which is much more) puniſhed vs for appealing, it is cleare by the teſtimonie of his owne Decrees, and other writings. *Prohibemus autem ſub pæna &c. We prohibite* (ſaith our Arch-prieſt in his Decree of the 18. of Nouember 1600.) *vnder paine of ſuſpenſion from diuine offices, & leeſing all faculties, that no Prieſt after any manner either by writing or word of mouth, do ſeeke or giue voyces in any cauſe ſoeuer, which is not certainely knowne to haue bene communicated before to vs, or to two of our Aſſiſtants.* Secondly, when ſignification was giuen to our Arch-prieſt (which was performed in the
Pag. 1003. letter that accompanied the Appeale, and is ſet downe before) that we intended to moue ſome moe of our brethren to giue their names to the Appeale, he preſently wrote a letter with this addreſſed, dated the 28. of Nouember 1600. *To the Reuerend and dearelie beloued in Chriſt my Aſſiſtants and felow-prieſts*, in which the words folowing are inſerted: *Quoniam ſunt quidam qui in eo cauillati ſunt, quod collectionem ſuffragiorum ad notitiam aut meam aut Aſſiſtentium deferri mandauerim; cognoſcite in hoc hunc fuiſſe meum ſenſum, quem ſic declaro, vt communicationem facerent collectionis ſuffragiorum cum Superiore, cuius conſenſus exquirendus & habendus eſt. Atque illud præcipuè intendimus: quod Decretum antecedentibus temporibus confirmatum fuit authoritate Ill^mi (bonæ memoriæ) Cardinalis Caietani.* that is, Becauſe there are certaine that haue cauilled, for that I commaunded the collection of ſuffrages to be imparted to me, or the Aſſiſtants, know ye in this thing, this to be my meaning, which thus I declare, that they ſhould communicate the gathering of voyces with the Superiour, whoſe conſent is to be asked and obteined. And this was that which we chiefely intended: which Decree in former times was confirmed by the authoritie of the moſt Illuſtrious (of good memorie) Cardinall *Caietane.*

By which paſſage, and that which was rehearſed out of the Decree, together with the cauſe, for which his Reuerence made this explication, it very plainely appeareth, that he forbiddeth vs either to appeale, or at leaſt to giue, or aske names for making of an Appeale without his conſent. And that this is no more nor otherwiſe, then our

Arch-prieſt

Arch-priest himselfe acknowledgeth, his words ensuing in the same letter do testifie: *Quod enim in suis literis posuerunt decreta quædam nostra 18. Octobris edita, plane constat eos non ignorasse duo illa potissimum, quæ in ipsorum literis cõtinentur, quibus sub grauibus pœnis præteritæ inobedientiæ defensionem & collectionem collationémue suffragiorum expresse prohibuimus: Quæ tamen illi omnes (si omnes quod non credimus verè subscripserunt) manifestè transgressi sunt. Quare nos sane non videmus, qua ratione ab illis pœnis liberi esse possint, quotquot huic friuolæ appellationi vel subscripserunt vel consenserunt.* That is. For that they haue put downe in their letter certaine Decrees of mine, set forth the 18. of October, it is very euident, that they were not ignorant especially of these two things conteyned in their letters, by which we expreslie forbid vnder grieuous penalties, the defence of their former disobedience, and the collection or ioyning of voyces. Which things they all (if all, which we do not beleeue, haue indeede subscribed) haue manifestlie transgressed. Wherefore we surely do not see by what meanes they may be freed *(that is, of suspension from diuine offices, and of leesing all faculties)* how many soeuer haue either subscribed or consented to this friuolous appeale.

What more euident, the premisses put together, then that our Arch-priest, stiling his prohibitions by the name of Decrees, and prohibiting vs vnder paine of suspension, and losse of faculties, to collect names for making an appeale, and after censuring vs to haue incurred the said penalties for collecting and ioyning names to and in one appeale, doth plainely forbid vs either to appeale, or at leastwise as we haue said, to seeke or giue names for appealing together without his obtained consent. And if either, as there can be no euasion in the latter, then considering his Reuerence did make this prohibition by the name of a Decree, it seemeth infallibly to follow, the same Decree being a violation, restriction, or abridging of *Ecclesiasticall libertie*, that he by making and publishing the same, incurred the 15. excommunication in *Bulla (o) Cœnæ domini*, and those that *(p)* wrote the same Constitution, or counselled or aided him in the making or publishing thereof, or haue presumed to iudge according to the contents, seeme also to haue incurred the excommunication of Pope *Honorius* the third, registred in the *(q)* Decretals.

That the aboue mentioned Decree of our Arch-priest is against the honour of *ecclesiasticall libertie*, it appeareth by seuerall heads. First, for that by the name of *ecclesiasticall libertie*, that *libertie (r)* (as all

(o) *Per Clement. 8. anno* 1598.

(p) *Gloss. in ca. nouerit de sent. excom. verb. scriptores.*

(q) *Ca. nouerit de sent. excom.*

(r) *Innocentius & Panor. in ca. nouerit n. 2. de sent. excom. S. Anto. 3. par. tit. 25. ca. 17. Angel. verb. excommunicatio 7. casu 12. nu. 1. Siluester verb. excom. 9. n. 31. Tabiena verb. excom. 5. casu 20. § 5. Caiet. verb. excom. ca. 31. vers. quinto nota. Nauar in man. cap. 27. n. 119. vers. 5. & Bart. in authen. cassa. l. de sacrosanct. eccles.*

writers affirme) is vnderstood, which the whole vniuersall Church inioyeth, and the facultie of appealing without the Superiors leaue, is a priuiledge, or rather a due right graunted to the vniuersal Church, not only by the law (*s*) of nature, or (*t*) example of S. *Paul*, who appealed to *Cesar*, but also by sundry Papall constitutions, as of Pope (*v*) *Anacletus: Omnis oppressus liberè sacerdotum (si voluerit) appellet iudicium, & à nullo prohibeatur.* Let euery one that is oppressed freely appeale (if he please) to the iudgement of (*x*) Bishops, and be hindered by none. Also of (*y*) Pope *Zepherinus: Ad Romanam ecclesiam ab omnibus maxime tamen ab oppressis appellandum est, & concurrendum quasi ad matrem vt eius vberibus nutriantur, authoritate defendantur, & a suis oppressionibus releuentur:* All persons especially the oppressed, may appeale to the Romaine Church, and haue recourse to her, as to their mother, that they may be nourished with her paps, defended by her authoritie, and relieued of their oppressions. According to which sayings, and many (*z*) moe like in the Canons, Pope (*a*) *Alexander* the third writeth: *Sacri Canones singulis faciunt facultatem appellandi:* That the sacred Canons do giue euery one leaue to appeale. Therefore the Superiors leaue is not necessarie, as Maister *Blackwell* in his decree exacteth, and consequently thereby abridging the rights of *ecclesiasticall libertie,* incurreth as we haue said the censure of excommunication in *Bulla cœnæ domini.*

(s) *Valent. to. 3. disp. 5. q. 13. punct. 3.*
(t) Act. 15.
(v) *Epist. 1. 2. q. 6. c. Omnis oppressus.*
(x) *Gloss. ibidem.*
(y) *Ibid. c. ad Roman. 2.*
(z) *2. q. 6. per totum.*
(a) *Ca. super eo 2. de appel.*

Secondly, the foresaid Decree of our Arch-priest impeacheth the right of *ecclesiasticall libertie,* because *illud statutum dicitur contra libertatem ecclesiasticam per quod prohibetur personis ecclesiasticis illud quod neque iure diuino, neque humano prohibitum est.* That constitution is against *ecclesiasticall libertie* (as writeth (*b*) *Felinus*) by which ecclesiasticall persons are forbid that, which neither by diuine or humaine law is prohibited. And it can not be shewed out of either law, that Priests be debarred either to seeke or giue voices for ioyning in one appeale, without consent and leaue of the Superior. We will here omit for breuitie sake what (*c*) *Caietaine* (*d*) *Baldus*, and (*e*) *Siluester* write in the explication of the word [*ecclesiasticall libertie*] and set downe the excommunication it selfe, which peraduenture best declareth, what is signified by *ecclesiasticall libertie.* (*f*) *Necnon qui statuta, ordinationes, constitutiones pragmaticas, seu quæuis alia Decreta in genere, vel in specie, ex quauis causa, & quouis quæsito colore, ac etiam prætextu cum suis consuetudinis, aut priuilegij, vel alias quomodolibet fecerint, ordinauerint, & publicauerint, vel factis, & ordinatis vsi fuerint, vnde libertas*

(b) *In ca. nouerit. de sent. excom. n. 4.*
(c) *In summa verb. excom. ca. 31. vers. quinta nota.*
(d) *In margarita sua super decret. verb. ecclesia.*
(e) *Verb. immunitas 2. n. 2.*
(f) *In Bulla cœnæ dom. Clemen. papæ 8 anno 1598.*

bertas ecclesiastica tollitur, seu in aliquo læditur, vel deprimitur, aut alias quouismodo restringitur, seu nostris & dictæ sedis, ac quarumcunque ecclesiarum viribus quomodolibet directè, vel indirectè, tacitè, vel expressè præiudicatur. The english. We excommunicate and anathematize all & singular persons, who shall make, ordaine, and publish statutes, ordinances, constitutions pragmaticall, or any other Decrees in generall or speciall, vpon any cause or deuised colour, and vnder pretence of any custome or priuiledge, or in what other sort soeuer, or being made or ordeined, shall vse them, whereby ecclesiasticall libertie is taken away, or any way diminished or depressed, or after any sort restrained, or preiudice inferred by any maner of way, directlie or indirectlie, couertlie or expresly, against our rights, or of the See Apostolick, or against the rights of what other Churches soeuer.

Now whether the state of *ecclesiasticall libertie*, by the foresaid Decree of our Arch-priest, especiallie expounded as himselfe enlarged it, and is before set downe, be either disanulled, impeached, diminished, or any way directlie or indirectlie, implicitiuely or expressely streited, we leaue to others to iudge, when as the same Decree forbade vs vnder threat of suspension from diuine offices, and forfet of all our faculties, either to seeke or giue voices in any cause soeuer, without his consent and leaue, and that we should not collect and ioyne voices in making an Appeale to his Holines, vnlesse we haue his assent thereunto, and hath sithence punished our attempt therein, both by declaring that we incurred the foresaid censure and penalties in breaking his Decree, by subscribing our names to the Appeale, and by suspending and taking away our faculties for the same cause, as the foregoings do most manifestlie conuince, and hundreds beside can witnes?

Tenaunts oppressed by their temporall Lord, may without his licence by all lawes conferre and combine themselues in one complaint, for reformation of their iniuries: likewise subiects receiuing wrong through the ignorance or corruption of any vnder officer, or vicegerent, may vnite themselues, giue, and gather names for manifesting their pressures by way of Supplication to their Prince and Soueraigne, without the parties consent or priuitie, who vniustly afflicteth them: yea the contrarie in either example or infinite moe that might be alleaged to the same purpose, were plaine tyranie in the secular state. And if in the ciuill regiment these things be alike lawfull, and sometime necessarie, can they be vnlawfull, or may they posſiblie be prohibited in eccleſiaſticall gouerment, and the rights of *eccleſiaſticall libertie* not infringed? No, no, the matter is plainer then it can be doubted of. And if ſo, then did our Archprieſt (as we feare) and ſome other cooperators who are comprehended vnder the Canon of *Honorius*, incur excõmunication in the nature of the fact: and becauſe the ſaid decree, is not yet cancelled, nor reuoked, but rather ſtill extended againſt vs, we thinke further that his Reuerence after abſolution falleth againe ſo often into that cenſure, as he maketh vſe of the decree againſt vs, which hath bin not ſeldome. And it is ſtrange, that the nature of the decree conſidered (which can by no ſhift of wit be truly ſalued from being againſt the rights of *eccleſiaſticall libertie*) our Archprieſt was not afraid to let paſſe in a common letter vnder his hand & ſeale, that the aboue mentioned part of the decree containing ſuch od ſtuffe, *was confirmed by Cardinall Caietane in his life time*. A report, which for the diſtaine it bringeth to the dead, we ſhould not beleeue. Or if it be true, yet we hope, it was but a ſlye fineſſe of father *Parſons*, winning the Cardinall to confirme what his grace looked not into; for that no Cardinall whoſoeuer, hath authoritie to decree any ſuch extremitie. But howſoeuer the ſame was, it can not but witnes a very ſeuere courſe intended, when ſuch a decree importing (if we miſtake not the caſe) ſacrilegious iniuſtice, was beforehand deuiſed & ratified.

Vbi ſupra.

28. of Nouẽber 1600.

A Fourth chief particular, wherein our Archprieſt ſeemeth to haue tranſgreſſed the lawes of holie Church, is, in that many of vs ioyning in one appeale, and alledging the ſame cauſes, his Reuerence admitted the Appeale for one, & reiected it in the behalfe of all the reſt. For either the ſaid Appeale was iuſt or vniuſt, in reſpect of vs all, or none, in that we were all vnited in the action, & yeelded the ſame reaſons. And if vniuſt, then did our Arch-prieſt violate the ſacred canons in approuing it towards one, becauſe they preſcribe, that when the appeale is vniuſt, the Superiour ſhould not defer thereunto. (g) *Appellationibus friuolis nec iuſtitia defert, nec eſt à iudice deferendum.* Neither doth iuſtice allow friuolous appeales, nor ought the Iudge to admit them. And the Gloſſe (h) goeth further, *Iudex à quo, non debet deferre appellationi friuolæ, quæ interponitur ſine cauſa, vel cauſa eſt irrationabilis, aut eſt falſa, imo ſi deferat, peccat mortaliter:* The Iudge from whom Appellation is made, ought not to admit a friuolous Appeale, which is interpoſed without a cauſe, or vpõ an inſufficient or falſe cauſe: nay rather if he defer thereunto, he committeth mortall ſinne. The like hath

(g) *Ca. cum appellationibus eod. tit. lib.6. & idem habetur cap. cũ ſpeciali. § porro.*
(h) *Ibidem.*

hath (*i*) *Panormitane*, though not in so plaine termes; and *Siluester* (*k*) calleth the deferring to an vniust appeale, *malice and imprudency*. And the reason why it is sinne, is plaine, because in receiuing an vniust appeale, the course of iustice is broken, and iniquitie patronised.

Of the contrary side if the appeale were iust, then did his Reuerence more grieuously offend in not admitting the same. (*l*) *Si à quoquam secus præsumptum fuerit ab officio cleri submotus, authoritatis Apostolicæ reus ab omnibus iudicetur: ne Lupi, qui sub specie ouium subintrauerunt, bestiali sæuitia quosque audeant lacerare*: He that shall presume (sayth Pope *Gregorie* the fourth) to reiect a lawfull and iust appeale, ought to be put from his office, and of all men to be iudged guiltie of contempt against authoritie Apostolicall, least Wolues that priuily entred in Sheepes clothing, should not feare to vexe and torment others with beastlie crueltie. Which vniustice of not deferring to a iust appeale (*m*) Pope *Alexander* the third tearmeth *a grieuous excesse*, and prescribeth, *that he who should presume to commit the offence is (if the appeale were made to the Sea Apostolicke) to be sent to the court of Rome, there to satisfye and be punished for the transgression.*

Or if finallie, the appeale were neither apparantlie iust, nor vniust, but doubtfull (as how it could so appeare we do not see, because the causes alleaged therein, were most weightie, demonstratiue, and proued by seuerall testimonies out of Maister *Blackwels* owne letters and other his writings) yet do the (*n*) Canons in this case appoint the Iudge to receiue the appeale, as both the (*o*) expositors of the lawe and (*p*) Summists testifie: *Si iudex de legitimatione appellationis dubitat (q) debet & (r) tenetur differre*. If the Iudge doubt of the lawfulnes of the appeale, he ought and is bound to deferre thereunto. And the reason is, because appellation doth alwaies implie an vniustice receiued, or intended: and in things doubtfull, the (*s*) diuine law, naturall and humane, declareth, that the case of the agrieued or sufferer is to be preferred.

A Fift essentiall point wherein our Archpriest seemeth likewise to transgresse the lawes of holie Church, is, that his Reuerence hauing admitted my appeale *à grauaminibus futuris*, from future agrieuances, & deliuered me my apostles or dimissory letters, would * some few weekes after, notwithstanding this his formall allowance of the Appeale, suspend, interdict, and redouble the taking away of my

(i) *In c. e. de priore de appel. nu. 2.*
(k) *Verb. appellatio, nu. 13*
(l) *2. q. 6. decreto.*
Note the punishment and censures of not admitting a iust appeale.
(m) *Ca. de priore de appell.*
(n) *Ca. Cum speciali de appell. § porro.*
(o) *Glossa in ca. Sacro de sent. excom. verb. dubitari. Durandus de appell. § 9. nu. 5. Panormita. in ca. vt debitus de appell. nu. 30. & VVamesius eod. tit. in ca. de priore nu. 7.*
(p) *Siluester verb. appell. nu. 13.*
(q) *Vbi supra.*
(r) *Vbi supra.*
(s) *Salon de iustitia q. 63. art. 4. contr. 2. concl. 2. & regula 11. de reg. iur. lib 6.*
* From the 20. of December to the 21. of February following.

See these things set downe in his own letter pag. 190.

faculties, and this vpon no new offence which was notorious, but euen for consenting to the prefixing of the causes before the appeale, which himselfe admitted, and for making answere to a lay Gentleman his letter, the copie whereof is set downe before, and lastly, for that three of the appellants did denye the giuing of their assents to the said causes which were prefixed.

(a) *Ca. super de appel. Ca. Romana, & ca. si à Iudice de appel. lib. 6. Panormitan in ca. ad reprimendam de off. iudi. ordi. nu. 9. Silu. verb. appellatio nu. 1.*

All (*a*) lawes and writers do assigne these two effects to euery appeale admitted, *viz.* the suspending of the superiours iurisdiction in the cause, from whome, and in which, the appellation was made, and the reuoluing of the said cause to the tryall of the higher Iudge, to whome the appellation was made. Hence it appeareth plaine that Maister *Blackwel* admitting my appeale, and after proceeding against me, in the very same kind of agrieuances for which I appealed: and this his proceeding against me chiefely for annexing the causes of the Appeale he allowed, without any new and notorious offence committed by me, as the fore-goings do manifestly conuince: hence I say it most euidently appeareth, that his Reuerence therein brake the lawes of holy Church, vnlesse his authoritie be a transcendant aboue all the written rules either of lawe or conscience.

This letter is set downe pag. 199.

A sixt particular wherein our Arch-priest exceedeth the limits of his authoritie as we verily beleeue, is, his opinion and practise touching the reuocation of faculties. What opinion his Reuerence holdeth herein, his letters to Maister *Charnock* of the 17. of Iune 1600. do manifestly shew, wherein amongst other things he writeth thus, *Facultatum concessio vt etiam duratio merè voluntaria censenda est, cum facultates delegatæ sine vllo prorsus crimine, solo nutu concedentis, vel ab eo potestatem habentis expirent:* As the graunt of faculties, so the continuation of them is to be counted meere voluntarie, sith delegatine faculties expire without any fault, vpon the sole will of the graunter, or of the party that hath authority from him. A strange position, and which cannot but prognosticate somewhat.

See *Panormitan. in ca. in singulis de stat. mona. nu. 7.*

* § 6. *vers.* 10.

Note a contradiction betweene the two opinions.

Cardinall *Caietaine* appointed Maister *Blackwell* Arch-priest, and gaue him Delegatine authoritie, as is plaine by his graces words, *cui vices nostras pro tempore delegemus,* to whome for the time we delegate our stead: and yet * father *Lyster* in his treatise against vs affirmeth, that *the Pope cannot depose him without a crime committed:* neither is the authority or office wherewith Maister *Blackwell* is inuested, a like meane of his maintenance, as the hauing of faculties is to Priests that liue in our countrey, which putteth a materiall difference

betweene

betweene the cases, and inferreth, that if Maister *Blackwell* may not, but vpon a crime be remoued by the Pope, much lesse may faculties be taken away from Priests in *England* without any crime foregoing.

The donation of faculties to Priests in their mission, seemeth not so to depend on the meere pleasure of the superiour, as our Arch-priest would pretend, but rather to be an implicitiue couenant, and the performance thereof due vnto them by iustice, vnlesse their owne misdemeanor bereaue them of the interest. For can their admittance into any of the Colledges; the addicting of themselues to the study of Diuinity; the taking of an oath to be made Priests, and goe into *England* when the Superiour shall appoint, promise lesse then a couenant on the Superiors side, to furnish them with faculties at the time of their going, vnlesse (as is sayd) their owne deserts shall make them vnworthie? sith the hauing of faculties is the chiefest meane of inabling thē to do good in our country, the end why they became Priests, and resigned the liberty of their former state. And as the giuing of faculties to Priests at their departure for *England*, is not to be counted a meere voluntarie fauour, being in truth the due hire of their trauels, and alteration of their state; so neither can the continuation of our faculties iustly be deemed to depend in such sort vpō the will of the graunter, as that at his pleasure they expire and determine, without any sufficient cause giuen. Vndoubtedly, the disgrace, and iniuries which accompanie such a fact, is an oppression that sendeth vp his cry to heauen for punishment vpon the imposer.

An extremitie, that men who haue left the Vniuersitie, forsaken the preferments of learning in their country, relinquished their patrimonies, lost the loue of their worldly friends, brought themselues in dislike with their Prince, and the State, deuoted their trauels to the gaining of soules, and hourely for that cause venture their liues, and floting beside in a sea of difficulties, must after all these, and in the middest of these, be spoyled of their faculties, yea, at the arbitrarie pleasure of another, and this *sine crimine*, without any blame or fault. But who seeth not how this doctrine of our Archpriest tendeth to bōdage and meere tyrannie? For haue Priests in our Countrey either Tithes, Parsonage, or Vicaredge, or any other help of maintenance (though they serue the Altar in more danger then any Priest in the Christian world beside) then the voluntarie charities of those, with whom they deale? And with whome can they deale, being depriued of their faculties?

The Councell of (a) *Trident* enacteth seuerall prouisoes, that Priests should not through necessitie of want be driuen to beg, holding the same a reproch to the order. The like also haue the auncient Canons (b) decreed, appointing that Priests, euen guilty of murder, when their liues are spared, should be allowed a competent portion for their maintenance, out of the benefices they had when they committed the fact. And touching the censure of suspension, all the Canons (c) agree, that when one is suspended from the fruites of his benefice *pro pœna*, for punishment of a fault, his necessities are to be relieued out of the same benefice: (d) *Licet clericus sit suspensus ab homine vel Canone, tamen ei relinqui debeat, vnde se & suos possit sustentare.* Albeit a Cleargie man be suspended by his Ordinarie or the Canon, yet there ought so much to be allotted vnto him, as wherewith he may honestlie maintaine himselfe and his familie. But our Arch-priest, as his owne writings declare, seemeth to haue little part of this consideration and good spirit, when he teacheth and diuulgeth that all our faculties (being the only meanes we liue by) may be taken away *sine crimine* vpon his only will.

The Cardinall in his ninth Instruction, calleth those Priests that are resident in Catholick houses, the parish priests of the same flock. Which if it be so, then haue they in respect of the said persons (e) authoritie *à iure communi*, to heare their confessions, and absolue them of all sinnes, from which ordinarie Curates may absolue their parishioners. Nor can this iurisdiction for any cause be taken away, so long as they remaine their Pastours, though the same may be suspended. But let this stand as it may, yet it is very apparant, and none can denie, but that our faculties here in *England* are in stead of Church-liuings vnto vs, & our only benefices. *Rebuffus* (f) writeth and (g) *Siluester*, and (h) *Archidiaconus* haue the same, *quod Papa post collata beneficia non habet potestatem auferendi ea sine causa,* that the Pope after induction hath not authoritie to depriue the incumbent, or take away the benefice without a cause: and the same Authour proueth the position by *Barbatia* (i) where he saith, that it was defined by the Councell, that none should be depriued of their benefices *nisi pro graui culpa,* but only vpon a sore and grieuous offence: Yea the contrarie seemeth to be, as (k) *Graffius* writeth, against the rights of morall equitie, namely, that one should be put from his benefice, which perhaps he atteyned to by much paine and expences, without any cause or fault foregoing, that could deserue the depriuation. Which if it be

true

(a) *Sess. 21. de refor. ca. 2. & seq.*
(b) *Dist. 50. ca. studeat.*
(c) *Panormit. in ca. pastoralis § verum nu. 16. Decius nu. 7 ibid. de appella. Felinus in ca. Apostolicæ de except. nu. 12. Geminianus in ca. si compromissarius de elect. li. 6. & aly.*
(d) *Glossa in ca. studeat dist. 50. verb. & fin.*
(e) *Henriquez de pœni. sacra. lib. 3. ca. 6. nu. 6.*
(f) *In repet. de rescrip. coll. 2. ad medium.*
(g) *In verb. Papa nu. 12. & 13.*
(h) *In 12. q. 2. non liceat.*
(i) *In ca. quod translationem de offi. legat. nu. 121. inuent. 16. qu. 7.*
(k) *P. 2. lib. 2. cap. 18. nu. 9.*

true in the ablation of benefices graunted, it holdeth more true and stronger in the reuocation of our faculties, for the causes abouementioned.

It appeareth by that little we haue said, how vnconscionable and extreme is the opinion, which our Arch-priest holdeth touching the voluntarie graunt and continuation of our faculties. Let vs now see the correspondencie of his practise; and as we haue alwayes alleaged his Decrees or letters for proofe of that we affirmed, so shall we do the like in this point also, being of importance. And to the end no exception may be taken either for abridging or dismembring his words, we will set downe the whole Instrument by which his Reuerence first tooke away faculties from some of vs.

Omnibus dilectissimis mihi Assistentibus, & Clero Anglicano salutem.

Sciatis nos antegressis temporibus duobus illis D. Ioanni Musho, & D. Ioanni Collingtonio facultates suspendisse propter eorum manifestam inobedientiam, & perturbationem pacis: postea autem eas restituimus ex ipsorum submissione. Quoniam autem illi tam defendunt causam suam, & satisfactionem petunt &c: & varias ad nos literas dederunt contumelijs siue calumnijs plenas, partim emissas in nosipsos, partim in alios etiam superiores: atque etiam hoc ipso tempore multa satagunt contra pacem &c. Ideo nunc, Nos Georgius Blackwellus Archipresbyter Angliæ reuocamus his duobus omnes facultates &c, iubentes vt omnibus catholicis id notum faciatis, ne ab ijs fortasse sacramenta recipiant. Plura ex communibus literis intelligetis; in quorum fidem hisce nostris literis sigillo nostro munitis, manu propria subscripsimus, Londini 17. Octobris 1600.

Vester seruus in Christo:

Georgius Blackwellus Archipresbyter Angliæ.

The English.

To all my dearely beloued Assistants, and to the English Cleargie, salutation.

BE it knowne vnto you, that heretofore we suspended Maister *Iohn Mush*, and Maister *Iohn Colleton*, from the vse of their faculties, for their manifest disobedience, and perturbation of peace; and afterwards restored them vpon their submission. But now because they defend their cause, and require satisfaction &c. and haue sent vs diuers letters full of contumelies and calumniations, partly published against our selues, partly also against other Superiours: and euen at this very instant do goe about many things contrary to peace &c. Therefore we *George Blackwell* Archpriest of *England*, do reuoke from these two all their faculties &c: commanding that you make the same knowne to all Catholicks, least perhaps they may receiue Sacraments at their hands. More of these matters you shall vnderstand by our generall letters: for credit of which matters we haue subscribed with our owne hand these our letters sealed with our owne Seale. From *London* the 17. of October 1600.

Your seruant in Christ George Blackwell,
Arch-priest of England.

Presently as I receiued the aforesaid Instrument, which was the seauenth day after the date thereof, I returned the letter following.

VEry Reuerend Sir, at this instant Maister *Heborne* deliuered me a Letter directed to your Assistants and the Cleargy of *England*, giuing them to vnderstand, that you haue reuoked all Maister *Mushes* faculties and mine, with an &c. And you specified foure causes thereof with a second &c. The first is, for that we defend our cause: then for that we aske satisfaction: thirdly for writing vnto you diuers letters full of contumelie or calumniations; partly published against your Reuerence, partly also against other Superiours; and lastly, for that at this present we busily bestir our selues in manie matters against peace, with a third &c. Moreouer you commaund the sayd Assistants and Cleargie of *England*, to acquaint all Catholicks with what you haue done, least haplie they receiue Sacraments of vs: concluding, that they shall vnderstand moe things out of your common letters. My humble request is, that you would vouchsafe to expresse these residues at length and plainely, as also what common letters you meane, and to whom we shall resort for a sight of them: otherwise in my poore iudgement the processe will appeare hard. For to diuulge in this notorious manner the taking away of our faculties, which heapeth discredit, and sundrie other damages vpon vs, and alike vnperfectlie or by halfes to recite the causes, and lay downe the punishment, as the reader through additions of *et-cetera-es*, is left, as it were to a wide scope,

ſcope,to conceiue what further bad matter or conſequence he liſteth of our demeanour, or ſtate of ſoule; and not vpon intreatie ſo much as to make a full and diſtinct declaration in the premiſſes, if the proceeding be iuridicall, or haue neighborhood with clemencie, either my bookes be falſe, or I vnderſtand them not. If your Reuerence tooke but all our faculties from vs, and the *et-cetera-es* adioyned implie no Cenſure nor a notorious damnable ſtate; then I deſire to know the reaſon, why we may not miniſter, and the Laitie receiue at our hands the Sacrament of the holie Eucariſt, baptiſme, or extreme vnction, which your cauſatiue *ne*, ſeemeth, and by congruitie of ſpeech can not, as I thinke, but denie. Concerning the cauſes alleaged, I acknowledge, as I euer haue, ſo do I continuallie maintaine that we were no ſchiſmatikes, for delaying to ſubiect our ſelues to your authoritie, before the arriuall of his holines Breue, and that I alſo inſiſt for the reuerſement of father *Listers* pamphlet, as moſt wrongfullie condemning vs of that deteſtable crime. For the other two offences your Reuerence chargeth me with, I denye them vtterly, and do beſeech you moſt humblie to name the Letter, and particular the contumelie or calumnes in which I abuſed your Reuerence, or forgot my ſelfe toward any other Superiour. The like I deſire touching my buſie practiſes againſt peace, and with greateſt inſtancie. Thus your Reuerence in few words ſeeth my grounds, and vnderſtandeth my requeſts: I humblie pray the graunt: and ſo with duetie do leaue, beſeeching God to guide you, & increaſe patience in me. 24. of October.

Your Reuerences,
Iohn Colleton.

Notwithſtanding which earneſt petition to our Arch-prieſt for his anſwere to the points, he, neuertheleſſe as if he had bin more then the Metrapolitane of *England*, and my ſelfe the meaneſt Prieſt on earth, returned me a ragged peece of paper, ſuch as would not much more then come about a mans thombe, with theſe words written in it, *legatur Suarez tom.3. diſput.16. ſect.1. & diſput.72. ſect.4. eod. to.* together with a few broken ſpeeches by word of mouth, either not appertayning, or not ſatisfying my demaunds, which alſo the meſſenger being a lay perſon, would not put downe vnder his hand nor atteſtate. The places he referred me vnto, teach, that Prieſts depriued of Eccleſiaſticall iuriſdiction, can not lawfullie miniſter any Sacrament, and how many wayes they ſinne mortallie that miniſter a Sacrament vnworthilie, or others in receiuing of a Sacrament at the hands of an vnworthie Minister. So that his intent in quoting the places was plaine, *viz.* that I could not, he hauing taken away all my faculties, administer any Sacrament at all, and that I liued in notorious mortall sinne, and therefore none, without sinning deadlie, could receiue a Sacrament of me. Wrongs, which as I pray God of his mercie to forgiue him, so do I hope, that neither he, nor all his adherents, shall be able to prooue, if they giue hands, and deuise all the quircks and quiddities in the world for bolstering vp the slaunder.

And before we descend to the examination of the causes, which his Reuerence alledgeth in the Instrument for the punishment he inflicteth, it seemeth necessarie to speake a word or two, explicating the beginning of his Letter, as also for declaring how and when he may take away our faculties by the authoritie graunted.

Some nine or tenne dayes before the arriuall of his Holines Breue, for confirmation of the new authoritie, Maister *Blackwell* suspended the vse of Maister *Mushes* faculties, Maister *Hebornes*, and mine, because we would not admit him, before he should shew his Holines Letters for proofe of the promotion. Which refusall being lawfull according to all lawes, he tearmeth *a manifest disobedience:* and our receiuing of him vpon the first appearing of the Breue, he nameth *our submission*; and the remouing of the suspension, *the restitution of our faculties,* all spoken vnproperlie, and the first also very wrongfullie.

See more of this matter pag. 52.

Touching the other point, how and when his iurisdiction authoriseth him to take away faculties, there can not be made a better declaration thereof, then are the selfe words of the Constitutiue Letter, being the set forme of his Commission, and from which he can not swarue a haires breadth, which are these: *To restraine or suspend the vse of faculties if there shall be neede, or to take them whollie away if necessitie constraine.* So that of force, either neede or necessitie must be the antecedent to his correction: neede, if he restraine our faculties, or necessitie if he take them away. And when is this? Marie as the same letter specifieth and seemeth to limite, *when his Reuerence hath summoned vs, and proposed with the aduise of his Assistants, the things which either he shall iudge necessarie to be obserued by vs, or shall thinke needefull to be written to Rome, or to Doctor Barret President of Doway, and we in the same matters shall shewe our selues disobedient, vnquiet, or contumaceous: then that his Reuerence after due admonitions,*

Gloss. in ca. cum dilecta de rescript.

admonitions, and reprehensions vsed in brotherlie charitie, may either take away, or suspend our faculties. Which passage (being the words of the Cardinals letter, and comming after the generall graunt of restraining or reuoking faculties, and in the place where his Grace deliuered the forme, how and when the Archpriest should vse the said punishing iurisdiction) appeareth to be the true, and intended exposition and limits of the former clause [*when there shall be neede, or necessitie constraine.*] Or whether this be so or no, yet it is euident by the discourse of reason, and the testimonie of the learned, that this *neede or necessitie* must be construed according to the truth of matters, and not according to the priuate conceipt or opinion of our Archpriest. For howsoeuer father *Parsons* the plotter and penner of the subordination, would perchaunce make our Arch-priest iudge in the matter, and not truth and reason; yet we haue no doubt, but the Cardinall the institutour, and are most sure, that his Holines the confirmer, would haue this [*neede or necessitie*] to be taken according to the veritie of the matter in it selfe, that is (*l*) for a certaine and manifest neede or necessitie, and not according to any mans formed fancie, or corrupt vnderstanding. And if the Cardinall, and his Holines had this meaning by the words, as we may not mistrust but they had, then can not our Arch-priest, (words especially deriuing iurisdiction, being (*m*) to be vnderstood not as they sound, but according to the intention of the speaker) suspend or take away faculties, but when there is a true and a reall *neede* or *necessitie*, which in this subiect (the nature of the punishment, and circumstances of place and persons considered) can not be, but a matter of mortall sinne, and such a mortall sinne, as is cleare by the euidence of the transgression it selfe, and that the delinquent was admonished before of the fault, and did not amend. For if admonition would morallie, or did reforme the partie, there can be no necessitie, or neede either of repealing, or suspending his faculties. Now to the examination of the causes.

Arg. gloss. in ca. vt debitus de Appell. verb. ex rationabile.

(l) *Arg. 11. q. 3. nemo Episcoporum & ca. sacro de sent. excom.*

(m) *Ca. intelligentia de verb. signif.*

The first cause that our Arch-priest alledgeth is, *for that we defend our cause.* O Lord, would not a man wonder to heare such a cause alleadged, if so he knew that we were neuer iuridicallie condemned, and lesse by such a superiour Iudge, as from whose sentence we neither did nor could appeale. Verily the ignorance or exigent must needes be great, when that is brought for a cause of robbing Priests of their faculties in such a countrie as ours, which the lawe of God, Nature, and all Nations doth allow, namely, the vncondemned to maintaine and defend their vnguiltinesse, and the reputation of their good names.

The second cause put downe, is, our *demaund of satisfaction.* Strange and very strange how the asking of satisfaction, that is a recompence (*n*) according to the equalitie of iustice for iniuries committed, can be reputed a cause of taking away faculties from Priests liuing in *England*; and the iniurie, for which satisfaction was demaunded, not disproued, yea, in the immediate and direct consequence approued to be a true and grieuous iniurie by the censure of a famous Vniuersitie. But what was the satisfaction demaunded, and which did alike aggrauate the matter, as for it our faculties must be taken away, without proofe of the cause or citation? Father *Lister* in a publick Treatise condemned vs of Schisme, our Arch-priest approueth the condemnation, and in seuerall letters not vnstiflie maintaineth the same: our ghostlie children by his and the Iesuites report, or defamations rather, were put in feare to haue spirituall participation with vs: and we desired the retractation of the said treatise, as also of the resolution which our Arch-priest sent abroade as receiued from *Rome*, charging vs with the same crime. And are not these, trow ye, capitall demaunds, being duties of iniustice by all lawes; if so we be cleare of the crimes pretended, as now the Pope himselfe on the first of Aprill last, after the full hearing of the matter, and after all the accusations, shifts, and descants, that father *Parsons*, his friends, and the aduocates of our Arch-priest could amplifie, hath declared for vs, and freed as well from the imputation of rebellion and schisme, as from the ignominie of the disobedience obiected, for not admitting the subordination, before the comming ouer of his Breue in confirmation of the same. Who is more blind, than he, that will not see? And holie scripture saith, *hæc cogitauerunt & errauerunt; excæcauit autem illos malitia eorum*, these things they haue thought, and they haue erred, for the faultinesse of their affection hath blinded their vnderstanding.

(n) *D.Tho. in 4.dist.15.q.1. art.1.q.3.*

Sapient.2.

The third cause rendred by our Arch-priest for the taking away of my faculties, is, *for that I wrote diuerse letters vnto him full of contumelies, or calumniations, partly published against himselfe, partly against other Superiours.* In my requests aboue specified, I besought his Reuerence to name the letter vnto me, or set downe the words, wherein I had misdemeaned my selfe, either towards him, or any other Superiour. What could I do more, my selfe not remembring any such thing,

thing, for comming to the vnderſtanding of my fault? But as reaſonable as this petitiō was, yet his fatherhood not liking, or not vouchſauing to anſwere me directly, only willed me to recount what I had written: and this was all that either then, or euer ſince I could receiue from him, touching the particulars of the foreſaid generall charge.

Let others iudge of the courſe, and how farre the ſame is from ſhow of all good dealing, that any Prieſt his faculties ſhould be taken from him, vpon any generall cauſe, without deſcending to the particular, or further proofe of the generall, then by willing him *to remember what he had written*. The Sheriffe of *London* commeth to *Symphronius* and taketh away all his goods, pretending that he wrote vnto him certaine letters, wherein ſundrie hye treaſons were contained. *Symphronius* robbed in this manner of his goods, demaundeth the Sheriffe who made the ſeiſure, to tell him what letters of his theſe were, and what were the treaſonable words in particular, for which he thus oppreſſeth him? The Sheriffe biddeth him remember what he wrote, and other aunſwere giueth none. Who will not admire the vniuſtice, the partie thus rifled, being neither condemned, nor the treaſons particularized, nor proofe made of any? Againe, how would our Countrie exclaime of the crueltie, if the Lord chiefe Iuſtice ſhould put a Counſeller from the barre, and forbid him his practiſe, alleadging for cauſe, that he had ſpoken diſhonourablie of him, but would not recite what ſpeeches they were, nor when he ſpake them, nor ſuffer him to pleade and prooue his innocencie in the accuſation? Our Arch-prieſt his vſage is in all points like: he tooke away our faculties before the fault was prooued, the vſe of them being the onely trade we haue to liue by; neither will he ſuffer vs to argue and defend our vnguiltines, but beſide the prohibition and iniuſtice, defameth vs in generalities: and requeſted to name the particulars, he refuſeth and biddeth vs to examine our ſelues: a reaſon that the greateſt tyrant in the world may yeeld for the fowleſt wrong that can be committed. Some of my letters vnto him are ſet downe before, others follow, as the contents of them do fall in with the matter treated, and the reader may iudge how full they are of contumelies or calumniations, that is, of (*o*) open reprochfull words againſt his, or any other Superiours honour, and of impoſing of (*p*) falſe and malicious crimes vpon either. Certes many of thoſe that haue already ſeene my letters, rather take my manner of writing to the Arch-prieſt for ouer-ceremonious and ſubmiſſiue, then for contumelious & calumniatiue. And I verily aſſure my ſelfe,

(o) *D.Tho.*2.2.*q.*72.*art.*1. & *q.*73.*art.*1.*c.*

(p) *Idem* 2.2. *q.*68.*art.*3.*c.*

that the partiallest reader who shall not wilfullie depose all regard of equitie and conscience, can not but witnes for me against the accusation; if he duly consider of the many iniuries his Reuerence hath done me, and the infinite prouocations which his common made letters haue giuen, especially that by name which he wrote to Maister *Iackson* the 18. of March. In which his Reuerence not onely calleth me the sonne of *Beliall*, but applieth besides this sentence of holie Scripture vnto me, *ab immundo, quid mundabitur, & à mendace, quid verum dicetur?* What shall be cleansed by the vncleane, and what truth can be spoken by a lyer? Which words as well the ordinarie glosse, as *Lyra*, and other expositours, do appropriate to the Diuell onely, and can be verified of none other, and much lesse of a Priest; who, how wicked and abhominable soeuer his inward life be, yet doth he ministeriouslie cleanse, either when he baptiseth or absolueth: and although the Diuell sometimes telleth truth, yet because he neuer telleth truth but to the end to deceiue, and for that such actes (q) take their denomination of the end: therefore the Diuell alwayes intending deceipt, no truth, as holie Scripture affirmeth, can be expected from him. Which kind of habituate and obdurate wickednes and reprobation, being not to be found in any mortall man, the place can not be truly spoken of any, but of the Diuell: and if of none except the Diuell, doubtlesse his Reuerence shewed either much splene, or some ignorance in applying this sentence to me, whom yet he hath not proued to be of so infectious vncleannesse and lying spirit, as that I defile whatsoeuer I haue hand in, and can tell no truth but to the end to beguile.

Eccle. 34.

(q) *D Th. 1. 2. q. 1. art. 3. & q. 19. art. 4. 6. & 7. & 2. 2. q 43. art. 3. & q. 64. art. 7.*

Let the premisses and other his writings be pondered, which are not scant in his letters, and I do not doubt but that my reioynders will seeme as temperate and respectiue, as reason, dutie, and priestlie mildnes did bind me vnto. To end this point, I do not remember that euer I mentioned any Superiour in my letters to him, saue onely father *Garnet*, neither him in any reprochfull or contumelious manner: which maketh me the more to muse, with what libertie of penne and conscience his Reuerence could pretend and diuulge the taking away of my faculties to be *for writing letters vnto him full of contention, or calumniation against other Superiours*; when I neuer touched in my said letters but one onely, and him after no vnseemely manner, his approbation of father *Listers* treatise, and the nature of his owne assertions considered, which were very false, iniurious, and shamelesslie detractiue against me in particular, as the specialties of the Appeale do testifie.

The fourth cause that our Arch-priest giueth for depriuing me of my faculties, is, *for that euen at the instant when he tooke them from me, I attempted many things against peace.* This he saith, but doth not specifie wherein, nor would his Reuerence, when after I wrote vnto him to know the particulars, answere me a word. The truth was, that vnderstanding our intention to appeale from him, and thinking Maister *Mush* and my selfe to be two of the chiefest in the action, he knew no meanes how better to take his peniworths of vs before-hand, then to disfurnish vs of our faculties. And to cloake the reuenge, his Reuerence deuised the foresaid foure causes, with a coople *etceteraes,* as loope holes to let in, what he, or his friends could afterwards espie out, of more truth or moment against vs. But let our encountering of father *Listers* paradoxe, and our withstanding the imputation of enormous disobedience, be exempted (which conscience & bounden respect of our good names tyed vs vnto) and the whole world can not giue an instance, wherein we hindered the making of peace: nay we aboue any others laboured and pressed the chiefe meanes of establishing true peace, as the discourse of the next Reason will demonstrate.

It appeareth by that litle which is said in answere to the reasons of our Arch-priest, that there was *neither neede nor necessitie,* nor any iust cause occurring, why he should bereaue vs of our faculties, especially before summons, and conuiction of the fault. To say, our misdemeanours were notorious, and therefore no neede of citing or triall before the inflicting of the punishment, is too bare a refuge, and ouer common, nor other, then may be alleaged in the wrongfullest accusation that can be imagined. The Canonists (*r*) teach, *Quod licet notorium non sit de necessitate probandum, tamen debet probari illud esse notorium,* That although there be no necessitie to proue that which is notorious or publick, yet there ought proofe to be made that the same is notorious. Which our Arch-priest hath not yet done, nor can euer be able to do by all the conioyned forces of the aduerse part. For that is (*s*) notorious in this case, *quod ita exhibet se conspectu hominum quod nulla potest tergiuersatione celari,* which so exhibiteth it selfe to the eye or vnderstanding of all men, as that it can not be hid or excused by any colour, or tergiuersation soeuer: Or as (*t*) *Panormitane,* and (*v*) *Archidiaconus* describe, a notorious fact or crime, *cuius testis*

(r) *Anto. fran. in ca. ad extirpandas de fil. presby. in lib. a. sub nu. 4. Gloss. in ca. ad nostram de emp. & vend. Speculat. li. 3. de notor. crim. § 1. nu. 9.*
(s) *Gloss. in ca. vestra de cohabi. cler. verb. notorium, & ca. tua, & ca. quæsitum eod. tit.*
(t) *In ca. vestra de cohab. cler. nu. 14.*
(v) *In 2. q. 1. ca. de manifesta.*

populus est, & dissimulationi locus non est, whose witnes is the people, and can not be dissembled. But the two first offences for which our faculties were taken away, that is, *for defending of our cause, and demaunding satisfaction*, do so litle offer themselues to the vnderstanding of most men in the nature and liuerey of notorious faults, as they hold the actions for most lawfull: and the latter two, *viz. the writing of contumelious or calumnious letters, and my frequent deuisings against peace*, how can they be notorious and manifest to others, or not admit deniall or dissimulation, when my selfe who should best know, as being most inward to mine owne action and intention, can by no examination of my conscience (holden neither for the dullest, nor the blindest) recount any such transgression?

It is a generall rule, without exception among the learned in the lawe (x) *Quod debet constare de notorio, ante quam super notorio disponatur:* That there ought to be a manifest constat, and greatest assurance, that the crime or fact be notorious, before any processe be made, or punishment imposed vpon the same. as notorious. Furthermore, if any processe be made, or ecclesiasticall penalty inflicted, without summoning the offender before, for a fault that is not publick or notorious, the processe or penaltie doth not bind. *Sententia lata contra non citatum, nulla est, nisi in facto notorio:* A sentence (as writeth (y) *Siluester*) giuen without citing the delinquent before in a fact that is not notorious, is voyd, and of no effect. And *Panormitane* writeth, (z) *Quandoque potest competere aliqua defensio, quod est quasi regulare, & tunc requiritur citatio, aliàs sententia non valebit:* Sometime in facts that are notorious, there may be place of defence, which is very common, and then citation is so requisite, as without it the sentence is of no validitie.

By which places and others before quoted it is very plaine, that our Arch-priest did not only exceede the bounds of the Constitutiue Letter, in the manner of taking away our faculties, but that he did also breake the lawes (*a*) of Nature, and holy Church in such his enterprise, and the fact neuerthelesse of no obligation: which may also be confirmed by other arguments.

There is nothing lesse doubtfull either in the (*b*) Canon, or (*c*) Ciuill lawe, then that no one can be depriued of the thing he possesseth, without iudiciall examination, and triall of the cause. Which without question holdeth also true, as (*d*) *Nauar* writeth, in ecclesiasticall rights. So that the possession and vse of our faculties being vnto vs

(x) *Anto. franc. in ca. consuluit de appell. sub lit. 6. verb. notorium. Card. in consi. 54. incipi. in elucidatione, & Ro. consi. 42. incipi. visis.*

(y) *Verb. citatio nu. 5.*

(z) *In ca. vestra de coha. cleri. nu. 18.*

(a) *Clem. ca. pastoralis de re iudica.*

(b) *12. q. 5. c. 1. & ca. 1. de causa poss. & prop. & tit. vt lite non contesta. per totum.*

(c) *L. fi. c. si per vim siue alio modo l. 2.*

(d) *In ca. accepta de rest. spo. solut. oppositionis octaue nu. 18. & 19. Pagi. 223.*

in steed of benefices, and in a sort, couenanted for, and deserued, as it hath bin before shewed; it followeth directlie vpon the same reason, that we cannot lawfully be dispossessed of our faculties before we be heard, and iudiciall examination had of the offence for which they are to be taken away. But of that, which may not lawfully be done, there can be *no neede or necessitie,* which are the limits and direction, when our Arch-priest may take away faculties, as appeareth by the Cardinals letter; therefore this not obserued but exceeded, (*e*)his fact therein may easily be mortall sinne to himselfe, but neuer of any effect in vs, because if he goe beyond his commission, he goeth beyond his iurisdiction, and going beyond his iurisdiction, his fact is of no force, nor obligation, but absolutely voyd in it selfe, as the fourth and fifth propositions teach.

(e) *D.Tho.22. q.60.art.2. & 6. Ricardus in 4.dist.18 art. 4. q. 4. Pag.25.*

Againe, the Diuines and Canonists agree, that regular or religious Priests, being once allowed by the Bishop to heare confessions, cannot againe be imbarred thereof, but (*f*) *causa cognita & probata,* vpon examination and proofe of the cause pretended. Much more then, the priests in *England,* being sent with like danger of life into our country, and hauing no other meanes of procuring harbour or maintenance, then by vse of their faculties, nor any way inabled, so much to reclaime or profit others, as by exercise of that function, should not, nor cannot by any lawe or rules of conscience (and the more for that also, the losse of their faculties is a defamation vnto them) be depriued of their faculties, but vpon iudiciall examination and tryall of the cause, and crime obiected.

(f) *Henriques li.3. de pœni. ca.6 nu.6. Benedict 11. in Extrauag. inter cunctas Pius 5. prop. mot. pro mendic. Sotus dist. 18. q 4. art.3. Siluest. verb. confess. 2. nu.11.*

Hence, as by other perticulars, the iniustice and oppression of our Arch-priest appeare great in dispossessing vs of our faculties, onely vpon the bare naming of a cause, without citation or proofe of the cause alleaged, a course contrarie to lawe, diuine, and ecclesiasticall, and contrarie to the forme of all practise in the christian world. Which measure also becommeth the more ouer-running in extremitie and iniustice towards vs, in that his Reuerence, notwithstanding the long want of our faculties, would not restore vs to our former state vpon the order, and commaundement of his Holines *Nuncio* in Flanders, to whom himselfe assigned me in his dimissories, as to the Iudge of my appellation; a more direct, and lesse iustifiable kind of disobedience by many degrees, then we can be charged with, notwithstanding the condemnation and outcryes that haue bin made and continued for a long space most violently against vs. The words of the

Nuncio his letter vnto him, belonging to this point, were these: *Eo casu mittendi aliqui erunt, sufficienti procuratorio & authoritate, ad ea quæ hanc in rem necessaria erunt peragenda instructi (si profectionem rationes & negotia admodum R^{dæ} D.V. incumbentia non admittant) interim eam monitam & rogatam cupimus, vt interea temporis omnia in antiquum statum reponentur.* To the end that all matters may be examined and discussed before the Priests that are come from *England*, go forwards in their iourney to *Rome*, some are to be sent with sufficient information and authoritie for accomplishing the things that are hereunto necessary, if your Reuerences charge and affaires may not suffer your personall repaire vnto me: in the meane season, whiles these matters be a treating, we admonish and will you to set all things in their old state.

Some weeke or more after I had sent the *Nuncio* his letter vnto our Arch-priest, and receiuing no answere from him, I addressed the Letter following.

Very Reuerend Sir:

I Sent you some few dayes past a Letter from his Holines *Nuncio* in Flanders, with a copie of an other of his to the Priests of our Countrie in generall. I doubt not but that you haue receiued them; and receiuing them, not I alone, but other also of my brethren do maruell (the contents and the solemnitie of the feast considered) that we haue not as yet heard from you. By reason of which delay, these are very earnestly to beseech you to aduertise vs, whether you determine to restore vs to our former state, as his Honour in the said Letter directed and willed you to do. Which due of iustice we expect the more to receiue at your hands, in regard the thing his Grace enioyneth you is none other then what the Canons of holie Church not vnstrictly commaund, the vse of our faculties being vnto vs in lieu of Ecclesiasticall liuings, and the meanes of our maintenance. Let vs therefore (we againe beseech you good Sir) vnderstand your full mind in the point, and receiue notice of the time you assigne, for the appearance of some of the Appellants before the *Nuncio*, there both to answere to that your selfe or your Procuratours shall obiect, and to proue the auowances in the Appeale, and other iniustices receiued: that so his Lordship hearing both parties face to face, may the more maturely iudge, and relate to his Holines at full (to whom other of our associates in the action are gone) the beginning, processe, and true

3.q.1.in multis ca. & eadem,q.2.ca. Oportet & ca. Si Episcopus.

true causes of the whole dissention betweene vs. Your Reuerence hath oft affirmed (and in that you haue published the same, our aduersaries make it an assured ground of diffidence or despaire in our cause) that your Proctours in Flanders and at *Rome* haue long expected, attending our comming, which how true soeuer it may happen to fall out at *Rome*, yet we are very sure, that the truth was otherwise in Flanders. For our brethren comming thither, neither found nor could vnderstand of any such Proctours, and lesse so amplie furnished as your * dimissories reported; yea, and which taketh away all colour of doubt that may be made hereof, the *Nuncio* himselfe in the Letter I sent you, wrote vnto you to send ouer (if your other affaires should not licence your personall repaire) some with full instruction from you to relate and negotiate the difference: a trauell and charge which his wisdome would neuer without doubt haue put you too, had your Proctours bin there attending, or so much as shewed them selues before his Grace, during the time of our brethrens being with him. And that your Proctours at *Rome* expect our comming thither, is an affirmation that likewise claimeth in our conceipt no great beliefe, because father *Parsons* (the onely man by all likelyhood who must prouide and informe them) hath laboured both the Popes holines and Cardinall *Fernesius* our Protectour, vtterlie to forbid our comming to *Rome* in the cause, and hath further solicited as well the *Nuncio* in *Paris*, as the *Nuncio* in *Flanders*, to dehort (for I will not say to stay, though that were the word that the partie vsed who sent the intelligence) our brethren at their comming by them, from going onwards to his Holinesse.

No more, but God giue vs all in our words and deedes to vse the sinceritie it becommeth, and then no doubt the controuersie will soone take a sound and a lasting end. Fare you well, with remembrance of duetie. The feast of the Innocents, 1601.

Your Reuerences,

I. Colleton.

* In which among other things these words were writ-ten, *Illic pro nostra defensione extabunt variæ Illmo Cardinalium literæ: illic prodibit Breue Apostolicum: illic patebunt omnes occultæ vestræ machinationes contra pacem: illic circa literas meas, fallaciarum vestrarum omnem caliginem discussam videbitis: illic calumniæ vestræ, & seditiosæ vestræ literæ proferentur, & rerum omnium vestrarum opertarum fiet vobis iniucunda patefactio.* There, for our defence shall diuers letters of most Illustrious Cardinals appeare: there shall come forth the Apostolicall Breue: there shall all your machinations against peace be laid open: there shall ye see all the darkenes of your craftie deuises about my letters put away and disparkled: there shall your calumniations, and your seditious letters be brought forth, and an vnpleasant discouerie shall be made of all your hidden matters. 20. of December. 1600.

OVr Arch-prieſt notwithſtanding this my Letter and earneſt requeſt, did not ſo much as returne one word in anſwere either by letter or meſſage, albeit I ſent twiſe or thriſe for his anſwere. Now to conclude this our fourth Reaſon, we hope the premiſſes haue ſufficiently ſhewed, that the authoritye which our Arch-prieſt poſſeſſeth, being very ample in it ſelfe, and infinitely more ample in the practiſe, maketh him a ſuperiour Prelate, and conſequently his Reuerence conteyned vnder the Extrauagant *Iniunctæ* afore mentioned. And if ſo, as the largeneſſe of his authority and the ſcope of his Iuriſdiction reaching ouer *England* and *Scotland*, cannot but conclude him vnder the ſame: then all the power, wit, and learning of the aduerſe part can neuer proue vs to be in the leaſt point diſobedient, either vnto his Holines, the Cardinall Protector, or to Maiſter *Blackwell*, becauſe the ſayd Extrauagant commaundeth, and enacteth vnder a heauie penaltie, not to admit any Superiour Prelate promoted by the ſea Apoſtolick to the dignitie he is choſen to, without he firſt ſhew the letters of the ſame Sea for proofe of the preferment. Of which kind, we are right ſure the Cardinals letter neither was, nor could be. Yea, to affirme a Cardinals Protectors letter, either patent or ſealed vp to be an Apoſtolicall letter, were groſſe error, and perhaps hereticall alſo, if ignorance do not excuſe. For ſuch letters only are called Apoſtolicall, and vnderſtood in the Extrauagant, *quæ Bulla ſunt munitæ*, whoſe ſeales carry the print or purtrait of a Bull, as *(g) Nauar, (h) Gomeſius*, and *(i)* others write, and the text of *(k)* the lawe ſeemeth to import. Neither can our aduerſaries winde themſelues out of the ſtraites they are in, by ſaying that Maiſter *Blackwell* was not promoted by the Sea Apoſtolick, but by the Cardinall Protector. For let this be ſo, yet what followeth, when the Extrauagant doth extend it ſelfe, as well to thoſe that haue their confirmation from the Sea Apoſtolick, *aut confirmationis munus recipiunt*, as to thoſe that are immediatly preferred by the ſame ſea: and none can denye, but that our Arch-prieſt had the confirmation of his office and dignitie from the Pope? If then, the authorities and reaſons afore-going do conuince, that we were not bound to receiue Maiſter *Blackwell* to the office vpon the ſole view of the Cardinals letter, it followeth, that no bond being, no ſinne could be, becauſe ſinne is alwayes the breach of ſome bond; and if no ſinne, no diſobedience: if no diſobedience, no rebellion: if no rebellion, no ſchiſme: and if no ſchiſme, no excommunication, no irregularitie, nor loſſe of faculties. And if none

(g) *In ca. accepta de reſt. ſpol. ſolut. oppoſit. 8. nu. 23.*
(h) *In reg. de non iudi. iuxt. form. q. 1.*
(i) *Gloſſ. regulæ Cancel. 69.*
(k) *Ca. licet & ca. quam graui de crimi. falſ.*

D. Th. 12. q. 71. art. 6.

none of all these, then what wrongs, what oppressions, what ignominies, and those also most grieuous & slanderous, haue father *Lister*, father *Garnet*, father *Holtby*, and our Arch-priest with their adherents, heaped in prodigallest measure vpon vs, and on the necks of our ghostly children: and haue not onely hereby most despituously massacred our good names, but also raysed sociall contention, turmoyled the inward repose of thousands, and set that on fire, which will hardly be quenched this twise tenne yeares as we feare. Our blessed Lord forgiue them, and graunt vs grace to redeeme our sinnes, by remitting their manifold trespasses done against vs.

The fift Reason.

THE fift and last Reason of iustifying our delay, was, that admitting there had bin no surreption vsed in the information to his Holines, or the Cardinall, and that the Cardinall had receiued an expresse commandement from his Holines, to erect this particular iurisdiction by name, and that his Grace had also signified the same in plaine termes in the Constutitiue Letter; and that we stood obliged to beleeue and rest vpon the Cardinals word in so preiudiciall a matter; and finally, that the *Extrauagant Iniunctæ*, did not as the same was either set forth by *Bonifacius* the eight, or as it hath bin since enlarged by (*a*) *Paulus* the third, (*b*) *Iulius* the second, and (*c*) *Iulius* the third, inuolue, or concerne the promotion and office of Maister *Blackwell*, as how little true all these things are, the former reasons haue sufficiently declared: yea we tooke the hard conceite and indignation which our Prince and the State carry against Father *Parsons*, (whom they reputed to be the chiefe deuiser of the subordination, and to haue the whole ruling thereof) as a iust excuse of not admitting the authoritie, especially at the first appearance thereof, vpon the bare sight of the Cardinals letter, directed also to no more then one. And the grounds why we tooke this to be a reasonable cause of iustifying our bearing off, were these that follow.

(a) *In constitutione quæ incipit cum à nobis.*
(b) *In const. quæ incipit Romani Pontificis.*
(c) *In const. quæ incip. sanctissimus.*

First, becauſe the Magiſtrates haue in their hands, and *de facto* haue ſhewed to ſome priſoners at the time of their examinations for proofe, and to exaggerate the diſloyalties and treaſons obiected, one, or mo letters which they affirme to be father *Parſons,* wherein his concurrance and furtherance to an inuaſion were expreſſed: then the mans reſtleſſe tampering in State matters, being reported to haue profered, and reprofered the Crowne of our Countrie to ſeuerall Princes, now to one, now to another, as the meeting of matters and oportunities could moſt recommend and credit his words, and entertaine the perſonage with hope thereof: thirdly, the inceſſant ſolicitation, which the Magiſtrate proteſteth, that he hath vſed with forraine Potentates, and the attempts, which, as the ſame Magiſtrate affirmeth, haue thereon enſued for a conqueſt of our countrie. So as the Magiſtrate vnderſtanding (as common fame could not but bring it to his hearing) that the ſubordination was the worke of father *Parſons,* our feare was, leaſt the politick State would deeme vs coadiutors and creatures combined with him, if we had admitted the Subordination vpon no greater compulſion, then the Protectors letter, and conſequently, that we were perſons who did deſerue to be abandoned, and to haue the extremitie of the lawes proſecuted againſt vs. Could we therefore in common reaſon do leſſe, matters ſtanding in theſe termes, then deferre our acceptance of the authoritie, vntill his Holines had commaunded vs by Bull, Breue, or other papall inſtrument, or verball meſſage, to ſubiect our ſelues thereunto; that ſo the State might ſee, our receiuing of the Subordination not to be for any liking we caried towards father *Parſons* proceedings, but for obedience only towards the Sea Apoſtolick, and in a matter wherein the obſeruances of our religion bound vs, and the ſame not iuſtlie preiudiciall to the temporall ſtate? Verily we tooke this for ſo reaſonable and iuſt a cauſe, as we could not but ſtand thereupon, vnleſſe we would in our owne vnderſtanding haue ſhewed our ſelues cruell to our owne innocencie; of ill deſerts towards the Magiſtrate, in not remouing his wrong ſuſpition of vs when and how we might; ingratefull to our benefactors; vnmindfull of our owne liues; betrayers of the cauſe we profeſſe; enemies to the profeſſors thereof; and iniurious to the honor of Prieſthood: for that all theſe (her Maieſtie and the State not reading in our actions, that we were true diſlikers of all and ſingular his diſloyall practiſes and platformes) were like to receiue increaſe of affliction & blemiſh,

by

by our admittance of the iurisdiction, before such time as his Holines had confirmed the same, & thereby through the vertue of his supreme authoritie, freed both it and vs, from hauing part in father *Parsons* intentions, so farre as they were any whit disloyall.

Neither is father *Parsons* holden onely of our Magistrate for a Statist, or marchandizer of the Crowne and Diademe, though this were enough to estrange & deforce vs from hauing any connexion, or partaking in ought with him: but his trauels and negotiations this way are become so notoriouslie knowne, that euen *Pasquine* in *Rome* (as intelligence is sent vs) speaketh in this manner of him:

If there be any man that will buy the Kingdome of England, *Let him repaire to a Marchant in a blacke square Cappe in the Citie, and he shall haue a very good pennyworth thereof.*

Touching the proper nature of our delaie vpon the foresaid cause, we thinke, that the same will not onely appeare iust and reasonable before any Tribunall vpon earth to our full excuse, but that it will be found of that qualitie in the day of iudgement, when * *Iustice will be iudged, and Ierusalem searched with a candle.* For what humaine cause can be thought iust or reasonable, if not the precedent, branching into so many seuerall and weightie consequences, as the premisses deliuer, and reason maketh manifest, if circumstances of time, place, and persons (the direction of a wise mans aime) be vprightlie considered? And if the cause were either in truth, or in semblance iust, we meane, either iust in it selfe, or so taken in good faith by vs, then our prolonging to subiect our selues (supposing the Cardinals letter had bin a binding precept vnto vs) was either no sinne at all, or not greater then a veniall. No sinne, if the cause were reallie iust, as witnesseth (*a*) Pope *Alexander* the third, (*b*) Saint *Thomas*, (*c*) *Archidiaconus*, (*d*) *Panormitane*, (*e*) *Siluester*, (*f*) *Nauar*, (*g*) *Graffius*, and others. Or not greater then a veniall, if the cause were but putatiuely iust, as writeth (*h*) Saint *Antonie*, (*i*) *Caietane*, (*k*) *Paludensis*, (*l*) *Siluester*, (*m*) *Nauar*, (*n*) *Gregorius de Valentia*, and others. Neither is this doctrine only true in the commaundements of inferiour pre-

* Psal. 5. Sophon. 1.
(a) *Ca. si quando de rescript.*
(b) 12. *q.* 96. *art.* 6. & 22. *q.* 147. *art.* 3. *ad* 2. & *in* 4. *dist.* 15. *q.* 3. *art.* 4. *ad* 4. *quæst. ad* 3.
(c) *In dist.* 76. *ca. vtinam.*
(d) *In ca. eam quæ de rescript. nu.* 4. & *in rubr. de obseruat. ieiu. nu.* 11.
(e) *Verb. lex. nu* 8.
(f) *In man. ca.* 23. *nu.* 43.
(g) *P.* 1. *li.* 2. *ca.* 36. *nu.* 16.
(h) 2. *P. tit.* 6. *ca.* 2. *ante* § 1.
(i) *In* 22. *q.* 147 *art.* 3. & *in summa verb. præceptum.*
(k) *In* 4. *dist.* 15 *q.* 4.
(l) *Verb. ieiunium nu.* 21.
(m) *Vbi supra.*
(n) *T.* 3. *disp.* 9. *q.* 2. *punct.* 5.

lates, but holdeth likewise true in the precepts of Cardinals, or of Popes them-selues, as both the text of the lawe, and the best writers do testifie. (o) *Si aliqua tuæ fraternitati dirigimus, quæ animum tuum exasperare videntur, turbari non debes, &c. Qualitatem negotij, pro quo tibi scribitur, diligenter considerans, aut mandatum nostrum reuerenter adimpleas, aut per literas tuas, quare adimplere non possis, rationabilem causam prætendas.* If we inioyne you any thing (sayth Pope *Alexander* to the Archbishop of *Rauenna*) that may seeme to stirre your mind, you ought not to be troubled therewith, but after diligent consideration had of the nature of the businesse, either reuerently to accomplish our commaundement, or yeeld a reasonable cause why you may not fulfill it. And (p) *Ioannes Andreas* writeth, *Is ad quem rescriptum Papæ dirigitur, debet illi parere, aut iustam causam ostendere, quare non paret.* He, to whome the Popes rescript is directed, ought to obey it, or assigne a cause why he doth not obey it. The same (q) hath *Felinus*; & (r) *Baldus* writeth further, *Quod si in literis Papæ dicatur districtè præcipuendo mandamus, tamen potest supersederi ex causa iusta:* That if the Pope do strictly cōmaund such a thing to be done, neuerthelesse the same may be omitted vpō a iust cause. Likewise the Glosse affirmeth, (s) *Quod oportet mandatum domini Papæ, adimplere nisi subsit causa non adimplendi,* That we ought to fulfill the commaundement of the Pope, except there be a cause of not fulfilling it. Also *Graffius* writeth, alleaging Saint *Thomas* and *Panormitane* for proofe of the position, (t) *Quod in omni præcepto legis positiuæ, admittitur exceptio causa rationabilis:* That in euery precept of a positiue lawe, the exception of a reasonable cause is admitted. And the reason hereof is, because the lawes of the Church, or commaundements of Superiours are not *secundum se* in their owne natures of the necessitie of saluation (as are the precepts of God, (v) being the precepts of the lawe of nature) but only by the institution of the Church, or decree of the Superior, and therefore some causes or obstacles may occurre, whereby a partie may not be bound to the obseruance of them. By all which it appeareth, with how little iudgement, or rather with what ignorance, and childish reasoning, father *Parsons* in the tenth leafe of the Appendix inueyeth, and inferreth against vs, for affirming, that one may vpon a reasonable cause deferre to fulfill the commaundement of the Superiour.

(o) *Ca. si quādo de rescript.*

(p) *In ca. si quando de rescript. nu. 1.*

(q) *Ibidem nu. 1.*

(r) *In ca. cum teneamur de præbend. in apostillis ad Innocent.*

(s) *In ca. cum teneamur de præbend.*

(t) *P. 1. li. 2. ca. 36. nu. 15. & 16.*

(v) *D. Thomas 22. q. 147. art. 4. ad. 1.* See the 7. 8. and 12. propositions pag. 27. See also pag. 47.

NOw for the more perspicuitie of all that hath bin hitherto said, it seemeth necessarie, that we put downe the whole race of the controuersie,

controuersie, and what offers of attonement we haue made from time to time, that so the reader may see whether side hath more inclined to peace, and sued for it. And to shew this, from the beginning of the difference, and how desirous we euer were to giue satisfaction to all parties who were scrupulouslie grieued at the manner of our proceedings, chiefely of mine, on whome most blame was layd: I will here set downe two Letters for testifying of such our willingnes, the one written to father *Garnet*, the other to an earnest lay-fauorite, and patrone of the aduerse part.

Very Reuerend Sir:

VNwillingnesse to shew my selfe either too quick in taking, or ouer-tender in brooking iniuries, hath hitherto not a little (as to me seemeth) staid both toung and pen from due questioning and complaining; and would haue done longer, but that reports are now growne to the like head, as euen feare of offending through too great neglect of my good name, necessarily enforceth a more respectfull consideration vpon me. My owne eares haue bin witnes (good Sir) and my friends euery where giue me to vnderstand, how sinisterly I am talked of, for wronging (that I vse but one, and no harder a tearme, albeit many and much harder be spread of me) the fathers of the Societie. These are therefore to beseech you, and in all right of charitie to intreate the receiuing of so much fauour, or rather not the vndue tribute of iustice from you, as to acquaint me with those particulars, wherein I haue reproueablie, either to your owne knowledge, or by such information as will be stood vnto, miscaried my selfe in word, deede, or demeanour against your selfe, or any of your societie. I expect my full charge, and do no way desire you to leaue any point vntouched, or not amplified to the most, whereof you hold me culpable. Adding, that the plainer you deale with me herein, the better cause I haue to like you. Aduertising besides, that for sauing some of your friends credit so farre as the deliuery of like vntruths do discredit, it importeth to alleage the most you can against me. If my leaue be desired as no neede, I yeeld it franckly, because I would not willingly dwell in ignorance of my sinnes, nor omit satisfaction where I am bound to make it. Thus in briefe you haue my request, and see the motiues, I praye affoord me the performance with the soonest. Fare you well with very good will, though the course (if with your priuitie) followed against me, sheweth little good will. Nouember 5. 1598.

By him whom plainenesse in the premisses maketh more yours:

I. Colleton.

SIr, I perceiue by the continuance of your hard speeches against me, vttered euen where they may worke me most hurt, that there will be no end of the euill, vnlesse some meanes be taken that both you may vrge whatsoeuer you can obiect against me, and I on the other side, haue leaue and hearing to make my answers. To which intent, I offer by these, to come where and when you shall appoint, and do further beseech you, that you would haue such present, as you thinke can speake most, and best proue your and their accusations against me. I shall come alone, only with the testimonie of my owne conscience; you may take to your selfe as many as you shall thinke good: and if you and they shall iustly proue me to be faultie, in that I goe charged withall, I wil forthwith, God willing, both aske you pardon, and be ready to make any satisfaction that shall be thought fit. In the meane, it were good we remembred what the holy Ghost writeth, *The abomination of men is the detractor.* By which words, the wisdome of heauen seemeth to affirme, that of all ill qualities which make men hatefull, and their companie to be abandoned, the vice of detraction is the first. Surely if the mouth speaketh from the abundance of the hart, then what suds must lodge in the hart of him, that deprau eth the good name of another, and incomparablie more in his, who calumniouslie accuseth his spirituall father? For such a one the lawes of holy Church reckon for an infamous person. No more but what I write to you, the same I meane to your sonne Maister *N.* Fare you well the 28. of Ianuary.

Yours howsoeuer you repute of me,

Iohn Colleton.

TO the latter of these Letters I receiued no answere at all; and of the former I receiued the answere that followeth, which I thought good to set downe *verbatim,* both to the end that others might see wherewith I was charged, and how I cleered my selfe: but chiefely because my reply could not be well vnderstood without the adioining of his answere, and for that some parts of my reioinder did most

most euidentlie protest our readinesse, of admitting Maister *Blackwels* authoritie, vpon notice of the first canonicall certitude that should appeare thereof, and consequently in all truth of learning, freed vs of father *Listers* calumniation imposed, and likewise conuinced the author and approuers of the same, either of very bold ignorance, or of vnworthiest demeanure against vs, they hauing the said replie of mine almost three moneths, if not full out, in their hands, before the setting forth of that proude and slanderous treatise, the only soule and life of the whole contention.

My very reuerend Sir :

IF you be sinisterlie talked of for wronging our Societie : blame not him (I beseech you) who, for all your strangenes ceasseth not to loue you : and whome, for your hurtfull proceedings, loue inforceth to pittie you. Father Garnets answere.

It hath bin alwayes my desire, since that we purged our selues (I hope sufficiently) from the malicious slaunders of some impudent libellers, that all things should (as much as is possible) be vtterly forgotten : and if all could not be induced to loue and affect vs, to beare their auersion with patience & silence, without following any course or pursuite against them : so, that if you heare either your selfe, or by any others, any sinister reports against you, you may examine them best, whether they be true, and the reporters are to giue account on what ground they vtter them.

True it is, that as it hath pleased God to giue our Societie part in many glorious labours which in his holie Church are continuallie atchieued : so also very often times, yea ordinarily, doth he make vs partakers of the afflictions and difficulties which do thence arise : and if any worthie thing be accounted worthie of blame, we are lightlie the first which are blamed. Note the matter of this our blame.

It hath pleased his Holines of late to ordaine a certaine gouernement among vs. It hath bin receiued with singular liking of the most and best. God forbid, but that I and all my brethren, should haue bin most ready to runne whither charitie and obedience did call vs, least by disobedience we should contemne our Superior, or by schisme and diuision be cut off from the head.

Some haue refused to acknowledge this head, much more to obey him. Their pretences are in euery ones mouth that haue heard of this authoritie : It is a thing deuised by the Iesuites : The Superior is one of their owne choosing: Why should the Iesuites app oint vs a Superior, more then we a Generall vnto them? It is the fine head of father *Parsons* that hath inuented this: He hath giuen wrong information to the Cardinall and his Holines: The Cardinall was alwayes partiall on the Iesuites side: Some of necessitie must be sent to informe better: The messengers must procure that some assistants be chosen, who may not be thought to be partiallie affected to the Iesuites: They must propound, to haue the gouernment of the Colledge enlarged, as being ouer-straite, or indiscreete for our nation: Yea they must make suite that the Iesuites be remoued from the gouernment of all Seminaries of our nation: And touching the mission of *England* in particular, all the Iesuites must needes be called away.

These and the like speeches hauing bin vttered by such, as either gathered voyces for another gouernment, or are knowne not to fauour this: what can it argue else, but that such oppose themselues against the Societie, as if no authoritie were to be liked, but which may beate downe the Iesuites, or set them and other *Reuerend Priests* together by the eares? And verily, the successe of matters since the authoritie of the *Reuerend Arch-priest* was diuulged, doth make many to feare, least the secret intention (yet not perceiued of all) of these which were the principall seekers, to erect a sodalitie, or other superioritie and subordination, was either ambitious, or seditious. For hauing now that very thing which they sought for (although imposed on other persons then they had designed) to reprehend and impugne the same, must needes make men suspect, that they doe it, either because they themselues are not chosen, or because such were not chosen as might deale peremptorily with those which they ought to tender. Both which affections, sheweth them doubly vnworthie of gouernment. For what is so vnfit for honor, as ambition? And what haue we done, that all should not affect vs? Yea by Gods great goodnes so it is (as we thinke) that if any affect vs not, the fault is in them, and not in vs. So that if they would haue themselues, or others that do not affect vs (though otherwise seeming neuer so vertuous) to be chosen heads, let them first affect vs (so farre as in vertue they ought) that they may be worthie of gouernment.

Then you see (good Sir) it wanteth not probabilitie, that if any giue out that you wrong vs, it is because you are thought to draw

backe

backe from your Arch-presbyter, which you knowe whether it be so or no. And although I verily perswade my selfe, that most of those speeches neuer proceeded from your mouth, yet those that will be part of a discontented companie, of force must be contented to beare the reproch of many things which are done or sayd amisse by a few, it being impossible that all men should distinguish, and applie euery particular to the true authour. And verily, as it grieueth me oftentimes to heare, and I reprehend it so often as I heare it spoken, that such a one, or such another who is not ioyned to the Archpresbyter, is condemned, as opposite to the Societie: and condemne such manner of speech for a fallacie, which we call as you know *non causæ vt causæ*: for in very deede, I would not haue them reprehended because they are opposite against vs, but because they acknowledge not their lawfull Superiour: so on the other side must I needes acknowledge that it is, and by Gods grace will I alwayes procure, that it shall alwayes continue: that those two things are so annexed one to the other, that whosoeuer is opposite against our reuerend Archpresbyter, must of force be consequentlie opposite against vs. And therein will we *gloriari in Domino*, if any be thought opposite to vs, who are opposite vnto him. Therefore (good Sir) there is nothing I more desire, there is nothing can be more honorable & profitable for your selfe, then that you vnite your selfe vnto him, whom God hath made your Superior: who like vnto him which is *Princeps Pastorum*, is in this our particular church *lapis qui factus est, non in offensionem, sed in caput anguli, qui medium parietem maceriæ soluat, qui faciat vtraque vnum:* is the onely meanes to ioyne vs all together in perfit loue and vnion, which we had long since enioyed, if his authoritie had bin admitted, as at this present there is no hinderance at all of vnitie, but the refusing of the same. So that wee finde true that which is most worthilie sayd by Sainct Paule, *Non tenens caput ex quo totum corpus per nexus & coniunctiones subministratum & constructum crescit in augmentum Dei.* And the cause of this refusing the head he expressed before: *frustra inflatus sensu carnis suæ.* With this head therefore must I hold, to him must I be vnited, to him must we cleaue. *Qui illi coniungitur meus est: qui cum illo non colligit spargit.* And vnfaignedlie I affirme vnto you, that I continuallie pray in particular for your vnion vnto him, in respect of the loue I haue borne and do beare vnto you: which shall not decay, although you would with neuer so great contrarietie of iudgements and opinions. And thus wishing you to follow that which is most to the glorie of God and your owne soules health, I ceasse. 11. Nouember. 1598.

Your plaine friend, as you wished
Henry Ga.

Very reuerend Sir:

PErusing your Letter, I find little to the purpose, wherein I intreated your answere. My desire was, to be aduertised of all such wrongs, as either in your owne knowledge, or by auowable information, I had committed against the Societie: and you altogether leauing this point, amplifie another matter. Neuerthelesse, sith you haue taken paines to write, what better pleased you then to satisfie my request, I shall not let for eauening your labour, to returne you also my opinion of that you haue written.

Touching my strangenesse, I pray consider, whether I can not with greater reason except the same against you, then you against me. For you know the way to me, I know not where to come to you: and while I did know, I was (as I verily thinke) oftner then ten times with you for your once being with me. Besides, in my knowledge, there was neuer any cause offered, why you should estrange your selfe, and moe then one giuen me, that might iustlie disswade my repaire to you, as namely, when out of good will vpon aduertisement I told the elder Gentlewoman of the safe shipping of her maide-seruant, she refused to take notice, making a like strange of my speeches, as if I had bin a person iustlie to be mistrusted, or not to be trusted with so small a secret. Againe, one of those that belong vnto you, and who was very well and long weeting to my free accesse in former time vnto you, made pretie shifts in dissembling the house and quarter where you abide. Both which in common reason, did, and must bid me doubt, least wonted good will or trust, or both, be decayed in you and in them towards me. If you shall say, that you haue sent for me once or twise, my being in Phisick at those times (as the messenger could informe from his eye) sufficiently excuseth my faile: and verily since my better health, I haue seuerall times wished for a guide to conduct me vnto you, so little I did affect to estrange my selfe, notwithstanding the vtter shew, or counterpleadings of the aforesayd discurtesies. Maister *Blackwell* in his last speech with me, sayd, the Fathers of the Societie had many exceptions against me, which was one principall cause,

cause, why I wrote vnto you in the tenor I did, but now if strangenesse be all, and the same no more deseruingly obiected, I see well a little can soone and easily be made much against me.

You say, *Loue inforceth you to pittie me for my hurtfull proceedings.* Good sir, in my iudgement you should haue shewed as much loue, and certes, loue better qualited, if it had stood with your good liking to haue forborne alike hardlie to mis-censure my proceedings. I wote not of what hurt my proceedings may be made the occasion, because the frailtie of man may make what is perfit good, to serue to shadow that which is ill. But how my proceedings may be the cause of hurt, which requiring an intention, doth make them truly hurtfull, and so denominate: this I see not, because I do not espye in my selfe any such intent and meaning. And if you say my proceedings be of that qualitie in their nature, you say more then I hope you shall be able to proue, and vntill you proue them so, why may not my nay perswade as much as your yea, or more, in regard you cannot be so priuie to my actions, their circumstances, and my intent, as my selfe.

Such as sinisterlie report of me, are (by the auowance of your own assertion) *to giue account on what ground they vttered their reports.* Father *Iones* reported & affirmeth the same in his Letter to me, that I should call your kind of gouerning the English Colledge in Rome *a Macheuilian gouernment, or worse.* And when by letter I wished him either to proue that I spake the words, or disproue himself for doing me the iniurie, he returned answere: *if I did purge my selfe of Fishers confession, I should satisfie him.* Verily as I wote not what the father meant by this kind of replie, so the probablest meaning that may be directlie gathered of his words seemeth to be, that *Fisher* hath appeached me of such plentifull & bad matter against your Societie, as vntill I cleare my self thereof, the good man cannot hold himself satisfied, and in the *interim* my good name forsooth to be so deepely wounded, and publickly depraued, as licenseth him to report as he did, or what he listeth further of me. My request is the performãce of your owne graunt, that he giue an account on what ground he vttered the report, & if so any detractiõ be found in me, I yeeld my self to fullest satisfaction: if in him, I demãd my right. And because this sore spreadeth in time like a canker by sufferance, the sooner satisfaction be made, the better. But here I cannot but greatlie meruaile, with what shew of charitable dealing Fa. *Iones* or any of the Societie can vpbraid me with *Fishers* confession, whome your selues call (as I vnderstand your letter) *a malicious slanderer, and an impudent libeller.* If you say the man is sithence altered, I hope you haue better proofe thereof, and I desire to know it, then that speaking to my reproofe, he must make no lye, and no fault at all to diuulge, or obiect the same against me: and in speaking to yours, he must tell no truth, and a crime to repeate it, or once to thinke it of you. Your fortune is good, my fauour little; neuerthelesse, if coniectures vpon likelihood of circumstances may perswade ought, they pleade for me against the assumption. For what can carrie more probabilitie, then that he, who being at libertie, free and out of feare, could and did dispence with his conscience for slandering a meany, and such a meany as your selues be, who haue so mightie partners euery where, would in his restraint, in the height of his distresses, and for sooner ridding himselfe out of trouble, make scruple perdy, to wrong or calumniate such a meane one as my selfe is, so farre off also, and without all acquaintance in that place? Againe, whatsoeuer it be that he accuseth me of, as what it is I cannot imagine, he must needes take the same from the mouth of another, or borrow it from his owne inuention: because he neuer knew me, nor I him, or euer had conference each with other, by messenger, word, letter, or otherwise. Neuerthelesse, sith Fa. *Iones* layes his confession to my charge in the discurteous manner he doth, I must needes thinke (or hold the Father very inconsiderate) that there is some surer proofe for the veritie of that I stand accused of, then the only presumption of *Fishers* bare confession. Or if there be not, as I request all that may be brought, to be brought against me, the measure is very hard which is offered, in that his sole word must be a currant truth against me, whome your selues condemne, and are bound thereunto, vnder losse of much credit, for a very vnhonest, malicious, and lying person.

Note these well.

You affirme, *that his Holines of late hath ordained a certaine gouernement among vs, and that Maister Blackwell is our lawfull Superior made by God.* Good sir, if you loue not our errors, or more, if you loue peace, proue your affirmations, and you end the difference. For vndoubtedlie our soules beare witnesse that you are faultilie mistaken, if you take vs for such, that will neither obey what our holie Father the Pope appointeth, or what God himselfe ordaineth. Belieue me I beseech you, that the reason why we delay in the manner we do, to subiect our selues to the new authoritie, is not because *we are in vaine puffed vp by the sense of the flesh,* as you wrongfullie insinuate: but because we neither see, nor can heare of any Bull, Breue, or other authenticall instrument,

ment, comming from his Holines, for atteſtation and declaration thereof. Which forme of proceſſe, being euer the cuſtomarie vſe of the Sea Apoſtolicke, euen in matters of much leſſe moment, and incomparablie of leſſer queſtion, and failing in this, maketh vs greatlie to miſdoubt, or rather putteth vs in vndoubted aſſurance, that his Holines was not the author thereof, nor the appointer.

His holie Fatherhood well knowes we haue no Church-liuings, but liue only of almes, and that our miſeries are in way of no other caſe, then the priſon, torture, and gallowes, euery miſcreant hauing ſufficient authoritie to apprehend vs : ſo that for his Holines to increaſe the number of our preſſures, to make the burden of our croſſes more heauie, not only by denying vs the choice of our owne Superior, (a freedome and benefite which the Cleargie euery where elſe, and by the Canons of holie Church enioyeth) but by impoſing alſo a Superior vpon vs, without all our vnderſtanding, and not with the leaſt notice of our liking, ſeemeth to our iudgements to be a courſe of much greater ſeueritie, then the mildnes of his Holines nature, and the ripe wiſedome of his aged experience, would euer deſigne, and leſſe enact, and put in vre againſt vs. Further, his Holines being for theſe fortie yeares ſpace our immediate Biſhop, how can we, without expreſſe certificate of ſuch his Holines pleaſure, admit another betweene his bleſſed Fatherhood and vs, vnleſſe we would thereby condemne our ſelues of want of loue and dutie towards his Holines, and of forgetfulnes for ſeuerall rich benefits receiued. They be in *England* who haue heard his Holines to ſay, that he would not appoint a gouernment in *England* before (to vſe his owne words) the good Prieſts there ſhould aduertiſe what kind of gouernment they thought fitteſt, and beſt liked. Therefore affirme what you liſt, and tell your fauorites, and the vulgar neuer ſo liberallie, and vntrulie to prattle of our miſconceiued diſobedience, yet we may not beleeue the new authoritie to be the ordinãce of that ſea, hauing (by the record of many) his Holines owne words to the contrarie. There is an eſpeciall *prouiſo* in the Cardinals letter, that if it happen the Archpresbyter to dye, or be taken, then the next ſenior aſſiſtant to ſupply that roome, till there be another choſen by the Cardinall. Verily if we had no other ground at all, but the hardnes of this *prouiſo*, there were cauſe enough to aſſure our ſelues that his Holines had no part in the new authoritie. For who weeting to the abundance of his fatherlie loue, care, and mild proceedings, can winne his thoughts, or once to feare, that his wiſedome and rare clemencie, would alike grieuouslie loade our miseries with so perpetuall a burden, as neither first, nor last, nor at any time to haue the choosing of our owne Superior, but must in all changes stand to the appointment of a stranger, vnacquainted with vs and our State, and who taketh wholie his aduertisements or direction from others that are not of our companie, but incorporate to another body, and who more labour the glorie and aduancement of their owne peculiar as reason leadeth, then the good of others, from whom they are by profession distinguished. Yea those that are the Cardinals informers, and whome his Grace most willinglie heareth and followeth, are the chiefe parties of the one side in the difference, for ouerruling whereof, the new authoritie was first thought on, sollicited, and at vnawares brought vpon vs. Now the truth of the particular being thus, as euery one sees who is acquainted with the issue of matters, and will not close his eye, I appeale euen to the good opinion which your selfe holds of his holines disposition, indifferencie, and iustice, whether if he had bin the institutor of this new authoritie, his wisedome and tender conscience would haue permitted the adding of so large a prerogatiue, or truer of so vnequall a *prouiso*. I thinke it an attribute of iustice, if not a decree in nature, that the bond of obedience ought euermore to bring some commoditie with it: as the obedience of the seruant to his maister receiueth wages: the obedience of the child to his parent, the benefit of education: the obedience of the wife to her husband, her maintenance and dowrie: the obedience of the religious to his superior, prouision of all necessaries: the obedience of the Priest to his Bishop, iurisdiction, and the appurtenances: the obedience of the subiect to his Soueraigne, protection and the administration of iustice: and generally wheresoeuer obedience is due, there followeth a correlatiue, I meane a good depending which maketh it due. You would haue vs to obey, and it is the scope of all your trauailes. I praye name vs the good that commeth to vs thereby, the whole authoritie consisting only in the taking away of faculties, and in distressing more our miseries? If the supposed authoritie had bin the action of the Pope, no doubt his Holines consideration for drawing mens obedience the sooner thereunto, would haue giuen to it some indulgence at least, if no temporall or other kind of spirituall commoditie. I shall be driuen to touch this point in mo places, being the directing cliffe to all, and therefore do omit here to stay longer vpon it, hoping what is alreadie said to be sufficient.

You proceede to the reckning vp of our pretences, for ſo it phanſieth your pen to by-name the reaſons following, as though all were falſe colours, and no truth at all: and thus you repeate them, as obiected by vs.

1. *It is a thing deuiſed by the Ieſuites.*

I truſt you will not make ſhew to deny this, the truth being ſo cleare as the light of the Sunne when it ſhineth. And if you do, a number of conuincing teſtimonies can be brought againſt you, and you by gaineſaying ſo euident a truth, will giue vs good cauſe to take heede, how farre we beleeue you in doubtfull and vnknowne matters.

2. *The Superior is one of the Ieſuites owne chooſing.*

This alſo we auerre for a certaine truth, and auow further, that not only the Superior, but all the aſſiſtants are likewiſe of your chooſing, as Maiſter *Blackwell* himſelfe, neither could nor did denie, nor ſeemed vnwilling to acknowledge. And what greater ſoueraigntie would you ſeeke to carrie ouer vs, if you might haue your wiſhes, being in the dignitie of prieſthood, and in the labours for our countrie by many yeares our iuniors?

3. *Why ſhould the Ieſuites appoint vs a Superior, more then we a Generall to them?*

If the reſemblance be not good, I praye ſhew the difference that diſproueth, and the reaſons why you may elect our Superior, and we not yours.

4. *It is the fine head of Father Parſons that hath inuented this.*

Omit the epitheton, I meane ſo farre as it carrieth the nature of a quipping word, and the reſidue we maintaine, belieuing there is no one, who will not wilfully blind himſelfe, but ſeeth ſo much. For what can be clearer if particulars be compared, or what leſſe denyable or more manifeſt, then that whereof his owne letters to Maiſter Doctor *Pearſe*, to Maiſter Doctor *Worthington*, and others beare witnes infallible? Therefore good ſir, where you let not to affirme, *that God hath made Maiſter Blackwell our Superior*, you are to proue, prouing your aſſertion, that father *Parſons* act was Gods deede, and what the one, the other did, which will be ſomewhat hard for you to do, in reſpect of the indirect dealing which father *Parſons* vſed in ſending ouer word vnto vs, to deſiſt from further proceeding to the choosing of a Superior, as from a matter I wot not of what ill consequence, and he himselfe notwithstanding to labour and effect it vnder-hand, contrary to the purport of his message and all our knowledges. The Cardinall addressed a letter (as you know) to two reuerend Priests while they were on the way to *England*, and in it made speciall mention of two apostolicall Breues, which his Holines had then newly set forth. The letter signed with his Graces seale, and subscribed with his owne hand, rehearsed the contents of both in manner following: *Sua Sanctitas Breue apostolicũ edidit, Datum apud Sanctũ Marcum sub anulo Piscatoris, die decimo octauo huius mensis septembris præsentis anni* 1597. *quo prohibet omnino, ne quis Anglicanæ nationis, quoad illud Regnum ad religionis Catholicæ, ac sedis Apostolicæ vnionem redierit, Doctoratus gradum in theologia vel iure accipiat, nisi post cursum quatuor annorum expletum, alios adhuc quatuor annos ad ea quæ didicit perpolienda impendat, neque tunc etiam nisi habeat suberioris Collegij in quo vltimò studuerit licentiam in scriptis, cum Protectoris vel vices eius gerentis assensu, & qui secus fecerit, illum pœnam excommunicationis ipsi sedi Apostolicæ reseruatæ ipso facto incurrere: neque præterea gradum, quem accepit vllum esse omnino sed prorsus inualidum. Edidit præterea sua Sanctitas aliud Breue exhortatorium, ac consolatorium ad Catholicos Anglicanos pijssimum illud quidem, ac verè Apostolicum, quo eos ad constantiam patientiam, longanimitatem, cœterasque virtutes hortatur præcipue vero concordiam, pacem, ac vnionem, quæ cœterarum omnium virtutum fundamenta sunt atque vincula, eosque vitent, qui seditiones, ac diuisiones seminant.* Good sir, as I may be deceiued, so perhaps I am, yet vnder correction I must thinke that there may be framed out of these a *dilemma*, or forked argument, that maketh euery way greatly for vs. Either the reported Breues were set forth, or not set forth. If set forth, then what should perswade, that his Holines wisedome and diligent regard, being alike circumspect and prouident in making forth his particular and speciall Briefes for ordering the precedents, would in enacting this new authoritie (a much more iealous and contentious subiect) forget, or neglect, or refuse, to do the like or more? Shall we attribute to his sacred fatherhood, prudence, vigilancie, and maturest consideration in small matters, & take them frõ his Holines in great? His Holines possesseth the Chaire, that hath the promis of diuine assistance. He is our holie Father, and therefore retaineth care of continuing peace among vs his children: as the dignitie requireth, so his Holines is full of charitie, benignitie, and compassion, and therefore much

This Breue was neuer seene, for ought we euer heard.

much vnlike, especiallie while the Magistrate is in drawing his sword against vs, that his Holines would appoint a meere punishing authoritie, that neuer had an example, and not so much as signifie to vs the constitution thereof, by Bull, Briefe, or other Papall instrument, but as if our case, function and trauels were despiseable, to leaue vs to the reports of others for notice thereof: who, as to his Holines knowledge deedes haue proued, incline more to fauour that is against vs, then to friend or causes. And to say, as some say, or as they say who say most, that his Holines wisedome omitted to make forth a Briefe thereof, for feare of trouble, and prouoking the State, is so light and superficiall a reason, as it best answereth it selfe in his owne weakenes. For what greater trouble could such a Briefe cause, which the institution of the new authoritie causeth not more? Neither do we demand the transporting of the Briefe, though we see no more danger therein then in sending ouer the Cardinals letters, yea much lesse, because the pot that goeth often to the water, is likelier at length to returne broken, then that which was vsed but once. The fauour and iustice we sue for, is only canonicall notice of that which is done. For this we call, for this we haue long and often called, and for this shall we still continue calling, being both iust and reasonable, and the performāce of no difficultie, nor requiring time, were the authoritie his Holines ordinance. On the other side, if no such two Briefes were set forth (as I am sure you will not grant) then must father *Parsons* the archdeuiser thereof be much too blame in getting the Cardinals hand, subscription and seale to the aforesaid Letter, and iust cause administred, why we should suspect the like peece of cunning in other letters that haue come from the Cardinall. There is one clause chiefely in his Graces letter of the tenth of Nouember, which bearing little shew of indifferencie, maketh vs the more to feare the like guile by father *Parsons*. For who euer heard, where there was but an outward face of iustice, that the Iudge shall commaund one aduersarie, to informe him of the life and manners of the other aduersarie, and to lay downe his causes and reasons for him in the matter in question betweene them? The partialitie appeareth such, as deforceth vs to thinke that euer his Grace read the Letter, but signed it, vpon confidence of father *Parsons* sinceritie and wisedome. A smooth meane to deceiue the best. You see good sir, how either part of the proposition (and one must needes be true) maketh in our excuse, for not stooping downe our necks to the yoake that father *Parsons* hath prepared, and by all meanes laboureth to inforce. If Maister *Standish* be asked the cause of his iourney to *Rome*, the perswasions vsed to him to that end, the helps he receiued, the companions he went with, his long expectance for father *Parsons* returne out of *Spaine*, who brought him to the presence of his Holines, the particulars of the oration he made, of whom he receiued the instructions, his Holines speeches in answere thereunto, he can informe enough, if your owne acquaintance with the plotting and processe of the matter be not light sufficient, to teach you who inuented the new authoritie, who layd the ground, who added the complements. I should stay my pen from writing it, if it auailed ought to be silent in that which euery man notes. It would make more to the praise of father *Parsons*, if being a religious man, he were either lesse actiue, or busied in matters directlier appertaining to his calling and charge. For what hath he to do with the Priests in *England?* How do we depend of him? At what back-dore vnknowne doth his authoritie or charge come in? Or what may the rich pleasures be that his wit and trauels hath stead vs in, and bound vs to him, why he should in this high presume of our patience, and yeelding to whatsoeuer he liketh to appoint? Sundry of his deuises, or to returne the same word back againe that he giueth vs, disturbances, haue so little made vs beholden vnto him, that neither we nor our Countrie haue receiued more preiudice from any that seemeth to loue vs. He happie, we happier, if religion were lesse worldlified in him, and state matter, and the designing of kingdomes had not so great a part in his studies.

5. *Father Parsons hath giuen wrong information to the Cardinall and his Holines.*

So farre as the coniectures of all likelihood may auerre a troth, this is no vntruth, because we can no way conceiue that the Cardinall or his Holines would euer haue decreed such a penall forme of gouernment, consisting only in taking away of graces, without bringing the least benefit to our countrie, or ease to our afflictions, if their wisedomes had bin fullie and rightfullie informed of the true state and termes of our aduersities. That I say nothing of the designes and petitions which many of the ancients in our realme had assigned, and were forthwith determined to exhibit them to his Holines view, iudgement, and approbation. Further, if father *Parsons* had giuen true information to the Cardinall and his Holines, it followeth necessarilie

cessarilie that his credit is right litle or nought with either (which you would not haue vs to thinke) yea and their loues and care also (which we shall neuer thinke) as litle or lesse towards the huge multitude of our manifold miseries, in reason their supreame authoritie and compassion cannot be drawne to graunt vpon his information, and sollliciting no other fauour then increase of penalties, and facultie to reuoke whatsoeuer our late Cardinall of blessed memorie had obtained of the sea Apostolick, as well to credit Priests the more, as also to manifest his greater affection towards our Countrie: yea, and as though this had bin too litle seueritie, to inflict besides that kind of punishment, without annexing the same to any crime or crimes, as no age since the beginning of the world (as I verily assure my self) yeelds in all respect a president. All which considerations commaund vs to belieue, that the Cardinall (especiallie his holines) had no part in setting downe the particulars of the authoritie, or were not well informed, but much more misinformed by father *Parsons*.

6. The Cardinall was alwayes partiall on the Iesuits side.

I wote not into what hard meaning the word partiall may be drawne, therefore we only affirme, that his Grace is no way a backfriend to your Societie, but euery way most ready to do you all the pleasures and the best furtherances he can.

7. Some of necessitie must be sent to informe better.

I verily belieue the necessitie hereof, was many wayes so importantlie great, that vnlesse our two brethren had out of their charitie and due considerations, aduentured vpon the difficulties of the iourney, for learning the truth, and his Holines pleasure in all things, there had bin much more alteration and questioning among vs about the validitie and bond of the authoritie, then now is, or hereafter can be, hauing by their labours made knowne our case, and submissiuelie referred our selues to his Holines arbiterment in what soeuer. That the Cardinall by the title of his Protectorship, should haue the like soueraigntie in *England*, as to inforce a Superior vpon vs, mauger our vnwillingnes, and without our priuitie, seemeth so strange a noueltie, as the like was neuer heard of in our countrie before, nor as I thinke euer had instance in any other country hereticall or catholick. Or if his excellencie haue this ample iurisdiction, by any other title, grace, or priuiledge, it were very meete we knew it, and after some authenticall manner, especially sith he delegateth authoritie, euen to take all authoritie from vs, graunted by whome soeuer, or when soeuer: yea, to remoue vs from the places of our acquaintance and residence, and by consequence to turne vs to seeke harbour and sustenance among strangers: an extremitie most seueare and most meruellous, the rigour of the lawes of our Realme, and the tearmes of the best condition that Priests liue in dulie considered, which is meane and base enough, without this new increase of our greater contempt and agrieuances.

8. *The messengers must procure that some assistants be chosen, who may not be thought partiallie affected to the Iesuits.*

Sir, admit this were so, albeit I thinke there will be many other motions made before, yet what kind of iniustice, or vncharitable dealing can you deduce from hence? Is there not good cause that at least some of the assistants (who haue by the veritie of Maister *Blackwels* words, euery one in his owne quarter, as large authoritie to execute all extremities as himselfe against vs) should be perfitlie vpright, without poize of biase or parcialitie? And I praye what reason can you yeeld, or any other complice of the new authoritie, why the Priests themselues of each quarter should not be franchised and allowed so much fauour, as to choose the assistant that must be ouer them, vnlesse we must be made yongmen still, or rather boyes or children, and you our tutors to gouerne and direct vs in all things, and giue our voyces for vs?

9. *The messengers must propound to haue the gouernment of the Colledge enlarged, as being ouer-straite or indiscreete for our nation.*

As I cannot affirme, so will I not denye, but they may peraduenture moue such a sute to his Holines, and the sooner by much, in regard we hold the same no preiudice, but a pleasure done to your Societie, as being the selfe sute which your Generall as your selues giue forth, hath made to his Holines, and that of late: and which also well established, could not faile to be but a meruailous good furtherance both to the making and keeping of a perfit peace among vs, and likewise to the augmenting of your greater, or more generall good name and estimation. For from whence commeth the cause of all, or most of our agrieuances, but from the manner of gouerning that Colledge?

And

And what so greatly weakeneth the good opinion which our Realme hath conceiued of your Societie, as the continuall discontentment of the schollers there, and the multiplicitie of their complaints here after their ariuall? Griefe and shame forbid me to rehearse their manifold exceptions, or to name the crimes, that were after their departure frõ the Colledge most iniuriouslie imposed vpon them, and as full detractiouslie read openlie in the Refectorie, and diuulged to their foulest infamie. I omit these as points more odious, then willinglie I would any way occupie my penne in, and do only beseeke you, to tell me with what indifferent person, you thinke it can find good hearing, that the Students there, must not talke nor conferre vnder three in a companie: nor those of one chamber speake or recreate with their fellowes of another chamber, and that they must haue strangers to their prefects, whereby the due honor of our nation, especiallie of the elder sort of Priests, and students (to whome that office alwayes hitherto belonged) must needs be much impaired, if not distained: also the number of schollers, which otherwise the reuenewes of the Colledge would serue to maintaine, lessened, by so many at least, as the companie of the externe prefects amount to.

10. *Yea the messengers must make sute that the Iesuites be remooued from all the Seminaries of our nation, and touching the mission of England in particular all the Iesuites must needes be called away.*

This amplifying speech and exaggeration is the addition of some cunning head, and happilie not by chance reserued by you for the last place, as by the pretexed impietie & mustering whereof, all that went before, might the sooner leese the credit of truth, and take vnto them the shew of words of malice, *ad excusandas excusationes in peccatis.* For my owne part I can say, and as I verily thinke all my associates can auerre the same, that vntill the reading of your letter, I neuer heard the least inckling of any such matter. Beside, grant we could so frame our consciences, yet vnlesse we should leese our naturall wits therewithall, we could not shew our selues so very fooles, as to propound the like motion to his Holines, being the assured meane of drawing rebuke to our selues thereby, and to stop his Holines eares against the hearing of other sutes. And to speake my mind plainlie as the quicknes of the premisses inforceth: without all question, it is a large freedome of toung, that many of your fauorites vse, if your selues be all cleare. The fault is generallie noted, begins to be appropriated, disinayes not a few,and cannot but ere long,purchase small commendation to your Societie,if it be not eftsoone reformed.

In the paragraffe following,you infer as it were a cōclusion,saying: *These and the like speeches hauing bin vttered by such as either gathered voyces for another gouernmēt,or are knowne not to fauour this: what can it argue else,but such oppose themselues against the Societie,as if no authoritie were to be liked,but that which may beate downe the Iesuits,or set them and other reuerend Priests together by the eares?* The franke libertie of your pen astonieth deare sir.For the disiunctiue cannot be proued,and your illatiue importeth much detraction, charging vs to haue no other marke in our eye in the association we laboured, but the beating downe of your Societie,& the setting of you & other reuerend Priests together by the eares. Alas, could not charitie & your loue of Priests, intreate your preiudicate conceipts so much, as to thinke there was some other cause lesse wicked & more excusable,why we imbrace not the new authority, then for that no authority liketh vs,but which treadeth the Iesuits vnder foote, and soweth discord? Hard,that nothing can be disliked in your actions, but by and by, it must be dubbed an opposition,and euery opposition also, to carrie the like vncharitable gloses. The forme of gouernment that was gone about by the assent & good liking of those,that were to liue vnder the same, was no whit in the outward letter preiudiciall to the Societie, as both you and father *Edmonds* did seuerallie approue, and the rules thēselues declare. And to presume a corrupt intention,to feare false measure, and to suspect the lurking of notorious impietie,where the ouert act is good,& the doers neuer detected of any treacherie: if it be pollicie, it is *sapientia huius mundi,* the wisedome of this world, contrary to the propertie of charitie, *quæ omnia credit,* which beleeueth all things, if not contrarie to our Sauiours prohibition, *nolite iudicare,* iudge not.

You verily sooth, *that the successe of matters,since the authoritie of the Reuerend Archpresbyter was diuulged, doth make many to feare, least the secret intention (yet not perceiued of all) of those which were the principall seekers, to erect a sodalitie, or other superioritie and subordination, was either ambitious, or seditious.* You still make little conscience to speake your pleasure of vs. Maister *Standish* was the first and principall mouer (as I haue bin told) of the sodalitie, and who vnderstanding that his parts were counted by vs not fit to beare office in the same, anon shifted sayles (vpon what intent you may better aske him) and so leauing vs, went to you, became an agent, and by his industrie or good fortune,

fortune, hath gotten an assistantship. If in the former charge you meane him, he is of age let him answere for himselfe. But if by it you point to me, and others, then let vs see how you fasten the fault of ambition or sedition vpon vs. You say because *hauing now that very thing which we sought for, although imposed vpon other persons, do neuerthelesse reprehend and impugne the same.* Like truth, like proofe. Is the new authoritie good sir, that very thing we sought for? I could wish that writing in a controuersie, you would be better aduised what you did affirme, & how you did contradict your selfe: for not seauen lines before, you called ours another gouernment from this, as indeede it is, and as different a gouernment, as chalke and cheese, white and blacke. For as chalke and cheese agree in whitenes, and white and black in that they are both colours: so this new authoritie with that we intend, agrees only in the name of a gouernment, and in all other points and properties, most discording and dissonant, as is manifest by comparing them together. Ours constrained none to accept thereof: this inforceth all. Ours communicated benefits: this penalties. Ours was to be instituted by the good liking of all their consents that were to obey: this enacted by whose meanes we know not, other then by the plotting of your Societie, vnwittingly to vs all. Ours a superioritie intreating: this full of commaunds. Ours neuer to haue proceeded, vnlesse the following of peace had bin sure by the opinion of all or the most and wisest: this the more vnquietnes it moues, the greater variance it stirreth, the stifflier and with the more earnestnes it is pursued against the refusers. Ours brought in it selfe consolations to our aflictions, reliefe to our needes, succour to our distresses, seuerall commodities to our countrie, spirituall and temporall, and a continuing mutualitie of good offices; not only betweene vs, that were of that sodalitie, but betweene vs and our other brethren, and also betweene the Cleargie and the Laitie: this, I meane as it hath bin hitherto practised, harroweth mens consciences, bringeth Priests in contempt, maketh laymen our controllers, rayseth slaunders, priuiledgeth the toungs of your followers, preiudiceth our best friends, decayeth charitable almes, breedeth faction, and putteth dislike betweene persons of neerest allance. And none of these heauie sequeles counterpoysed, by any spirituall good ensuing, either to vs, or our countrie thereby; nay both receiue detriment in this kind also, as the new authoritie is now and euermore may be demayned against vs; as namely, trouble, cumber, vexation of mind, scandall, and stumbling blocks, euen in the way of the good. Thus you see good sir, how little in our account, the new authoritie is that very thing we sought for. And admit it were the selfesame with ours, as you affirme it to be, yet haue I to demaund of you, why fauouring the new authoritie with the maine force of all your endeuours, by praysing, writing, subscribing, counselling, directing, soliciting, imployment of your friends, and what way soeuer you could, or can most grace, recommend, and promote the same, did so little countenance and set forward the association we purposed, being as you will needes haue it, the selfesame thing with the other: I say, did so little countenance and set it forward, as some of your brethren (what part soeuer your selfe had therein) spake liberally against it, dispraised it, condemned it, gainestood it, and by cunning preuention ouerthrew it? Againe, if ours and this be all one, what may Maister *Blackwels* reasons be, why he, hauing written, and to so great liking of himselfe, against that which we purposed, would or did accept of this with all readines and applause, being as you confidentlie affirme, the very thing which ours was, and which himselfe before improued with many words? I will go further, and aske you that which is hardlier assoyled. What moued Maister *Blackwell*, if this and ours be one, to discommend and glaunce so oft and pretilie as he hath done, both in speech and writing at the one, and so exceeding highly commend and extoll the other? If he or you seeke to guild the matter, in respect, that this hath the strength and louer of authoritie, which ours had not, the shadow which hereby you would seeme to lay on, is nothing, because there is neither of you both, but well knew, that it was neuer our intention to haue the fellowship we solicited to proceede, be in force or in esse, before the Popes Holines had ratified and confirmed the particulars. And the motiue why we did acquaint the number of our brethren with the designe, before we sought for confirmation thereof, from the chaire of his Holines, was not for an idle vaunt, or for an vntimely, or incongruent publication of our purpose (as Maister *Blackwell* is still pleased to hold the opinion) but for that we would not giue our brethren cause of offence, as iustlie we had done, by procuring the allowance, and establishing of the association without their priuitie, aduise and agreement first had thereunto.

You demaund, *what you haue done that all should not affect you, affirming, that if any affect you not, the fault is in them, and not in you.* Good sir, I know not your faults, or if I did, I should refuse to compose the Letanie:

Letanie: yet do I not thinke, you beare that kind of hatred to your selues, as telling your owne tale, you would hurt your owne credits. There is no doubt but there are many that do not affect all your proceedings, but where the blame resteth hereof, that is the doubt: you lay it in vs, we returne it to you, and I beseech the mercies of Almightie God, that we may euery one see his owne fault, agnize, and amend it.

You hold on, and make the degrees of affection which euery one beareth towards your Societie, a touchstone as it were for trying who are fit, who vnfit to be Superiors. I will repeate your owne words as they lye together, to the end I be not thought to misconsture, disioynt or wrong place them. *If they would haue themselues or others that do not affect vs (though otherwise seeming neuer so vertuous) to be chosen heads: let them first affect vs (so farre as in vertue they ought) that they may be worthie of gouernment.* The first parenthesis sheweth nought that glistereth to be gold, vnlesse it hath your opinion for foile. The residue layeth in, as it were a caueat, or rather giueth order, that such as would be heads, must first affect you *(so farre as in vertue they ought) that they may be worthie of gouernment.* I must take leaue to aske you who shall iudge of this measure and qualitie of affection, which of like necessitie you require? Others or your selues? If others, who are they, and who made them the like officers? If your selues be the men, in what assurance can you put vs, that you will alwayes iudge aright? Forsooth the whisperings of your owne thoughts, the construction you shall be pleased to make of other mens words, deeds, and demeanour, shall be the aime, rule, compasse, and light to direct you. And what may this be other then for your selues to beare rule, which if it be not your desires so to do, truly there is an vntruth conceiued of you, and which hath many belieuers, and which in the contriuing, and managing of these latter actions, is no more hid, then what is most visible. But I praye, what may the full meaning be of the condition you set downe, and which maketh those only capable of superioritie, or head-ship, that are qualited therewith? Do they *only affect you so farre as in vertue they ought,* that haue but one yea and one nay with you, and can dislike nought, and will approue all, whatsoeuer you say or do, or go about? Or may they be said to *affect you so farre as in vertue they ought,* who carrie a reuerent respect towards your Societie, and towards your persons also, yet not so affectionatlie, but will see and can dislike that is amisse in your actions, and be further willing, to put their most helpe to the redresse? No doubt if this measure be of the size that contenteth, there are as many or more fit, left vnchosen as chosen, vpon suspect and ielousie only, that they affected you not, so farre as in vertue they ought. I haue little feare but that Maister *Blackwell* well cleared himselfe of all suspition that way, and *affected you so farre as in vertue he ought,* when in your behoofe, and not without preiudice to the schollers, he wrote a Letter to *Rome,* witnessing vnder his hand, that there was no dislike or difference betweene the fathers of the Societie, and the Priests in *England,* albeit your selfe with shew of griefe voluntarily acknowledged the contrary vnto me not long before; yea complained thereof, and expostulated the causes. He also *affected you so farre as in vertue he ought,* when for making vp the fuller measure of your purgation, letted not (as the report goeth) to touch three Priests at once with disgrace, by writing vnder their testimonies and censure which they gaue, concerning the particulars of the memoriall: *Hij tres patres non bene informantur &c.* as if the three good Priests had bin altogether strangers to the State and truth of matters, or carried so loose consciences, as in so waightie an affaire, would affirme they knew not what, and to testifie vnder their hands what themselues were ignorant of. Likewise that partie *affected you so farre as in vertue he ought,* who writing somewhat (as it was thought) with the largest in your and your brethrens behalfe, and being demaunded by a familiar friend of his, how he could verifie the words, answered, he could do it by the figure *hyperbole.* If such dealing and excesse of truth be the meane of farming your good conceipts, I would be loath to become tenant, if I might haue, as this good man had, an assistantship for vantage. Others who spake and wrote their conscience, and deliuered no more, then what their knowledge, iudgement, and integritie led them vnto, and that also vpon charitable considerations, and to good purpose, were notwithstanding deemed thereby not *to affect you so farre as in vertue they ought,* and thereupon by the decree of your owne order, reputed not worthie of gouernment. The particular is knowne, and after an vndenyable manner, as from his mouth, who carieth greatest regard with you. By all that I haue said, I would say, that this your strange caueat or canon, and correspondent proceedings, as well in appointing of our Superior, as in the choise of the assistants, and in the deuising of the instructions and forme of gouernment, shew apparantlie enough, how little you seeke to haue the ordering and swaying of all things.

You

You affirme, *that in very deede, you would not haue any reprehended, because they are opposite against you, but because they acknowledge not their lawfull Superior.* I praye sir, how do these words comport with that you said before, where you will haue the want of affection towards you, a barre against election? Will you make men vneligible, without a fault, or without such a fault as is worthie of reprehension? or will you haue such faults as make men vneligible, to be soothed in them and not reprehended? One of these must needes follow; by the sequele of your order: and either concludes more then my selfe sees reason to maintaine. But let this be as it may be, assuredly all men are not perswaded, and some do feele, and will sweare, that not only the reprehending of your oppositors, but the punishing of them also, and with extreame rigour enough, setteth but as a gentle corrasiue to your hearts, howsoeuer you grieue now, and would haue that none be reprehended for being opposite against the Societie.

You giue vs to know, and seeme to take a liking therein, *that you will by Gods grace, procure alwayes, and to your vttermost, that who soeuer is opposite against the reuerend Archpresbyter, must of firce be consequentlie opposite against you & your brethren.* Howsoeuer you please your self in the needlesse vttering of these voluntarie speeches, my dulnes cannot conceiue how this spirit agreeth with that of Saint Paule, *factus sum infirmus infirmis vt infirmos lucrifacerem,* by compassion of the infirmities of all sorts I became weake to the weake, that I might gaine the weake. If it be a fault to oppose our selues in the manner we do against the new authoritie challenged (as we acquiet our conscience to the contrarie, and thinke our selues well able by sound and good arguments to vphold the lawfulnes thereof against whome soeuer in our countrie) yet your Societie being no partie, nor bound to intermedle, more indifferencie, and lesse taking against vs, had beene in my poore opinion, as charitable and more wisdome. For by making your selues a partie without cause, and so professed and forward a partie, what could you get but aduersaries, and haue debarred your selues from being mediators in the difference, *si fieri potest, quod ex vobis est, cum omnibus hominibus pacem habentes,* if it may be, as much as in you, hauing peace with all men.

That you say *you will gloriari in Domino, if any be thought opposit to your Societie, who are opposite to our reuerēd Archpreslyter:* I say no more, but hope, that notwithstanding your *gloriari in Domino,* your glorie in our Lord, yet our Lord wil not be in this, *gloria vestra nec exaltās caput ve-*

strum, your glorie, nor the lifter vp of your head.

You auouch, *that the new authoritie is the only meanes to ioyne vs all together in perfit loue and vnion, and that there is now no hinderance at all of vnitie, but the not admitting and refusing of the same.* Sir, I can easily belieue you in this, for God forbid I should liue the while, to account you, or any of you, so ouerloaden with frailties, or surcharged with ill nature, that hauing your desire, will refuse to contract loue and vnion with those that graunted it vnto you, and further, surrender themselues to your disposing.

That which followeth in the same paragraffe maketh me somewhat to muse, by whose authoritie or example, you applie the words of Saint Paule, *non tenens caput*, not holding the head, to the Archpresbyter. For if the holie Fathers of Christes Church, and the Popes themselues, other then in a generall terme, euer abstained for reuerence to the Apostles, from vsing their kind of blessing and salutation, *gratia & pax à Deo Patre & Domino nostro Iesu Christo*, grace and peace frõ God our Father, and our Lord Iesus Christ, I see not why you might not very well for reuerence sake, haue forborne the application of that passage to Maister *Blackwell*, being literallie and euer principallie referred to our Sauiour, and neuer secondarilie applied to any but a Pope, nor can be but incongruously, as my small reading and iudgement giueth me. A bold charge, hard measure, that, for bearing off to subiect our selues to the new authoritie, vntill the returne of our two brethren with true certificate of his Holines pleasure therein, we must be counted by you, *non tenere caput ex quo totum corpus per nexus & coniunctiones subministratũ & constructum crescit in augmentũ Dei*, not holding the head, wherof the whole body by ioints and bands being serued and compacted, groweth to the increase of God: which is by the prime and proper signification of the place, to apostatate or forsake Christ, and in the second and largest sense, to be an hereticke or schismaticke. Take heed good sir, least for reprouing others, you vtter what is not worthie of your self. I know you had not so ill a meaning, but the inferences be direct, and therefore I wish you againe to take better heede to the running of your pen hereafter.

The infusings shewed I was deceiued herein.

You say, *the new authoritie is receiued with singular liking of the most and best, and that who is ioyned to Maister Blackwell is yours*, and *qui cum illo non colligit spargit*, he that doth not gather with him scattereth. First, you forget comparisons to be odious, and continue the citing of places vnprouable against vs. Then you sooth more then can be

truly

truly auerred in the eye of the world: for by generall opinion, there are of as good parts, and of as good deserts, and of no lesse name, that haue not, as haue submitted themselues thereunto. And for the number (a gay coate-card in all your mouthes) I thinke if there were authoritie from the sea Apostolicke, willing euery Priest to deliuer his conscience which of the two kinds of gouernment he most liked, or deemed fittest, either this of your and father *Parsons* deuising, where an Archpresbyter, the lowest Prelature in holie Church, and now worne out of vse, must absolutely commaund and prescribe to the Cleargie of a whole kingdome: or the other that we now principallie sue for, which is the Ecclesiasticall & only vsuall regiment throughout all Christendome: I say, if there were such authoritie graunted, for comming to the true knowledge of euery priests opinion herein, there would be, as I am most assured vpon good grounds, ten for one, if not twẽtie, or rather hundreds of the Cleargy & Laity with vs against you.

And this time the Laitie were not comprised vnder the authoritie.

Now sir for conclusion, if the points of your Letter to me, or more, if the contents of your Letters to others, whereof I haue had some vnderstanding: or more then either, if the seueritie vsed in *Rome* and in *England* against our cause and brethren, were vprightlie and iudiciallie weighed, doubtles in my opinion there would appeare little ground for the truth of that you say in the beginning of your Letter, to wit, *that if all could not be induced to loue and affect you, you would yet beare their auersion with patience and silence, without following any course or pursute against them.* I praye, if the Societie, I meane the English and your adherents, should do their worst, what could there be more done then is done against vs? Could there be more horrible crimes obiected? Could what is obiected be more openly or more against conscience diuulged? Could promises be lesse kept? Could conditions be worse performed? Could dissimulation be finelier masked? Could Priests sustaine greater triall of patience, then is heaped on them? Could the burden of their afflictions take increase? Could their friends be more earnestlie laboured to withdraw their good liking and charities from them? Could there be mightier shoouing, to remoue some of that coate from their places of residence? Could all assayes, almost euery way, to that end be lesse forborne? Could detraction be rifer? Could calumniators swarue more? Could mo pratlers be found to tenise their obloquies? Could harder censures be giuen of them or more liberallie? Could their liues be ript vp from a further period? Could their faults be liuelier depainted? Nay, could faults of no faults be plentifullier created? Or could all this, or more, go freer without satisfaction, lesse check, rebuke, or controulement? Lamentable, that men suffering for being Priests, and suffering the like extremities they do, should be deuoyded of faculties, and haue doubts thrust into their heads, and by parties of speciall name, to be also vnlawfull for them either to vse the altar, or to practise preaching. So that if particulars be belieued, small is the patience, lesse the silence, and sharp is the course or pursute that is followed against vs. I write not these things to the end I do or would charge any in particular, and much lesse you, then any other: whome my loue hath a long while reuerenced for vertue, and other good habilities: but I rehearse them (and verily with teares) to moue pitie, to stir vp compassion, and if I might be so happie, to procure also the surceasing and redresse of these our common, but no common miseries. And one thing seemeth more strange then all, that acquainting as we did M. *Blackwell* himselfe with our purpose of sending to *Rome* for full vnderstanding of his Holines mind, and to intimate to his wisedome the true state of our countrie, and the tearmes of Priests, as his holie Fatherhood (by the relation of those that heard the speeches) required vs to do, yea some hauing made their appeale also from him, yet that in this short *interim* till our iust doubts be cleared, neither he, nor your societie, nor your copartioners, can be intreated to breath, and let the difference sleepe, till our brethren bring, or your selues shew his Holines resolution, but will needs with tooth and nayle, and with all earnestnes pursue the challenged authoritie against vs, and stop at nothing that lieth in your way, be it the generall disturbance of vs all, and the disquieting of the whole realme, that I say nothing of the scandall nor of the edging of other persons. A better temper would more commend. Vndoubtedly, if our two friends returne not the sooner, nor you perswaded to desist from the busie course begun, assure your selues you wil baile our pens, and inforce vs for defending of our good names, to make knowne to the whole realme, the full state & processe of all matters in *Rome* & in *England*. Wherein, if there fall out ought, as it is feared there will fall out much, little to the commendation of some of your proceedings, you are to impute the blame to your selues, that thus mainely vrge the occasion. Good counsell to remember before hand, that had I wist is too late. Neither were it amisse if you did lesse follow the begging of names to *Olim dicebamur*, especially with lesse importunitie; an office fullest of suspitiõ for you to take vpõ you: but all shews frõ whence the plot came, and whither it tends, to haue our heads vnder your girdles, in making & ruling our Superior, and by consequēce in working your pleasures in whatsoeuer vpon vs. Patience. For taking my leaue, I beseech you to consider the dissention at *Rome*, to consider the differēces in *England*, to looke into the causes & maintenance of them both, and if you do not espy that we haue more to say against you, then you against vs, yet to thinke that our purgation when it commeth forth, wil shew you so much, & proue vs also to haue vsed more plainenesse, forbearance, truth, silence and charitie, then our oppositors haue done in their cariages against vs. Thus haue I (beloued sir) tyred my selfe, and long troubled you, beseeching you humblie of pardon, if I haue any way offended: and truly, if I knew the word, line, sentence, or particular which were against bounden charity, I could labour rather to blot it out with teares of bloud, then euer suffer it to come to reading. Fare you well most hartily.

A post-Script.

GOod sir, let the length of my answere excuse that it commeth in an other bodies hand, and the reason why it commeth so long after yours, was an ague-doubtfulnes, whether I should reioyne or no: fearing least if I did, I might moue offence, which I am loath to do, and would not haue set vpon the aduenture, had your side taken vp in any time, or obserued any measure in their hard speeches against vs. The excesse and surfet whereof, hath bin and continueth so great, that had men and women a charter to speake what they list, of Christ his annointed, and that there were no such thing as the restitution of fame, I see not well, how they could either lesse restraine, or more enlarge their ignorant and slanderous babling. I hope, conscience binding, and all lawes permitting vs to defend our guiltlesnes against whome soeuer, you will not dislike, and lesse misconsture, and lesser misinforme against this our inforced appologie, but rather vnderstanding the grounds of our refusall, procure with all speede canonicall certitude of that you would bring vpon vs, which must and shall presentlie stint all disputes, & find vs readily obedient in what soeuer. Fare you well againe, and our Lord protect you, and giue me of his grace to see his holie will, and follow it.

Yours in true loue,
Iohn Colleton.

NOtwithstanding the serious and seuerall auowances interlaced in the former Letter, that the least Canonicall notice, such as the lawe in like cases prescribeth, should presently without further question, haue vs ready vpon the first shewing thereof, to subiect our selues to the authoritie: yet did father *Garnet*, and father *Lister*, the one in a Letter communicated to many, the other in a diuulged Treatise, censure and condemne vs of schisme, and alike violently prosecuted their opinion, as if the same had bin the sentence of all the learned, or rather the declaration of the Sea Apostolick. Neither did this their headie presumption correct it selfe in any time, but the passion indured, and not indured only, but increased also to the heaping of most excessiue and vntollerable iniuries vpon vs. Neuerthelesse, our thirst after peace and quietnes was such, as we sent the conditions following to Maister *Blackwell* (who had now allowed the said Treatise of father *Lyster*, and taken on him the patronage of father *Garnets* positions) that his Reuerence conferring the matter with the Fathers of the Societie, the difference might be composed, & our selues reunited in former loue.

Conditions offered to Maister Blackwell *by the Priests, who delayed to receiue him to their Superiour before the comming ouer of his Holines Breue.*

AS alwayes we haue, so now expressely againe we do admit all Authoritie, whatsoeuer his Holines hath instituted, and are most readie actuallie to obey the same, when authenticall proofe thereof shall be shewed vnto vs.

Further if that can not be shewed, yet for auoyding slanderous reports, and to the intent we may more peaceablie exercise our functions, benefite and edifie others, we are well content voluntarily to subiect our selues and obey this forme of gouernment, with these Conditions following.

First, that we may be sufficientlie aduertised, how farre this Authoritie extendeth particularly ouer vs, and that we may haue a copie thereof.

Secondly, that you and the Societie will consent with vs to the sending ouer of certaine, who may thereby haue the freer accesse to his Holines, both to informe him in our cause, and vnderstand his holie Fatherhoods determination therein : Alwayes prouided, that

that if their audience be preuented directlie or indirectlie by your or the Societies meanes, that then we fullie reuoke all obedience here offered.

Thirdly, in consideration that two of our brethren imployed in this busines, haue bin, by information from hence, discredited and imprisoned, and so still continue for ought we know: our desire is, that we may receiue from you notice of the crimes or misdemeanour laid against them, or haue your testimonie for their good cariage and behauiour whilest they liued here, or at least, that you knew no defaming ill by them.

Fourthly, that whereas we all in generall, and diuers particularlie haue bin iniured and defamed by a Treatise of Schisme, diuulged by one of the Societie, the same may be reuersed, and we againe restored to our credits.

Fifthly, that you would let vs haue your accord, and letters ouer, for procuring order from his Holines, that hereafter the Arch-priest may not be elected otherwise then by the consent and voyces of our owne bodie. Likewise that the Assistants in respect they haue (as it is affirmed) equall authoritie with the Arch-priest in the places where they gouerne, may not be chosen but by suffrage of the Priests, who reside in the Shires or circuite ouer which the Assistant shall be authorised.

Sixtly, that euery one that shall be made either Arch-priest or Assistant, shall for auoyding tumult or perpetuall contention through the confounding and mixing of the two distinct States together, Religious and Secular, protest by the word of a Priest, that he is not by vow, obedience, or other tye, in subodination or incorporate to any other bodie or companie then our owne, and that he will manifest so much, and surrender the place and authoritie he holdeth ouer vs, whensoeuer he shall be throughlie determined to change his state and vocation.

Lastly, that forsomuch as the State is alreadie maruelloulie incensed against vs, and the indignation increasing dayly by the meanes of bookes, letters, and plots touching State matters, neither meete in these times, nor belonging to our function: our most earnest request is, that all proceedings of this qualitie be by you vtterlie & presentlie forbidden: and that you, with the ioynt petition of all the Assistants, would make instant supplication to his Holines for expresse prohibition thereof.

THe offer of these conditions, how well soeuer the same was meant by vs, was neuerthelesse alike offensiuely taken by our Arch-priest, as his Reuerence did not only most peremptorily reiect them all, but returned in his answere, *that impenitencie of heart, and an obstinate will of sinning being the more grieuous phrensie, drew vs to the making of the requests:* and that our petition of hauing the Arch-priest and the assistance to be chosen hereafter by the voyces of the Priests who were to obey, was *the destruction of peace, and the perturbation of order in the Church,* being in truth the expresse decree of holie (a) Canons, and the customarie forme of electing Superiors ouer the whole Christian world. Againe, his Reuerence teamed our demaund of hauing the treatise of schisme reuersed, *an vnreasonable request, because* (as he gaue the reason) *the medicine ought not to be remoued, before the sore be thoroughly cured,* applying besides these words of scripture vnto vs, *stiffe-necked, and of vncircumcised hearts and eares, alwayes resisting the holy Ghost,* with many other alike exciting speeches.

That is called by our Arch-priest a destructiō of peace and order, which the Canons of holie Church appointed for the preseruation of peace and order.

(a) *Ca.1.de electi.*

Not long after the exhibiting of the aforesaid conditions, his Holines Breiue arriued, and we presently without any stay, receiued Maister *Blackwell* to our Arch-priest, and yeelded him our obedience: yea, such was our affection to vnitie, as for desire thereof, we were content to pardon all the iniuries and defamations past, being many in number, and in qualitie most grieuous. At this very time our Archpriest wrote likewise a common Letter, willing and commaunding all Priests not to vpbraide and impute the fault of schisme any more vnto vs. Which fauour (so to call the surceassing of most grieuous wrongs) we know not whether it moued sorrow or no in the Iesuites (who perhaps had conceiued some feare, least the concord begun, might diminish the authoritie and sway they carryed with the Archpriest, being linked now to his body, and brethren) but most certaine it is, that not many weekes after the making of this generall attonement, father *Iones* a Priest of the Societie, gaue forth, and defended the assertion, that *whosoeuer should stiffely maintaine that our refusall to the subordination appointed before the arriuall of his Holines Breue, did not make vs schismatickes, incurred by such his patronage of our case the censures of holy Church.* Which vnreasonable position, our Archpriest, my selfe acquainting him therewith, affirmed to be true; as there hath bin nothing hitherto written or spoken by the Fathers against vs, which his Reuerence, how vnprobable and iniurious soeuer the same was, hath not soothed, and to his power sought to iustifie. Neither

ther did his Reuerence after the aforesaid prohibition, only allow and defend this strange saying of father *Iones*, but also he himselfe diuulged a resolution, both declaring that we *were schismaticks by our refusall,* and directing all Priests not to apply the benefite of absolution vnto vs, vnlesse we did acknowledge the offence, and make satisfaction for it. Which reuiuall of matters rising so directly, and in points of like importance, both from the Societie, and from our Archpriest, and for that also some of our fellowes were thorough the diuulging of the foresaid resolution denyed absolution in the sacrament of penance, and not suffered to celebrate in some places where they came, and where before they had bin well accoumpted of, we, not seeing a fitter meane either of easing our distresses, or of relieuing our good names, framed the Petition following to our Arch-priest.

Verie Reuend Father:

WE humblie beseech you, that the extreame necessitie of the hard tearmes our good names are brought into, may both excuse the boldnes (if bounden indeuour to put off so great a hurt may be called boldnes) and encline your consideration to take in good part the proposing of our request. Your Reuerence and others do still affirme, and seeme to auow the opinion more and more, that we incurred the crime and penalties of schisme, in not absolutely admitting your Authoritie before the ariuall of his Holines Breue, our first certaine notice of his priuitie thereunto. Would God therefore it might please you (deere sir) for perfit tryall of the truth, & the thorow ending of the controuersie, to licence, that we may conferre, reason, or dispute the case with the conditions vnder specified. Good manners, and more, the duties of obedience, forbid vs to name, or request you to be one of the disputants, being our Superior, but if your owne desires shall carrie you to the yeelding of your most help, for better declaration and strengthening of the issue, we shall hartilie greete the fauour, and rest fuller satisfied, in respect we wish the vttermost that can be said and vrged against vs. For certes, if we see our selues, we do neither affect to be misled by errour, or dwell in ignorance, or, presupposing that we are deceiued, seeke for ought more, then to haue the noted crime, fortified with the proofes that may most reproue and conuict our guiltines. Among all the meanes our poore wits could thinke of, this appeared of most force and the readiest, as well to let the miſtaken ſee their faile, as alſo to mediate a generall attonement, in regard the rules of conſcience bind to acknowledge a truth when it is euidentlie ſhewed, and the agnizing induceth to ſatisfaction, and ſatisfaction hath right and authoritie, as well to cancell iniuries paſt, as alſo to inuite loue for the time to come. Two ſoueraigne effects, and being the natiue begetters and nourcers of peace, cannot but bring great ioy and edification to many. If therefore your better iudgement ſhall like to ratifie this courſe, and vouchſafe to giue vs notice, the aduertiſement will much glad vs, and ſhall indebt vs for dutifull thanks to your Reuerence for the kindnes. Neither without good cauſe: for if the difference be not after this way decided, alas we ſee no remedie, but of conſtraint our good names bleeding alike pittifullie as they do, and the wound ſo oft and hardlie rubbed on as it is, we muſt either wittinglie ſuffer perpetuall infamie to come vpon vs, or take our pennes in hand, & cleere our ſelues as we may. A proceſſe that feareth, becauſe great likelihood our apologie ſhall receiue an anſwere, the anſwere require a reply, the reply occaſion a reioynder, and ſo the difference become a circle, that is to ſay, without end, vnleſſe it be that lamentable end which the Apoſtle ſpecifying, ſayd, *quod ſi inuicem mordetis & comeditis videte ne ab inuicem conſumamini*, if ye bite and deuoure one another, take heed leaſt ye be not conſumed one of another. To flye this gulfe, and eſchue ſo idle waſt of ſo much time, that we ſay nothing of the ſcandall, we moſt ſubmiſſiuely intreate your good Reuerence, to graunt for your ſelfe, and ſolicite the Fathers, that we may in this ſort (the ſhorteſt as we deeme, and the quieteſt of all others) ſtint and end the variance. And hauing now good ſir, propoſed our requeſt, and giuen you a feeling of our deſires, it followeth that we ſuppliantlie beg of your good Fatherhood, which our hearts performe in moſt reſpectiue manner, that you would not ſtretch our words beyond our intention, which is only to make to appeare, how earneſtlie we couet a friendlie conference, to heare what can be ſaid, and be heard what we can ſay; to the end the queſtion to and fro largely diſcuſſed, the truth may lye open, and all further contention dye for euer. Which being the all only ſcope and marke of our deſigne, propounded alſo vpon hope of leaue and vnder correction, we truſt there is no cauſe why we ſhould feare to haue our interceſſion for a conference, named a challenge; our inforced defence, a voluntarie oppoſition; ſatisfaction to others, a breach of obedience; and the ſeeking of repoſe to our owne ſoules, vndutifulnes to our

How neere is this prediction true.

our Superior, or contempt of Authoritie. An intreatie that would make our case most miserable; loaden till we be forced to bemoane our agreeuances, and then more loaden for making way to ease them. But our hope is better, and we misdoubt no part of the precedent, in respect of your owne construction; but because the addresse (the purport so beseeking) remayneth to be imparted by you to others, and perhaps not euery one in readines to vnderstand our meaning to the best; therefore we haue presumed the more expressely to signifie what we would not haue conceiued amisse. And thus (reuerenced sir) being come to the end of that we would say, we leaue, with humblest request of pardon, and like defrayment of dutie.

The first condition.

FAther *Wallay*, Father *Lister*, and whome and how many soeuer of the Societie they shall thinke good to choose vnto them, to be reasoners, debatours, or disputants of the one side: and of the other, three such Priests of our companie as we shall nominate.

The second.

The grounds, reasons, arguments, answers, reioynders of both sides, vpon full discussion and agreement to be set downe in writing.

The third.

The vmpeers or arbitratours, to heare and determine of the waight, truth, and coherence of all that shall be said or alleaged by either side, to be two or three of the senior Assistants, and Maister *Doleman*. And that it be in the choice of your Reuerence to admit such of the Laitie to be hearers of the dispute, as to your wisedome for the qualitie of occurrances, shall seeme meete.

The fourth.

That each of the foresaid arbitratours shall faithfullie promise in the word of a Priest, to proceede to the giuing of sentence, vpon the proofe and disproofe of either side, according to the dictamen of their consciences, and inward perswasion, without delay, colour, mitigation, and all partialitie.

The fift.

If the said arbitratours shall iudge that our case was schisme, and our selues schismaticks, then we to be bound most humblie to aske pardon on our knees of your Reuerence, and the Societie, for hitherto defending the contrary, against the veritie of their & your affirmance: If of the other side, they shall censure or deeme that we were no schismaticks, then the Societie, especially the penner, and the approuers of the pamphlet of schisme, to acknowledge their errour, reuerse the tract, and make vs some ratable satisfaction for the heape of iniuries and infamies sustained.

The last.

That it be lawfull without offence or prohibition, for either side, after sentence giuen and fulfilling of the premisses, to seeke (if it so please) a resolution in the difference, from the Vniuersities beyond the seas, vpon shew and euidence of the said written dispute, grounds, reasons, proofes & arguments, subscribed with the hands of the vmpeers and disputers of both sides, to the end, it may manifestly appeere to be the same, and no place left to the other side to suspect any indirect dealing, either by adding, changing, or subtracting ought, to, in, or from the originall, and that none of the foresaid arbitratours or disputants refuse or deferre to put to his name, being requested thereunto.

An Appendix.

DEere sir, after the writing of these, no weake doubt began to arise in our minds, whether we had done well or ill, in not descending fuller into the causes that induced, or truer constrained vs, to the making of the foresaid Supplication. And the more we chewed the doubt, the greater it waxed, and the plainer we sawe, how we had therein omitted the particularizing of that, which would most iustifie the mouing, and best pleade the graunt of our sute. May it therefore stand with your good leaue, that we here supplie the defect, for what you giue not leaue to, the same we reuoke, and beseeke, it be holden vnwritten.

1 The head sourse whence our agreeuances do chiefely spring, is the retractation or vnperforming of that, which your selfe did set downe vnder your hand, and the testimonie of one of your Assistants, namely, a prohibition, willing, and if that were not sufficient, commaunding all parties to desist to inueigh or follow the note of schisme against vs, but contrariwise, to suffer all matters past to quaile, and to english your owne Latine phrase, *lye buryed in perpetuall obliuion.* Which

Which charitable ordinance, and many wayes most needefull, for making and conseruing peace, how much and how oft it hath bin gone from, let the particulars declare that follow. One of vs informed your Reuerence, that a Father of the Societie (whome he named) affirmed, and stood to the iustifying of the assertion, that whosoeuer beleeues, or to vse his owne word, holds opinion *dogmatizando*, that we were not schismaticks, incurreth *ipso facto* the censures of holie Church. Which licence of speech (at leastwise outwardly) you no way seemed to dislike, but answered, the position was true. And if true, and we not deceiued in the signification of the word, how many good sir, of very good conscience, do there abide in a right dolefull and a most miserable plight of soule? All our ghostlie children, not few in number, and some of them of good qualitie, and infinite others beside hold opinion, nay firmely, & most resolutely, and with boldest assurance beleeue, we were no schismaticks: and will the Father say that we, and they all, through this our beliefe, liue and continue in a damnable state, and vnder the heauiest curse vpon earth? Pardon, we can neuer thinke it, nor count it lesse in our selues then rashest temeritie, euen but once to surmise the same: yet vnlesse the Father be mistaken, or our selues beguild in the darke or incongruent senses of his speech, we see no auoydance, but we must needs more then thinke it, being bound, if his position be true, to belieue and teach the veritie therof. Verily deere sir, this touch, or somewhat more, sitteth so neere, is of that nature, reacheth to so many, and goeth vested with like circumstances, as by no warrant of conscience, we may neglect the disproofe (were we through the vertue of humilitie, or the holie contempt of our selues, neuer so greatlie proane and willing thereunto) as teacheth *Saint Tho. quodl.* 10. *quest.* 6. *art.* 13. and may be auouched by that knowne saying of *Saint Augustine: Qui conscientia sua confidens famam negligit crudelis est:* He is cruell, that neglecteth his good name vpon the cleerenesse of his conscience. And againe, by that exhortation of the Apostle, *prouidentes bona non tantum coram Deo, sed etiam corã omnibus hominibus,* prouiding good things not only before God, but also before all men. And the reason is apparant, for being pastours, and labouring in the busines of gaining soules, the report of a good name is as important to vs for the good of our neighbour, as a good conscience for our selues.

2 Further, your Reuerence being sued vnto by the whole number of Priests in the *Clinck* for vouchsafing to restore *M. Benson* to the vse

of his faculties, you refused, or thought it not meete so to do, vnlesse among other points he did first acknowledge & sorrow his long adherēce to the schismaticall conuenticle, meaning & so naming our companie. Which forme of speech, and manner of proceeding, cannot but make plaine to euery vnderstanding, how desperatly grieuous you repute our state, and what miscreants we come to be reckoned, when our Superiour letteth not to tearme our fellowship a schismatical conuenticle, and that also by pen, whereunto then to a sodainnesse of speech, a farre more mature deliberation concurreth. Consider (in the name of our Sauiour we humble the request vnto you) the place you hold, the authoritie your words beare, your writings more; and how thereby the waight of our affliction, with the hauock of our credits dayly increaseth, all or most men taking your word for warrant against vs.

3 Againe, there is a Letter auowed to be written by your Fatherhood, as the tenor can agree to no other, and the copies common, wherein the words following lye word for word, without change or interposition. *We haue receiued a resolution from our mother citie, that the refusers of the appointed authoritie were schismaticks: and surely I would not giue absolution to any that should make no conscience thereof. Do they thinke that the scandall that did arise thereof, that the discrediting of our Protectors authoritie, that the opprobrious speeches against the Fathers vttered by them, that the danger they drue me vnto, may be free from sinne? I hope they haue not so senselesse a conscience. And therefore my direction is, that they do make accompt thereof, and do make satisfaction before they do receiue the benefit of absolution. The order and manner of satisfaction, I referre vnto the discretion of their ghostlie fathers which haue not bin marked with this note of schisme.* O good Lord help vs, is our demaund & standing off, only for canonicall proofe, that the designed authoritie was the ordinance of his Holines, or that it had his Holines approbation adiudged to make vs schismaticks, and the maiestie of the place remembred to credit our dome the more? And hereupon, as if all were by and by an vndoubted truth, whatsoeuer is aduertised by some persons against vs, you, first soothing what you would do your selfe, commaund all other, that we make satisfaction, ere the benefit of absolution be imparted vnto vs. An ordinance only, and that seldome, annexed to publick and horrible crimes: but patience must be our remedie, & much patience seemeth not vnneedfull, albeit our hope is, there may be some as meane schollers in *Rome*, as there are elsewhere,

elſewhere, or how ſingularlie learned ſoeuer he or they were, that thus hardlie concluded, it inferreth not much, becauſe as the euidence and information were deliuered, ſo without all doubt were we ſentenced: and if theſe were either not true or vnperfit, as we aſſure our ſelues of the one or both, then muſt the iudgement depending thereon needes take the ſame dye, & be of like veritie. And if it be replied, that true and full information was giuen, then we aske, why it is not added to the reſolution, or otherwiſe ſhewed vnto vs, to the end our ſelues and others may be witneſſes thereof, and haue whereupon we may iuſtlie alter and repent our contrarie opinion? Beſides, it were to good purpoſe, and to our ſeeming not vnrequiſite, that as well the names of the reſoluers, as alſo the moſt ſubſtantiall reaſons of ſuch their opinion, were likewiſe ſet downe, and adioyned to the reſolution. For without theſe or other good ſpecialties, what man or woman of conſcience in the world, vpon view or hearesay of an vnauthored reſolution, without ſhew of proofe, reaſon, inſtance, example, or authoritie, will condemne ſo many as are of our ſide of ſo irreligious a crime, and criminall outrage, whoſe proper entitie and nature requireth in the doer wittingnes, deliberation, obſtinacie, and rebellion, and that immediatlie or mediatlie, againſt our high *Pontifex*, and as *Pontifex* or head of our Church: for vpholding and maintenance of whoſe prerogatiues, we haue ſuffered, and dayly do, many ſorts of preſſures, calamities, and death it ſelfe. A ſtrange propoſition, and much incredible. In like manner how is it poſſible, that ſuch a bare and naked reſolution ſhould weigh ought with vs, ſtanding as we are verily perſwaded we do, vpon diuerſitie of aſſured grounds for the contrarie, eſpeciallie when we conſider, who wrote the reſolution ouer, a puney in Religion, and fellow Ieſuite with the creatours of our ſchiſme: at what time? when a feare was conceiued, leaſt we had ſent to the Sorboniſts for their opinion: why? becauſe the vſuall aduertiſer either had not (as may be coniectured) or would not be ſeene to haue his finger in ſo great an vnright, condemned ere we were heard to ſpeake, or asked the reaſons why we did prolong our ſubmiſſion. To draw neerer, would not the ods in the iudgement of all men good ſir, fall on our ſide, if to counteruaile this vnſtrengthened reſolution, we ſhould oppoſe the opinion & cenſures of our engliſh Students and Doctors at *Doway*, who (as an honeſt Prieſt reported that came from thence) make the diſcourſe and proofe of our ſchiſme, a meere ieſt and matter of recreation, to ſport themſelues with by the

Maiſter Beiſley.

fire, and cannot beleeue but the author trauelled when he penned it, in some forgetfulnes of his schollership, or distemper of head? Or, if we should seeke to incounter the said resolution by the suffrage euen of such our fellow Priests here at home, as *haue not bin marked with this note of schisme,* who being eye and eare witnesses to all particulars, and not without some knowledge in the state of most of our soules, and therefore by probabilitie, as likely to see as farre into the point, as strangers, were we anon cast in the closing, or should we leese thereby? If reports be true, or many of good vnderstanding not deceiued, there are few of our said brethren either reuerēt for yeares, or speciallie counted of for learning, vertue, wisedome, iudgement, discretion, true courage in Gods cause, or for any other good part, who do not greatlie meruaile at this strange resolution, and not a little grieue to see and heare, how sharplie, how vncharitablie, how iniustlie, we are dealt with, and what bond of endlesse discord the pamphlet of schisme (the occasion and origin of all) hath most vnfortunatelie cast among vs, which notwithstanding we do not rehearse, that when the difference commeth to tryall, we intend to make benefit of such their opinions, hoping without that help, to be able with sounder proofes to confirme what we hold, then with such allegations. Now touching your Fatherhoods charge, and our culpablenes in the other offences specified, we omit to say much, partlie, in regard of dutie, partlie because we would not be thought tender in taking, nor full of defending, partlie also, for *that the raising of scandall,* must fall in fine to their part, to whome the lawfulnes or vnlawfulnes of the vsed processe, and more the truth or vntruth of our schisme after deciding, shall prescribe and giue it. And as for the other three kinds of sinne, *of discrediting our Protector, of vttering opprobrious speeches against the fathers, and of drawing your selfe into danger,* our only answere is, that because the mentioning of them in this sort, bringeth a suspition of their vngodlines vpon vs all, we most hartilie beseeke you, to nominate and take condigne punishment of the guiltie, and thereby free the residue of so foule a staine. Doubtlesse, if the taunts of our schisme composed, and the pluralitie of by-words which he spent in that paradox with lesse modestie against vs, yea, if his condemning vntruths, in sentencing vs to be rebels, schismaticks, fallen from Gods Church, offenders against all faith and humane authoritie, excommunicate, irregular contemners, and treaders downe of due obedience to the Sea Apostolick, scandalizers of all the godlie, infamous throughout euery mans

mans mouth, no whit better then soothsayers and idolaters, and to be counted of as ethnicks and publicans: if these we say with other intollerable defamations, dispersed and sent to *Rome* against vs for deeper deprauing our designes and persons (which we can proue, some by letters yet extant, others by testimonie of credible relatours) were vprightly ballanced, with that which we haue said or written against the Fathers, it would soone appeare, and as manifestlie as light at noonetide, who haue most exceeded, who haue surfeited, and who remaine obliged to satisfye, for vttering, we may say lauishing, of loose, bad, & opprobrious speeches. Is it possible, we meane not for religious humilitie, or morall courtesie, but for gaule it selfe, or a worse humour, to exaggerate matters heauier vpon vs, then to affirme, *that if those whome we haue begotten to Christ, or who are our ghostlie children, should receiue sacraments at our hands, they seeme to receiue poyson in place of medicine from vs, yea also to commit grieuous sinne if they do but intreate vs to celebrate, or shall but help vs at Masse.* Surely, surely, had we defiled our pennes against the Fathers with like stuffe and doctrine (Lord) how francklie had we bin exclaimed against with open mouth, if not all the bels both in towne and country rung out *Crucifige* vpon vs long since, to our euerlasting ignominie? But the abhomination and execration of our schisme commerited and importuned this, and a fuller measure of bitternes to be powred vpon vs. Be it so, though we hope by all authorities to cleere our selues from any such tainder: yet the same being neither decided by sentence of holie Church, nor in talke nor in the least suspition, before it pleased the Fathers to raise and spread the calumniation of vs, we cannot but thinke we haue reason, to blame them of course and homely dealing, that hauing alwayes honored them in the degree we haue, and they being neither our superior, against whome our offence, if any were, was committed, nor in any way with vs in subordination vnto him, but a distinct body from him and vs, thus peremptorily, thus eagerly, thus violently to censure and condemne their long welwillers, and ioint-labourers with them in one vineyard. To say charitie induced them to so exceeding a processe against vs, were to speake voluntarilie beyond all likelihood of truth: for, if charitie had bin the motiue, charitie being as the Apostle writeth, *patient, benigne, not prouoked to anger, suffering all things, hoping all things, bearing all things,* they would either haue deferred the denouncing of their cruell sentence vpon vs, knowing that we had long before that time sent to his Holines for

Father Garnets words in his letter to me of the 7. of March 1599.

vnderstanding his pleasure, or haue vsed ciuiller tearmes, or at leastwise not interlaced so many frumps, and mightily inciting scoffes, as they did in the treatise, fitlier beseeming a Stage-player, then a religious person.

4 There remaineth one materiall point yet vnremembred, and which putteth vs in feare of mo troubles at hand, *viz.* that part of your letter to Maister *Clearke*, wherein you signifie, that *you are content for the time to suffer vs in our opinion of schisme, as the lesse euill, and will not deale as yet as a prelate may do for appeasing the same.* What course you intend against vs good sir in these your words, we know not in particular, but a warning they must needes be vnto vs, either to addresse our selues, to take vpon vs without demerit, the turpitude of schisme, and thereby discredit our nation, staine our function, leese our faculties, loade our consciences, wrap our selues in censures, and turmoile, if not agonize, the soules of our ghostlie children, in breeding doubts, whether their confessions made vnto vs, or hereafter to be made, be good or no. On these mischiefes, great, and many, and very fearefull, we must wittinglie put our selues as is said, or prepare our patience to beare, whatsoeuer it shall like our hard friends to aduise, and your selfe to impose vpon vs. Lamentable to remember how much the former glorie and renowne of our english schollers and priests at *Rome*, are sithence the death of our blessed Cardinall, eclipsed, or rather blotted, or rather then either, if we may so say, defamed. Which euill hitherto outlandish and confined chiefely to that place, begins now alas to creepe hitherward apace, nay hath alreadie, found large welcome in our realme, and gauled the reputation of Priests, impeached the increase of Catholicks, decayed the reliefe of prisoners, and raysed the like mutinies and debates in our country, as the generall and Gods cause lyeth groueling, amitie pineth, peace droopeth, our aduersaries reioyce, and dissention and faction seeme only to raigne. Our good Lord for the infinitenes of his mercy, guide and graunt you good Father, the happines to reforme all, and pardon the causers whosoeuer they be, that they feele not the smart of the misdeede, in the reckoning of their last accompts. For conclusion, we appeale honored sir, to the indifferencie of your owne thoughts, whether (these, and mo of like agreiuance, which if we would, we could alleage, being the aduersities of our present state) there be not greatest necessitie of mouing and recommending this sute vnto you, accounting the graunt thereof, as we do, the ablest meane of acquieting

all

all differences, and of reducing vs againe to peace, loue, and vnion. *Qui pacis ineunt consilia, sequitur eos gaudium,* ioy followeth the counsellers of peace.

To take our leaues, we beseech you on our knees of pardon, louing Father, if error in our vnderstanding hath misguided our pen in ought: for as for our will, we do assure she is not accessarie, & we hope we carry the minde, what decay soeuer other of late may note in vs, that we would not wittinglie do the thing, which our vnderstanding shall giue vs to be vnlawfull. We misdoubted the direct and lawfull procurement of the authoritie vpō more then pregnant coniectures: we did morallie assure our selues, that it was not the commaundement of his Holines: we eftsoone to our great charge, sent two of our brethren to *Rome,* for vnderstanding the full truth therein: we acquainted your Reuerence with our intent: we gaue you a copie of such things, as we purposed to moue to his Holines: we offered to obey you in the meane time, and did in fact obey you, as by seuerall particulars we can prooue, though we deferred to subiect our selues absolutely vnto you before receipt of notice from our brethren or other canonicall certeintie, that the authoritie was the ordinance of his Holines. When the Breue came, we by and by without any delay, submitted our selues, laboured our friends to do the like, shewed our selues ready to any seruice, and hauing bin almost infinitely wronged, as the particulars before touched do in part declare, neuerthelesse for peace sake, and to make vp vnion againe, we were content and willing to remit and forgiue all that was past. What could we do in reason, or out of reason, more then we did, and were most desirous thereof, and now to haue matters reuiued and prosecuted afresh against vs, what may our afflicted Church and our selues hope for, but to fall from lesse quietnes to lesse, if the sole cause of difference after this or by some other good way be not remoued and cut off? Which our all-mercifull God, through the bleeding wounds of our sweete Sauiour, and the intercession of all our english Saincts, graunt to the honor of his owne name, and the weale of our country. Fare you well most hartily, remayning obediently your Fatherhoods children, who although we omit to subscribe our seuerall names in respect of the time, yet not vnknowne vnto you by the imputed marke of schisme.

After the receite of these, our Arch-priest wrote an answere vnto vs, wherein he did not only deny the graunt of our foresaid pe-

In his letter of the 14. of March 1600

tition, but threatned in the manner as followeth: *If euer I can finde hereafter, that either by word or writing you iustifie your enormious disobedience, as voyde of sinne, this being a signe of want of grace, and defence of sinne, which is an high pride, and tending to the stirring vp of new tumults, and disturbance of our wished peace, I will suspend you from your function, as not worthie to exercise the same.* Hereupon, seeing our best indeuors could receiue no more fauour from our Arch-priest towards the remouing of the accusations, wherewith we were charged, we sent the state of the question (taking this for the next remedie) to the Vniuersitie of *Paris*, earnestly requesting that venerable companie to giue vs their resolution in the case. Who resoluing it to be no schisme, nor any sinne in the nature of the fact, our Arch-priest presentlie vpon the first notice of their censure, published a decree, *forbidding vs vnder paine of suspension from diuine offices, and losse of faculties, to be incurred in the fact it selfe, either to maintaine, or defend, directlie, or indirectlie, in word, or writing, the said censure; and he likewise forbad the Laitie the same, vnder paine of being interdicted in like manner, that is, in the fact it selfe.*

Of the 29. of May 1600.

Againe not long after the said decree, his Reuerence published an other of the 18. of October 1600. wherein he declared, that *we had vndoubtedlie disobeyed the sea Apostolicke, and rebelled against his office, and did also therein prohibit vs and the Laitie vnder the foresaid penalties, to defend the contrary any manner of way whatsoeuer.* Now what refuge was there left vnto vs, saue only to flye to his Holines by way of appellation, and by laying downe vnto him the particulars of our agreiuances? which our Arch-priest reiected, allowing it but in the behalfe of one only, whose faculties he had taken away before. Further, when his Reuerence had thus wronged vs, and also suspended, interdicted, and dispossessed some ten of vs of our faculties, Maister *Mush* not many weekes before he began his voyage to *Rome*, sent the conditions following to Maister Doctor *Bauine* the senior assistant, to the end that thorough his mediation and furtherance, they might the sooner be accepted of by our Arch-priest, and all matters accorded.

The first condition.

Conditions of attonemét offered by Maister Mush.

THat our Arch-priest with his Assistants, and the fathers of the Societie, would be content to declare by a publick instrument, that our forbearing to admit the new authoritie before the arriuall of his Holines Breue, was no schisme, nor any such disobedience, but that

that wee, notwithstanding the same, might lawfullie and with safe conscience celebrate diuine mysteries, and minister sacraments.

The second.

That his Reuerence would make knowne by some common letter, that who soeuer hereafter should renew this controuesie, he was and ought to be taken by all men for a seditious person, and enemy to our churches peace, and the common good of the Catholick cause.

The third.

That after the aforesaid two publick declarations, our Arch-priest would restore euery one to his former state and faculties.

The fourth.

That his Reuerence would likewise be content that what Priest soeuer should be accused, either to himselfe, or to any of his Assistants, or informed against for any crime or misdemeanor, he the said Priest should not be condemned, nor any way punished, before he were found guilty of the fault by iust tryall, and personally heard to answere for himselfe.

The fift and last.

That his Reuerence would recall all his penall decrees, and not make any hereafter, the burdens of the time considered, without vrgent necessitie, and with the aduise of eight or sixe of his Assistants, which conditions as reasonable as we tooke them to be, either did displease, or not content, because we receiued no answere vnto them.

And now hauing thus signified how matters passed betweene vs, we leaue the discreet reader to iudge whether side in their actions haue shewed greater desire of peace: we who receiued the wrongs, and did both pardon them, and offered seuerall conditions of reuniting our selues, or they who doing the iniuries, neuer made profer of reconciliation; nay sued vnto, did exact such kinde of submission at our hands, as without defaming our selues vniustly, & deadly belying our soules, we could not yeeld thereunto. And that these may not appeare bare words, without particular proofe, we will here *verbatim* rehearse both the declaration that our Arch-priest made touching *M.Drury*, and the forme he sent him, wherein and how he should submit himselfe, and acknowledge his guiltinesse.

Uniuersis Catholicis Anglis Salutem. That is,

To all english Catholicks greeting.

THese are to giue you to vnderstand, and are to declare, that Maister *Robert Drurie* Priest, hath incurred the paines of suspension, and of the losse of all his faculties, not in respect of Appeale (which I do not denie to any) but for his disobedient breach and contempt of my fourth and fifth penall decrees published 18. *Octobris, Anno Domini* 1600. of which he taketh notice by his subscription to the Letter and the pretended Appeale, dated 17. *Nouembris* 1600. And to this my declaration I haue subscribed with mine owne hand, and thereunto set my Seale this 7. of December 1600.

Georgius Blackwellus Archipræsbyter
Catholicorum Anglorum. That is,

George Blackwell Arch-priest
of the English Catholicks.

The forme of the submission.

Pag. 120. *EGo N. confiteor & agnosco me ex nulla iusta causa de grauaminibus, atque immensa iniuriarũ mole mihi à Rmo D. Archipræsbytero illatis, conquestum esse, & in ipsum dissidiorum tumultuum, atque bellorum intestinorum culpam coniecisse, eiusque salubria quædam decreta transgressum esse, quorum omnium veniam, facultatum restitutionem, censurarumque si quas incurri sublationem humiliter peto, ac superiora omnia reuoco, eaque à me dicta vel scripta, vel approbata minime fuisse vehementer cupio. Insuper iuro in posterum pacifice, & obedienter erga eundem superiorem meum me gesturum, atque vt alij idem faciant, quantum in me erit, & officij mei ratione curaturum.*

The English.

I N. do confesse and acknowledge to haue complayned vpon no iust cause of the greeuances, and exceeding great masse of iniuries imposed vpon me, by the most Reuerend Archpresbiter, and to haue layd the fault on him, of the discord, tumults, and ciuill dissentions, and to haue transgressed certaine wholesome decrees of his, for all which

which I humbly aske pardon, and the restitution of faculties, and absolution from Censures, if I haue incurred any, and do reuoke all the former, and very hartily wish, that these things had neuer bin spoken, or written, or approued by me. Moreouer I sweare, that I will cary my selfe hereafter peaceablie, and obedientlie, towards the sayd my Superiour, and in regard of my dutie, procure so much as in me shall lye that others do the same.

THe disobedient breach and contempt which our Arch-priest obiected against Maister *Drury* was, *for that he gaue his name to an Appeale to his Holines, without acquainting his Reuerence therewith before, and without his licence; and because he by appealing presumed to defend the disobedience that was imputed to such as refused to admit the subordination vpon sight of the Constitutiue Letter.* Two great offences comparable to the saying of a *Pater noster*, and touching the former. One and the first of the sixe Articles (*a*) in which Saint *Thomas* of *Canterbury* resisted the Constitution of King *Henry* the second, was, *Quod non appelletur ad sedem Apostolicam sine licentia Regis:* That no appellation be made to the Sea Apostolick, without licence of the King. Which gainestanding of Saint *Thomas* was counted so little a fault in him, as he was Canonized for the fact, and God himselfe proued his vertue by testimonie of most glorious and infinite miracles. Our Arch-priest decreed, that *none vnder paine of suspension, interdiction, and of losing their faculties, ipso facto, should giue their names or suffrages in any cause whatsoeuer, vnlesse he did before make his Reuerence priuie thereunto, and had his assent,* comprehending vnder the clause [*of any cause whatsoeuer*] appeales to *Rome*, as himself interpreteth the words in his common letters to his assistants, and maketh the same most euident, in this his fact of declaring Maister *Drewry* to haue falne into the said Ecclesiasticall penalties, *by his subscription to the pretended appeale. Stapleton* in the life of the former Saint, affirmeth, that the abouenamed Constitution substituted the King in the place of the Pope, by attributing that power vnto him, which is proper to the Pope, and that it expressely contradicted the generall Councell of *Sardis*, and taketh away from that sacred consistory the pontificiall primacy which was giuen to *Peter* by our Sauiour, and to those that should succeede him to the worlds end. Which if it be true, as we are sure our Arch-priest will not deny, what can be lesse inferred, then that his sayd decree and declaration doth by so much the worse, and

These two branches of the decree are set down pag. 191.

(a) *Stapletonus de tribus Thomis p. 36. Quadrilogus lib. 5. ca. 8. Surius in vita eius Matheus Parisiensis pa. 135.*

See pag. 216.

Cap. 7.

the more vnworthily violate the rights of *Ecclesiasticall libertie*, aboue King *Henries* Constitution, by how much the office and person of an Arch-priest, is inferior to the state and royall soueraigntie of a King, because the presumption of violating such prerogatiues, taketh his degrees of deformitie from the parties state and condition, who letted not to decree and publish such prohibitions to the preiudice and infringing of the said Ecclesiasticall rights and liberties? But of this matter we haue spoken before in our fourth Reason, where it is shewed, that not only the makers of such lawes or Constitutions, but those that shall vse or iudge according to the iniustice of them, are excommunicated in the Bull of *Cœnæ Domini*.

Concerning the other offence, for which our Arch-priest declared Maister *Drewry*, who had long before, euen at the first comming of the Cardinals letter, most absolutely subiected himselfe to his authoritie, to haue incurred the foresaid censures and penaltie, *viz.* for that by putting his name to the Appeale, he adiudged him to maintaine the disobedience obiected. We hold it also for no greater fault (admitting *the subscription of his name to the Appeale*, were a defence of the disobediēce pretended, as we do no way see, how it could be) then is the doing of a good deed, & perhaps of bounden charitie, according to this saying of Pope *Alexander*, recorded in the Canons, *Qui ex vestro collegio fuerit & ab auxilio vestro se substraxerit magis schismaticus quam sacerdos esse probabitur*: He that is of your colledge or coate, and shall withdraw himselfe from assisting you, doth therein more approue himselfe to be a schismatique then a priest. By which it appeareth, how vndeseruingly our Arch-priest inflicted his punishments, and how vnconscionably contrary to all truth and iustice, he would haue vs in our submission to bely and defame our selues. For it is to be noted, that this forme of submission, or iniurious condition of release, was not sent to Maister *Drury* alone, but the same was exacted also of Maister *Mush*, when he wrote to the Arch-priest for the restoring of his faculties, and of vs all, especially of my selfe, when Maister *Iohn Benet* vpon direction from father *Parsons*, labored to compose the dissention (into whose hands at that time as himselfe can witnes, I committed my whole particular, for him to make what end he thought fit, so willing I was of peace, howsoeuer our Arch-priest held me therein auerted:) which manner of proceeding & exaction, so greatly distasted Maister *Benet*, as whereas before he would not graunt to set his name to the Appeale, he then presently gaue his consent

3.q.1. Nulli dubium. Let such of our brethren well note this place, as beleeued in their conscience we had wrong, and would not for feare giue their helps towards the redresse, either by appealing with vs, or by manifesting their opiniō for the better resolution of the doubtfull.

sent

ſent thereunto, ſaying, that he now ſaw no hope of compounding the controuerſie by any other more peaceable meane then by appellation. The Prophet writeth, *Erit opus iuſtitiæ pax,* Peace ſhall be the worke of Iuſtice. And the Euangeliſts do note vnto vs, that our Sauiour ſtood in the middeſt of his Diſciples, when he ſayd *Pax vobis,* Peace be vnto you, ſignifying thereby that indifferencie begetteth, and continueth peace. A vertue which our Arch-prieſt hath not hitherto much obſerued, but rather ſhewed himſelfe euer moſt partiall betweene the Ieſuites and vs, as the particulars aforegoing do conuince: and ſo alſo may the words which he vſed to me, at my laſt ſpeaking with him, to wit, *that whatſoeuer we ſhould ſay, or do againſt the Ieſuites, he would take the ſame to be done as to himſelfe.* Which conſidered, the nature of their iniuries done againſt vs, and how little they ſeeme to incline to ſatisfie, or deſiſt from increaſing of them, may eaſily appeare, and iuſtly put vs in diſpaire of enioying peace, ſo long as his Reuerence holdeth his place and opinion. Our good Lord turne all things to his honor.

Eſay. 32.

Luke. 24. & Iohn. 20.

To fold vp the whole diſcourſe, we do, and euer did very certainely aſſure our ſelues vpon the reaſons afore-going, that our deferring to receiue the new authoritie, was lawfull before God and man, as either commaunded, or directed by the Canons of holy Church, and not repugnant to the doctrine of any good writer, auncient or moderne. Idle therefore and vngrounded, are the exceptions which our oppoſitors pretend, and the ſlaunders they haue rayſed of vs (or if they will not haue ignorance to diminiſh their fault, the calumniations) toto exorbitant, and exceſſiue. Wherefore we hope, they will make vs ſatiſfaction, eſpecially for the temporall loſſes, that haue directly accrued vnto vs by ſuch their defamations: and more, through the wrongfull taking away of our faculties. They know the *(b)* rule of the law, the ſame *(c)* being the maxime of Saint *Auſten: Peccatum non dimittitur, niſi reſtituatur ablatum:* The ſinne is not remitted, except what is taken away be reſtored, and ſatisfaction made, where *(d)* there is abilitie of the domages incurred. And they know alſo, that *(e)* reſtitution implyeth a negatiue precept, and conſequently *(f)* that it bindeth them to make the ſame forthwith. Neither are they ignorant that this right of ſatisfaction *(g)* being conteined vnder the firſt concluſions of the law of Nature, remaineth vndiſpenſable by any power vpon earth: ſo that knowing to what they are bound, our demaund and affiance is, that they will diſcharge the bond, and not as witting

(b) *Reg. 4. de reg. iur. li. 6.*
(c) *Ad Macedoniũ epiſt. 54.*
(d) *D. Tho. 22. art. 2. & 4.*
(e) *Ibidem art. 8.*
(f) *Ibidem 22. q. 35. art. 2. c.*
(g) *Silueſter verb. Papa nu. 16.*

Luke. 12. offenders, deserue to be beaten with many stripes. They haue the whole realme and a great part of the Christian world to their lookers on, and therefore it would vndoubtedlie redound to their obliquie, and scandalize not a few, if they should make no satisfaction for so grieuous iniuries and detriments.

Pag. 85. 86. & 238. It hath bin proued once or twise before, that the prorogation of yeelding our obedience to *M. Blackwell,* was neither disobedience against his Holines, nor the Cardinall, nor against himselfe, notwithstanding the contrarie assertion of our aduersaries, and the laying of a much fouler crime to our charge; a crime, which for the obiect, or noblest good it impugneth (being the *(h)* vnitie of Gods Church his Doue & spouse) is worse then theft, adultery, murder, or patricide, and worse then the most detestable outrage that can be committed against our neighbor. We of purpose omit here to refute the vnworthines of the imputation, because his Holines himselfe hath giuen sentence against the same, and not only cleered our delay from the accusation of schisme and enormious disobedience, but from all kind of disobedience. And verily we cannot but greatly maruell, how possibly so many of our aduersaries, carying the reputation of learning and iudgement, could conspire in so great an error, vnlesse the wisedome of God thought it fit for some cause to humble them, or check the high opinion which many carry of their worthes, to the disgrace, if not to the contempt of others their fellow-laborers, and perchance of equall deserts with them, in the worke they iointly haue in hand. Obstinate disobedience (and without *(i)* obstinacie, there can be no schisme) may be considered three manner of wayes, either against the thing commaunded, or the person commaunding, or against the office of the commaunder, in not recognising him for his Superiour. And this later kind of rebellion only maketh the crime of schisme, as *(k)* Saint *Thomas,* and all his *(l)* expositors, with the *(m)* Summists do witnesse.

(h) *D. Tho. 22. q. 39. ar. 2.*

Note the grieuousnes of our defamation.

(i) *D. Tho. 22. q. 39. art. 1.*

(k) *Ibidem ad 2.*

(l) *Caiet. ibidem & in summa verb. excommunicatio. 7. Banues ibidē Valentia Tho. 3. dispu. 3. q. 15. punct. 1.*

(m) *D. Antoninus 3 par. tit. 22. ca. 5. §. 11 Archidia. 3. par. tit. 13. Siluester verb. schisma ante nu. 1.*

Hence it followeth demonstrably, if our refusall to receiue Maister *Blackwell* to our Arch-priest, did, or could any way possibly make vs schismaticks, that the only and principall cause of such our refusall, was, and of all necessitie must needes haue bin, for that the Pope (note our words) or the Cardinall by his commission, had (instituting the subordination) appointed him for our Superior: which how farre it was and is from all truth, let our sending to *Rome* declare; let the protestations we made in our first letters, *that the least canonicall notice,*

which

which should come from his Holines, should presently stint all disputes, and Pag.269.
finde vs readily obedient in what soeuer: let our often repeated demaund, and continuall insisting for a Breue, Bull, or other Papall instrument, for testimonie of the Institution: let our prompt and reall yeelding of our obediēce vnto Maister *Blackwell* so soone as his Holines Breue arriued: let other our seuerall actions and conclamations beare witnes, decide, and denounce to the whole world, whether we refused to receiue him, because the Pope appointed him Arch-priest, or for the reasons alleaged in the discourse before. Verily the paradox of our schisme, seemeth so ridiculous, and childish, and without all shew of learning, iudgement and sense, as we cannot thinke, but that the opinion, especially the long maintenance thereof, was in the authors *pœna peccati,* the effect and punishment of sinne past. And because there can be no demonstration or argument made so cleare, but that he who is disposed to wrangle, may easily deuise somewhat to reply vpon, we thinke it most conuenient for the thorow satisfaction of all parties, to set downe here a copy of the Letter which our brethren wrote vnto vs of late, aduertising what his Holines had declared in the controuersie.

Pag.255.

Admodum reuerendis in Christo patribus, & fratribus nostris Ioanni Collingtono, Antonio Heburno, & cæteris consocijs.

ADmodum reuerendi in Christo patres fratresque, exhibuimus Illustrissimis Card. Burgesio, & Arigone (quos sanctissimus arbitros constituit in causa nostra, viros tam pietate & virtute insignes quam legum scientia, rerum experientia, & animi candore omnibus gratos) rationes quibus ducti distulimus Archipræsbytero, ante aduentum Breuis Apostolici, obedire. Quibus cum sanctissimo communicatis 11. *Aprilis, placuit Illustrissimis Cardinalibus Sanctitatis suæ mentem eodem die nobis significare; nimirum quod propter dictam dilationem, nec schismatici, nec rebelles, aut inobediētes extiterimus: & quod confessiones factæ sacerdotibus, qui ob huiusmodi rationes distulerunt, essent validæ, & nullo modo reiterandæ, nisi aliud forsan interueniret impedimentum quam quod à tali dilatione haberet originem. Hæc vobis significanda duximus, partim vt multorum conscientijs satisfiat, partim etiam vt ad omnem vos modestiam, charitatem & humilitatem excitemus, tam literis quam exemplo. Quod reliquum est habemus clementissimum patrem, æquissimos arbitros, neque est quod du-*

bitetis de pristina pace & tranquillitate breuissime recuperanda. Valete in Domino, Rome 15. Aprilis.

R.D.V. fratres & serui in Christo humillimi,

Iohannes Cecilius.
Thom. Bluet.
Iohannes Mush.
Anthonius Champneus.

To the Reuerend Fathers in Christ, and our brothers, *Iohn Colington, Anthony Heburne*, and the rest of their associates.

VEry reuerend Fathers and brothers in Christ, we haue exhibited to the right noble Cardinals *Burgesius*, and *Aragone*, (whom his Holines hath appointed for arbitrators in our cause, men renowmed for their knowledge in the lawes, and experience in all occurrences, and gratefull vnto all men for their sinceritie) the reasons whereby we were induced to deferre our obedience to the Arch-priest before the receipt and comming of the Apostolicall Breue. Which being signified vnto his Holines vpon the 11. of April, it pleased the right worthy Cardinals to signifie vnto vs his Highnes mind the same day, namely, that in regard of that our foresayd delay, we were neither schismatiques, nor rebels, or disobedient, and that those confessions which were made vnto such priests, who for these reasons deferred their obedience, were in full force, and ought in no sort to be reiterated, except perhaps some other cause or let did happen, then that which tooke his originall from the former dilation. These things we haue therefore thought good to signifie vnto you, partly that many consciences might be thereby satisfied, partly also that we might excite you vnto all modestie, charitie, and humilitie, as well in writing, as in example. The conclusion is, we haue a most pious and mercifull Father, and a most iust Iudge, neither haue we any cause to suspect, but that very shortly we shall recouer our auncient peace and tranquilitie. *Rome* the 15. of April. 1602. Your Reuerences brethren and humble seruants in Christ,

Iohn Cecil.
Thomas Bluet.
Iohn Mush.
Anthony Champney.

Harum

Harum literarum exemplar cum vtroque Card. reliquimus, qui, communicato cũ sua Sanctitate negotio, responsum tulerunt, Sanctitatem suam velle & iubere vt hac ad vos scriberemus.

A copie of these Letters was left by vs with both the Cardinals, who communicating the contents thereof to his Holines, receiued answere that his Holines willed and commaunded to write these vnto you.

We hope none will thinke that either our brethren in *Rome* whose names are subscribed, or our selues would deuise or faine such a letter: and the same being taken to be a true letter, we haue a great hope, that our aduersaries will now change their opinion, and from henceforth call vs no more *the contentious Priests,* because *(a)* contention importeth an alteration against the truth. And therefore our standing in the maintenance of truth and our good names against them, cannot be called contention in vs (being a thing *(b)* laudable and *(c)* obliging) but in them only who so iniuriously oppugned both truth, ecclesiasticall order, and our good names.

(a) *D. Tho. 22. q. 38. art. 1. & Caieta. ibidem.* (b) *D. Tho. & Caieta. vbi supra & Valentia T. 3. disp. 3. q. 14. punct. 2.* (c) *12. q. 1. Nolo. D. Tho. quodl. 10. q. 6. art. 13. Nauar. t. 1. in cap. inter verba. 11. q. 3. concl. 2. nu. 15*

Likewise the aduerse part obiecteth scandall vnto vs, but with lesse colour of pretence, then it imputeth contention. For he that can be sayd to scandalize, must haue (as *(d)* Saint *Thomas* and all his expositors do vniformely teach) either a formall and expresse intention to draw others into sinne, or do an act which of his proper nature entiseth to sinne: or thirdly (which is called scandall by accident) do an act whereat others take scandall, albeit neither the nature of the act, nor the intention of the doer, gaue any such cause. Touching the first member of the diuision, we are sure our aduersaries will not say, that we had in our deferring a formall intention to scandalize: and touching the second member, it appeareth that our sayd deferring was not of his owne nature induciue to sinne, because the same was no other then what the Canons commaund, or allow, as the former reasons haue shewed, and as his Holines by his late declaration hath made more manifest. It resteth therefore, that if our sayd deferring occasioned scandall, that is the spirituall ruine of others, it was meerely through the ignorance, or infirmitie, or the malice of such as tooke scandall thereat. And before this actiue scandall by accident can be imputed a sinne to the giuer, it is of necessitie (as all Diuines agree, and common reason telleth, for auoyding many grosse absurdities which otherwise would follow) that he *(e)* who this

(d) *22. q. 34. art. 1. ad. 4. & art. 3. Caieta. & Banues ibidẽ Valentia To. 3. dispu. 3. q. 18. punct. 1.*

(e) *Valentia vbi supra puncto 2. & 4.*

way is ſcandalized, muſt firſt note, or be bound to note, both that another will take ſcandall at ſuch his fact, and that himſelfe be bound to deſiſt vpon the ſame notice, or aduerſion. Which two points and circumſtances our aduerſaries will neuer be able to proue to haue concurred in the act of our deferring. But of the other ſide, we little doubt, but that the condemnation which they paſſed vpon vs for the ſayd delay, and the great ſtirres, which by the nature of ſuch their actions haue followed, haue occaſioned both many, and moſt lamentable ſcandals.

Concerning the ambition wherewith ſome of vs goe charged by our aduerſaries, we would know whether they accoumpt vs voyde of all iudgement: for if they do not, how can they report vs to be ambitious, when there is not ſcarce any one of meaneſt vnderſtanding in our country, but knoweth, that no Engliſhman either of the Cleargie or Laitie, can come to preferment in *Rome, Spaine, Flanders,* or any place where the Ieſuites liue, but only or chiefely by their mediation or countenance? Yea, what Prieſt in *England* can come into credit with the Arch-prieſt, or hold ſo much of his fauour as he poſſeſſed before, if the Ieſuites do not like well thereof? Alſo touching the future, none can be ſo blinde, as not to ſee, that the Ieſuites affect, and hope to haue the diſtributing of promotions, and the ruling of all things, if our countrie happen to turne Catholicke. Of which hope and deſigne of theirs, though there be many other ſtrong preſumptions, yet none ſeeme to conclude the ſame ſo apparantlie, as doth Father *Parſons* Babell, that is, his Caſtle in the ayre, or booke of Reformation, preſcribing rules to all eſtates. So that our aduerſaries knowing vs voluntarily to haue diſcontinued familiaritie with the Ieſuites, and broken off all dependance on them, and neuertheleſſe vpbraiding vs with ambition, they muſt needes take vs to be very fooles, not onely in ſtriuing to ſwimme againſt the ſtreame, but alſo deſiring promotion, whereas we abandon all the likelieſt meanes of attayning thereunto. Or let theſe things pleade for vs as they may, yet becauſe my ſelfe by report am moſt condemned by name, for trauelling in the humor of ſeeking ſuperioritie, I muſt here craue a fauorable conſtruction from the reader of my intents, for laying downe the particulars following, being inforced thereunto by the neceſſitie of my owne purgation.

When the ſodalitie, or clergie aſſociation (ſo earneſtly inueyed againſt,

against, both in the Letter of the sixe assistants to his Holines *Nuntio* in Flaunders, and in seuerall places of the Apologie) was first intended to be erected, there were of that companie who labored me, that I would not refuse to accept of the superioritie: but can any one say, that euer I graunted thereunto? Maister *Standish*, one of the chiefest promotors at that time of the sayd Sodalitie, and whose testimonie is freest from suspition (being now become an aduersary thereunto) can witnes no, and that I still insisted to haue the Superiour chosen by two third parts of such, as should vnite themselues for the institution of the sayd Sodalitie. Againe, to the end that the Superior might this way be chosen, I named fiue or sixe auncient Priests, out of which the election (as I thought might well be made; offering beside to contribute largely towards the taking and furnishing of a house, for the vse of the sayd Sodality, so as they would exempt me, and make choyse of an other.

Now if the precedent refusall and offer do not cleere me of being desirous of superioritie, because the one may be interpreted for an externall shew of humilitie only, and both dissembled by me, to the end to draw them the more cunningly onward to the continuing of their purpose, of making me the superiour: yet surely the speeches which I vsed to Maister *Blackwell* himselfe about the same matter, will (I hope) free me with all men. Not long before the instituting of the new authoritie, Maister *Blackwell* dealt earnestly with me, that I would desist from making or furthering any innouation through the erecting of the Sodalitie, affirming, that it argued an ill affected humor in me, to intreate others (for so he sayd, he vnderstood that I did, though in truth it was not so) to be of the Sodalitie, whereof my selfe was designed the head. Whereupon, I then presently gaue him my word to be his bondman, if euer I accepted thereof; and yeelded him harty thanks for his speeches, as hauing giuen me a sufficient cause by them, to deny all my friends for euer taking vpon me the office, by how many soeuer the same might be importuned, and layd vpon me: which I trust is so plaine and sincere a disproofe of that which is imputed vnto me, as it can admit no exception.

Moreouer, when Maister *Bishop* and Maister *Charnock* were resolued to go to *Rome* for giuing his Holines to vnderstand what kind of gouernment the Cardinall Protector had instituted in our country, and how inconuenient the same was in many respects, and withall to manifest vnto him the lack of Bishops, which our yonger Catholicks had for the ministring of the sacrament of Confirmation; and how greatly that benefit was desired by many, I requested Maister *Bishop*, that if they should winne his Holines to graunt Bishops, that in no sort he would name me for any, assuring him, that if I thought he would, I should neither be willing he went the iourney, nor would contribute a penie thereunto. To speake yet more foolishly, finding my selfe not so strong as I did desire against all such temptations, and willing to strengthen my selfe more, I enioyned my selfe a yeres pennance (as the day of Iudgement will declare) for the better subduing of them, which spirituall taske I performed, and found (God be euer thanked for his infinite mercies) long before the penance expired, that holie feare and hatred of like dignities, as I would not, nor I hope yet will stoupe to the ground to take vp the best Bishoprick in the Christian world with the charge. Small reason therefore had our Arch-priest to write as he did of me, and to diuulge the copy of his letter, namely, *that I was a man clowded in my vnderstanding, if not cloyed about my heart with too many fumes of ambition:* And as little cause also haue many others (who perchāce lesse know me) to prattle and inlarge their backbitings of one, as they do.

In his Letter to Maister Hebborne of the 2. of March. 1599.

Further, if there be any Priest, or lay person in *England*, with whome, at any time I haue conferred about deriuing Superiority to my selfe, let him not spare to publish whatsoeuer I sayd vnto him: but I thinke there is not that creature liuing which can charge me with any such matter.

Of the other side, if either Father *Parsons* or our Arch-priest wrote the Epistle of *pious griefe* (as few doubt but one of them did) it is strange to see the praises they deliuer of them selues. And as for Father *Parsons* it is noted, that he writeth no booke, discourse, nor scarse any letter of these stirres, wherein he doth not make mention of the Colledges he erected, or recount some other good act of his owne. Amongst many, the man is thought to be ill neighbored, in that he is thus driuen to praise himselfe, and few do thinke it religious modestie, to farse bookes with their owne commendations, and to set them forth in other mens names: an exercise, that neuer any Saint or humble man practised. By which course of his, and some other of his dealings it is vehemently suspected, lest he direct his labours to the making of himselfe popularly famous, and prepare the way to a Cardinals hat.

By the erecting and managing of the Colledges, he commeth to haue store of money for euery expence, which otherwise he was like to faile of, nor could he spend fiue or sixe crownes a weeke (as by credible relation he doth) in postage for Letters only. Againe, the same imployment and care of his in erecting and prouiding maintenance for the Colledges, serueth his turne for liuing in places of concourse, here, there, and euery where, but in a colledge of his order. A libertie, which himselfe many yeares since so hartily desired, as he perswaded some Priests to write to his Generall, how greatly it concerned the common cause, and the good of our whole Nation, that he occupied himselfe in the affaires thereof, and liued abroade in the world, where the doing of most good should demaund his presence. Moreouer, by this oportunitie, and by hauing the Colledges vnder his owne gouernment, he inioyeth fittest meanes of picking out the finest wits of our Students, and furnishing his owne Societie with them. A seruice not vngratefull, and which increaseth his reputation with the Generall, and other chiefe persons of the Societie. In briefe, through these meanes also, and for that he presumeth to be able to do much (poore man that he is) in making our next King or successor to her Maiestie, he getteth acquaintance with men of State, Princes, and Kings, and entreth conference with them about the same. An affaire of no small contentation to the outward man (whom he is thought not as yet to haue fully cast off) and as potent and forward a help, as ordinarily any can be, of working his owne aduancement, and of gaining a scarlet cap. These, and other like respects are suspected to be the ends his trauels tend vnto, and the cause of such a suspition, seemeth doubtlesse to be strong. For if he sincerely intended the good of our Church, and the increase of learning, he would not haue dealt with one of the ancientest Priests of our Nation, about the dissoluing of the Colledge at *Reames*, nor would he haue suppressed the Lectures of the Colledge at *Doway*, whereby in short time, through the discontinuance of the studie, and practise of schole diuinitie, we shall haue no one of our secular Clergie fit to reade, or grounded in the facultie, but all esteeme and helps that way, must come from the Iesuites, a great honor to them, and dishonor to our Clergie. Further if Father *Parsons* affected to haue our Seminary Priests learned (a thing more requisite in the secular, then in the Religious) neither he, nor any other Iesuit-Rector of the Colledges, would send away the young Priests (if they resolued not to be Iesuites, or did not shew themselues zealous for them) before the finishing of their whole course. Neither would they vpon dislike, turne sufficient able wits for the studie of schole doctrine, to positiue diuinitie. In few words, if the credit of secular Priests, or the good of many were sought for, and not rather the drawing of all things to the Iesuites more speciall reputation and aduancement, how could Father *Parsons*, and some other English Iesuites, make a *Monipolium*, ingrossing all things into their owne hands, so much as no Priest in our country, can send ouer his friend (how perfectly soeuer he know him to be fit) to any of the Colledges, except the Iesuites be the meane and doers thereof, or one other, whome they most absolutely direct, or rather rule, as the maister doth the seruant? Vndoubtedly this was not the custome whiles good Doctor *Allen* was President, nor yet whiles he liued Cardinall: and if such policies, and seeking to sway all things (this latter being a demonstration of highest ambition) do long stand, or redound to the authors credit in the end, many are mistaken, who rather feare these sayings of holy scripture to be thereby the sooner exemplified: *Comprehendam sapientes in austutia eorum, & deposuit potentes de sede & exultauit humiles*: God will comprehend the wise in their owne wiles, and put downe the mightie from the seate, and exalt the humble.

1.Cor.3. Luke 1.

Fol.99.

In his Letter to me vndated, beginning, Sir, I admonish you to reflect, &c.

Vbi supra.

An other thing, which the Author of the Apollogie obiecteth against me in particular, and whereof our Archpriest also would make a hard prognostication, is *for that I had left the religious order of the Carthusians*. No doubt they carry a good will to discredit me, and the terme, scope, drift of the exception, do make it euident. Yea, some of their speciall fauorites (whome I can name) haue so earnestly labored to wound me for this cause in the conceits of my best friends, as they haue spared no perswasion to withdrawe their affection and good opinion from me. The Apollogie affirmeth, *that Maister Mush returning into England, and the Cardinall soone after dying, he ioyned with an other of his owne humor, that had left an other religion, namely the Carthugeans, and they two with some few other determined to make a new Hierarchie of their owne, calling it an association of Clergie men with two Superiours as it were Archbishops, the one for the South, and the other for the North.* The vntruths that abound in the Apollogy, are very many, equall to the number of the leaues, or perhaps of the pages, if not exceeding either. Amongst which rable, the passage recited, hudleth vp

foure

foure fayles in one. For neither did Maister *Mush* after his returne into *England* ioyne himselfe with me, neither did we two with some few others, determine to make the *Hierachie* mentioned, and lesse to make the same with two Superiours, and least of all, to make these two Superiours as it were Archbishops, the one, for the South, the other for the North. The falcitie of euery member of this quadrible auowance, appeareth manifest in this onely, for that I neuer saw Maister *Mush*, nor he me, nor had any conference each with other by letters, or messengers after his arriuall from *Rome*, vntill some fortnight before the comming ouer of his Holines Breue in confirmation of the Arch-priests Authoritie, more thẽ twelue months after the first institution thereof. So that, neither seeing Maister *Mush*, nor hauing any correspondẽce with him, nor he with me, during the whole time that the association was in speech, nor in many yeares before, how can it be sayd with any truth, that he ioyned with me, or that we two determined to ordaine a new *Hierarchie* with two Superiours, & these to be as Archbishops? Further, so many as euer heard me talke of the Sodalitie, or association intended, knew that none in *England* more misliked the making either of two Superiours, or of certaine other ordinances then my selfe, and therefore the error was very great in affirming that we ioyned in that, wherein we were most contrary. But to let these passe, and come to the maine point.

I confesse that I verily thought to haue bin a *Carthusian*, and was in probation with them full neere eleuen months: I acknowledge further, that I resolued on that state of life in the exercise vnder father *Cullume* the Iesuite then resident in *Louane*, when I was about some three or foure and twentie yeres old. But what, did I euer make a vow of religion, or was otherwise obliged by any law of God, or man, to continue that state? No, my vpbrayders, nor any other whosoeuer can say it. For what cause then do they lay this as a reproch vnto me? Was my conuersation misliked during my being with them, or was I put from them? I hope none will be so impudent as to auerre it, there being some liuing at this day, who can witnes that the Prior was hartily grieued for my departure. What then was the cause why I did not continue? I may alleage sicknes, for that I was long sick in the order, and so remayned after, till I was Priested, and returned to *England*. Likewise I may alleage a mightie oppression of sleepe, not remoueable by any meanes that could be wrought or thought on.

But neither of these impediments moued me to leaue the order. I could neuer learne to sing nor tune sixe notes, although I had during my stay with them, the change of sixe teachers, so little willing was the Prior and the Couaunt to leaue me. Father *Slade,* one that had bin of the Queenes Chappell, & taught the Countesse of *Oxford* to sing, was my last teacher, and who after long paines and tryall, deliuered my vnaptnes to the Prior in these tearmes, That he could teach a Cow to bellow in tune, as soone as me to sing in tune.

Further, my state of body, and vnaptnes to sing was such, that two of the Senior Monks of the house, aduised me to content my selfe with an other state of life, namely, to take Priesthood and go into *England:* Yea, Father *Cullume* who was priuy to all the motions that induced me to make choyse of the Carthusian life (which was chiefely my impediment of speech, for that I thought my selfe thereby fitter for a contemplatiue, then an actiue life) wrote me a Letter, perswading me (vnderstanding the difficulties I trauelled in, by relation of others, and not from my selfe) to come forth, and betake my selfe to some other state of life.

Now this being the truth, what cause hath father *Parsons,* or our Arch-priest to twite me with leauing the *Carthusians?* Verily if father *Parsons* were the setter downe of this exception against me in the Apologie, and that the same was not added to the copy by father *Garnet* or Maister *Blackwell* (the ouerseers of the worke, and vnto whome father *Parsons* gaue authoritie to adde, and detract what they thought good therein) I wish that he would remember the speeches which himselfe vsed to me in *Roane,* and thereupon correct his bad nature. For there, falling in talke with me after my banishmẽt, he told me, he vnderstood, that I had some motion of entring into Religion, a course which he thought not good for me, because he had learned how much I was inclined, and cumbred with melancholy, and therefore aduised me not to change my state of life. So that for him to except in so spitefull a manner against me, for not perseuering in that state of life, the like, which himselfe dehorted me from, and gaue his reason for the same, argueth both the want of good nature in him, and of honestie. But their anger being shewed, let vs see how Diuines, and the Canonists censure the case. Saint *Thomas (a)* writeth, *Melius est intrare religionem animo probandi, quam penitus non intrare,* It is better, or of more merite, to enter into religion, with a mind to make tryall

(a) 22 q. 189. art. 4. ad 1m.

tryall thereof, then not at all to enter. Which if it be true, as no approued author denyeth, then why doth Father *Parsons*, Maister *Blackwell*, and some other of their complices, impute my fact a fault vnto me, whẽ Saint *Thomas* (receiued of all men in the same) preferreth the doing before the omission, or the not doing thereof. If they reply, that they do not blame, or vpbrayde me for making tryall, and entring into religion, but for that I did not remayne still in it: I aske them, what they count my discontinuance? sinne, or no sinne: and if sinne, what sinne? Pope *Gregory* the eight defineth the question in this sort *(b) Statuimus nouitios in probatione positos ante professionem emissam, ad priorem statum redire posse libere infra annum:* We decree, that Nouices in their probation, before they be professed, may freely returne to their former state within the yeare. Freely, that is, as *Panormitan (c)* and *(d) Siluester* expound the word, *sine licentia petita ab aliquo,* without asking leaue of any one. And *Caietane (e)* writing of this point, sayth, *Annus probationis à iure conceditur cum libertate exeundi sine aliqua causa,* The yeare of probation is graunted by the lawe with freedome to goe forth without rendring of any cause. This, without all question, is most true in the exteriour court, and in face of the Church; but how doth the same hold in the tribunall of conscience, and before God? Saint *Thomas (f)* auerreth, *Quod ille qui religionem ingreditur si exeat ex rationabili causa, facit quod est licitum ei facere:* That he who entreth into religion, and goeth out againe vpon a reasonable cause, doth that is lawfull for him to do. And *Siluester (g)* writeth somewhat plainer in that case, *Qui solum proposuit perseuerare non vouendo, potest intra annum ad sæculum redire, de iure quo ad ecclesiam, & sine peccato quo ad Deum, si redeat ex iusta causa:* Who only proposeth to perseuere in religion without vowing it, may within the yeare lawfully returne to the world, as far as concerneth the Church, and without sinne before God, if he come forth vpon a iust cause. Nor is the act of such his comming forth scandalous, as both *(h)* Saint *Thomas* and *Caietane* testifie, and the later of the two teacheth further: *(i) Ingressus religionem si ex sola libertate retrocedat, venialiter tantum peccat.* He that entred into religion, making no vow thereof, and afterwards goeth out againe vpon no greater cause then for that he hath a will thereunto, sinneth no more then venially.

(b) *Ca. statuimus de regul.*

(c) *Ibidem nu. 2.*

(d) *Verbo. religio. 5. nu. 8.*

(e) *In 22. q. 189. art. 4.*

(f) *Vbi supra ad 2.*

(g) *Vbi supra.*

(h) *Vbi supra.*

(i) *Ibidem.*

Now it only remayneth to know what is a reasonable and iust cause, sith no Diuine but holdeth, that it is lawfull for any Nouice

during the time of his probation, to alter and discontinue his pur-
(k) *Vbi supra.* pose, of being religious, vpon a reasonable and iust cause. *(k)* Saint *Thomas, Caietane, Siluester*, and others, giue debilitie or weakenes of bodie for instance of a iust cause. Which if it be so, as I thinke my discreditors will not gainesay, then the same cause concurring, as it did in amplest manner, in respect I was not only some moneths sick in the order, but so continued a yeare and more after, and did not recouer, vntill I had bin some while in *England*. Yea it was misdoubted, least my disease, being an agew with a swelling, and voyding bloud at my mouth, would in short space haue ended my life, if I had continued fish dyet, as of necessitie remayning in the order, I must haue done. Neuerthelesse, neither this, or any other weakenes, or mightiest oppression of sleepe, was the chiefe cause, whereupon I left the order, but my vnaptnes, or truer, the impossibilitie, I trauelled in for euer, learning to sing, was that, which most of all discomforted me to tye my selfe, because being professed and Priested, I was bound by the rules of the religion, to sing Masse, when my weeke came by turnes, and lightly some verse alone, which I could neuer attaine to. This was the principall let, this the cause, which I tooke, and so did Cardinall *Allen* of good memorie, Doctor *Stapleton*, Father *Cullume*, with others, to be a most reasonable and iust cause, or rather an inforcing compulsion of leauing that holie and most religious order. The A-
Rom. 11. postle writeth, *Quis cognouit sensum Domini?* Who hath knowne the purpose of our Lord? I hope he inspired the motion whereupon I made the tryall, and I trust also it was not against his good pleasure nor ingratitude, or inconstancie in me (finding my selfe vnfit to proceede) to leaue the same, after tryall and experience made of my disabilitie. To conclude, whatsoeuer my vpbrayders are pleased to write or report of me, I would not for a million (looking vpon the inferiour and second causes of things) but that I had changed my purpose, considering that by my returne into *England*, my father, brothers and sisters became all Catholicks, which morally otherwise, was vnlikely, and most of them haue sithence indured imprisonment for the cause, and my father ended his life in Gloster ioale for the same. Againe since that time, which is now seauen and twentie yeares past or thereabouts, I haue felt that incombrance of melancholy, as God knoweth, what effect it would haue wrought in me if I had bin sequestred from companie, and liued a solitary contem-

platiue

platiue life: Whosoeuer therefore doth, or shall mislike me, for that I left the Carthusians order, I hope to beare his, or their aduersions with patience, if not with contentment.

Thus hauing yeelded the reasons of our delay, and answered all the obiections of moment that our aduersaries alleage, we surcease, submitting the whole to the censure of the Catholicke Church, and hartily desiring the Reader to informe himselfe of the truth without partialitie.

FINIS.

Faults escaped in the Printing.

Page 25. line 30. for attentiue, reade attentatiue. page 48. line 35. for we, reade well. page 82. in the margent, for 80. reade 70. page 64. in the margent to the cotation out of *S. Leo*, adde in *episto. decret.* 84. *ca.* 5. page 77. line 27. for one, reade our. pag. 108. line 14. for *Ireland*, reade *Scotland*. page 110. line 37. for take vigor, take that vigor. pag. 117. lin. 21. for ignorant inference, reade an ignorant inference. pag. 123. lin. 30. for their superiours, reade the superiours. pag. 149. lin. 27. for *Blackwell* our superiour, reade *Blackwell* to our superiour. pag. 160. lin. 9. for highly you esteeme, reade highly soeuer you esteeme. pag. 161. lin. 18. for which followeth, reade which follow. pag. 179. in the marginall note the tenth of Nouember, reade the 7. of March. page 184. lin. 5. for his reuenge, reade his reuerence. pag. 189. line 3. for other reade oath. page 204. line 34. for *peccata causa*, reade *peccati causa*. pag. 216. line 17. for this addressed, reade this addresse. pag. 218. lin. 38. for *cum suis*, reade *cuiusuis*. pag. 232. lin. 27. for his writings, reade his incitings. pag. 239. lin. 24. for yea, reade yet. pag. 249. in the marginall note, for this, reade their. pag. 256. lin. 17. for hath, reade haue. pag. 272. lin. 7. for asisistance, reade assistants. pag. 280. lin. 34. for composed, reade composer. pag. 293. *Harum literarum &c.* should be put after the latine Letter on the other page. 292. Of other faults, we desire to be his owne corrector, and to mend the ill pointing in some places.

JOHN SWEET

A Defence of the Appendix

1624

A Defence of the Appendix.

OR

A REPLY

TO CERTAINE AVTHORITIES alleaged in Anſwere to a Catalogue of Catholike Profeſſors, called, *An Appendix to the Antidote.*

VVHEREIN

Alſo the Booke fondly intituled, *The Fisher catched in his owne Net*, is cenſured. And the ſleights of *D. Featly*, and *D. VVhite* in ſhifting off the Catalogue of their owne Profeſſors, which they vndertooke to ſhew, are plainly diſcouered.

By L. D.

To the Rt. VVorshipfull Syr Humphry Lynde.

Eccleſ. 7. v. 30.

Solummodo hoc inueni, quod fecerit Deus hominem rectum; Et ipſe ſe infinitis miſcuerit quæstionibus.

Permiſſu Superiorum. M. DC. XXIIII.

TO THE RIGHT VVORSHIPFVLL Syr Humphry Lynde.

SYR. It may be you will take it vnkindly to ſee vnawares your ſelfe and your papers thus in print. But I was moued to doe it by due cõſideration of that which followeth. I receaued them not as ſecret, neyther do I thinke you gaue them to be concealed. You wrote againſt a printed Catalogue of Catholike Profeſſors, wherof a deare friend of mine is the Author, giuen you vpon a former Conference which your ſelf procured betweene ſome other of my Friends and your Doctors, concerning a Proteſtant Catalogue; which Conference though priuatly intẽded, was afterwards victoriouſly printed. Wherefore writing them as you did, againſt ſuch a

Booke, and vpon such an occasion, you might easily thinke they would be answered; and it is not strãge they should come to be printed. As the great opinion which others had of your deepe learning, and your owne profession of your great skill and reading in the Fathers, made me diligently to peruse those authorityes alleadged by you: so hauing well examined them, I thought my selfe diuers wayes obliged to giue a large & full Reply vnto them. And being as you are most extremely, and most vehemẽtly distant in opinion from me; no maruell, if to be better vnderstood, I speak so lowd that all the Land may heare me. And for the same cause you must pardon me, if I rather choose to expose both you & my selfe to the iudgment of others, then hauing takẽ some little paynes in this matter to make you the only iudge of my labours. The old *Maister Buggs* being carried away with *Ecce in Penetralibus*, thinketh to haue found the Messias in your study, and was wholy transported with those chosen places, and selected authorities contayned in your papers; which tending to no lesse then the losse of his soule, merited great compassion: the like may happen to others which deserueth preuention. Your owne Doctors haue already adorned the Pageant of their victory with the publication of your Names: Vnto you is giuen the driuing on of the Chariot: and the old *Maister Buggs* is led in Triumph. Some perchance haue been taken in the net of the Title, and may be freed againe by the net of Christ; which therefore should

ſhould not hange in the Riuers of priuate papers, when the other flyeth in the ayre, but ſhould be caſt into the Sea of the wide World, to gather and draw togeather all kind of fiſhes. In this net the Fiſhers themſelues are happily taken, and all they that are not taken, are loſt for euer. The other of the Heretikes is but a net to catch flyes, which though cũningly wrought, muſt in tyme be ſwept away togeather with the Spiders. They haue printed againſt vs, and renewed an old Decree againſt our printing: if no Reply ſhould be made, ſome of them would thinke, that now they might lye by Proclamation. What greater ſigne of falſhood, thẽ hauing told your owne tale to ſeeke to ſtop the mouthes of your Aduerſaries with old Statutes? But the State neuer intended to make a Law againſt God, his Word will not be tyed. All Princes ſhould ſerue it, and all printing Preſſes muſt be ſubiect vnto it. Therfore no maruell, if the taking of one Preſſe do ſet two more on worke, and that your Doctors by ſeeking to ſuppreſſe the Truth, do preſſe it forward. You know then what moued me to diuulge your papers. giuing the Fathers their due, I haue told you your owne, but ſparingly; and if you knew my hart, you would ſee, and confeſſe that I had done it friendly, *Belieue, and you ſhall vnderſtande*, Belieue the Fathers and you ſhall vnderſtand the Fathers, *He that heareth not the viſible vniuerſall Church, is no better then a Heathen*, and belieueth neyther Church nor Fathers: but the *vnlearned* not knowing the doctrine of the

Church, and the *vnstable* forsaking that which they haue knowne, as they *peruerte the Scriptures*, so also they preuert the Fathers *to their owne damnation*: from the which I beseech God deliuer you, praying you likewise to thinke no otherwise of me, then as of.

Your vnfaygned Friend, and seruant in Christ.

L. D.

THE

THE AVTHORITIES ALLEADGED BY *Syr Humphry Lynde*, agaynſt the *Appendix*.

Of Myracles.

EPIPHANIVS conuinceth not *Ebion* of falſe beliefe, becauſe neyther he nor any of his faction had the gift of working Miracles, but becauſe *Ebion* lykened himſelfe to Chriſt for his Circumciſion, and for his Birth: and he anſwers him, he could not be lyke to God, for that he was but a mortall Man, and was not able to rayſe *Lazarus* out of the graue, nor heale the ſicke &c. If he would be lykened to Chriſt, he bid him to doe thoſe things; the which things, if he had required at *Epiphanius* hands, I thinke noe man but would haue doubted of the performance of them ——————

—— *Read the place at large, and you ſhall find it hath no ſuch meaning, as is heere alleadged.*

Myracles were neceſſary before the world belieued, to induce it to belieue, and he that ſeeketh to be confirmed by wõders now, is to be wondred at moſt of all himſelf, in refuſing to belieue what all the world belieueth

lieueth besides himselfe. *De Ciuit. Dei, lib. 22. cap. 8. in principio.*

Shewed to be falsified.

Now we for our parts, say not, that we must be belieued, that we are in the Church of Christ, because *Optatus* or *Ambrose* hath commended this wherein we are, or els because that in all places of the world where our Communiō is frequēted, there are so many Myracles wrought of healing diseases &c. For all these things that are done in the Catholike Church, are approued in asmuch as they are done in the Catholike: *And not that it is therfore Catholike, because such things are done there. August. de vnitat. Eccles. cap. 16.*

Tertullian. They will say (sayth he) to excuse themselues for hauing followed Heresy: that their Doctours haue confirmed the Fayth of their Doctrine: that they haue raysed vp the dead, restored the sicke, foretould things to come, so as they were worthily taken for Apostles. As if (sayth he) this were not written, that many should come working great Myracles, to fortify the deceitfullnes of their corrupt preaching. *De Præscrip. cap. 44.*

S. Hierome. The Galathians had the gift of Healing, and of Prophesy, and yet they were insnared by the false Prophets; and it is to be obserued, that powers and signes are seene to be wrought in those that hold not the Truth of the Ghospell, which may be sayd agaynst the Heretikes, that think their Fayth is sufficiently proued if they haue wrought any Myracle, who in the day of Iudgment, shall deserue to heare this saying: *I know you not, depart from me. In Epist. ad Galat. cap. 3.*

S. *Augustine.* Let no man sell you fables. *Pontius* hath wrought a Myracle. *Donatus* hath prayed, and God hath answered him from Heauen. First, either they are deceaued, or so deceaue. *In Ioan. tract. 13. Et cont. Faustum Manichæum. lib. 13. cap. 5. Et de Ciuit. Dei, lib. 20. cap. 19.*

Answered, Sect. 5.

Of

Of Iustification by Fayth only.

THis is the worke of God, that he which belieueth in Christ, should be saued without workes, freely (by *Grace* only) receauing the pardon of his sinnes. *Amb. cap.1. in Corinth.*

What is the Law of Fayth? Euen to be saued by Grace. Heere the Apostle sheweth the goodnes of God, who not only saueth vs, but also iustifieth and glorifieth vs, vsing no workes heerunto, but requyring (*Fayth* only.) *Chrys. Hom. 7. Rom. 3.*

Basil. This is true and perfect reioycing in God, whẽ a man is not lifted vp with his owne righteousnes, but knoweth himselfe to be voyd of true righteousnes, and to be iustified by (*Fayth* only) in Christ. *Homil. de humil.*

Theodoret. We haue not belieued of our owne accord, but being called we came; and being come, he exacteth not purity & innocency of life at our hands, but by (*Faith* only) he forgaue our sinnes. *Coment. 2. Eph.*

Bernard. Whosoeuer is touched with his sinnes, and hungreth after rightneousnes: Let him belieue in God, that iustifieth sinners, and being iustified by (*Fayth* only) he shall haue peace with God. *Cant. Serm. 22.*

Answered, Sect. 6.

Of Free-will.

B*Ellarmine*. Man before all Grace, hath Free-will, not to things morall and naturall, but euen to the works of piety, and things supernaturall. *De Grat. & lib. Arbit. l. 6. cap. vltim.*

Basil. There is nothing left in thee O man, to be proud off, who must mortify all that is thy owne, and seeke for life to come in Christ, the first fruits wherof we haue already

already attayned in Christ; *owing all, euen that we liue, to the Grace and gift of God*. For it is God that giueth both the Will, and the Deed, according to his good pleasure. *Basil. conc. de humil.*

Bernard. To will, is in vs by Free-will, but not to performe nor will. I say, not to will eyther good or euill, but only to will; for, *To will good, is a gift of Grace*, to will euill, is a defect. Free-will maketh vs well-willing, from Free-will we haue power to will, but to will well cometh of grace. *De Grat. & lib. Arb.*

Augustine. It is certaine that we are willing when we are so, but it is he that maketh vs so, of whome it is sayd, It is God that worketh the will in vs: It is certayne that we worke when we doe so, but it is he that giueth vs this working power, by adding vnto our will, most effectuall strength, as if he sayd, I will make you work. *De bono perseuer. cap. 13.*

False cited, and shewed to be falsified.

Idem. Except God first make vs to be willing, and then worke with vs being willing, we shall neuer bring to passe any good worke. *De Grat. & lib. Arbit cap. 16.*

Idem. We must confesse, that we haue Free-will, both to good and euill, but in doing euill, euery man, iust and vniust is free, but in doing good, none can be free, in Will & Act, vnles he be freed by him that sayd; *If the Sonne free you, you are truely freed. De Corrept. & Gra. cap. 1.*

Augustine. We will, but it is God that worketh in vs to will; we worke, but it is God that worketh in vs to worke, according to his good pleasure. This is behooffull for vs both to belieue and speake. This is a true Doctrine, that our Confession may be humble and lowly, and that God may haue the whole: we liue more in safty, if we giue all vnto God, rather then if we commit our selues, partly to our selues, and partly to him. *August. de bono*

bono perseuer. lib. 3. cap. 6.

False cited.

Augustine. Farre be it from the Children of promise, that they should say: Behold, without thee we can prepare our owne harts; let none so thinke but those that are proud defenders of their owne Freewill, and forsakers of the Catholike Fayth: for as no man can begin any good without God, so no man can perfect good without God. *Contr. duas Epistol. Pelag. lib.* 2.

Augustine. Why doe we presume too much of the power of Nature? It is wounded, maimed, vexed, and lost: let vs confesse it freely, and not defend it falsely; therefore let vs seeke Gods Grace, not to forme, but to reforme it thereby. *De Natur. & Grat. cap. 35.*

False cited.

Non volentis, neq; currentis, sed miserentis est Dei, vt totum Deo detur, qui hominis voluntatem bonam & præparat adiuuandam, & adiuuat præparatam. August. Enchir. ad Laurent. cap. 32.

Answered, Sect. 7.

Of the Sacrament.

C*Yprian*. The Bread which our Lord gaue to his Disciples, not in Shape, but in Substance or Nature, changed by the Omnipotency, of the Word, is made Flesh.

1. The words of *Cyprian* are, *Panis non effigie, sed natura mutatus &c.* which you haue translated in Substance or Nature: where there is no word of Substance in *Cyprian*.

2. The Chapter of *Cœna Domini*, where this place is vrged, is none of *Cyprians*. *Extat inter opera Cypriani Sermo de Cœna Domini, qui Cypriani Episcopi Carthaginensis esse non videtur (inquit Bellarminus) lib. 2. Euchar. cap. 9. Author*

Sermonis de Cœna Domini, non est Cyprianus, sed aliquis posterior. Bellarm. lib. de Euchar. 4. cap. 26. Author Sermonis de Cœna Domini, est ignotus, inquit Garetius. De veritate Corporis Christi. fol. 181.

Cyprian. The Lord in his last Supper wherin he did participate with his Apostles, gaue Bread and Wine with his owne hands: but he gaue his Body to be crucified on the Crosse, to the hands of his souldiars &c. *Vt diuersa nomina vel species ad vnam reducerentur essentiam, & significantia & significata ijsdem vocabulis censerentur. De Vnctione Chrismatis.*

Shewed to be falsified.

Whereunto you adde, pag 47. in the Margent. *Tertullian; Hoc est corpus meum, hoc est figura corporis mei. cont. Marci. lib. 4. Aug. Christus figuram Corporis sui Discipulis commendauit. In Psal. 3. Ambros. de Sacram. lib. 4. cap. 5. Hier. ad verb. Iouin. lib. 2. Aug. in Leuit. quæst. 57. Gelasius cont. Eutichem. Aug. de Doctr. Christian. lib. 3. cap. 16.* It is a figure commaunding vs to lay vp in our Remembrance, that his Flesh was crucified and wounded for vs.

Answered Sect. 8. & sequent.

A·DEFENCE OF THE APPENDIX.

TO THE RIGHT Worshipfull Syr Humphry Lynde.

Section I.

The Fisher freed, and the Catcher catcht. In reference to the first point of the Appendix, *shewing the continuall Visibility of the Catholike Church.*

Our owne Doctors in your owne house professed, as you know, *The true Church must be able to name Professors in all Ages*; & made it the very groūd of their Argument, in that Dispute. Wherefore in all reason, before you went about to answere the Booke, which you receaued of the Catalogue of our Professors, you should haue giuen another, or referred vs to some booke of another of yours. And that so so much the more, because hitherto such a Catalogue on your side hath byn held impossible to be found, made, or produced. And hauing beene euermore demaunded and required for a hundred yeares togeather, could neuer as yet be seene nor obtayned.

Certainly, those your Champions which were chosen by your selfe, and with great expectation vndertooke to doe it, when they came to the Tryall, performed nothing; and all that they did, was but cunningly to auoyde the Question, giuen in these expresse termes.

Whether the Protestant Church was in all Ages visible, especially in the Ages before Luther; and whether the Names of such visible Protestants in all Ages can be shewed, and proued out of good Authors?

Wherein euery man may see, there was nothing els demaunded, but a playne Catalogue or Table, of the Names of your Professors in all Ages proued by good Authors. According wherunto, they receaued also another paper before the meeting, which there was publickly read, that ech partie should produce their Catalogues out of good Authors, and then interchangably by termes defend them. But this Table or Catalogue of the names of our Professors seemed a Lyon in the way of your Doctors, which therefore they durst not come neere nor behold, but sought by diuers straines to eschew it, and to turne the eyes and eares of the audience from their expectation of it.

As first they sought to make two Questions of the Question propounded; and flying the latter part, insteed of shewing the visibility of their Church, they would haue proued it *à Priori* (as they tearmed it) without shewing their visible Pastors, which was the poynt demaunded.

Secondly, they deride their Aduersaries, for demaunding the Names of their Professors, as if they had impertinently called *for a Buttry Booke,* of the Names of those, that

that euer were admitted into the Church of Christ; irregiously comparing the Histories of the Church wherein the Names of her Bishops, Martyrs, and other holy Men, were carefully recorded, to Buttry Bookes of Names. And for the same cause calling their Aduersaries *Nominalls*, they boasted themselues to be *Realls*; as if their Aduersaries had demaunded, no Men, but only Names of Men: or as if the Professors of the true Faith, like Knights Errants, or those of the round Table, had been no reall Men at all, but only names; which is asmuch to say, as that the Hystories of the Church were meere fables.

Thirdly, they sought to flinch by propounding sũdry tymes, diuers other Questions to be disputed. Which was, as it were, to put vp many Hares before the Hoũds, thereby to conceale the Kennell of that Fox which was then hunted.

Fourthly, they endeauoured to diuert the Question, from prouing themselues the true Church, by naming the visible Professors therof in all Ages, which was the thing demaunded; to proue the same by assuming they held the truth, that is to say, in euery particular Controuersie; as for Example, in denying of Transubstantiation, Merits of Works and the like. Which was as plaine a *Transition*, as if in case the Question had byn about Transubstantiation, their Aduersaries should haue gone about to proue it, by prouing themselues to be the true Church that held it. For both these kinde of proofes by a remote *Medium* do euidently transferre the Question; the one from a generall to a particular point, which was your Doctors fault: the other from a particuler to a generall, as in the other Example.

Fiftly, being called vpon by the Hearers, and especially by the Protestants themselues, which were ten to one, and confided much in their owne cause, to giue the Names of their Professors in all Ages; they named only Christ and his Apostles, with others, one or two

more

more of the first Age alone. Which according to the question vndertaken, they should haue proued to be Protestāts, by naming Protestants that succeeded them in all Ages following; but seeking euermore to auoyde that Rocke, they would haue stayed there, and before they went any further, vrged to proue the Professors of the first Age to be Protestants, not by naming their Successors, but by examining their Doctrine; Which againe had been to diuerte from the matter, and to runne from the generall point then in Question, to all particular Controuersies.

Sixtly; Therefore when none of these deuises could satisfy the expectation of the Hearers, fearing as it seemed, least, according to the words of the Question and playne intention of that meeting, they should haue byn vrged againe by the Hearers, to set downe a full Catalogue of all Ages, as once before they were importuned to doe, they suddenly brake off, and so departed.

Seauenthly; My L. *of Warwicke* imagining perchāce that this proceeded not so much from lacke of ability, as from want of due preparation, on their behalfe promised a Catalogue within 2. or 3. dayes, which though sought agayne by letter, neuer yet appeared.

Eightly; The Answerers themselues repayred the next day to your owne house, agayne offering to deliuer their Catalogue with one hand, so they might receaue yours with the other. Which another stāding by, whome they also tooke to be a Protestant Minister, affirmed to be very reasonable and indifferent. But you answered, You knew their minde for that point, and that they would neuer doe it, before the Names of the first Age were tryed, and so of the rest in order.

Ninthly; a printed Catalogue was sent to your selfe in particuler, hoping it might serue as an engine to importune, and as it were to extort another from you, or from your Doctours. But all in vayne, which maketh many

many much to feare, that this Catalogue of your Professors, will neuer be produced, and consequently that your Church, cannot possible be the true Church of Christ.

And now no maruell if some of the Hearers, when they saw the Booke of *The Fisher catched in his owne Net*, writen as it were in triumph of your victory in that Dispute, compared it to those other Puritan Bookes, which haue been lately printed of the great victories of the Protestants in their Warres against the Catholiks beyond the Seas: whereas in truth, not the Catholikes, but the Protestants themselues, haue beene alwayes notoriously vanquished and ouerthrowne. And presuming it came forth from his owne fingers that hath the principall part therin, they spare not to say, that it better deserued to be called, *The feates, and lyes of Doctor Feat-Lye*, then the other Title; which in falshood well agreeing with the Booke it selfe in that respect alone, might iustly seeme a fit lace or facing for it. For besides the sundry shifts and slights of the Doctors contayned in it, they accuse it also of many grosse vntruthes without end or number; in relating things out of due place and order, to their owne aduantage; in daubing and amplifying the speeches of D. *Featly* with much addition, and substraction of matter: As for Example.

1. That *M. Bugges*, the old Gentleman, who first desired the former Dispute, was sicke, and solicited in his sicknes by some Papists about him to forsake his Religion: And that it was feared he would haue fallen from his Fayth, if he had not recouered of his sicknes: which is altogeather false.

2. That he was much confirmed in his Religion, by hearing the former Disputation: which vnlesse he did extreamly forget himself (hauing often sayd the contrary) is also false.

3. That you *Syr Humfrey*, found *M. Fisher* by chance

in *Drurie Lane*; whereas you know, you came of purpose to offer him a friendly Conference with D. *White*.

4. That M. *Fisher* hauing written the Question, added vnder his owne hand, he would answere vpon it negatiuely, *As challenging and expecting Opposers*; which was false, for he was first asked by your self, whether he would oppose or answere: wherupon he wrote he would answere.

5. That you *Syr Humfrey*, tould *M. Buggs*, if M. *Fisher* would come with foure, or six at the most, they should be admitted for his sake, whereas it was expressely agreed on, that *D. White* and M. *Fisher*, should only bring an Assistant, foure Witnesses, and a Writer, and no more, with each of them, and that the matter should be kept secret, thereby to make the meeting very priuate. Which M. *Fisher* duly obserued, but when he came he found the house full of Protestants contrary to former agreement.

6. That *D. White* and *D. Featly*, being inuited by you to Dinner, and staying a while after Dinner, had notice giuen them (as it were by chance) that some Iesuits were in the next roome, ready to confer with them, and that the Doctors were at last perswaded to haue some Conference with them. As if forsooth they had neuer heard of the meeting before; when the truth is, that some daies before, *D. White* had receaued the Question, and vndertooke to oppose agaynst it, though afterward for more security he vsed *D. Featly* for his Champion, and both of them came thither of purpose, to make good the former challenge.

7. The Question was falsely and sophistically printed, by putting into the midst therof the figure of (2) in fauour of the Opposer, who sought to make it a dubble Question.

8. Before the Disputation began, *D. Featly* hauing propounded many other poynts of Controuersie to diuert the Question, That *M. Sweete* should answere they were

were scholasticall poynts not fundamentall. Which was not so; only he affirmed they were nothing to the purpose. Which he was moued the rather to say, because a little before he had desired two things of the Auditorie. 1. That all bitter speeches might be forborne. And 2. that nothing might be heard or spoken which was beside the Question.

9. That M. *Fisher* being charged to haue slaundred Doctor *White* in a former Conference, answered nothing: which is false, for he stood vp, and solemnely protested vpon his Conscience, that he neuer slaundred him.

10. And againe, that being charged to answere vpon his Conscience, whether he belieued Christ and his Apostles taught the Protestant faith, he refused to answere. Which is meerely false. It is true, that D. *Featly* before he began to dispute, coniured *M*. *Fisher* after an insolent manner, to answere according to his conscience, which *M*. *Fisher* accepted, and wished him to doe the like.

I omit many other such *Feates*, which the Hearers when they read, affirmed to be plaine *Lyes*, from whome soeuer they proceeded. If the Doctors according to their vndertaking, had giuen a sufficient and full Catalogue of their Professors in all Ages, *The Fisher had beene taken indeed in his owne Net*, and caught in the Question which himselfe propounded; but contrarily hauing taken more vpon them then they were able to performe, and not being able to set downe the Catalogue, which according to the issue of the Question was then expected, the Doctors themselues were manifestly taken in the Net of the Fisher. Wherein, by professing as they did, that, *The true Church must be able to Name Professors in all Ages*, they haue so intangled themselues, that howsoeuer they may dance in this Net to their owne shame and confusion, they can neuer get out, vntill they name them.

And now to come home againe to your selfe (endeauoring in the meane tyme as you doe to ouerthrow the succession of their Church, and not being able to shew another of yours) what do you get, or what do you seeke therby, but only the ruine and demolishment, both of your Church and theirs, leauing no true Church vpõ the earth, which cannot subsist without a visible succession of Professors to be named in all Ages, as you and your Doctors haue vrged? And by conseqnence, for wãt of such a visible Church, you leaue no true Fayth at all, nor true Religion in the world. *And who is a Naturall, but he that denyes it?*

Wherefore to conclude this Section, your Doctors with a great deale of noyse, hauing filled the aire with nothing but smoke. If now their Aduersaries should turne their owne Ordinance against them and reason thus, it is not your valor that would be able to defend them.

The Church that is Catholike as it ought to be, or the Church whose fayth is Eternall, or the Church of Christ and his Apostles, must be able to name Successors in all Ages. But the Protestant Church is not able to name the Professors of their Fayth, nor the Successors therein, to Christ and his Apostles in all Ages. Ergo, *the Protestant Church is not Catholike as it ought to be, nor the Church whose Fayth is eternall, nor the Church of Christ and his Apostles.* The *Maior* is their owne, and publickly produced by thẽ. The *Minor* cãnot be denyed vntill the Names be shewed. Wherefore vntill this Fort be built, how can you defẽd them, or where will you hide them from the power of this Gun-shot? And yet as this worke is plainly impossible to be raysed or performed, so it is no lesse impossible, that the Protestants should be found the true Church, & by Consequence, that any may be saued remayning in it.

Section II.

In reference to a second point of the Appendix, *shewing their Conuersions in all Ages.*

HAD you giuen vs such another Catalogue of your Professors, as you receaued of theirs, to make your party good agaynst thẽ, you should haue shewed the like Conuersions of Heathen Nations to the Fayth of Christ by your Ministers in all Ages; as that Booke hath shewed, by their Apostolicall Preachers. And that especially after those tymes wherin you pretend their Church was fallen, and the spirit of God was departed from them. As for Example, in the third Age were conuerted Donaldus King of Scotland, his Wife, Children, and Nobility. The Court of the Prince of Arabia, pag. 20. In the fourth Age, the Bessites, Dacians, Getes, and Scythians, pag. 26. In the fifth Age, the Sarazens, the Scots, the Irish, pag. 32. In the sixt Age, the Pictes, the Gothes, the Bauarians, the English, pag. 36. 38. In the seauenth Age, diuers Sweuians, the Westphalians, and many of our Nation, People of Teisterbandia, of Westphalia, of Holland, the King and Queene of Persia, with forty thousand Percians, pag. 42. 44. In the eight Age, Saxons, Borucluatians, the Frisians, the Hassits, the Thuringians, the Catti, the Erphordians, two Saxon Dukes, pag. 48. In the ninth Age, the Danes, Swethens, and people of Aquitania, the whole Iland of the Rugians, the Bulgarians, the Ruthens, or Russians, pag. 52. 54. In the tenth Age, Worziuous the last Pagan Duke in Bohemia, the King of Norway, the Polonians, the Sclauonians, and Hungarians, Heraldus King of the Danes, and Sueno his Sonne, pag. 60. In the eleuenth Age, the Prussians, the Vindians, also Pannonians and Transiluanians, the lapsed

sed Hũgarians, pag. 64. 66. In the twelfe Age, the Pomeranians, the people of Norway, Magnus King of the Gothes, pag. 70. 72. In the thirteenth Age, the Liuonians, the Lituanians, innumerable Tartarians, pag. 76. 78. In the fourtenth Age, the Canary Ilandes, the Chumans, the Lipnensians, Bosnians, Patrinians, and other Sclauonian Nations, pag. 84. In the fifteenth Age, Samogessians, the Kingdomes of Bentomine, Guinæa, Angola, and Congo, Zerra Iacob Emperour of the Abissyns, pag. 90. In the sixteenth Age, the Kingdome of Manicongo in Africa, the Kings of Amanguntium and Bungo, innumerable Indians, Iaponians, Brasilians, and other Westerne and Orientall people, more Countries and Kingdomes then all Christendome before. In the seauēteenth Age, the King of Sarra Leæna in the East Indies, with his Brethren and Children, besides many other in China, Iaponia, Persia, and other Nations.

This Argument taken from the *great increase of fruit which continueth, and abideth among them*, *Ioan. 15. 16.* and from the wonderfull propagation of their Religion, not only in the first fiue hundred yeares after Christ, but also much more in the Ages following to this present tyme; is surely a most forcible and strong perswasion, that they alone among all other sortes of Christians, are the company, and people whome God had blessed. Haue Idolaters been chosen and preserued by Almighty God, before his owne Seruants, to perswade in the force of his word innumerable people from tyme to tyme, to renoūce and tread vnder their feete the Auncient Gods of their Forefathers, in whome they so much confided; and to receaue him for their true and only God, who whipped and crowned with thornes, was nayled to a Crosse in the sight of the world, and so dyed? Haue all these seuerall Countries and Kingdomes, so extremely different in clymats, in tongues, in affections, in customes, and in natures beene voluntarily reduced to the vnity of one and the and the same Fayth in Christ, and to the obedience of one Pastor vnder Christ, by the followers of Antichrist? Haue the limmes of the Diuell reformed the sauage, brutish, and wicked manners of so many People and Nations, changing their hartes, and bringing them vpõ their knees, to serue their Creator, with piety and humility, and in exercise of all kind of vertue?

Then I must needes confesse, it seemeth vnto me, that eyther God himselfe must be in loue with Idolatry, or Christ himselfe must become Antichrist, or the Diuell himselfe hauing forsaken his malice, is now changed to be a seruant of Christ. Neyther do I see how possibly you can deny these innumerable Nations to haue beene conuerted by the true Church, recommended vnto vs in holy Scripture, vnlesse we deny both Church and Scripture. For by these Conuersions of Nations in all Ages, your Aduersaries doe manifestly proue themselues to be that Church which must in the end conuert all Nations, and was therefore surnamed Catholike or Vniuersall. And thereby it cannot be denyed they make it most apparent (the promises thereof in the Law, *Gen.* 22. 17. *Gal.* 3. In the *Psalmes*, 2. & 71. 6 & 21. & 28. In the Prophets, *Isa.* 2. 2 & 11. & 60. & 61. & 62. *Hier.* 33. *Ezech.* 33. 22. *Dan.* 2. 44. &c. In the old and new Testament, *Matth.* 24. 14. & 28. 19. *Luc.* 24. 47. being so euidently performed by thẽ) that they alone are the spirituall seede of Abraham, *Rom.* 4. 13. *Gal.* 3. The inheritance of the Sonne of God, *Psalm.* 2. & 47. The Mountaine on the toppe of Mountaines, *Isa.* 60. 12. The Mountaine filling the world, *Dan.* 2. 44. The glorious Citty, *Psal.* 86. whose gates must be alwayes open, that the strength of the Gentiles & their Kings may be brought vnto it: and the Nation and Kingdome, that will not serue it, must perish, *Isa* 60. 11. 12. That blessed Company *Isa.* 61. 9. whome our Sauiour promised to assist all dayes, or euery day, teaching and baptizing all Nations vnto the end of the

the world. *Matth.* 28. & 24. Heere againe (as in the end the former Section) if they should argue Syllogistically against your Doctors in this manner, though you had the strength of Hercules, I think you would hardly be able to defend them. *That Church which conuerted Nations in all Ages, is the true Church of Christ and his Apostles, recommended vnto vs, in holy Scripture. But the Catholike, and not the Protestant Church, hath conuerted Nations in all Ages.* Ergo, *the Catholike, and not the Protestant Church, is the true Church of Christ and his Apostles, recommended vnto vs in holy Scripture.*

Section III.

In reference to a third point of the Appendix, *shewing their Religion to haue byn confirmed by Myracles in all Ages.*

HAd you giuen vs a view of so many Nations reduced to the Faith of Christ by your Professors as he hath named conuerted by theirs, that your Church might not appeare altogeather inferior to theirs, you should haue shewed some points of your Religion confirmed by Myracles against them, as that Booke hath declared many points of theirs in all Ages, miraculously authorized, and as it were subscribed by the hand of God against you; & those so euidently testified not only by Auncient Histories, but also by the holy Fathers themselues, not liable to any exception, in the first fiue hundred yeares & downewards, as they seeme to enforce all good Christians to belieue them.

As for Example, in the second Age, *Narcissus* Bishop of Hierusalem, turned water into Oyle for the vse of the Church, *Eusebius lib. 6. Cap. 8. & 9 S. Balbina* and her Father restored to health by touching the Chaynes wher-

with

with Pope *Alexander* was bound, *Baron. An.* 132. *n.* 2. Cures wrought by the Bodies and Sepulchers of Martyrs. *Iustin. quaest.* 28.

In the third Age, the Myracles of *S. Gregorie* the wonder-worker, & some of thē wrought by the signe of the Crosse, *Nissen. in vita Greg. Thau.* And S. *Basil. de Sp. Sanct. cap.* 29. Also Myracles confirming the *Eucharist, & Reall Presence. Cyp. ser. de Lapsis.* Also S. *Cecily* shewed to *Valerian* the Angell Guardian of her virginitie. *Metaphrastes* and *Surius* in her life.

In the fourth Age, a sicke Woman cured, and a dead Bodie restored to life, by the wood of the Holy Crosse, whē it was first found out by Queene *Helen. Ruffin. Hist. lib.* 10. *Cap.* 7. *&* 8. *& Seuer. Sulpit. Hist. sacra lib.* 2. *Paul. Epist.* 11. *Niceph. lib.* 8. The same myraculously multiplyed to satisfy the deuotiō of all Christiās throughout the world. *Paul. Ep.* 11. *Cyr. catech.* 10. Many other Myracles wrought by Reliques, *Chrys. orat. cont. Gentes.* By holy-Water, *Epiph. haer.* 30. By adoration of the Blessed Sacrament, *Naz. orat.* 11. By prayers to our Lady, *Nazianz. in S. Cyp.* By the merites of Martyrs. *Ambros. serm* 91.

In the fifth Age, many Myracles wrought by Reliques of S. *Stephen, Aug lib.* 22. *de Ciuit. cap.* 8. By the signe of the Crosse, *Constantinus lib.* 1. *cap.* 22. *apud Surium, Tomo* 4. by *S. German.* Also Myracles wrought by *S. Hierome*, lying on his death bed, and after his decease, the blinde, deafe, dumbe, and sicke were cured: some by touching, some by kissing his Corpes, *Eusebius Cremon. Ep. de morte eius.*

In the sixt Age, Myracles wrought to confirme the Sacrifice of the Masse, *S. Greg. l.* 4. *Dial. cap.* 57. and Reall Presence, *Euag. lib.* 4. *Hist. cap.* 35. *Ioan. Diac. lib.* 2. *de vita S. Greg. cap.* 41. To confirme the honour and inuocation of Saynts, *Procop orat. de Edificat. Iustin. Euag. loco cit. Greg. de Myrac. S. Martini l.* 2. *cap.* 5. 6. 7. The vse of Images in Processions, and how by one of our Blessed Ladyes, painted by S. *Luke*, a contagious Pestilence was dispelled in Rome, *Ciac. in Greg. 1.* From another Image stabbed by a Iew, issued bloud, *Greg. Turon. de glor. Mart. cap. 22. Sigeb. ann. 560.* Holy Oyle flowed from a Crosse, and from an Image of our Blessed Lady, curing many diseases. *Baron. ann. 564.* Thus the Author of the Catalogue you receaued; And the like Myracles he sheweth in the rest of the succeeding Ages. As many more he might haue added aswell in the first fiue hundred yeares as after, but that he thought it not necessary, and therefore spared the labour to recollect them.

Which myraculous attestations, we must eyther belieue, and by consequence must also confesse those poynts of Religion confirmed by them, or els we shall not only condemne all Christian Antiquity of lying, and belieuing of lyes, but must lykewise reiect all euidence of credibility founded vpon human testimony; which is no lesse then to destroy the very foundatiōs both of Church, and Common-wealth, and all Society. Wherefore to binde this Burden also on your backe, that it may sit the closser, I will winde it vp in this manner. *That Church whose Doctrine hath beene confirmed by Myracles in all Ages, is the true Church of Christ and his Apostles. But such is the Doctrine of the Catholike, and not of the Protestant Church.* Ergo, *the Catholike, and not the Protestant Church, is the true Church of Christ and his Apostles.*

Section

Section IIII.

In reference to a fourth poynt of the Appendix, shewing the Doctrine of the Protestants to haue beene censured, and condemned by the Fathers in all Ages.

HAd you likewise confirmed your Doctrine by such diuine Authority, you should haue shewed some one point of their Religion censured by any of the Fathers, or condemned by any lawfull Counsell, as that Booke quoteth aboue twenty of yours notoriously opposed and condemned by them.

As for Example; Iustification by Fayth only, and Deniall of Iustice by Workes; condemned in Symon Magus, *Iren. lib.* 1. *cap.* 20. Extrinsecall Iustice by imputatiō only; in the Gnostickes, *Iren. lib.* 1. *cap.* 5. That no sinne can hurt them that are indewed with Fayth; in Eunomius, *Epiph. hær.* 76. *Aug. hær.* 64. That sinne abideth in the regenerate; condemned in Proclus, *Epiph. hær.* 64. That Baptisme doth not washe away sinne; condemned in the Messalians, *Theod lib.* 4. *hær. fab.* Neglect of the ceremonies of Baptisme; condemned in Nouatus, *Euseb. lib.* 6. Of holy Chrisme and the seale of our Lord (which is the signe of the Crosse so called) condemned in Nouatus and his Disciples, *Theod. lib.* 3. *hær. fab.* Derisions of Exorcismes, and Exufflations in Baptisme; condemned in the Pelagians, *August. de Nat. & concupis. lib.* 2. *cap.* 29. The Absolution of Priests not auaileable, and the abolishment of Confession; condemned in Nouatus and his Disciples, *Socrat. lib.* 4. *cap.* 23. *Cornel. apud Euseb. lib.* 6. *cap.* 43. *Theod. lib.* 3. *hær. fab. Pacian. lib. aduers. eos.* Denyall of inioyned Pennance; in the Audians, *Theod. l.* 4. *hær. fab.*

Denyall of the Reall Presence; condemned in Iudas Iscariot, *Claud. Xanct. Rep. 2. de Eucha. cap.14. Chrys. hom. 46. in Ioan. 6.* In the Simonians and Saturnians, *Theod. Dial. 3.* condemned likewyse by *Iren. l. 4. cap. 34. post medium.* Impugning the reseruation of the B. Sacrament; condemned in the Anthropomorphites, *Cyr. ad Calosyr.* Denyall of Oblations, and Prayers for the Dead; condemned in Aerius, *Aug. hær. 53. Epiph. hær. 65.* Denyall of Freewill; condemned in Symon Magus, *Clem. Roman. Recog. lib. 3.* In the Manichees, *Aug. lib. cont. Fortunat. Manic.* Ordination and Predestination to sinne, and by consequence, that God is the Author of sinne; condemned in the Predestinate, *Sigeb.415, Geneb. in Zosimo.* condemned likewise in Symon Magus, *Vin. Lirin. adu. prop. hæret. nouitat. cap 34.* And in Florinus, *Euseb. lib. 5. cap. 20.* That Saynts are not to be inuocated; condemned in Vigilantius, *Hier. cont. Vigil. cap. 2. & 3.* The Images of Christ and his Saynts not to be worshipped; condemned in Xenaias; *Niceph. lib. 16. cap. 27.* Worship of Saints Reliques to be Idolatry; condemned in Eustachius, *Socrat. l. 2 cap. 33.* and condemned likewise in Vigilantius, *Hier.* 161.

Impugnation of single life, and vowed Chastity, and that Marriage is equall to Virginity; condemned in Heluidius, and Iouinian, *Hier. cont. Heluid. & Iouin.* Disallowance of prescript Fasts; condemned in Aerius, *Epip. hær. 75. August. hær. 53.* and in Eustachius, *Socrat. lib. 2. cap. 33.* Noe difference of Merits in Heauen; condemned in Iouinian, *Hier. lib. 2. aduers. Iouin.* Good vse of Riches, preferred before Euangelicall Pouerty; condemned in Vigilantius. *S. Thom. opusc. 17.*

Denyall of one Chiefe Pastor in Earth; condemned in Nouatus, *Euseb. lib. 6. cap. 43.* Denyall of vnwritten Traditions; condemned in the Valentinians, *Tertul. lib. de Præsc. & hist. Eccles. lib. 5. cap. 16. lib. 3. cap. 36.* That the visible Catholike Church, might remaine in one parte, and perish in the rest of the world; condemned in the Donatists, *Aug. cont. lit. Petil. l. 2. cap. 108. & lib. de Vnitat. Eccles. cap. 2. & per totum librum.*

Thus the Author of the Catalogue; whereunto if I should adde out of the Protestât Apology page 74. and page 127. and pag. 207. how insolently and impiously the most and best learned Protestant-writers doe likewise censure, and condemne the Fathers of the first fiue hundred yeares, I know you would be ashamed to reade them. But this may suffice, to giue the Reader iust occasion to admire the little conscience of your late English Doctors, in challenging the Fathers of the first fiue hundred yeares, wherein if their Aduersaries might come to an indifferent and equall tryall with them, the very *Titles* of the Fathers Books against them, were sufficient to ouerthrow them. Only in this place I will giue the Reader this short *Notandum*: for the which if he desire sincerely to know and belieue the Doctrine of the Fathers, he shall haue cause to thanke me. When any of the holy Fathers, do censure any poynt of Doctrine, taxing it of Heresy, or noteth it as the particuler opinion of some Heretike, or reproueth it very much, or wondreth at it, especially if it be such a thing as euery learned Man may easily know, or was necessary to be taught, and that no other Father did therein oppose himself against him; It is an euident Testimony, that his Doctrine therein was the generall Doctrine of the Church at that tyme; and ought to be so receaued of the Ages that follow. Wherefore the Author of that Booke, hauing shewed so many poynts of your Doctrine to haue beene so notoriously cēsured and condemned by the Auncient Fathers of the first fiue hundred yeares in the Hetetikes of those tymes, besides many other poynts and some of those also condemned by Fathers and Councells in after Ages (whereunto you haue not answered a word) it is for ought I can see, or perceaue, a cleare demonstration, that the Fathers of those tymes were theirs, and that, eyther your Professors were none at all, or no other then those, that were condemned by them.

Thus, all things with them are infallibly certaine, easie to be knowne, and most conspicuous. They follow the streame and current of that Doctrine, which, by many knowne Successions of holy and learned Men, Martyres, and Bishops, as it were by so many Channells, they deriue from Christ and his Apostles. They follow the fame and greatnes of that Church, which by conuerting Countries and Nations in all Ages, is become eminent and apparent aboue all other sortes of Christians, like a *Citty vpon a Hill*, aboue the Moale-hills; or like the *Little Stone in Daniel*, which growing to be a Mountaine, filleth the world with it's greatnes. They follow the security of those Letters-Patents which the hand of God hath signed with his owne Seale, and cōmended to the world, by Attestation of many Myracles in confirmation of their Doctrine. And lastly they follow the infallible and powerfull Authority of that Body, which by Cēsures of Doctors, & Decrees of Coū-cells from tyme to tyme hath euer confounded all those that opposed themselues against it; While you in the meane tyme, without any lineall Descente from those whome you preteud to haue beene your Auncestors; without the Progenie of any Gentills conuerted by you; without any warrant of Gods hand, or sentence of his Iudges for you, do still remayne in the darcknes of your inuisible Church, tossed in the Sea of Error, *with euery winde of new Doctrine*, not knowing certainly whome to follow, nor what to belieue, vntill at the last, euen the wisest of you being wearie of seeking, and desperate of finding that which they seeke, come to hold all opinions probable, which is in effect to belieue nothing.

Good Syr, had you produced such a Successiō, such cōuersions of Nations, such Myracles and Censures, in the defence

defence of your Church, as that Booke hath shewed in confirmation of theirs, all zealous Protestants had been bound to haue fallen at your feete, and to haue honoured you for euer. But now, on the other side, against such weighty and massie matters, such cleare and conuincing proofes as these, not being able to giue in euidence so much as one Professor in euery Age, nor in any Age the conuersion of any Nation, or the testimony of any Myracle, or the Censure of any one Father in fauour of your Religion; who seeth not, that insteed of reason there is nothing but passion on your part; and certainly for the honour of your cause, it were better to hold your peace, then reply so weakely in a matter of such importance.

For besides all that hath beene sayd against many other most expresse Sentences of the Auncient Fathers, in those very poynts which you haue chosen to touch; you haue only produced a few dribling Authorities, as it were on the Bye, some falsely translated, and some falsely cited, and some in respect of other expresse words agaynst you, plainely falsified; that, not to accuse you of a bad Conscience, though you make profession to be much versed in the Fathers, yet the Reader must needes think, you neuer saw, or read so much as those few places which your selfe haue cited, but only tooke them by retaile frō others. And howsoeuer, though they were admitted and taken as you giue them vp; yet in my poore opinion, they eyther touch not your Aduersaries at all, or being a little considered, make rather with them, then against them. Which sheweth great want of iudgment in you: and I verily thinke, if you will be pleased to examine them with me, I shall make you see it. Wherefore as in the former Section, soe that you may know in this also, how far you are chargable, I giue you the summe of your accompt in this manner. *The Doctrine of that Church which was condemned by the Fathers of of the first fiue hundred yeares, was condemned by Christ and his Apostles. But the Doctrine of the Protestant Church, was condemned by the Fathers of the first 500. yeares, as the most and best learned Protestants themselues haue also confessed. Ergo, the Doctrine of the Protestant Church, was likewise coudemned by Christ and his Apostles.*

Section V.

Myracles defended to be a sufficient Testimony of Truth, and the Doctrine of the Fathers therein declared.

WHerefore to begin, as you doe, with Myracles, most certaine it is, that no true Myracle can be wrought, but only by him, *Qui facit mirabilia magna solus*; and therefore whēsoeuer any true Myracle is shewed, or sufficiently testified vnto vs, in confirmation of any point of Doctrine; it is an euideut proofe of the truth thereof. For a Myracle in that case, is the Testimony of God, who speaketh by workes, as men by wordes (sayth S. *Aug. Epist.* 49. *quæst.* 6.) and is the subscription (as it were) of his hand and seale vnto it. And certainly if Myracles were no sufficiēt proofes of true Doctrine, they would neuer haue beene called, *Signes and Testimonyes in holy Scripture*. God would not haue giuen Moyses power of working Myracles, *Exod. 4. That the People of Israel might belieue he had appeared vnto him*. Our Sauiour would not haue sayd, the Iewes had not sinned in not receauing him, *If he had not done those workes which no man els had done before him. Ioan. 15.* And in vayne should he haue promised, that *Signes should follow those that belieued*, and haue *cooperated* and *confirmed* the Doctrine of the Apostles by them. Neyther could he in Iustice

stice haue commaunded the world vpon paine of damnation, to belieue a thing so incredible, as that Christ being Crucified, was risen againe in his owne flesh, and ascended into Heauen, if many other Myracles which the Apostles wrought in confirmation therof, had not made it euidently credible, as S. *Austen* disputeth in his booke *de Ciuit. Dei lib.* 22. *cap.* 7. and in the former *Epist.* 49. *quæst.* 6. albeit he well obserued, that this kind of proofe was euer lowdly and extremely laught at, by the wicked Pagans: yet most true it is, which there he also affirmeth, that we should not belieue, Christ to be risen againe frõ the Dead, if the Fayth of Christians did feare in this point of Myracles, the laughter of Pagans.

Wherefore to answere those places of the Fathers which you obiect, not only agaynst so many of their owne Testimonies alleaged by your Aduersary, but also against Scripture, and against Christian beliefe it selfe, grounded vpon Myracles as hath beene noted; you must further vnderstand, that the world hauing beene once perswaded by myraculous operations and workes of wõder to belieue the Doctrine of the Apostles with this firme promise, that it should alwayes remaine with them and their Successors, the visible Pastors of the Catholike Church, vniuersally spread ouer all the world; it ought not to belieue any other Doctrine, or any other Myracles pretended to be done in opposition to that Doctrine which by continuall Tradition hath beene receaued frõ them. For as there can be no after-word of God, contrary to that which was first preached; soe there can be no latter Myracles contrary to the testimony of those, by which the world first belieued; but rather as S. *Paul* saith, If an Angell from Heauen should preach otherwise then we haue receaued, we should hold him accursed. This made *Tertullian* in the Booke you cite *de Præsc. cap.* 44. to protest against all Myracles supposed to be done against the Tradition of the Church; whereof S. *Augustine* in his

Booke *de vnit. Eccles.* obiected by you, giueth the reason yet more plainly, shewing that the Catholike amplitude or vniuersality of the Church, by conuersions of Nations in all Ages, doth more euidently proue it to be the true Church of Christ, then any other worke which is done therein; for it is more manifest to sense and human reason, that the cleare Prophesies of the true Church in holy Scripture are fullfilled and accomplished only in the Catholike Church, which accordingly in all Ages doth visibly spread it selfe ouer all the world, then it can possibly appeare, that any worke of admiration is truly a Myracle surpassing the force of Nature, or power of the Diuell; whereof it followeth, that the true Church is more manifestly knowne by the accomplishment of those promises, then by the wondrous effects of any Myracles; and that Myracles doe not soe well, and cleerly proue any Church to be Catholike, as the Church being visibly Catholike, doth manifest those Myracles to be true, which are approued by it.

Whereof it followeth againe, that all Myracles which are done against it, or agaynst the vnity thereof, are as firmely and constantly to be reiected. Which is it that he also teacheth, *lib. 13. cont. Faust. cap. 5.* and *Tract. 13. in Ioan.* and *lib. 22. de Ciuitat. Dei, cap. 8.* obiected by you. And heere by the way I beseech you to note, how much Saint *Austen* esteemeth the former Argument of the conuersions of Nations in all Ages, according to the promises therof in holy Scripture, which he maketh such an euident marke, and such an infallible proofe of the true Church, that he preferreth it before Myracles. And for the same cause, *lib. 22. de Ciuit. Dei, cap. 8.* he spareth not to say: *That he who seeketh to be confirmed by Wonders now, is himselfe to be wondred at, in refusing to belieue, that which all the world* (or the visible Church through the world) *belieueth.* Which your selfe also hauing obserued, you may wõder at your self, both in refusing to belieue, what you know the visible Catholike Church, for a thousand yeares, through the world, belieued, and (wherin I also wonder my selfe) at your not obseruing, that S. *Augustine* doth wonder at you in that very place, wherein you suppose he agreed with you, as by and by I shall make it appeare.

Adde in the meane tyme to that which hath beene sayd, that the Myracles whereunto the holy Fathers, alleadged by you, forbid vs to giue credit, as vnto Arguments not sufficient to proue the Truth of Religiō, were eyther Myracles in apparence only, and such wherewith Heretikes *might easily be deceaued, or so deceaue*, as S. *Augustine* speaketh in the former place vpon *Ioan*: not such as might reasonably induce any prudēt man to belieue thē. As Dreames, and Visions, and exauditions of Prayers, like vnto those of the Donatists, against whome wrote *Saint Augustine lib. de Vnit. Eccl. cap*. 16. Or such as were Testimonies of the Iustice and mercy of God in generall, and not of Doctrine in particuler, as were those whereof S. *Hierome* speaketh: Or finally such as being wrought by wicked men, exceeded not the power of the Diuell, as S. *Augustine* obserueth, *lib*. 20. *de Ciuit. Dei cap*. 19. *& Tract*. 13. *in Ioan*. Or were not sufficiently testified, but rather sayd then proued, which *Tertullian lib. de Præscr.* derideth and sayth, that the power of Heretiks was nothing like, but rather contrary, to the power of the Apostles; for their vertue was not to rayse the Dead, but rather to kill the liuing, literally fullfilled in Caluin, *Bolsec. in vita Caluini*, who pretending by his prayer to rayse a counterfaite dead man, being then truly aliue, was thought to be the cause, that he was instantly slaine, eyther by God, or the Diuell. In the same sense also *Epiph. lib. 1. de hær. cap*. 30. vrgeth *Ebion*, to rayse some dead man &c. assuring himselfe that he could not doe any true Myracle, *by meanes of his false Faith, yea though he called vpon the name of*

 Christ.

Christ. Not so the Myracles alleaged by your Aduersary, which hauing beene wrought and belieued, and most authentically testified by soe many most holy, most prudent, and learned Witnesses, in confirmation of that Doctrine which is professed against you, need no more to feare the laughter of Protestants, thē the Myracles of former tymes, as *S. Austen* saith, had cause to feare the laughter of Pagans. And such as belieue them not, may iustly feare to be condemned as Pagans, for belieuing nothing. To deny therefore this Doctrine of Myracles, seemeth noe lesse impious, then to deny Christianity it selfe: and to affirme that myracles haue ceased sithence the tyme of the Apostles, were noe lesse vnreasonable, then to reiect all humane Testimonies, and in particuler the Authority of *S. Augustine* himsefe, in those very places obiected by you.

For in that very place of *S. Aug. de Ciuit. Dei, lib. 22. cap. 8.* which you alleage against Myracles, *That they were necessary before the world belieued, to induce it to belieue*: And, *That he that seeketh to be confirmed by wonders now, is himselfe to be wondred at, in refusing to belieue that which all the world* (or the visible Catholike Church through the world) *belieueth*: which being well considered, maketh little for you. In that very place (I say) you could not choose but read these other words directly against you; *That now also Myracles are wrought in his Name, eyther by his Sacraments, or by the prayers, and memories of his Saints*; togeather with the relation of many Myracles done in his owne tyme, and of those in particuler wrought by the Reliques of S. *Stephen*, which though not necessary after the World had once belieued, as *S. Austen* there disputeth; yet God in his mercy hath euer shewed them in all Ages, as well to confound the obstinate that would not belieue the visible vniuersall Church, as also to confirme those in their Fayth, that already belieued. In this place there-

therefore you haue plainely falsified the sense of the Author, eyther very fraudulently, or very ignorantly, choose you whether.

Section VI.

Merits of VVorkes defended, according to the Doctrine of the Fathers: and Syr Humphry answered.

IN the next place against the Merit of Workes, you obiect many places of the Fathers, but none to the purpose. You know full well, that the Catholikes distinguish betweene works that goe before Faith, & workes that follow. Workes going before Faith, and proceeding only from the light of Nature, or from the knowledge of the law of Moyses (called therefore by S. *Paul Rom. 3. The workes of the Law*) your Aduersaries doe all hold, neyther to saue, nor to be needfull to saluatio; according whereunto S. *Paule* also saith; *That a Man is iustified by Faith, without the workes of the Law*. But that workes following a liuely Faith, formed with Charity, and proceeding from it, doe iustifie, and are needfull to saluation, your Aduersary proueth not only by expresse Scripture, *Iames cap. 2. Yee see then how that of workes a man is iustified, and not of Faith only:* But also by the lyke Testimonies of all the holy Fathers, noting and condemning the contrary opinion of the Protestants as hereticall, in Symon Magus, in the Gnostickes, and in *Eunomius*, as hath beene shewed. And further he alleadgeth S. *Aug. de fide & oper. cap. 14.* testifiyng of the Apostles themselues, that because this opinion of Faith only, sprung vp in those dayes, by peruerting the words of S. *Paules Epistle* before related, the *Epistles* of *S. Peter, S. Iohn,*

S. Iames, and *S. Iude*, were principally written, *vt vehementer astruant*, vehemently to vrge, and contest that Fayth without workes doth profit nothing. Agaynst all which manifest proofes, you bring only some Authorityes of the Fathers, shewing that *our owne workes and righteousnes* (as *Basil. hom. de Humil.*) *or workes of the Law*, going before Fayth (as S. *Chrysos.* with S. *Paul. Hom.* 7. *in* 3. *ad Rom.*) and before Sinne pardoned (as S. *Ambrose*) and forgiuen (as *Theodoret comment.* 2. S. *Bernard in Cant. Ser.* 22.) doe not iustifie, but *only Fayth* without them; which is nothing to the purpose because therein your Aduersary agreeth with you. But you bring not a word to proue that workes following Faith doe not iustify, nor are needfull to Saluation; which opinion of yours, your Aduersary hath shewed to haue beene often tymes condemned by the Apostles themselues, & by the Auncient Fathers in other Heretikes that haue gone before you.

Section VII.

Free-will defended: and Syr Humphry answered.

IN the Controuersy of Free-will, you seeme first to suppose your Aduersaries belieue, that Man hath Free-will to performe supernaturall actes and workes of Pietie without Grace, and then you proceed to dispute against them. How can you imagine, they are so absurd as to thinke by the power of Nature alone to doe that which they thēseues confesse to be aboue the power of Nature, wherin there appeareth not only a great deale of passion in you, (which hanges lyke to a Cloud betweene the Eye of your minde, and the light of truth) but also (as it seemeth) great want of conscience.

For

For you know they hold, that without grace, it is impossible eyther to belieue, or to do any other acte which may auayle, or so much as dispose to Saluation. This also you know to be the Doctrine of *Bellarmine* euery where in that whole Booke, out of which you seeme to cite his words in a contrary sense: and the words that immediatly follow in the very place you cite, do plainely shew, that against your Cōscience you falsify his meaning. His words are these: *A Man before all grace hath Free-will, not only to naturall and morall workes, but also to workes of piety and supernaturall*, as you faythfully cite them: but then it followeth, *Thus S. Augustine teacheth, l. de Spiritu & litera, cap.* 33. where he sayth; *That Free-will is a naturall and middle power, which may be inclined to fayth, and infidelity*. Thus Bellarmine; whereby it is manifest his meaning to be, that by Grace, Free-will is not made, or giuen vnto vs, but that we haue the power thereof by Nature, which afterward by Grace is inclyned and strengthned to doe those things which by the force of Nature, without Grace, we are not able so much, as to will, or to thinke, much lesse to performe or perfect; according whereunto, in the same place, he citeth also *S. August. de Praedest. Sanctorum, cap.* 5. teaching, that the *Posse, or power to haue Fayth and Charity, is in man by Nature.* And in the same Booke, *cap.* 11. he alleageth *S. Augustine* againe *Epist.* 49. *quaest.* 2. to the same purpose, saying: *Free-will is not taken away, because it is holpen* (by Grace;) *but because it is holpen, therefore it is not taken away*. If it be giuen by Nature, and not taken away by Grace, most certaine it is, that still we haue it. In this sense therefore, your Aduersaries not only affirming, that we haue Freewill by Nature, but also teaching that it is so excited and strengthned by Grace, as we cannot so much as thinke, much lesse accomplish or performe any supernaturall acte without it; they would easily graunt with *S. Basil, con. de Hum.* that we owe all, euen that we liue, *to the Grace and gift of God*; but that you falsely translate it.

They

They graunt with *S. Bernard de Gratia & lib. Arbit. That to will Good, is a gift of Grace.* And with S. *Augustine. That it is God, who maketh that we worke, by adding to our will most efficacious strength. That vnlesse he make vs willing, and then worke with vs, we shall neuer bring to passe any good worke.* And againe with S. *Augustine de correp. & grat. cap.* 1. *That though we haue Free-will to doe good, yet none can be free in will and acte to do it, that is to say, perfectly, or in actu secundo,* as the Scholmen speake, *vnlesse he be freed by the grace of God.* And againe: *That all is to be giuen to God, not the first part vnto our selues, & the rest vnto God,* as the Pelagians did, against whome S. *Augustine* disputeth, but all vnto God, and vnto our selues nothing that is not of God. And againe, *That without God we cannot prepare our owne harts.* And againe, *That Gods grace doth not forme, but reforme our* Nature, by giuing it the grace wherewith it was first formed. And finally, *Ench. ad Laurent. cap. 32. That of his mercy he prepareth our will to be holpen, and helpeth it being prepared.* Whereby (condemning your Aduersaries as you doe, and yet eyther not knowing what they hold, or maliciously mistaking their meaning) you may see at the last, that with a great deale of labour, for want of a little learning, if not for want of Charity, you haue rather confirmed, then censured their Doctrine.

But now that we haue no Free-will to any act at all, in such manner, as it lyeth not in our power to doe it, or not to doe it; and that all things are done necessarily, though willingly, because all things are done by the ineuitable decree of God, being the point you should haue proued; none of the Fathers you alleadge, eyther thought or sayd, but haue condemned it for Heresie and Error in Simon Magus, and in the Manichees: yea, and because it followeth from hence, that God is the Author of sinne, euen for more then Heresie, in Florinus, *vt refert Euseb. l. 5. cap.* 20. Heere againe I must friendly admonish you, that negligently or ignorantly being deceaued by others, you haue falsely quoted S. *Augustine de grat. & lib. Arbit. c.* 16. *Except God first make vs willing &c.* And againe, *de Nat. & Grat. cap.* 35. *Why doe we presume so much &c.* which wordes with the rest that follow, are not to be found in those place : neyther if they were, would they make any thing for you, as your selfe will iudge by that which hath beene sayd. And againe you alleage *S. Augustine lib.* 13. *de bono perseuer. cap.* 6. there being but one single Booke of that Argument, and in that Chapter, those wordes are not found which you haue there alleaged. You cite him also, *cont. duas Epist. Pelag. lib.* 2. which second Booke hauing 10. Chapters, you quote no Chapter. Will your Reader impute so many imperfect and false quotations only to the error of your pen, and not rather to your ignorance, or want of due perusall?

But how will you defend your selfe, in alleaging these other words out of *S. Austen: It is certaine that we worke, whē we do so, but it is he that giueth vs this working power, by adding vnto our will, most effectuall strength*; as if he had sayd, *I will make you worke*. Whereby you will make your Reader belieue, that according vnto *S. Austen* we haue no power of Free-will by Nature, but that God giueth it, by adding his Grace; which is not so: for *S. Austen* doth not say, It is he that giueth vs this working power, by adding strength to our will as you alleage, but that, *He maketh vs to worke, by adding strength to our will* (or which is all one) *to the power of our will*; which therfore proueth, that we haue power of will by Nature, though not sufficiētly able to do any supernaturall act, before he adde the strength of his Grace vnto it. Againe you finde not in S. *Augustine* these other words of yours: *as if he sayd, I will make you worke*; but they are by you fraudulētly foisted in, to cut off, & cōceale the words that follow. For wheras Pelagius, to proue that we are able by Nature without Grace to keepe the Commaundements obiected out of *Ecclesiasticus: Si volueris, seruabis mandata*, if thou wilt, thou shalt keep the Commaundements: *S. Augustine* answereth, he knew as well as Pelagius, that they that will, shallbe able to keepe them, yet not by Nature as he would haue it, but by Grace, holding it for certaine, that we are able to keepe them, but so as that God is he who worketh in vs both to will and to performe them. The words of S. *Augustine* are these that follow: *It is certaine, that we will when we worke, but it is he that maketh vs to will, of whome it is sayd; It is God that worketh in vs to will; It is certaine that we worke when we worke, but he maketh that we may be able to worke, giuing most efficacious strength vnto our will, who sayd; I will make them walke in my Iustifications, and to keepe my Iudgments, and to doe them.* Which last wordes you partly changed, and partly omitted, to conceale the Doctrine of *S. Augustine*, and his proofes out of Scripture, shewing that by Grace we are able to keepe the Cõmaundemẽts, which the Protestants haue euer held impossible. Lastly as if you meant not to be discouered, you cite the former words out of his Booke *De bono perseuer. lib. 13. cap. 6.* which are only to be found in *De Grat. & lib. Arbit. cap. 16.* Let this be ignorance in you, which in another were plaine forgery.

Section VIII.

S. *Cyprian falsly alleaged by Syr Humphry, against the Reall Presence.*

FInally concerning the B. Sacraments, you only taxe one Authority cited by your Aduersary out of S. *Cyprian* in his Sermõ *Of the supper of our Lord*, and alleadge another against it out of the same Author, in his Sermon *Of the Vnction of Chrisme*, which Chrisme (as it is there recorded) was vsually made at that tyme vpon holy Thursday of Oyle and Balsamum (as now also it is accustomed) for the vse of the Church in Baptisme, and

other

other Sacraments: So hard it is for one of you to alleage any thing out of the Fathers, which one way or other doth not make against you. The words alleaged by your Aduersary are these: *The Bread which our Lord gaue to his Disciples, being changed not in shape, but in Nature, by the omnipotency of the Word, is made flesh.* A place so playne for Transubstantiation, or change of substance in the Sacrament, that when I read it, it makes me blush at the bouldnes of those Diuines who dare to auouch that Trāsubstantiatiō was neuer known before the Councell of Lateran. Now in this sentence, (*forgetting the beame in your owne eye*) *you seeke a mote in the eye of your Brother*, accusing him, because to be vnderstood, he translated the word which signifieth Nature, to signify Substance, or Nature. If you were as good a Philosopher, as you pretend to be a great Diuine, you could not be ignorant that these three wordes, *Nature*, *Substance*, and *Essence*, are all equiualente, signifying the same thing in diuers considerations; that which is called *Nature* in order to motion, is called *Substance* in relation to the Accidents, and *Essence* in reference to the definition of it. And I pray you Syr, there being nothing in Bread but shape and substance, he who sayth, *That Bread being changed, not in shape, but in Nature, by the omnipotency of the Word, is made Flesh*, what doth he affirme, but that it is changed in substance?

Secondly, you accuse him for alleaging those words out of *Cyprian*, which Bellarmine himselfe *lib. 2. de Euch. cap. 9.* holdeth to be none of *Cyprians*; Wherein you must giue me leaue to tell you, that your selfe much more deserue to be accused. For first, albeit Bellarmine doth say, he thinketh that Sermon *de Cœna Domini*, not to be *S. Cyprians*, yet he addeth immediatly in the same place, that it is, *The Sermon of some auncient, most holy, and most learned Man, as the Aduersaries* (meaning Protestants) *do confesse*; which words (that you might with more shew eleuate, and auoyd the former Authority) were fraudulently concealed by you. *It is the worke of some learned Man of that Age*, sayth *Erasmus* in his annotations vpon the workes of *S. Cyprian*. *In tyme not much inferior to Cyprian*, sayth *Fulke*, *in* 1. *Corinth. cap.* 11. Wherefore doe we reuerence the Authority of *S. Cyprian*, but because he was an Auncient, holy, and learned Father? If therefore the Author of this Sermon, was a most holy and learned Man, as Bellarmine sayth the Protestants themselues confesse, and of the same Age with *S. Cyprian*, or in tyme not much inferior vnto him, as I haue shewed that the Protestants themselues doe likewise witnesse, why should any Protestant reiect him?

Besides, though Bellarmine thinketh this Sermon to be none of *Cyprians*, yet many other *Deuines of great name Cypriano tribuunt, doe iudge it to be the worke of S. Cyprian, as well for the likenesse of the stile, as for the dignity of the matter*, sayth *Gaulortius* a learned Protestant in his annotations thereupon. Why then may not your Aduersarie follow heerein, the iudgment of many other great Deuines? In fine, your Aduersary may alleage for himselfe in this matter, the testimony of *S. Augustine cont Donat. lib.* 4. *cap* 22. his words are these: *From that Theefe to whome, not being baptized, it was sayd; This day thou shalt be with me in Paradise*; the same *S. Cyprian tooke no sleight document, that paßion* (or death, or Martyrdome) *doth sometyme supply the place of Baptisme*. According whereunto both in sense and words in the same Sermon *de Cœna Domini*, it is sayd (and therefore according to *S. Augustine*, by *S. Cyprian*) *That our Lord &c. deferred not his benefit, but with the same speedy Indulgence he gaue presently aswell a document, as also an example thereof, saying vnto the Theefe; This day thou shalt be with me in Paradise. He had his condemnation and punishment for robery, but his contritiō of hart changed his payne into Martyrdome, and his bloud into Baptisme*. Why now may not your Aduersary cite that Sermon as Saint *Cyprians*, which Saint *Augustine* himselfe so long a goe alleadged vnder the name of *Cyprian*?

First, therefore heerein you deserue both blame and shame,

shame, insimulating your Aduersary of fraud for misalleaging *S. Cyprian* by the testimony of Bellarmine, and fraudulently cōcealing those words of Bellarmine in the same place; which euen the testimonyes of Protestants themselues do shew the words alleaged by your Aduersary out of *Cyprian*, to be of no lesse Authority, then the words of *Cyprian*.

Secondly, you deserue the more blame heerein, because you alleage agaynst it another place out of S. *Cypriā*, which according to the opiniō of Bellarmine in the same place, in the same Chapter, is none of *Cyprians*. And plaine it is, that the Sermon of *the Supper of our Lord*, alleaged by your Aduersary, and the other of *Chrisme* alleadged by your selfe, are both the Sermons of the same Author; for the whole Booke contayning 12. Sermons, is intituled, *Of the Cardinall workes of Christ*, and dedicated to Pope *Cornelius* the Martyr, who liued in the tyme of *Cyprian*: And therefore he that denyeth the one, hath no reason to affirme the other to be the worke of *Cyprian*. How then out of the same mouth could you breath both hoat and cold? And how out of the same Bellarmine could you proue the Sermon alleadged by your Aduersary to be none of *Cyprians*, and affirme agaynst Bellarmine the other alleaged by your selfe, to be the worke of *Cyprian*?

Thirdly, the like foule fraude cōmitted by you appeareth yet more grossely in the words which you cite out of the same Author, who when you take him to be with you, is *Cyprian*, but not *Cyprian* when he speaketh against you. The words of the Author are these: *Our Lord therefore at that Table wherein he made his last Feast to his Apostles, with his owne hands, gaue Bread and Wine: but at the Crosse he gaue his Body to be wounded by the hands of his Enemies; that sincere verity, and true sincerity (being more secretly imprinted in the Apostles) might expound to* Nations, *how the Wine and the Bread was Flesh and Blood: and after what manner the causes agreed with their effects: That diuers shapes might be brought to one*

Essence, and the things signifying, and the things signified, might be called (and knowne) by the same names. Thus S. *Cyprian*. But not thus Syr Hũphry, for hauing alleaged the words which seemed to make for him, *he gaue Bread and Wine to his Apostles, but his Body to his Enemies*, he chopt off with an &c. the words following, *That sincere verity, and true sincerity, (being more secretly imprinted in the Apostles) might expound to Nations, how the Wine and Bread was flesh and Blood*: which as euery man may see, are expressely against him, and serue to expound the meaning of the Author in the rest of that Sentence; which though otherwise beeing a little obscure, yet being a little considered, may be thus explained. Our Lord sayd to his Apostles, *This is my bodie, which shall be giuen for you*, when at the table he gaue to them visibly Bread and Wine, but at the Crosse he visibly gaue his owne Body; that his Apostles thereby might visibly see, he had giuen them inuisibly his owne Body; because he gaue them the same Body into their owne hands, which was giuen for them, into the hands of their Enemies. 1. *That the sincere verity, and true sincerity heereof, being thus secretly imprinted in the harts of the Apostles, they might confidently expound to all Nations, how the Bread and Wine of that table, was truly and sincerely Flesh and Blood*. 2. *How the causes agreed with their effects, & the words of our Sauiour, which were the causes going before, agreed with their effects, both at the Table, and at the Crosse, that followed after*. 3. *How vnder diuers shapes of Bread and Wine at the Table, was contained but one & the same Essence, because the same shapes remayning, the Natures of Bread and Wine, by the omnipotency of the Word, were changed, or reduced into the Nature of his Body*; as before you haue heard out of his former sermon. 4. *How the thinges signifying (which were the shapes of Bread and Wine remayning) and the things signified (which were the Body and Blood of our Sauiour) came both to be called by the same names, because the one did signify, exhibit, and containe the other*. By all which it appeareth (the Author hauing his right brought backe againe, and his owne

owne breath being restored againe vnto him, which you had thought to steale and smother) that he plainely confesseth the Bread and Wine to be Flesh and Blood, and that the Nature of the one being changed into the Nature of the other, they are both reduced into one Essence; which is the same Doctrine, that your Aduersary professeth, and maintayneth against you.

Your Aduersaries affirme, the Bread to be made a Sacrament and the Body of Christ, by the words of Consecration, for the which cause they not only adore it before they receaue it, but also they haue euer held, that it might be lawfully giuen to Infants, and that which remaines thereof they are wonte to reserue to be giuen afterward to the sicke, or to others that come to receaue, as occasiõ requireth. You Protestãts affirme on the other side, that it becõmeth a Sacrament, and a Seale of the Body of Christ vnto you, without any change in the thing, by the liuely Faith of the Receauers, and consequently you giue it not to Infants, because they cannot receaue it with that Faith which makes it a Sacrament: and that also which remaineth thereof, after the whole Action, you take to be no better then common Bread, and soe you vse it. As custome is the best interpreter of the law, so the practise of the Church is the best interpreter of her owne Doctrine. Wherefore to know what S. *Cypriã* with the Church of God in the secõd Age after Christ belieued at that tyme, concerning this point of the B. Sacrament, there can be no surer way, then to examine what is practized in communicating the same to Infants, and in reseruing of it, to be taken as need required. Which S. *Cyprian* in his sermon *De Lapsis,* his owne vndoubted worke, hath not obscurely recorded: for he relateth (*Teste meipso*) *& sacrificantibus nobis; my selfe being witnes, and we our selues offering sacrifice*, that an Infant hauing beene fedde with a sopp of wine before an Idoll, and being afterward brought to Church, was much tormented during the

the tyme of the Sacrifice, and when it's turne came to receaue, it resisted so vehemently, that the Deacon was faine perforce to open it's mouth, *and to power in somewhat of the Sacrament that was in the Chalice*; but (sayth *S. Cypriā*) *The drinke sanctified into the Bloud of Christ, brake out of her polluted bowels &c.* In which Sermon he likewise testifieth: *That a certaine Woman when she would with vnworthy hands haue opened her coffer, wherein was reserued the Holy Thing of our Lord, there sprung vp fire from thence, wherewith she was so terrified, that she durst not touch it.* And, *That another defiled Person presuming to receaue with others, could not eate, nor touch the Holy Thing of God, for in his opened hands (insteed thereof) he found Ashes. By Document whereof* (sayth *S. Cyprian*) *it is shewed, that the Lord doth depart when he is denyed.* By which Documents of reseruing the *Eucharist*, and giuing it to Infants, they (who will not be obstinate) may also learne out of *S. Cyprian*, that the *Eucharist* after the words of Consecration, was belieued to be really the Body of Christ, and not figuratiuely by Fayth only, to him that doth worthily so receaue it. Wherefore to conclude this Dispute, concerning the Testimony of *S. Cyprian* for Transubstantiation, and Reall Presence, as it was false that your Doctors claymed him in the former Conferēce, so being plaine agaynst them in this point, besides many other of no lesse importance, it was fondly done of you, to say they claymed him.

Section

Section IX.

S. Augustine falsly alleadged by Syr Humphry, against the Reall Presence.

FYnally against the Reall Presence you obiect other places of the Fathers, affirming the Sacrament to be a figure of Christs body, which your Aduersaries deny not. For they define all Sacramēts to be signes and figures, according whereunto they also holde, that as the Sacrament of the *Eucharist* is a figure, in respect of the Shape or externall accidents therof, so it is the Body of Christ, in respect of the thing contained in them.

But now that the *Eucharist* is only a figure, or that it is not the Body of Christ, which you should haue proued against them, or els you proue nothing, none of the places alleaged by you do shew; neyther is it possible in all the Fathers to find so much as one place, that doth sufficiently proue it. While they in the meane tyme (besides many most expresse Scriptures, *Matt.26. Marc.* 14. *Luc.22. Ioan.6. 1. Cor. 11.* confuting also your principall obiection, that the Body of Christ cannot be in two places, *Act. 9.5. 22. 8.23. 11. 1. Cor. 15. 8.*) They, I say, on the other side produce so many superabūdant Authorities from the Fathers & Councells in all Ages, conuincing the holy *Eucharist* to be the Body of Christ, that I must needs say, they haue discouered more bouldnes (if not impudency) thē learning or conscience, who eyther in bookes or in Pulpits haue pretended to shew, that the Fathers in this point are plainely against them. To make this appeare, it may suffice at this tyme, briefely to set down the beliefe only of those Fathers in particuler, which your selfe in your papers haue produced for you, *Tertullian*, S. *Austen*, S. *Ambrose*, S. *Hierome* and *Gelasius*, shewing, how

 euident.

euidently they teach the cōtrary Doctrine aswell in their writing elswhere, as in those very places which your selfe haue cited. First therefore let vs begin with *Saint Augustine*; who in his Workes making often mention of the Sacrament, giueth vs these particulers of his Doctrine
,, therein; That before the words of Consecration, that which was offered is called Bread; but after the words
,, of Christ haue beene pronounced, now it is not called
,, Bread, but it is called the Body, *Serm. 28. de verb. Domini.* That if Children had neuer seene the likenes of those
,, thinges, but only when it is offered, and giuen in the
,, Celebration of the Sacrament, and that it should be tould vnto them with most graue Authority whose
,, Body and Bloud it is, they would belieue nothing els,
,, but that our Lord had neuer appeared to the eyes of
,, Men, saue only in that likenes, *lib. 3 de Trin. cap. 10.* That Childrē were wont to receaue it, *apud Bedā, in 1. Cor. 10.*
,, Who haue not the mouth of Faith to receaue it. That
,, it pleased the Holy Ghost, & was vniuersally obserued that our Lords body enter into the mouth of a Christiā
,, before other meates, in the honor of so great a Sacra-
,, ment, *Epist. 118. cap. 6.* which must needes be meant of the mouth of the Body. *That we receaue with our hart and*
,, *mouth the Mediator of God and Man Iesus Christ, Man giuing*
,, *vs his Flesh to be eaten, and his Bloud to be drunke, although it*
,, *seeme more horrible to eate Mans flesh, then to kill it, and to drinke Mans bloud then to spill it, lib. 2. cont. Aduersar. legis*
,, *& Prophet. That we doe not eate dead flesh dilaniated, and cut*
,, *in peeces, as the Capharnaites vnderstood it*; for this indeed were horible, and would profit nothing; but we eate
,, the flesh of Christ, as it is liuing flesh, *vegetated with his*
,, *Spirit*, which is Christ himselfe entirely as he is now in Heauen, *Tract. 27. in Ioan. & 63* That no man eateth
,, that Flesh, before he adore it, *in Psalm. 93.* That the
,, rich men of this World cōming to the Table of Christ,
,, do receaue his Body and Bloud, which though they

adore,

„ adore, yet are not filled with it, because they doe not imitate it, eating him that is poore, but contemning „ pouerty, *Epist. 120. ad Honoratum*. That the Apostles „ did eate the Bread which was their Lord, *Panem Dominum*; though Iudas did eate but the Bread of our Lord, „ *Panem Domini, Tract 59. in Ioan.* For our Sauiour was not truly his Lord, because Iudas was not truly his seruant; And if at the day of Iudgement he should say, *Domine, Domine*, our Lord would answere, I know thee not.

Protestants may well say with Iudas, that they eate the Bread of our Lord, if our Lord did ordaine it to be a figure of his Body, but they cannot say with the Apostles, that they eate the Bread which is their Lord, because they deny it to be their Lords Body. That Iudas Iscariot „ receaued *That* (sayth he) *which the faythfull know, the price* „ *of our Redemption, Epist. 162. ad Glor.* That our Sauiour did literally beare himselfe in his owne hands whē „ he gaue it, *Conc. 1. in Psalm. 33.* That Bishops and Pres„ biters in the Church of Christ, are properly Priests, „ *de Ciuit Dei, lib. 20. cap. 10.* Which doth infer, that properly also there are Priests and Sacrifices, & that Chri„ stian Priests doe properly offer Sacrifice vpon *Altars*. „ Wherefore making often mention of MASSE, *Serm. 91. de Tempore, & Serm. 251.* he sayth likewise, that our „ Sauiour changed the Sacrifice according to the order „ of *Aaron*, and did institute a Sacrifice of his owne Body and Bloud, according to the order of Melchisedech, *in* „ *Psalm. 32. & in Psalm. 39. & lib. 17. de Ciuit, Dei, cap. 20.* „ That he prayed God, to giue him contrition & a fou„ taine of teares, when he assisted at the holy Altar, to offer that marueilous & heauenly Sacrifice, which Christ „ the immaculate Priest did institute and commaund to „ be offered, *in Manuali*. That a Priest of his offered the Sacrifice of the Body of Christ in a house infested with „ wicked spirits, which was thereby freed, *lib. 22. de Ciu.* „ *Dei, cap. 8.* That he desired all Priests (whome he cal-

„ led his Bretheren, and his Maisters) who should read
„ his Booke of Confessions, to remember his Mother at
„ the *Altar*, where she also desired to be remembred after
„ her death, *lib 9. Confess. cap. 13.* That it is not to be doub-
„ ted, the dead are holpen thereby, because the vniuer-
„ sall Church receauing it from the Fathers, obserued
„ that it should be offered for those, who departed this life
„ in the communion of Christs Body, *Serm. 32. de verbis*
„ *Apostoli.* He reckoneth it amongst the Heresies of *Aerius,*
„ that he denyed Oblations and Prayers for the Dead,
Hær. 53. Could any Catholike at this day, or Bellarmine himselfe if he were now aliue, more fully declare his owne Doctrine in this point of the *Reall Presence*, and of the Sacrifice of the Masse, then doth *S. Augustine* against you? though in other things you may retaine some difficulties, yet in this me thinkes you should freely acknowledge, that you are wholy conuinced.

Finally, vpon *Leuiticus, quæst.* 57. in the very place which your selfe haue cited, where there is nothing that may sound for you, but only that the figure is sometymes sayd to be the thing figured, (which as I take, it is only in
„ those cases, where it is knowne and presupposed to be
„ a figure) he demaundeth why the people should be so
„ much forbidden from the Bloud of the Sacrifice of the
„ old Law, when as none were forbidden to take for
„ their nourishment, the Bloud of this one Sacrifice,
„ which was signified by all the former; but all that de-
„ sired life, were rather exhorted to drinke it.

Now therefore heereupon, might not your Aduersaries deeply charge you, that you had egregiously abused *S. Augustine*, and plainely peruerted his meaning?

Section

Section X.

S. Ambrose falsly alleaged by Syr Humphry, against the Reall Presence.

LEt vs now come to S. *Ambrose*, who conuerted S. *Augustine*, that we may see how the Maister & the Scholler agree togeather; he maketh mentiō of the MASSE, and that himselfe sayd MASSE, *Epist. ad Sororem Marcellinam*. He repeateth a great part of the *Canon* of the MASSE, which is now vsed: *We offer vnto thee this immaculate Host; this reasonable Host; this vnbloody Host; this holy Bread, and Cup of life euerlasting &c. And we pray thee to receaue this Oblation as thou didst vouchsafe to receaue the gifts of thy seruant Abel the iust, and the Sacrifice of our great Father Abraham, and that which the high Priest Melchisedech did offer vnto thee, lib. 4. de Sacramentis, cap. 6.* He sayth: *We daily adore the Flesh of Christ in the Mysteries* (that is to say, in the MASSE, or Sacrifice) *lib. 3. de Spirit. Sanct. cap. 12.* He maketh his prayer vnto that Bread, *to heale his infirmity, to come into his hart, to clense both his flesh and his spirit from all that defileth*, in his prayer preparatory before *Maße*. And in his Booke *De Mysterijs init. cap. 9.* he obiecteth in this manner; *Perchance thou wilt say, I see another thing, how dost thou affirme vnto me, that I receaue the Body of Christ?* Whereunto he answereth: *How many Examples haue we to proue it, not to be that which Nature hath formed, but that which Benediction hath consecrated: And that Benediction is of greater power then Nature, because by it, euen Nature it selfe, is changed?* And then declaring many Myracles wrought by *Moyses, Helias,* and *Helizæus*, he concludeth: *If human benediction were able to change Nature, what shall we say of Diuine Consecration? If the speach of Helias was able to bring Fyre from the Heauens; Shall not the speach of Christ be able to change the formes of the Elements?*

If the word of Christ were able to make of nothing that which was not, can it not change the things that are, into that which they were not? For it is no lesse matter to giue new Natures vnto things, then to change their Natures. And a little after he sayth: *It is manifest that a Virgin brought forth agaynst the ordinary course of Nature, and the Body which we* (Priests DOE MAKE) *is of the Virgin: What dost thou require the order of Nature* (to be obserued) *in the Body of Christ, who was borne of a Virgin against the order of Nature?* Could the Doctrine of Transubstantiation, or change of Nature in the Sacrament, be more auouched, or better proued by any moderne Papist? Who likewise *lib. 6. de Sacram. cap. 1.* thinketh it no blasphemy to say, as he doth, *That as our Lord Iesus Christ is the true Sone of God, not as man by grace* (or by Fayth) *but as the Sonne of the substance of his Father; so* (as he himselfe hath sayd) *it is true Flesh which we receaue;* That is to say, not by grace, or by Fayth only, but in Truth, and in Substance.

Finally in the place which you cite for your selfe, *lib. 4. cap. 5. de Sacram.* (where there is nothing to be found in your fauour) he hath these expresse words. *Therefore before Consecration, it is Bread; but after the words of Christ come to it, it is the Body of Christ. And before the words of Christ, it is a Cup full of Wine and Water; when the words of Christ haue wrought, then it is made the Bloud which redeemed the People. To conclude, our Lord Iesus testifieth vnto vs, that we receaue his Body and Bloud; Ought we to doubt of his Fayth and Testimony?* Heere if I had concealed the name of S. *Ambrose*, would not the Reader thinke, the man had liued in our tyme, that wrote so forcibly and vehemently agaynst you?

Finally, in the former Chapter of the same Booke he saith againe: *The bread, is bread before the words of the Sacrament, but after the words of Consecration, of Bread is made the flesh of Christ.* And againe in the same little Chapter, as if by often repeating the same thing he meant to vexe or confound euery obstinate Protestant that should reade it, he saith: *Therefore, that I may answere thee; It was*

was not the Body of Christ before Consecration, but after Consecration, I say vnto thee, it is the Body of Christ. And agayne a little after, repeating the same againe, as if he had now conuinced his Readers, he concludeth: *You haue therefore learned; that our Bread is made the Body of Christ, and that Wine & Water is put into the Chalice, but is made Bloud by the Consecration of the heauenly Word: But it may be thou wilt say, I see not the forme of Bloud. But it hath the likenesse; for as thou hast receaued the likenesse of death, so thou drinkest also the likenesse of Bloud, and not the visible forme of Bloud, that there might be noe horror of Bloud; and yet the price of our Redemption, which is the Bloud of Christ, might worke in vs. Thou hast learned therefore, that thou receauest the Body of Christ.* Which you also might haue learned, if you had read him your selfe, and not trusted others that read him for no other purpose, but only to wrest his words against his meaning.

Section XI.

S. Hierome falsly alleaged, by Syr Humphry, agaynst the Reall Presence.

NOW come we to S. *Hierome*, who thinketh it noe blasphemy to say *Epist. 1. ad Heliod. That Priests with their sacred Mouthes doe make the Body of Christ. And, Epist. ad Euag. That his Body and Bloud is made at their prayer.* And, *in cap. 25. Matth.* writeth as followeth: *After the typicall Passouer was ended &c. he taketh Bread and passeth ouer to the Sacrament of the true Passouer, that as Melchisedech the Priest of the most high God had done, offering Bread and Wine to prefigure him; he also might represent the truth of his Body and Bloud.* That is to say, as Melchisedech offered Bread and Wine to prefigure him; so he also taking Bread and wine, offered the truth of his Body and Bloud to ful-

fill

fill the figure. According wherunto, in *Ps. 190.* speaking to our Sauiour he saith: *As Melchisedech offereth Bread and Wine; soe thou also offerest thy Body and Bloud, the true Bread and the true Wine.* In that sense, true Bread, as in *Epist. ad Hedibiam, quæst. 2.* he saith, that Moyses *gaue noe true Bread*; And as our Sauiour sayd, *Ioan. 6. That his Father gaue them true Bread from heauen.* Where also S. *Hierome* hath these words: *Let vs heare the Bread which our Lord brake, to be the Body of our Lord and Sauiour.* And he adeth a little after. *He sate at the Banquet, and was himselfe the Banquet; he the eater, and he that was eaten.*

Finally, *lib. cont. Vigil. cap. 3.* he reprehendeth *Vigilantius*, for speaking against Reliques in this manner; *Therefore* (according to thy speach) *the Bishop of Rome doth ill, who vpon the Bones of Peter and Paul (which we call venerable, but thou esteemest most vile dust) doth offer Sacrifices to God, and maketh their Tōbes to be the Altars of Christ.* According wherunto *in Prouerb. 11.* he also saith; *That after this life, small sinnes may be taken away, by paine, by prayers, and almes of others, and by celebrations of MASSE.*

Lastly in his Booke against *Iouinian*, which you cite at randome without any number, I find nothing but this that may any way please you: *In the type of his Blood he offered not Water, but Wine, lib. 2. cap. 4.* This testimony I find alleaged by your Doctours as S. *Hieroms*, for their meere figuratiue or typicall Presence; wherin they discouer eyther ignorance or desire to deceaue their Readers. For whosoeuer shall take the paynes to peruse the place, will find the aforesayd words not to be S. *Hieroms* but *Iouinians*, whose discourse against Abstinence from flesh and wine, S. *Hierome* there setts downe in that Heretike his owne wordes, whereof these are a part, *In the Type of his Bloud he offered not water but wine.* And S. *Hierome* afterward cōming to answere this obiection against drinking of water, and Abstinence from Flesh sayth, that Christ neuer vsed wine nor dainties, *excepto mysterio quo Typum suæ passio-*

nis

nis expreßit, & pro probanda corporis veritate. Where the Saynt tearmes the holy Eucharist a Type, not of the Body and Blood of Christ, as the Hereticke did; but of his Passion, which is represented in the Mystery of the Masse, which is the ordinary Catholike Doctrine and phrase.

Notwithstanding, seeing this Heretike, erred not agaynst the Catholike Doctrine of the Reall Presence, his wordes haue a true sense, and make agaynst you Protestants. For you deny, that in his last Supper, he offered any thing at all, and say, that only vpon the Crosse, he offered himselfe once for all, not only suffiiciently by his Bloud and Passion, *Heb.* 2. but also effectually, agaynst *Mal.* 2. without any other *cleane oblation*, for the application of the merit of his Passion vnto vs. This place therefore maketh not for you, neyther is it any way against them though it were *S. Hieroms*, for they graunt he offered Wine in type or figure of his Bloud, but he offered also his Bloud, answering the figure in Truth and Substance. As he was Priest after the order of Melchisedech, in Bread and Wine, he offered Bread and Wine in figure: As the offering of Melchisedech was a figure of his offering, he offered also his Body and Bloud, which was the Truth or Substance of that figure. Which to be the meaning of *S. Hierome*, may sufficiently appeare by that which hath beene sayd, and these other wordes of his *Epist. ad Marcellam*, doe make it yet to appeare more plainely saying: *Melchisedech in the Type of Christ offered Bread and Wine, and dedicated the Mystery of Christians, in the Body and Bloud of our Sauiour.*

Section XII.

Tertullian and Gelasius falsly alleaged by Syr Humphry, agaynst the Reall Presence. And S. Ignatius absurdly claymed by the Protestant Doctours.

THere remayneth behinde of the Authors you alleage, *Tertullian* and *Gelasius*. Tertullian is cleare for them, who in his Booke *De resurrectione carnis*, to proue that our flesh shall ryse agayne and be saued, vseth these words that follow: *The flesh is washed, that the Soule may be clensed. The flesh is annointed, that the Soule may be consecrated. The flesh is fed with the Body and Bloud of Christ, that the Soule may be fatned.* Though the Soule may feed on Christ by the metaphoricall mouth of Fayth; yet the flesh hath no such mouth to feede vpon him, and if it had, being only fed metaphorically therewith, nothing would follow thereof, but that it might rise and be saued only metaphorically; and so Tertullian should haue proued that which he there impugned. In fine, as the flesh is heere sayd to be truly washed and annointed, so also it must be vnderstood to be truly fed, and not to be fed by fayth only, or in figure.

Which Argument to proue the Resurrection, *Tertullian* seemeth to haue learned of *Irenaus lib. 4. cont. Hær. cap. 34.* whome also he calleth *Omnium Doctrinarum curiosissimum Exploratorem, lib. cont. Valent. prope initium.* And therfore becanse the Doctrine of *Irenaus* in that place doth serue very well to confirme both the doctrine of Tertullian, and the Reall Presence heere in question, I will giue you his whole discourse. *Quomodo constabit ijs &c.* (sayth he of the Heretiks against whome he wrote) *How can they assure themselues, the Bread wherein thankes are giuen, to be the body of their Lord, and* (the Cup to be) *the Cup of his bloud; if they do not confesse him, to be the Sonne of him that made the world? And how againe doe they say that, that flesh must go into corruption, and not receaue life, which is nourished by the body and bloud of our Lord? Therefore eyther let them change their opinion, or let them cease to offer the things aforesayd. But our Doctrine agreeth with the Eucharist, and the Eucharist againe confirmeth our Doctrine; for we offer* (therin) *vnto him those things that are his*, (because being the Sonne of God, he maketh thẽ by his omnipotency his owne Body & his owne Bloud) *and consequently we teach the communication and vnity of* (his) *Flesh, and of* (his) *Spirit* (with vs; (our flesh being fed with his Body and Bloud, and receauing thereby his Spirit to liue for euer.) *For as the bread which commeth from the Earth, receauing the vocation* (or word) *of God, is now no more common bread, but the Eucharist, consisting of two things, the one earthly* (comming from the earth) *and the other Heauenly,* (the Body and Bloud of the Sonne of God:) *so also our bodies receauing the Eucharist* (by the communication and vnitie of his flesh with ours) *are no more corruptible, hauing now the hope of Resurrection*. So that according to these auncient Fathers; as we belieue our Sauiour to be the Sonne of God: so must we belieue the *Eucharist* to be his Body and Bloud. And as we belieue the Resurrection of the Flesh: so must we belieue that our flesh is fed with the flesh of Christ. And eyther you must change your opinion, or els, as now you haue ceased to offer these things, and to feed your flesh with the body and bloud of Christ; so you are also in danger to change your beliefe as well of the Diuinity of Christ, as also of the Resurrection of your owne bodyes.

But it may be, the place which your selfe haue cited, *lib. 4. cont. Marcionem*, out of the same Author, is no lesse with you thẽ was the former agaynst you: his words are these: *Professing therefore that with a desire he desired to eate the Pasche as his own* (for it was not seemly that God should desire to eate the Pasche of another) *hauing taken the Bread, &c. he made it his owne body, saying: This is my body; that is, the figure of my body. But the figure had not beene, vnlesse there were a true body.* Whereof citing imperfectly, but halfe the Sentence: *This is my body, This is the figure of my body,* and changing *that,* into *this,* to make it sound more fully for you, you guilefully omit the other halfe; *The bread which he tooke he made his body, saying, This is my body:* which are euidently against you. The words also which you cite, wherein the Author seemeth to say, *This is my body; that is to say, this is the figure of my body,* and no more, your Aduersaries do clearly shew to haue another meaning.

First, because otherwise, he should not only teach that which is directly contrary to his former Doctrine in the place before alleaged, but also should contradict himselfe in this very sentence: for according to our expositiō he should not haue sayd, that Christ tooke bread & made it his body, which is false, if it be only a figure of his body; but that he tooke bread, and made it the figure of his body, saying: This is my body, that is to say, the figure of my body, and consequently in the words that follow, he should haue sayd, *But it were not a figure vnlesse there were a true body;* and not as he doth, *but there had not beene a figure,* if there were not a true body. For if the figure and the body were both at the same tyme, why should he say of the one, that it had beene, and of the other, that it was?

Secondly, your Aduersaries therefore do say, the meaning of those words, *This is my body,* that is, *the figure of my body,* to be; *This is my body,* that is, *the figure of my body in the Law, now by me fullfilled;* Or, *This is my body,* that is to say, *this is the bread which was a figure in the Law signifying my body, and is now fullfilled by me;* hauing relatiō to the words of the Prophet *Ieremy* which a little after he citeth and expoundeth, and sheweth to haue beene then fullfilled by

our

our Sauiour. As in the like sense *S. Iohn Baptist*, for example, when he saw our Sauiour might haue sayd, *This is the Messias, that is to say, The Lambe of God which was the figure of the Messias in the Law*, to signify, that the Prophecy of the Lambe of God in *Isa.* 16. was then fullfilled in our Sauiour.

Therfore that Tertullian meant to say, *This is my Body, that is to say, the figure of my Body*, now fullfilled &c. your Aduersaries doe plainely proue. First, because it is euident that Tertullian in this place intended to shew how our Sauiour in his *Pasche*, fullfilled the law, against *Marcion*, who being an Enemy of the Old Testament, contended that our Sauiour came to dissolue it; and Tertullian argueth against him in this mãner. The Bread of Christ in the law did signifie the Body of Christ, which he proueth out of *Ieremie* 11. saying: *Come, let vs put Wood on his Bread:* that is (sayth Tertullian) *the Crosse vpon his Body.* But our Sauiour gaue his Apostles, that Bread which he made his Body, saying, *This is my Body*, therefore he fullfilled the law, in giuing that Body which the law figured in Bread, and was therefore called Bread in *Ieremie*.

In the same manner againe he proueth, that giuing his Bloud in the forme of Wine, he fullfilled the law, because he gaue that which the law figured in Wine, and therefore *Gen.* 49. was called Wine, where it was prophesied of our Sauiour; *That he should wash his stole in Wine, that is,* (sayth Tertullian) *his Flesh in bloud*; So sayth Tertullian, he, *qui tunc vinum in sanguine figurauit*, who then made Wine a figure of his Bloud, now consecrated his Bloud in Wine.

Secõdly, your Aduersaries proue the same, because Tertullian vrgeth these former words, to proue also against *Marcion*, that our Sauiour had a true Body, and not the shadow or phantasme only of a Body as he contended. Which supposing that his Body was (as Tertullian speaketh) the figure of his Body then fullfilled; he proueth, becauſe vnto the figure of a Body to be *Crucified*, there muſt anſwere a true Body: *for of a Phantaſme* (ſaith he) *there can be noe figure.*

Secondly heproueth the ſame, *Becauſe in the mention of the Cupp, instituting his Testament ſigned wih his Bloud*, he cōfirmed the ſubſtance of his Body. That is to ſay: he confirmed his Body to be no ſhadow, but a ſubſtance; for, ſayth he, *the proof of Bloud, is a proof of Flesh; and the proof of Flesh, is a proofe of a true body*. Wherefore hauing giuen Bloud in his Teſtament, he gaue alſo a true Body.

Theſe Arguments therefore haue place, if according to the ſenſe which your Aduerſaries make of the words of Tertullian, *Our Sauiour fullfilled the law, by giuing that which was figured in the law*. But if according to your expoſition he gaue only a figure of his Body and Bloud; he gaue not that which was figured in the law, as Tertullian himſelf expoūdeth the law; for that which was figured in the law (ſayth Tertullian) was that Body which was to be crucified, & by conſequence he fullfilled not the law: which notwithſtanding was the Hereſie of *Marcion*, there condemned by Tertullian. And againe, if our Sauiour had giuen that which was only a figure of his Body, Tertullian could not haue proued thereby, that our Sauiour had a true Body anſwerable to the figure therof, in the Prophet *Ieremie*. For if there might haue beene a figure of a figure, there might haue been alſo a figure of a Phantaſme. And if in the mention of the Cup, he had not ſigned his Teſtament with true, but only with figuratiue Bloud, his Teſtament had not beene true, but only figuratiue; neyther had he thereby confirmed, that his Body was a true Subſtance. For figuratiue Bloud, could haue proued but figuratiue fleſh, and figuratiue fleſh could haue proued but a figuratiue Body.

Add vnto this, that if in your ſenſe Tertullian hath ſayd, This is my Body, that is, the figure of my Body: *Marcion* might as well haue ſayd in lyke manner: This is my Body, that is to say, the shadow, or Phantasme of my Body. And so in effect, Tertullian had agreed with *Marcion*, whose Heresy he there condemned; and had impugned the Truth of the *Eucharist*, which he there mētioned; for as *Ignatius* long before obserued the Simonian and the Saturnian Heretikes, *did not admit Eucharists and Oblations, because they did not confesse the Eucharist to be that flesh of our Sauiour which suffered for our sinnes*, Epist. ad Smyr. *vt citatur à Theodoreto Dial. 3.* Wherefore if *Tertullian* had not confessed the Eucharist to be the flesh of Christ, he must also haue denyed the Eucharist and the oblatiō thereof; and for the same reason the Protestants denying it to be the flesh of Christ, and consequently denying the oblation thereof, it is euident that they admitt not the Eucharist of Ignatius, no more, then the Simonian and Saturnian Heretikes haue done before them; but insteed of the Eucharist which was in his dayes, they haue suppostitiously brought in another of their owne inuentiō.

This is that S. *Ignatius* Martyr, the disciple of S. *Iohn*, thought to be that Boy, who was found to haue the fiue Barly loaues and two fishes which our Sauiour multiplyed, that thereby the harts of men might be the better disposed to belieue the locall multiplication of his owne body in the dreadfull Mystery. Euen frō thence he tooke a great deuotion thereunto, and was euen then ordayned to be a witnes of the admirable Doctrine thereof. *I delight not*, sayth he, Epist. ad Rom. post med. *in the nutriment of corruption, I desire the Bread of God, the Heauenly Bread, which is the Flesh of Christ the Sonne of God, and the drinke which is his Bloud*, And as he had beene fed with the bread, which was Christs flesh while he liued, so when he came to dye, he desired that his flesh might be grown'd as in a Mill with the teeth of Lyons, that he might be made cleane bread for the mouth of our Sauiour. Where also he sayth: *It is not lawfull without a Bishop* (that is to say, without orders receaued from a Bishop) *to baptize, nor to immolate Sacrifice.*

And

And what Protestant Minister will take vpon him, to immolate Sacrifice? Or what Protestant Bishop, eyther can or will giue him power to doe it? For which cause the Centurists, *Cent.* 2. *cap.* 4. affirme those wordes of his, to be incommodious, *Col.* 55. dangerous, and as it were the seedes of errors, *Col.* 167. Yet this is that *Ignatius* of the first Age, whome your Doctors with vnspeakable bouldnes claymed to be theirs, as you know in the former Cōference; and in their Booke would make fooles belieue, that the Catholikes when they heard him named, much reioyced, taking him to be *Ignatius Loyola*, the founder of the Society of IESVS. But the truth is, your Doctors might aswell haue claymed the latter as the former. For if his Religion be tryed by Workes, or Epistles that are extant, then your Authors disclayme from the former no lesse then from the later. Your M. *Wotton* being vrged with the saying of *Ignatius* in the behalfe of Merit, taken out of his Epistle to the Romans, vndoubtedly his, as both *S. Hierome* and *Eusebius* acknowledge, yea *S. Irenæus* (*lib.* 3. *aduers. hæres. prope finem*) doth alleage a sentence of this Epistle yet to be found therein: being I say, pressed with this testimony, your Doctor in his defence of *Perkins pag.* 339. answereth in these wordes: *I say plainely, this mans testimony is nothing worth, because he was of little iudgment in Diuinity.* What more could he haue sayd in contempt of the testimony of S. *Ignatius* of *Loyola*? But your Grand Maister *Caluin* yet speaketh more plainely in his Institutions *l.* 1. *c.* 14. §. 44. *Ignatium quòd obtendunt, nihil nænijs illis quæ sub Ignatij nomine edita sunt, putidius.* Whereas they produce the testimony of *Ignatius*, I say nothing is more rotten or corrupted (with Papistry) then those trifling Epistles that go vnder his name. If nothing be more rotten, that is, more Papisticall, and contrary vnto Protestants then the Doctrine of the writings we haue of S. *Ignatius* the Apostles Disciple, then is he asmuch for vs as S. *Ignatius* of *Loyola*. And the same M. *Caluin* in his booke

Booke *de participatione Christi in Cœna*, whereas *Westphalus* the Lutheran alleadgeth the testimony of *Ignatius* cited by *Theodoret* in his 3. *Dialogue*, out of his Epistle *ad Smirnenses*, where he chargeth the *Menandrian* Heretikes with his Caluinian hereticall Doctrine, *Non confitentur Eucharistiam esse carnem Saluatoris nostri Iesu Christi*, they do not belieue the Eucharist to be the flesh of our Sauiour Iesus Christ; *Caluin*, I say, not without disdayne frameth this answere: *What ingenuity is this to cite the Epistle of Ignatius which euen an ordinary* (Friar or) *Monke would hardly acknowledge as his owne? They know that haue read those toyes that they contayne nothing but tales of Lent, of Chrisme, of Tapers, of Fasting, and festiuall dayes, which through superstition and ignorance crept into the Church after Ignatius his dayes.* Thus *Caluin* speakes of the Epistle cited by *Theodoret*, by *Eusebius*, by S. *Hierome*, for the Epistle of *Ignatius*. So that as I sayd, if the Religion of S. *Ignatius* the Disciple of S. *Iohn*, be tryed by his writings, which all antiquity acknowledge as his, he is found, euen by the confession of Protestants, as very a Papist as was *S. Ignatius* of *Loyola*, to wit, more then any ordinary Friar or Monke. What desperation then was it of Doctour *Featly*, & to what a *Non-plus* was he brought, when he was forced to giue vnto *Ignatius* and his writings the first place after the Apostles in the Catalogue of Caluinian Professors? For this Author can no more be coupled togeather with *Caluin* in the same Religion and Church, then light can agree with darknes, Christ with Beliall. Which (besides what hath beene sayd) may appeare in the Preface of his Epistle to the Romans, by the great *Encomium* he maketh of that Church, *Quæ præsides in Regione Romanorum*; which presidence must needs be vnderstood of the Church of Rome aboue other Churches.

Thirdly, to draw to an end of this point, Tertullian seemeth to proue, that our Sauiour gaue his true body, because he professed, *That with a desire he desired to eate the Pasche as his owne; for that it had beene vnseemely, that God should*

should haue longed after the flesh of the Iewish Lambe (or quid alienum) or after any thing els that was anothers. But if he had desired to eate bread with his Apostles, he had not desired to eate his owne, but that of another; and it had beene no lesse vnseemely, that God should haue longed to eate the bread of another with his Apostles, then to eate flesh of another with the Iewes.

Lastly, if this sentence of Tertullian be obscure, it must be expounded by the other place before alleadged where he sayth, without any ambiguity, that our flesh is fed with the body and bloud of Christ. For it were agaynst all reason that the plaine words thereof should be expounded by this other place, which seemeth to contayne two contrary senses, and therefore is often alleadged by vs agaynst our Aduersaries, and by our Aduersaries against vs.

As concerning *Gelasius cont. Eutichem,* the last Author that you alleage; I wilbe content that *Chemnitius* a learned *Lutheran,* and as great an Enemy of *Transubstantiation* as your selfe, be iudge betweene vs, whether that place doth fauour it, or doth sound any way for it: his words are these *Examen. part. 2. pag. 88. Gelasius sayth, that the Wine and the Bread of the Eucharist, by the work of the holy Ghost, doe passe* (or conuert) *into the diuine Substance of the Body and Bloud of Christ; and verily these words do seeme to sound very strongly for the establishing of Transubstantiation. For that which passeth into another substance, and that by the working of the holy Ghost, certainely doth seeme, not to remaine in his former Substance.* If you had seene this place, or if passion had not blinded you, had it beene possible you should haue cited *Gelasius* against *Transubstantiation*, which by the iudgmēt of such a professed Enemy thereof, doth make so strongly for it?

Section

Section XIII.

The Conclusion of this Treatise.

Thus much concerning the Authories of the Fathers alleaged by you, partly false cited, which may be pardoned; partly falsified, which seemeth to touch your Honour; and all of them eyther wholy peruerted, or far from the matter; which cōming from a Knight sheweth an excusable ignorance in this kind of learning: But against the substance of the booke you receaued, as I haue shewed in the 4. first *Sections* of this Treatise, you haue answered nothing. Now therefore, good Syr, if according to your Degree, you will doe your owne selfe Knights seruice, indeed set to your shoulders, and vnderprop your Church, as *Atlas* was faigned to support the heauens; for as you haue heard and seene in the former *Sections*, it is so mainely battered with fower such peeces of great Ordinance, that vnlesse it be mightly sustained, the sound of thē alone is sufficiēt to shake it downe and ouerthow it. 1. Their visible Succession in all Ages. 2. Their Conuersions of Nations in all Ages. 3. Myracles in confirmation of their Doctrine in all Ages. 4. Censures of Fathers and Councells, for the condemnation of yours, in all Ages.

For 1. your Doctors did but beg the Question, when they made clayme to Christ and his Apostles, and began at the wrong end, making that their Argument, which should haue beene their conclusion, & was to be proued, by nominating Protestants to succeed them in all Ages, and especially in the Ages before *Luther*, according to the words of the Question, which they vndertooke, to answere. What foule shame, and extreme confusion is it to your Cause, when being vrged to name or bring forth but one Protestant in 500. or 1000. yeares, before *Luther*, you are eyther constrained to answere it is not necessary, or els supposing the ignorance of those that heare you, yow are inforced to cloth your nakednesse, with the raggs of *Wyckliffe* & *Waldo*, and other such accursed Heretikes; all of them holding some points with your Aduersaries against you, and being for other grosse heresies noe lesse detested by them, then condemned by you. Rather let the bowells of *Oxford Librarie* be ripped vp, and ransacked from end to end: Or els neuer leaue digging, vntill you haue wrought your selues into those caues where Protestants liued for so many hundred yeares, to find some Volumes, some Commẽtaries, or some Records of the Actes and Gestes of your Auncestors. If nothing can be found in Europe, recommend the matter to the East Indian Cõpany, or to the Westerne *Voyagers*, to seeke and search among furthest Nations, for Protestants, lineally descended from Christ & his Apostles; which being discouered, were better found then Mynes of gold. For vnlesse by some such meanes, the Professors of your Ghospels may be brought to light, your Church cannot long continue aboue ground, but the former Question alone, will suffice to coniure it downe againe into her auncient darkenes.

2. What can be more vnworthy, thẽ whẽ *Priests, Iesuites,* & other *Religious men* execute the cõmãdemẽt & cõmissiõ of our Sauiour in carrying his Ghospel to the ends of the Earth, as their Auncestors haue done in all Ages before them, thereby prouing themselues their true Successors, whome our B. Sauiour, according to his promise, *Matt.* 28. hath euer assisted, and will alwaies accõpany, *Teaching and baptizing all Nations, Omnibus diebus, vsque ad consummationem sæculi*, all dayes, or euery day vnto the end of the world: that your wiued Ministers in the meane tyme, fatned with their benefices, should only execute their owne malice in rayling vpon those laborious men, and deprauing their Christian endeauours, thereby shew-

ing

ing themselues to be that peruerse and bastard generatiõ, which insteed of cõuerting Infidells doth labour only to subuert belieuers; insteed of planting the faith of Christ, only indeauor to extirpate that Faith, which they found to be already planted; & insteed of sowing the first corne, only scatter cockle and darnell vpon that corne which was first sowed by others. Rather set forth whole fleets of Ministers, with their numerous families both for the East, and for the West, to bring those miserable Nations vnto the liberty and light of the Ghospell, that haue layne so long captiue vnder the foule bondage and execrable Tiranny of the Prince of darknes. Then it would be quikly tryed whether in those parts the diuells would submit themselues, and fly before them: or, *Whether like the strõger party Luc.* 11.18. as hitherto in Virginia they haue shewed thẽselues, *they would be able to keepe in peace the soules and vessells which they haue there soe long possessed*; vntill there come others stronger thẽ your Ministers that may be able to bind them.

3. What can be more impious, then whereas your Aduersaries, like true Christiãs confirme their doctrine in all Ages by those signes & myraculous operations, which were promised to follow the true belieuers, *Marc.* 16.17. you on the other side should haue nothing to answere, but only like Iewes and Pagans to laugh at them, and at the holy Fathers themselues that were so simple, as eyther to testify or to belieue them. Rather ioyne your harts and your hands togeather, that once in your tyme, you may see a Generall Councell from all Protestant Prouinces meete togeather, where out of so many Religions sprũg vp amongst you, hauing chosen one by Lot to be generally professed, beseech him, who heareth all those that with a true Fayth doe call vpon him, to confirme that chosen doctrine by some ostension in the *Sunne*, or in the *Moone*, or with some such notorious signe from Heauen, as might no lesse exceed the former Myracles of the Pa-

pistes then the wondrous workes of *Moyses*, confounded the magicall practises of the Egiptian Sages.

4. And lastly, what can be more voyde of shame and conscience, then to clayme those Fathers of the first 500. yeares for yours, that haue so impartially censured so many seuerall points of your Doctrine in the Heretikes of their tymes (for the which I refer me to the fourth Sectiō of this Treatise) as he that considereth them, may iustly esteeme the body of your Religion to be almost nothing els, but only a confarcination or bundle of old Heresies, condemned by them. Rather ioyne all in prayer, that if your Cause be true, as Almighty God vouchsafed in his owne person, to iustify *Iob*, against his friends; so that our Sauiour would be pleased with a voyce from Heauen, to iustify you agaynst the Fathers. But ouer Shooes, ouer Head and Eares, sayth the Prouerbe; according whereunto, if being once entred into a bad cause, it be resolued, that still you must needes goe forward; ceasing to falsify the words, and to peruert the meaning of those holy Fathers, least God in his iustice double your punishment, as you double your iniquity, hold your selues to the Scripture alone, and to your owne interpretation of Scripture (with M. *Luther*, and M. *Caluin*, and those learned Protestants of your owne Nation for so many yeares togeather) not fearing to reiect the Fathers that were but men, and directly refuting their errors; for in so doing, though you should want verity, yet God might be pleased at the length, to haue mercy vpon you for your sincerity.

O Mercifull God, the Author of all truth! If you be in the truth, why should you defend it by fraud and falshood? And how can it stand with his good will and pleasure, that against so many powerfull Arguments and euident demonstrations to the contrary, you should any longer thus contentiously hold it? And obstinately so continue to professe it?

Certainly

Certainly those 4. Considerations before remembred and reported more at large in the 4. first Sections of this Treatise, do make it so euidẽt vnto me, that theirs & not yours is the only true visible & vniuersall Church ordayned and founded by Christ and his Apostles, to teach the world; that I wonder in my hart how any learned Protestant can be so blinde as not to see it, or so voyd of honesty, as not to confesse it. Neyther if I were now a Protestant should any thing with-hold me from ioyning my selfe vnto them, vnlesse it were only in honor of that Religion wherein I was bred, to expect a little, *Whether the foresayd Catalogue* of the Names of your Professors in all Ages, and especially in the Ages before *Luther*, might be found and produced. The Question is now very happily set on foot; I hope it wilbe soundly followed; and it were to be wished, that no other Controuersy might be imbraced, before this, which is but matter of fact and the key of all the rest, be fully cleared. If Satisfactiõ may be giuen in this poynt, you may the better hope to be satisfied in the rest. But if not so much as one man can be produced in 500. yeares before *Luther*, that held not some maine points of Popery against you, or some other grosse errors condemned by you: if when *Luther* first began, not one Protestant can be named, that did not first fall from the Religion wherein he was bred, or which he had first receaued; then certainly it is not to be marueiled, if thousands and thousands ere it be long, doe renounce & abandone (with prayer for those to come after thẽ, whom they shall leaue behind them) that vpstart Fayth which was new when *Luther* began, and none at all before *Luther*.

ALmighty God, inspire the hart of his Majesty, whom it importeth noe lesse then our selues, that whereas the Catholike Recusants were neuer as yet accused of heresy, according to forme of Ecclesiasticall iustice, much lesse sommoned and called to make their answere, or iuridically

ridically condẽned; & that their Enemies formerly cẽsured by Generall Coũcells according to the Auncieẽt Law and receaued custome of the Church, haue notwithstanding, beene hitherto admitted, not only as accusers, but also as witnesses and iudges against them, whereby the people of the Land, being constrained to heare the one party, and restrained from hearing the other, haue been morally compelled to loue the one and hate the other, to magnify the one and detest the other; his Maiesty would be pleased to grãt vnto all his louing subiects, for the saluation of their poore Soules committed to his charge, that now at the lẽgth they might be allowed both their eares, to heare both sides indifferently, to weigh and ponder both causes, and well to cõsider of both Religions. Lest vnder the plausible name of spirituall liberty, they be cunningly held in miserable captiuity: being flattered with the shew of light, they be insnared in dubble darkenes: & being deluded with presumption of knowlege, they be bound and buried in most dredfull ignorance. A request soe fauorable both in the sight of God and Man, and so agreable to the principles of Protestant Religion, as I thinke it can be vngratefull to none, who doe wish vnfainedly, that only falshood may be suppressed, and the truth maintained. For the which all those that sincerely desire to serue God vprightly, shallbe infinitely obliged to pray for his Maiesty; not only as for their Gratious King, but also as for their deliuerer from the thraldome of conscience wherein he found them, and for the Author of their chiefest liberty wherin he should place thẽ.

FINIS.